Literature and Human Rights

Law & Literature

Edited by
Daniela Carpi and Klaus Stierstorfer

Volume 9

Literature and Human Rights

The Law, the Language and the Limitations of
Human Rights Discourse

Edited by
Ian Ward

DE GRUYTER

ISBN 978-3-11-055302-4
e-ISBN (PDF) 978-3-11-036855-0
e-ISBN (EPUB) 978-3-11-039263-0
ISSN 2191-8457

Library of Congress Cataloging-in-Publication Data
A CIP catalog record for this book has been applied for at the Library of Congress.

Bibliographic information published by the Deutsche Nationalbibliothek
The Deutsche Nationalbibliothek lists this publication in the Deutsche Nationalbibliografie;
detailed bibliographic data are available on the Internet at http://dnb.dnb.de.

This volume is text- and page-identical with the hardback published in 2015.
Typesetting: jürgen ullrich typosatz, Nördlingen
Printing: CPI books GmbH, Leck
♾ Printed on acid-free paper
Printed in Germany

www.degruyter.com

Contents

Literature and Human Rights: Interdisciplinary Reflections on the Law, the Language and the Limitations of Human Rights Discourse

Introduction

The intellectual conjunction of law and literature is now well-established. Lawyers have become familiarised to the thought that the law is not something that simply exists, but is something that is written and something that is read. As Kieran Dolin has recently confirmed, all "law is inevitably a matter of language."[1] It is textual, for which reason the kinds of things that literary scholars contemplate, such as how we read or how we interpret, matter to lawyers too. Equally, it has become apparent, perhaps most obviously in the classroom, but also perhaps the courtroom, that reflection upon the presentation of legal dilemmas in literature might assist lawyers in their everyday work.[2] Conversely, for literature scholars, the engagement of legal texts has helped to enrich myriad areas of literary analysis and criticism. At the same time, it must be admitted that the evident benefits of such a cross-disciplinary engagement have proved to be variable. Criminal lawyers, for example, appear to have embraced the possibilities offered by literature rather more enthusiastically that those whose intellectual attention is focused on international conventions which address commodity exchanges or secured transactions; in large part perhaps because good novels on commodity exchanges are few and far between, poetic muses on secured transactions still fewer and further. Some areas of law simply lend themselves more readily to the literary and the poetic. And few it might be argued lend themselves more readily than human rights and human rights law.

The very term "human rights" invites cross-disciplinary speculation, and more especially the complementary speculation of lawyers and literary scholars. The idea of rights lies at the heart of modern liberal democratic jurisprudence; from its earliest articulation in texts such as John Locke's *Treatises of Government*; through its grander statement in the great Enlightenment constitutions of 1776 and 1790, and the treatises written in due deference, such as Kant's *Metaphysics*

---

1 Kieran Dolin, *A Critical Introduction to Law and Literature* (Cambridge: Cambridge UP, 2007), 2.
2 See here C.R.B.Dunlop, "Literature Studies in Law Schools," *Cardozo Studies in Law and Literature*, 3 (1991): 63–110, and Ian Ward, "The Educative Ambition of Law and Literature," *Legal Studies* 13 (1993): 323–31.

of Morals and Tom Paine's *Rights of Man*; through to more recent articulation in international documents such as the UN Declaration and the European Convention on Human Rights, and its complementary contemplation in the writings of John Rawls, John Finnis and Ronald Dworkin. Lawyers, legal philosophers more especially, are supposed to know about "rights." There is no such expectation however in regard to the "human." Such a proposition would, of course, do an injustice to the student of Kant or Rawls or Finnis or Dworkin. But it is otherwise arguable. Whilst law students are invited to spend many of their hours contemplating the meaning of right, they are less commonly instructed to go away and think a little more about what it means to be human. And the reverse might be just as readily argued. It is difficult to spend long with Shakespeare or Wordsworth or Dickens, without stopping to think a bit more about humanity and its fate. But it is quite possible to spend a lifetime reading their poetry and novels without reflecting on the ambiguities which nestle in the word "right." The eighteen essays that comprise this collection are designed to nurture precisely this reflection, to confirm the importance of engaging matters of human rights from an inter-disciplinary, and still more particularly, "law and literature" perspective. They invite us to think rather more deeply about rights, about humanity and about the necessary tensions that play along their margin.

In their different ways, each of the essays which follow invite still closer contemplation of two intimately related themes. The first is the condition of the "other." The second is the role which language plays in the experience of exclusion. The supposition that the literary text might be better suited to this contemplation has been consistently argued by the likes of Richard Weisberg. According to Weisberg, "Stories about the other" can "induce us to see the other, and once we do so, we endeavour consistently to understand the world from the other's optic."[3] The same aspiration is articulated by Drucilla Cornell. A literary jurisprudence is something "driven by an ethical desire to enact the ethical relation."[4] And by Martha Nussbaum, who opens her *Poetic Justice* with the assertion, "I defend the literary imagination precisely because it seems to me an essential ingredient of an ethical stance that asks us to concern ourselves with the good of other people whose lives are different from ours."[5] A literary and a liberal education moreover does something more, as Nussbaum emphasises. It makes us care, and it does so by enhancing our appreciation of "imagination,

---

3 Richard Weisberg, *Poethics: and other strategies of law and literature* (New York: Columbia UP, 1992), 46.
4 Drucilla Cornell, *The Philosophy of the Limit* (London: Routledge, 1992), 62.
5 Martha C. Nussbaum, *Poetic Justice: The Literary Imagination and Public Life* (New York: Beacon Press, 1995), xvi.

inclusion, sympathy and voice."[6] As she argues in *Cultivating Humanity*, a liberal humanist education is defined as one which places at its centre a refined "narrative imagination." The exercise of such an imagination:

> Means the ability to think what it might be like to be in the shoes of a person different from oneself, to be an intelligent reader of that person's story, and to understand the emotions and wishes and desires that someone so placed might have.[7]

The relation of the empathetic and the normative in our perception of the "other" is the animating theme in the first set of essays in this collection; each of which treads what we might term the margins of human rights discourse. More closely still the first two essays, by Helle Porsdam and Richard Mullender, actively engage Nussbauam's defining supposition, and the consequences it draws for human rights and human rights law. In "Empathy, literature and human rights: the case of Eliot Perlman, *The Street Cleaner*," Helle Porsdam deploys Perlman's muse on the nature of human suffering in the twentieth century, from the Holocaust to the American civil rights movement, as means by which to alert us to the necessary tensions that pervade our attempts to achieve that vital balance between the immediacy of empathy and the reason of morality in our contemplation of human rights. What can happen when we fail in this endeavour is vividly described in the essay which follows, Richard Mullender's "Privacy, Blighted Lives and a Blindspot in British Law." The "depressing" failure of British courts to develop privacy rights, according to Mullender, is a failure of "compassion," the consequence of a juridical culture which owes rather too much Dickens's Gradgrind, and resembles rather too closely the "ruthless" morality identified by Thomas Nagel.

Unfortunately, as both Maria Aristodemou and Ricardo Baldissone suggest in the two essays which follow, there is a certain sad predictability here. In her "A Squeamishness about existing: Fernando Pessoa's Quiet Rejection of the Human in *The Book of Disquiet*," Aristodemou engages Pessoa's insinuation that modern human rights discourse should be understood as an expression of existential anxiety rather than Enlightenment optimism, revealing a greater determination to guard against the prospective threat of others than a desire to appreciate their needs. It is the same spectre which haunts Baldissone's "I and Another: Rethinking the Subject of Human Rights with Dostoyevsky, Bakhtin and Simondon." As a construct of competing narratives, contexts and subjectivities, Baldissone sup-

---

6 Nussbaum, *Poetic Justice*, 118–119.
7 Martha C. Nussbaum, *Cultivating Humanity: A Classical Defense of Reform in Legal Education* (Cambridge Mass.: Harvard UP, 1997), 10–11.

poses, there can be no stable demarcation between self and other, for which reason there can be no stable definition either of human or of human right. The very idea of human rights is questioned.

The same essential questions are contemplated further in Daniela Carpi's "Dehumanizing the Enemy: How to Avoid Human Rights." Carpi's attention is drawn more closely still to the place of 'dignity', not just in formal human rights declarations, but in human rights discourse, political and literary. Inviting the reader to revisit the familiar case of Shylock, as depicted originally in Shakespeare's *The Merchant of Venice* and then later in the writings of Arnold Wesker and Charles Marowitz, Carpi confirms that without a proper appreciation of "dignity" there can be no sensible protection of human "rights." The invitation that Carpi makes is the first in a series which might be said to establish a typology of exclusion. A second, revisited by Patrizia Nerozzi Bellman in her "'Am I not a man and a brother?' Notes on the Representation of Slavery in Eighteenth Century English Art and Literature," is just as familiar. It might again be hoped that the image of the enchained slave would today be of merely historical interest. But it is not. Much the same might be said of another historically inscribed exclusion; a very familiar one. The exclusion of women, as Ian Ward argues in his "The Rights and Wrongs of Marriage: Article 14.2 UDHR and the Case of Edith Dombey," is inscribed not just by history, but by language and by law "The Rights and Wrongs of Marriage: Article 14.2 UNHCR and the Case of Edith Dombey." As readers of Charles Dickens's 1848 novel *Dombey and Son* were to discover, if they did not already know, nineteenth century English matrimonial law was written to confirm the exclusion of married women, for which reason it was also written to excuse their violation.

The reality moves against the rhetorical pretence of universal human rights. It always has. And it is in this context that literature or art, historical or contemporary, matters, serving to sharpen not only our sensitivity to the idea of right, but also our sensitivity in regard to what it means to be human. In evidently similar ways, addressing their particular exclusions in their particular historical moments, Carpi, Nerozzi Bellman and Ward are seeking to articulate those "voices" which, to quote Ariel Dorfman, otherwise remain "hidden, at the bottom of the rivers of silence of humanity;" even if as they do so they betray the same residual anxiety discernable in the essays of Aristodemou and Baldissone.[8] And alongside the Jewish moneylender and the enchained slave and the abused wife can be placed an array of other more or less familiar categories of excluded

---

[8] Ariel Dorfman, *Other Septembers, many Americas: Selected provocations 1980–2004* (London: Pluto, 2004), 232.

"other." There are, for example, those who are deemed to be mad. In her "Mental Illness and Human Rights in Patrick McGrath's *Asylum*," Chiara Battisti revisits a long and troubling history of juridical de-humanization in English law; one that more recent statutory enactments including the Human Rights Act and the Disability Discrimination Act has only begun to address. And then there is the dead, as Sidia Fiorato suggests in her "The Role of Forensics in Human Rights Discourse: Kathy Reich's Crime Fiction and the Rights of the Dead." The disciplinary here focus moves within medical science, from psychiatry to forensic, from the dismemberment of the mind to the dismemberment of the physical body. The contention that any credible vision of "human rights" must be founded on an appreciation of human "dignity" is by now familiar. It recurs throughout this collection. There is however a paradox in Fiorato's consideration; the supposition that by reinvesting the identity of the anonymous corpse, the forensic anthropologist, also re-humanizes it. The rights of the dead like those of the insane and the enslaved might be said to be hard cases. They test the jurisprudential mettle of our human rights discourse.

It is in this context that Roxanne Doerr and Carla Dente turn our attention in the following too essays to a very contemporary exclusion, that of the supposed terrorist. In doing so of course they insinuate subversion, encouraging us to contemplate that which is deemed to be taboo, the prospective humanity of the terrorist. In "Rumpole and the Rights of Accused Terrorists," Doerr invites contemplation of the tensions that exist between Convention jurisprudence and English statutory provision in two of John Mortimer's "playful" Rumpole novels. In both cases Rumpole finds himself in the perhaps unexpected position of human rights champion. The situation is not however quite so simple, for it is apparent in both cases that there is a considerable divergence between the textual instantiation of Convention rights and their application in the more prosaic world of legal practice. The same distinction is written still more plainly in Carla Dente's "Reality, Theatre and Human Rights," except that here the question is not the difficulty of pressing human rights in the courtroom so much as the absence of any courtroom in which to make the case. The focus of Dente's essays is what Lord Steyn famously termed the "black hole" of Guantanamo. In the absence of a formal legal procedure, in which the possibility of human rights might be raised, theatre provides a vital alternative space. Vera Brittain's *Guantanamo*, the principle literary focus of Dente's essay, is one of a striking number of recent examples of documentary or verbatim drama written to this purpose.

The second set of essays takes a closer look at the textuality of exclusion. Here again, literature contributes a further dimension to the jurisprudential contemplation of human rights, its limitations and disappointments. Language includes and language excludes, as it always has; an insight which Paola Carbone engages in her essay on the linguistic exclusion of women on the sub-continent, "Manju Kapur's *Difficult Daughters* and the Cause of Female Literacy in India." The historical moment may be different, and the geography, but the misogyny and its consequence is not. It shares the same critical denominator. The margins of law are prescribed by those who assume political power, for whatever reason of pretended religious or cultural prejudice; and for centuries this has been men. The theme of linguistically constructed exclusion also animates the contributions of Liza Lanzoni and Matteo Nicolini. In both cases moreover the experience of exclusion is again intensified by particular geo-cultural context. In her *"The Trial of Jomo Kenyatta*: Oral Tradition and Fundamental Rights" Lanzoni revisits Montagu Slater's account of the 1955 Kenyatta trial. The exclusion here is generic, and ironic; the marginalisation of a jurisprudential tradition precisely because it is oral, the specific silencing of voice. Lawyers like rights to be written down somewhere. And then read by those who matter; a point which Nicolini reaffirms in his *"'n Droe Wit Seizoen in die Stormkap*: Andre Brink and the Fundamental Rights of the *Afrikaners* in Apartheid South Africa." Here Nicolini investigates the peculiar prejudices which underpinned Afrikaaner conceptions of right; prejudices which, as Andre Brink concluded, were rooted in an avid "linguistic purism."

And it is the same theme, of linguistic exclusion, which is pursued in Alessandra Tomaselli and Lino Panzeri's "The Definition of 'Linguistic Minority': Linguistic versus Legal Perspectives." Here again the problem lies less in the aspiration, written in Italian law to preserve the rights of linguistic minorities, but in the practice. Defining a linguistic "minority" is no easier than defining human "dignity." Or indeed the very idea of an "environmental" human right, as Valentina Adami argues in her "Rights of Humans/Rights of Nature: the Language of Environmental Rights in United Nations Documents." The greater the number of UN reports that are written on the state of the environment, the greater the number of prospective definitions of environmental human rights, and the greater the linguistic, and conceptual, "vagueness." The global environment faces many challenges. The blight of linguistic indeterminacy is just one of them.

As indeed Cesare Beccaria might have predicted. It is Beccaria's discussion of linguistic indeterminacy at the very dawn of the Enlightenment in the mid-eighteenth century which is the subject of Mara Logaldo's "On Crimes, Punishments, and Words: Legal and Legal Issues in Cesare Beccaria's Works." Beccaria would have been an advocate of human rights. But he would also have appreciated the limitations that apply to their mere enactment, the way in which the very language which aspires to liberate can be a language which limits and excludes. For which reason he would have been unsurprised to learn that violence and exclusion have retained their sad familiarity two and a half centuries on. There is indeed much that disappoints about human rights. Beccaria's caution has proved to be well-founded. But there is also much that we might celebrate and cherish. Beccaria was, in the end, an optimist. He preferred to imagine a better future. And it is this same possibility which animates the final essay in this collection, Jeanne Gaakeer's "Dignity and Disgrace in Law and Literature." Gaakeer's panoramic contemplation of suffering and dignity moves around a reading of JM Coetzee's acclaimed novel *Disgrace*. In many ways it revisits a number of now familiar themes. The re-inscription of human rights so as to incorporate a more empathetic appreciation of human dignity is perhaps the most obvious. But there is also the irreducible necessity of voice, the centrality of language, and literature, in the cause of political, social and cultural liberation. If we are to imagine a better future we need to keep these aspirations close, for without a more nuanced appreciation of the human there will be no realisation of the right. Each of the essays which comprise this collection is written in this spirit.

Helle Porsdam

Empathy, Literature and Human Rights: The Case of Elliot Perlman, *The Street Sweeper*

Characterizing, in a blog post in February 2013, fiction as "an empathy workout," *The Atlantic Wire* correspondent David Wagner wondered what it is that "makes bookworms such bleeding hearts."[1] His wonder had been spurred by a new study, coming out of the Department of Management & Organization, VU University Amsterdam, according to which reading fiction may affect a reader's empathetic skills over a period of time. The researchers had university students read either texts of fiction or newspaper articles. Assessing the students' empathetic abilities and self-reported emotions before and after the reading, they concluded that fiction readers had noticeably higher levels of emotional engagement than non-fiction readers. The key to this effect seemed to be the reader's level of emotional engagement with the text: Fiction readers who were not emotionally engaged were less empathetic after participating, just as non-fiction readers did not display these effects to any significant degree.[2]

The findings of this study are probably not all that surprising to literary scholars who are so well aware of the importance of emotional engagement when it comes to the reading of fiction. Writers of fiction aim at eliciting emotions, knowing full well that fiction is an unrivaled medium for the exploration of human social and emotional life. They exploit the feeling readers get from becoming part of the community described in the narrative they are reading – a mechanism which satisfies the deeply human need for belonging. "Fiction at its best isn't just enjoyable. It measurably enhances our abilities to empathize with other people and connect with something larger than ourselves," maintains Keith Oatley, an emeritus professor of cognitive psychology at the University of Toronto.[3] Having written a number of books on the influence of adversity on emotional

---

1 David Wagner, "Reading Fiction Can Make You More Empathetic," *The Atlantic Wire*, February 22, 2013, available at http://www.theatlanticwire.com/technology/2013/02/reading-fiction-can-make-you-more-empathetic/62443/ (July 18, 2013)
2 See P. Matthijs Bal, Martijn Veltkamp, "How Does Fiction Reading Influence Empathy? An Experimental Investigation on the Role of Emotional Transportation," *PLoS ONE* 8.1 (2013), available at http://www.plosone.org/article/info%3Adoi%2F10.1371%2Fjournal.pone.0055341 (July 15, 2013).
3 Keith Oatley, "Changing Our Minds," *Greater Good* (Winter 2009) available at http://greater good.berkeley.edu/article/item/chaning_our_minds/ (July 18, 2013).

disorders such as depression, and on human emotions more generally, Oatley has come to see fiction as simulation of real life: "In terms of 21st-century psychology, we might best see fiction as a kind of simulation [of our emotional and social worlds]: one that runs not on computers, but on minds."[4]

Oatley's research is in line with recent developments in empirical fields such as developmental psychology and neuroscience that have emphasized empathy as a natural human faculty and as the basis for altruism and morality. Empathy, argues renowned primatologist Frans de Waal, for example, comes naturally to a great variety of animals, including humans – it is what makes us willing to reach out to others and to understand their situation.[5] Indeed, empathy research seems to be thriving. In the humanities, too, there is an increasing focus on emotions, especially those involved in moral thought and action.

The historical dimension of emotions and affect is currently attracting increased attention among historians employing a wide range of theoretical perspectives and methodological approaches, for example. U.S. historian Lynn Hunt's *Inventing Human Rights* from 2007 is one – very influential – case in point. Hunt traces the rise of rights to the changing ideas of human relationships displayed by novelists, playwrights and artists in the seventeenth and eighteenth centuries. Novels, Hunt argues, such as Samuel Richardson's *Pamela* (1740) and *Clarissa* (1747–48) made people aware of the needs of their fellow human beings, including those not of their own gender or class. The spread of empathy beyond local communities would in the end make people reject torture, just as it would make them push for the expansion of self-determination for various disenfranchised groups.[6]

If we are to believe Hunt, the belief in law's empowerment is grounded in empathy and how others think. In what follows, I will look at the relationship between empathy, literature and human rights. I will do so against the background of Elliot Perlman's novel, *The Street Sweeper*, first published in Australia in 2011. As more than one reviewer of Perlman's bestselling novel has pointed out, *The Street Sweeper* may not be among the best works of literature, but it is surely among the most emotionally gripping ones. "Tell everyone what happened here" – this is the moral imperative that Perlman has his characters repeat over and over again. Spanning over fifty years and ranging from New York to Mel-

---

4 Oatley, "Changing Our Minds."

5 See e.g. Frans de Waal, *Our Inner Ape: A Leading Primatologist Explains Why We Are Who We Are* (New York: Riverhead, 2005) and Frans de Waal, *The Age of Empathy: Nature's Lessons for a Kinder Society* (Broadway, Portland: Broadway Books, 2010).

6 Lynn Hunt, *Inventing Human Rights: A History* (New York and London: W.W. Norton & Co, 2007).

bourne, Chicago, Warsaw, and Auschwitz, his novel tells us a captivating story about the Holocaust and the U.S. civil rights movement which stirs our empathy on numerous levels and in numerous ways.

The stories of "what happened here" appeal not only to our emotions, however. Making the world a better place to live in, Perlman implies, is not something that can be done overnight – by means of bursts of emotion, however powerful these may be. The author of *The Street Sweeper* stresses the importance of continuing the fight for one's beliefs over longer periods of time – of staying dedicated even when that fight seems to be much too slow, and when reasoned argument is called for instead of bursts of emotion. Anger, as one of his main characters will learn from none other than Justice Thurgood Marshall, only gets in the way: "Anger could sabotage the benefit of the passion. It could be the enemy of a good lawyer." Known to his co-workers as a "gradualist," as "someone who wanted change to come but gradually,"[7] Justice Marshall epitomizes for Perlman the perfect combination of the *emotional* and the *reasoned* moral fight.

Having surveyed current research on empathy in part one of this article, I will move into a discussion on Perlman's novel in the second part. My argument will be that while the capacity of a work of fiction to make us feel compassion with and to make us recognize the points of view of others is undeniable and important, there is a downside to the present enthusiasm for empathy – at least when human rights are involved. Empathy may lead people astray. It may lead them to care more about attractive victims than unattractive ones, for example – or to react to shocking incidents such as a tsunami, while ignoring more permanent conditions like global hunger or preventable diseases. Human rights is not just about putting oneself in someone else's shoes. There is a normative dimension to human rights which is downplayed, if not excluded, by the present focus on compassion and empathy.

1 Empathy and the "Affective Revolution"

1.1 The Case for Empathy

Responding to the massive attention currently paid by scholars across the board – from the humanities to the empirical sciences – to empathy and emotions and attempting to summarize it, popular writer Daniel H. Pink uses the phrases "L-Directed" and "R-Directed thinking." The former concerns the kind of thinking

---

7 Elliot Perlman, *The Street Sweeper* (London: Faber and Faber, 2012), 97, 28.

and attitude toward life which is characteristic for the left part of the brain – keywords being "sequential, literal, functional, textual, and analytic."[8] By contrast, "R-Directed thinking" is the kind of thinking that goes with the right hemisphere of the brain. Pink uses the words "simultaneous, metaphoric, aesthetic, contextual, and synthetic" to describe it, and he argues that "R-Directed thinking" is currently perceived to be more important:

> Left-brain-style thinking used to be the driver and right-brain-style thinking the passenger. Now, R-Directed Thinking is suddenly grabbing the wheel, stepping on the gas, and determining where we're going and how we'll get there. L-Directed aptitudes – the sorts of things measured by the SAT and deployed by CPAs – are still necessary. But they're no longer sufficient. Instead, R-Directed aptitudes, so often disdained and dismissed – artistry, empathy, taking the long view, pursuing the transcendent – will increasingly determine who soars and who stumbles.[9]

Through a combination of affluence, technological progress and globalization we are currently moving into what Pink calls the "Conceptual Age" – an age in which the most important characters are the creators and the empathizers, pattern recognizers and meaning makers who are able to master R-Directed Thinking. They are the ones who can detect patterns and opportunities and who can craft these into a satisfying narrative, thereby helping their fellow human beings make sense of it all.

Along somewhat similar lines, Anne Kreamer (former Executive Vice President for Nickelodeon) provides us with "The Business Case for Reading Novels" in a 2012 *Harvard Business Review* blog post. Emphasizing, like Pink, that the ability to be empathetic is essential in a globalized economy, she writes that "emotions also have an impact on the bottom line" and offers an interesting list of "great literature about business and organizational behavior" which may shape "your mind to be more emotionally acute."[10] On this list, we find such writers as Anthony Trollope, Jane Austen, Charles Dickens and William Gaddis – all writers who understood, Kreamer claims, that empathy is vital to success in the world of business, as indeed in any collaborative enterprise.

Among the studies that Kraemer refers to are a couple by cognitive psychologist Keith Oatley. Summarizing his work (undertaken alone or together with other

---

8 Daniel. H. Pink, *A Whole New Mind: Why Right-Brainers Will Rule the World* (New York: Riverhead Books, 2005/2006), 26.
9 Pink, *A Whole New Mind: Why Right-Brainers Will Rule the World*, 27.
10 Anne Kreamer, "The Business Case for Reading Novels," *Harvard Business Review* Blog Network, January 11, 2012, available at http://blogs.hbr.org/cs/2012/01/the_business_case_for_reading.html#.Tw7nkGZGHAI.twitter (June 22, 2013).

scholars) in a 2009 "Synopsis of Our Results," Oatley states: "Our empirical results on effects of fiction are of two kinds. One kind is correlational. We have used a measure of lifetime reading that tells us whether people read predominantly fiction or predominantly non-fiction [...] The second kind of result is experimental." Both kinds of empirical data, obtained over a number of years, led Oatley et al. to "think that fiction primes readers to think about people and what they are up to in their interactions."[11] As their titles imply, Oatley's two most recent works, *Such stuff as dreams* (2011) and *The passionate muse* (2012)[12] – the latter being a short novel interspersed with chapters that analyze the emotional impact of that novel on the reader – build on these findings and specifically focus on how identification with fictional characters occurs and improves social abilities.

The findings by Oatley and other psychologists are not self-evident, as Jonathan Gottschall puts it in *The Storytelling Animal* (2012): "If anything, stereotypes of nerdy bookworms and introverted couch potatoes might lead us to expect that fiction degrades social abilities rather than improving them."[13] Lovers of fiction therefore rejoice in these findings – seeing in them the ultimate repudiation of rumors about the death of the novel and/or of storytelling. Indeed, argues Gottschall, human beings are but storytelling animals for whom most events unfold as narratives. For once, the latest research in neuroscience, psychology and evolutionary biology seems to support the kind of things that people like Gottschall and other humanities scholars believe in – and that they teach to their students. If we are moving toward Pink's 'Conceptual Age' in which R-Directed Thinking is the name of the game, then the core disciplines of the humanities may experience a renaissance – a prospect that seems very alluring at a point in time where science and technology increasingly seem to operate in an expanding universe whereas the humanities seem to inhabit a diminishing one.

The way in which the findings of neuroscientists and psychologists are related by Kraemer and others to cross-cultural understanding and a globalized economy fits neatly with the theories on identity politics, migration and multiculture that have been such an important part of the humanities for the past many years. In a review of cognitive scientist Steven Pinker's *The Better Angels of Our*

---

11 Keith Oatley et al., "Synopsis of Our Results," *On Fiction: An Online Magazine on the Psychology of Fiction*, January 19, 2009, available at http://www.onfiction.ca/2009/01/synopsis-of-our-results.html (May 31, 2013).
12 Keith Oatley, *Such Stuff as Dreams: The Psychology of Fiction* (Oxford: Wiley Blackwell, 2011) and *The Passionate Muse: Exploring Emotion in Stories* (New York: Oxford University Press, 2012).
13 Jonathan Gottschall, *The Storytelling Animal: How Stories Make Us Human* (Boston & New York: Houghton Mifflin Harcourt, 2012), 66.

Nature (2011), literary scholar Elaine Scarry writes approvingly, for example, of the way in which for Pinker 'empathy' means "not the capacity of literature to make us feel compassion for a fictional being (though literature certainly does this), but rather the capacity of literature to exercise and reinforce our recognition that there *are* other points of view in the world, and to make this recognition a powerful mental habit."[14]

What interests Scarry is the ethical power of literature and the question of whether or not literature can help reduce acts of injury. Pinker argues as much, as we shall see, but like Lynn Hunt on whose work he draws, he focuses on the role of the novel during what he calls the Humanitarian Revolution of the late seventieth and early eighteenth centuries. As Scarry sees it, there are a number of antecedents to the novel. The most important one is poetry. From the *Iliad* to Petrarchan form and Shakespearean sonnets, disputes are built which "bring us face to face with acts of deliberation." There are parallels in the Eastern tradition and "in their own time, these poems helped to give rise to new civic institutions in which disputation was carried out obsessively."[15] It was through such debate and disputation that poetry – and later literature – did help diminish real-world injury by making people more tolerant and by opening their eyes to the fact that there are many different points of view.

1.2 The Case against Empathy

The Better Angels of Our Nature (2011) has received a lot of attention. Scarry's is but one of a series of reviews and articles that discuss Pinker's many interesting and provocative arguments. One of these concerns the legal reforms and protective laws of the late seventeenth and early eighteenth centuries. Like Hunt, Pinker sees these as the result, in part, of increasing literacy. Once people started reading novels, they became sensitized to the suffering of their fellow human beings and began to question the brutality of acts such as torture and the burning of alleged witches. Empathy is one of the four 'better angels' to which Pinker alludes in his title. The other three are self-control, a moral sense, and reason, and over the years, Pinker says, certain historical forces have helped our peace-loving motives keep our more violent ones at bay. Among these is 'the escalator of reason' – an "intensifying application of knowledge and rationality to human affairs," which

---

14 Elaine Scarry, "Poetry Changed the World: Injury and the Ethics of Reading," *Boston Review*, July 1, 2012, available at http://www.bostonreview.net/poetry-arts-culture/poetry-changed-world-elaine-scarry (July 10, 2013)

15 Scarry, "Poetry Changed the World: Injury and the Ethics of Reading.".

"can force people to recognize the futility of cycles of violence, to ramp down the privileging of their own interests over others', and to reframe violence as a problem to be solved rather than a contest to be won."[16]

While empathy and literacy have been important factors in the decline of violence that Pinker traces, other factors – self-control, a moral sense, and reason – have been no less important. Indeed, according to Pinker, reasoned analysis and deliberation may in the end serve us better than gut feelings of empathy. In a recent *New Yorker* article, Paul Bloom picks up on this.[17] A professor of Psychology at Yale University, Bloom has explored in his own research how children and adults understand the physical and social world, with special focus on morality, religion, fiction, and art. In "The Baby in the Well: The Case against Empathy," he stresses that the current interest in empathy "isn't just theoretical. If we can figure out how empathy works, we might be able to produce more of it."[18] Behind the many studies investigating the link between empathy and moral action lies the hope of discovering whether – and if so, how – empathy can make people willing to act and fight for a better world.

Many of these studies are well-researched and faithfully engage with existing scholarly literature on empathy. In their conclusion, they typically advocate that we should cultivate empathy because it makes us better people. This befits the times, writes Bloom, but their "enthusiasm may be misplaced [...]. Empathy has some unfortunate features – it is parochial, narrow-minded, and innumerate. We're often at our best when we're smart enough not to rely on it."[19] Why is it that events such as Hurricane Katrina elicited a major outburst of empathy in the United States in 2005 while very few Americans showed any interest in the genocide in Darfur that was unfolding at the same time – or in their fellow human beings around the world who were dying from preventable diseases or from malnutrition? And why is it that people have such a hard time relating to the larger picture – say, in the case of global warming – and to the long-term consequences of our current inaction? Most often, we put the blame for not enacting sensible policies on our politicians who want to be reelected and are therefore more interested in short-term cures and/or in not hurting powerful money interests, but "the politics of empathy is also to blame.

---

16 Steven Pinker, *The Better Angels of Our Nature: Why Violence Has Decline* (New York: Viking Books, 2011), xxvi.
17 Paul Bloom, "The Baby in the Well: The Case against Empathy," *The New Yorker*, May 20, 2013, available at http://www.newyorker.com/arts/critics/atlarge/2013/05/20/130520crat_atlarge_bloom?currentPage=all (August 15, 2013)
18 Bloom, "The Baby in the Well: The Case against Empathy."
19 Bloom, "The Baby in the Well: The Case against Empathy."

Too often, our concern for specific individuals today means neglecting crises that will harm countless people in the future [...] Our hearts will always go out to the baby in the well; it's a measure of our humanity. But empathy will have to yield to reason if humanity is to have a future."[20]

One piece of work that highlights some of these paradoxes of empathy and to which Bloom refers in his *New Yorker* article is Philosopher Jesse J. Prinz's "Is Empathy Necessary for Morality?"[21] Prinz offers a skeptical response to the question raised by his title. Defining empathy as "a kind of vicarious emotion: it's feeling what one takes another person to be feeling,"[22] he notes that claims for empathy, being an important part of morality, are typically made in studies relating to moral judgment and development – or to the motivation of moral conduct. Prinz challenges all of these claims by arguing, first of all, that "we can have moral systems without empathy." Even in the absence of empathy, other emotions such as e.g. anger, guilt or shame have been demonstrated to be sufficient for moral judgment.[23] Various studies have shown, he furthermore claims, that empathy is also not a major player when it comes to moral development. And most importantly in this context, nor does it seem to be a great moral motivator that will lead to action:

> Its contribution is negligible in children, modest in adults, and non-existent when costs are significant. Other emotions, including those associated with approbation and disapprobation appear to have much greater impact. Thus, the hypothesis that empathy is necessary for moral conduct – or even important – enjoys little support.[24]

What makes us help others, Prinz writes, is not empathy but instead happiness. Temporary bursts of positive emotion seem to promote altruism. In one experiment from the early 1980s, researchers planted a dime in a phone booth. Eighty-seven percent of the people who found the dime offered to help a person who dropped some papers nearby, compared with only four percent who did not find a dime. This sort of behavioral pattern repeats itself, other studies show, even when there are costs involved to the people doing good things for others – something

---

20 Bloom, "The Baby in the Well: The Case against Empathy."

21 Jesse J. Prinz, "Is Empathy Necessary for Morality?," in *Empathy: Philosophical and Psychological Perspectives*, eds. Amy Coplan & Peter Goldie (New York: Oxford University Press, 2011), also available at http://subcortex.com/IsEmpathyNecessaryForMoralityPrinz.pdf. In the following, my references are to the latter.

22 Prinz, "Is Empathy Necessary for Morality?," 2.

23 Prinz, "Is Empathy Necessary for Morality?," 2–3.

24 Prinz, "Is Empathy Necessary for Morality?," 10.

which contrasts strikingly with empathy "which does not motivate moral behavior when there are significant costs."[25]

Moreover, empathy may make people do things on the spur of the moment which they would not do, had they stopped to think more carefully. Prinz offers a "laundry list of worries about empathy" that he invites his readers to think about: Empathy may lead to preferential treatment and can be easily manipulated. Juries have been shown to give lighter sentences to defendants who show sadness, for example, and people are easily swayed by salient, newsworthy events. Empathy may influence people to care more about cute than ugly victims, just as it can be very selective and in-group oriented. In sum,

> empathy has serious shortcoming. It is not especially motivating and it is so vulnerable to bias and selectivity that it fails to provide a broad umbrella of moral concern. A morality based on empathy would lead to preferential treatment and grotesque crimes of omission. Empathy may do some positive work in moral cognition, such as promote concern for the near and dear, but it should not be the central motivational component of a moral system.[26]

All of this, but perhaps especially this latter point – that people tend to show much more understanding for and to care about those they perceive as being like themselves – has obvious consequences for the international human rights situation. To Prinz, as to other skeptics about empathy as a useful moral motivator, the way to go is not directly to suppress empathy, but to make it work in such a way that not only our own near and dear become its target, but also people in distant parts of the world who need us to act. What we ought to do, by means of intellectual detachment and reason, is to further a cosmopolitan understanding of the needs of others: "What we really need," Prinz concludes, "is an intellectual recognition of our common humanity and combined with a keen sense that human suffering is outrageous. If we could cultivate these two things, we would achieve greater commitment to global welfare [...] When confronted with moral offenses, it's not enough to commiserate with victims. We should get uppity."[27]

1.3 The Street Sweeper

Eliot Perlman knows how to manipulate us and our feelings. But the argument he makes in *The Street Sweeper* is also a highly moral one – he does get "uppity" with

---

25 Prinz, "Is Empathy Necessary for Morality?," 10.
26 Prinz, "Is Empathy Necessary for Morality?," 16.
27 Prinz, "Is Empathy Necessary for Morality?," 17–18.

us. Perlman is the son of second generation Jewish Australians of East European descent. He is a barrister and worked for a few years in a New York law firm. These biographical details show in the plot and the thematic choices Perlman makes in the novel. *The Street Sweeper* begins in contemporary New York and focuses on the racism that the civil rights movement set out, but ultimately failed, to combat; then moves to Europe and back in time – all the way to the Second World War and the Holocaust.

In a 2011 interview for *The Sydney Morning Herald* Perlman was asked why he drags his readers through page after page of the most unbearable details of what happened to the doomed men, women and children when they entered the gas chambers in Auschwitz. "I would like them to know," Perlman answered. "It was qualitatively different to pretty much everything that happened in human history [...] This is the gold standard of human rights abuse." "In a sense," he furthermore told his interviewer, "this book is a little advertisement for the inalienable dignity of the individual."[28] This is Perlman the lawyer speaking – using a version of what Mary Ann Glendon once called "rights talk."[29] I have suggested that there is a European parallel to the American "rights talk" – a "human rights talk."[30] In *The Street Sweeper*, Perlman makes use of both kinds of rights talk.

Since Glendon first used the expression, many scholars have challenged the belief in law's empowerment that both "rights talk" and "human rights talk" represent. This does not seem to have made much of an impression on Perlman who, especially in the first part of the novel which concerns, in part, the American civil rights movement, plays on exactly the kind of legal mystique that has always served the American legal profession so well.[31] Except, perhaps, in the sense that they may not have been the best of fathers, the civil rights lawyers we hear about are heroes who attempted to use the law to do good. And their boss, Thurgood Marshall, who was later to become the first African-American on the U.S. Supreme Court, is portrayed with both awe and admiration. Adam Zignelik, the Jewish American Australian character who is the most like Perlman himself, is driven by his loathing of racial hatred and injustice. Unlike his father, Adam does not

---

28 Jane Sullivan, "Interview: Elliot Perlman," *The Sydney Morning Herald*, October 29, 2011, available at http://www.smh.com.au/entertainment/books/interview-elliot-perlman-20111027-1mkla.html#ixzz2aosVDNgU (October 1, 2012)

29 Mary Ann Glendon, *Rights Talk: The Impoverishment of Political Discourse* (New York: Freedom Books, 1991).

30 See Helle Porsdam,*From Civil to Human Rights: Dialogues on Law and Humanities in the United States and Europe* (Chatham, UK: Edward Elgar, 2009).

31 This is a theme that I develop in *Legally Speaking: Contemporary American Culture and the Law* (Amherst, MA: University of Massachusetts Press, 1999).

become a lawyer but instead a historian. He very fittingly writes his dissertation on the importance of the civil rights legal strategy, though.

1.4 The Portrayal of the U.S. Civil Rights Movement

We first encounter Adam in Part Two of the novel when he wakes up with "a montage of images in his mind" which has induced "a series of increasingly violent bodily tremors." The images are "from another time, his father's time" and "mainly of black people."[32] There is Emmet Till who was murdered in Mississippi in 1955 at the age of 14 after reportedly flirting with a white woman. There are Carole Robertson, Cynthia Wesley, Addie May Collins, and Denise McNair who were killed – the first three fourteen years old; Denise only eleven years old – by white segregationists in the Birmingham, Alabama 16th Street Baptist Church bombing in September 1963. There is fifteen-year old Elizabeth Eckford, one of the so-called 'Little Rock Nine,' a group of African-American students who, in September 1957, made an unsuccessful attempt to enter Little Rock Central High School in Little Rock, Arkansas after the most famous of all U.S. Supreme Court opinions, *Brown vs. Board of Education of Topeka* (1954) had made integration in U.S. primary schools mandatory. Of the *Brown* decision, more later.

And then, there is Adam's father – Jake Zignelik. Snippets of conversation between Adam as a boy and his father keep popping up and interrupting the montage of images that haunts Adam. Adam's parents divorced when he was only four, and his mother took him with her back to her native Australia. Until Jake's death when Adam was 16, Adam paid infrequent visits to his father in New York, and it is the conversations he had with his dad during those visits that keep coming back to him – especially those that concerned the importance of civil rights. "The enemy," Jake would explain to his son, "is racism. But, see, racism isn't a person. It's a virus that infects people [...] We have to fight that wherever we find it. That's what good people do."[33] This "mantra" makes a big impression on Adam who subsequently adopts it as his own and tries to act on it.

Along with the legacy as a major civil rights lawyer, this mantra is about all that Jake left his son. One of the problems Adam has when we first meet him is that his marriage is faltering because he does not want to father any children. His long-time girlfriend wants children but Adam does not want any child to feel the same sense of abandonment that he himself felt because Jake was always much

---

32 Elliot Perlman, *The Street Sweeper* (London: Faber and Faber, 2012), 19.
33 Perlman, *The Street Sweeper*, 29.

more interested in his work than in his son. And it is not just his marriage that lies in ruins. Adam is also heading for professional disaster. Since his dissertation, which was a great hit both with his fellow-historians and with the general public, and which landed him a job at Columbia University, he not only has not been able to produce any new academic work; he also has no clue as to what kind of research he might wish to pursue. Both he and the head of the History Department at Columbia, Charles McCray, who also happens to be one of Adam's best friends, know that he will not get tenure.

Charles is the son of William McCray, an African-American attorney and veteran of both World War Two and the civil rights movement – and also best friend and colleague of Jake Zignelik. Unlike Jake, William has been a good father to his son – but like Jake, he "was forever fighting the good fight." Adam "loved this man"[34] and it is no co-incidence that it is William who gives him the idea to look into the rumors about black soldiers being among the American soldiers who liberated Auschwitz. This eventually leads Adam to the forgotten papers of psychologist Henry Border, whose story is taken up in Part Seven of the novel – a story that provides Adam (and his author) with one of many links between the civil rights movement and the Holocaust. Reflecting the fact that there is no agreement among historians on the role of black soldiers in the liberation of German concentration camps, Perlman wisely leaves it somewhat unclear who was indeed involved in the liberation of Auschwitz – and only uses William's idea for Adam to look into this as a way of getting the other and, in the context of this particular novel, more important story going: the one about the first interviews, made by European-American psychologist Henry Border, with Holocaust survivors.

Jake and William met when they both signed up with the NAACP Legal Defense and Educational Fund. About Jake we learn that he

> had been there in 1954 in the US Supreme Court when Thurgood Marshall had argued *Brown versus Board of Education*. In 1949, fresh from Columbia Law School, Jake Zignelik, a New York Jew, went to work for what would later become known as the NAACP Legal Defense and Educational Fund, later simply known as the LDF. He went on to be mentored by Thurgood Marshall. In a long career he represented Martin Luther King and many others, arguing numerous civil rights cases before the US Supreme Court.[35]

Jake would later become the director-counsel for the LDF – a job, we are given to understand, that William also wanted, and that many thought ought to have been given to an African-American. This never ruined the friendship between the two

---

34 Perlman, *The Street Sweeper*, 152.
35 Perlman, *The Street Sweeper*, 27–28.

attorneys, though, and many years later William will think back on his first day of work and the "nervous excitement" he felt "when he couldn't have imagined the momentous events in the nation's history and in the stop-start history of Western Enlightenment in which he and his colleagues would play a part."[36]

Perlman's choice of words here is significant. In the canon of US Supreme Court decisions, as in US (legal) history in general, *Brown* is considered to be one of the proudest moments. In declaring state laws establishing separate public schools for black and white students unconstitutional, the Court – in a rare, unanimous (9–0) decision – overturned the *Plessy v. Ferguson* decision of 1896 (which had allowed state-sponsored segregation in public schools). The Court referred to the Equal Protection Clause of the Fourteenth Amendment to the US Constitution, which requires each state to provide equal protection under the law to all people within its jurisdiction, and thereby helped dismantle racial segregation and discrimination against various other minority groups. Together with the Thirteenth (abolishing slavery, ratified in 1865) and Fifteenth (granting voting rights to people of color, ratified in 1870) Amendments, the Fourteenth Amendment belongs to the so-called Reconstruction Amendments which were intended to guarantee freedom and civil rights to African-Americans after the Civil War.

It was in his capacity as Chief Counsel for the NAACP that Thurgood Marshall argued for the desegregation of public schools in the US. His victory in the *Brown* decision turned him into a national icon. He would serve on the US Court of Appeals for the Second Circuit and then as Solicitor General, until President Lyndon B. Johnson appointed him to the US Supreme Court in 1965. *The Street Sweeper* reflects all this. It is from Justice Marshall, as previously mentioned, that Jake and William learn the valuable lessons concerning the importance of "gradualism" (change coming gradually) and anger being the enemy of the good lawyer. It is a version of this advice that Adam gives to his history students when he teaches his popular course, "What is History?"

> Pay attention to the small details. It is the mark of a professional. When Adam Zignelik said this to his students he was referring to the craft of a professional historian. More than fifty years earlier William McCray learned the same thing as it pertains to lawyers. He learned it from Thurgood Marshall not merely through it being said but also by simply watching him and the way he worked.[37]

"Is any of this true?," Adam asks his students as he lectures about Gandhi, Harlem, Christ, Jews in Europe, Dietrich Bonhoeffer, and a black man living on

---

36 Perlman, *The Street Sweeper*, 99.
37 Perlman, *The Street Sweeper*, 103.

Broadway in the Union Theological Seminary in 1930. Is there a connection between these people, places and ideas, moreover – and if so, who is to find this connection? The answers toward which Adam works together with his students is that yes, there *are* connections – and that it is precisely the job of the historian to find these. As he winds up his lecture series, he refers to historians Barbara Tuchman and G.M. Trevelyan who thought that, "ideally history should be the exposition of facts about the past, in their full emotional and intellectual value to a wide public by the difficult art of literature." The best historians know their stuff inside out – but they combine their knowledge with imaginative powers which help them "leap into the lives, into the skins of the people who came before us."[38]

Human beings are totally unpredictable, but what makes history courses such as the one Adam is teaching so useful is that "while history can't tell us exactly what's going to happen next, it can suggest certain things we should or should not do the next time something similar happens again." History can show us what people have been through before and this can provide comfort in difficult times. History is a "way of honouring those who came before us," Adam tells his students. "We can tell their stories. Wouldn't you want someone to tell your story? Ultimately, it's the best proof there is that we mattered."[39]

1.5 The Importance of Storytelling: Henryk Mandelbrot's and Henry Border's Stories

Throughout the rest of the novel, there are especially two stories that demand our attention: that of Holocaust survivor Henryk Mandelbrot and that of psychologist Henry Border. Both concern the mass murder of European Jews before and during World War Two, and both are related in various ways to events before and during the civil rights movement. The former is told by Mandelbrot himself to Lamont Williams, the humble African-American janitor with whom the novel opens. Lamont works in a New York cancer hospital on probation after release from prison for his unwitting involvement in an armed robbery when he meets and befriends Mandelbrot. The friendship that develops between Lamont and Henryk Mandelbrot is a very unlikely one – one of the many strange coincidences that make up Perlman's novel and that critics have commented on.[40]

---

38 Perlman, *The Street Sweeper*, 122–23.
39 Perlman, *The Street Sweeper*, 128.
40 See e.g. David Gates' review of *The Street Sweeper* in the *New York Times*, "Connecting the Lowly and Mighty in New York,"January 27, 2012, available at http://www.nytimes.com/2012/01/

When, toward the end of the novel, Lamont is dismissed from the hospital probationary program for allegedly having stolen a silver menorah which had been given to him by the dying Henryk Mandelbrot, it is his ability to pay attention to detail that saves him. He has so carefully memorized Mandelbrot's life story that he is able to convince Mandelbrot's relatives that he did indeed know the Holocaust survivor well enough for the latter to give him the menorah as a gift. Adam is called in to testify at the meeting that is called between the hospital authorities, the Mandelbrots and Lamont. He explains that only very few people have known all the minute details that Lamont knows about the Jewish 'Sonderkommandos'. This helps to persuade the hospital authorities that Lamont is innocent and should keep this job.

Through Mandelbrot, Lamont – and the reader – learns what happened to the men, women and children once they arrived at the gas chambers of Auschwitz. As a Jewish 'Sonderkommando,' Mandelbrot was involved in getting thousands of victims into those gas chambers in order then later to dispose of their bodies. His character is based on Henryk Mandelbaum, one of the few surviving Jewish 'Sonderkommandos' whom Perlman met and interviewed for the novel.[41] When Lamont asks Mandelbrot how he could possibly live through all the gruesome and terrifying events he witnessed, the latter answers: "At the start of your shift you want to die… But all the time you're thinking that somebody has to survive just to tell what happened. Somebody has to get the story out."[42]

Mandelbrot's answer is echoed by Rosa Rabinowicz, one of the participants in a 'Sonderkommando' rebellion shortly before the Russian liberation of Auschwitz. Before she is hanged, she calls out: "Tell everyone what happened here!"[43] Rosa's story is of particular interest in that it feeds into the larger story of Henry Border. Born Chaim Broder, Border is a Polish Jew who fell in love with and married Rosa during the war. They had a daughter together, Elisa, but one day Broder surprised Rosa in bed with her former boyfriend. Broder reacted by fleeing Warsaw and Europe for the US. He took Elisa with him to Chicago where he started a new life as Henry Border and eventually became a professor of psychology at the Illinois Institute of Technology.

Obsessed, for obvious reasons, with what was happening to Europe's Jews, Border managed to find funding for a research trip back to Europe where he interviewed Jewish Displaced Persons – later known as Holocaust survivors. It is

---

29/books/review/the-street-sweeper-by-elliot-perlman-book-review.html?pagewanted=all&_r=0 (August 15, 2013)

41 See Acknowledgements Perlman, *The Street Sweeper*, 553.

42 Perlman, *The Street Sweeper*, 380.

43 Perlman, *The Street Sweeper*, 452.

the transcripts of these interviews (some, but not all of which have been published in a book) along with the original magnetic recording "wires" themselves that Adam accidentally discovers when he is persuaded by William to go to Chicago to try to find out if African American soldiers had been involved in the liberation of Dachau. Though not a Holocaust scholar himself, Adam immediately sees the importance of these interviews which he thinks may indeed be the first ever made with Holocaust survivors, and which make Henry Border one of the first oral historians.

One of the oral interviews turns out to be different. Whereas Border in the other interviews kept cool and stayed in the background only to ask questions which would get the interviewees going, in this particular interview he became very emotional. "Who will sit in judgment over all this," Adam hears him mumble – "and who is going to judge my work? [...] Who is going to judge... me?"[44] Adam becomes interested in finding out why Border should be so afraid of the judgment of others and discovers the truth about his leaving Rosa behind out of disappointment and anger – forgetting his promise to her that he would take care of her. Instead, she died in the Holocaust and Border, who had never even told his daughter about what happened, has found it very difficult to live with his guilt.

2 Concluding Remarks

There have been attempts the last few years to see the American civil rights movement as part of a transnational human rights movement. In *From Civil Rights to Human Rights: Martin Luther King, Jr., and the Struggle for Economic Justice* from 2005, the historian Thomas F. Jackson discusses how King increasingly came to see his and his fellow-Americans' fight for civil rights as a part of something bigger: a more global fight for human rights.[45] And in this global fight, Jackson shows, the legal battles fought for formal *de jure* equality by the NAACP came to be viewed by King and his followers as not going far enough – King eventually realizing that without economic justice, African-Americans (along with minority groups and victims of colonization around the world) would never reach an equal standing with the white majority.

---

44 Perlman, *The Street Sweeper*, 237.
45 Thomas F. Jackson, *From Civil Rights to Human Rights: Martin Luther King, Jr., and the Struggle for Economic Justice* (Philadelphia, PA: University of Pennsylvania Press, 2005).

Thomas Borstelmann reaches a somewhat similar conclusion in *The 1970s: A New Global History from Civil Rights to Economic Inequality* (2011).[46] For Borstelmann, as for Jackson, what was happening in the US in the middle of the 20th century was but part of a global development; as a result of which, in considerable part, civil rights movements in America have gained much more formal equality. However, the 1970s witnessed not only a drive for ethnic equality, but also a demand for deregulation and privatization which has had the effect of making US society much more economically *un*equal. At one and the same time, that is, the US became ethnically equal, but financially unequal. The civil rights fight was not just about domestic civil rights or 'rights talk,' American-style. It was about 'human rights talk' or global human rights. It concerned not just civil and political rights (or what some human rights scholars would call 'first generation' human rights), but also economic, social and cultural (or 'second generation') rights.

In linking the US civil rights fight with what happened during the Holocaust, *The Street Sweeper* reflects the (global) commonality of human suffering. The most explicit theme of the novel is the importance of history and memory: the necessity of remembering and retelling the stories of the oppressed and the persecuted. Slowly but surely, the threads of the many sub-plots lead back to Auschwitz and to the Holocaust – that "gold standard of human rights abuse."[47] The Auschwitz scenes are the most forceful. They are based on the talks Perlman has had with real-life survivors and thus testify to that importance of attending to details, which he promotes throughout the novel. "There is sometimes the feeling from well-meaning people: maybe they know too much, they have 'done the Holocaust'," Perlman said in an interview a couple of years ago. "I think that arises because they are so familiar with the imagery, the iconography. But they're almost totally starved of the facts."[48]

Fiction allows a writer to go into his or her characters' minds and to make up linkages that were not there in real life[49] and thus to cater to the reader's empathy. But Perlman does not just want his readers to feel empathy with the victims of the terrible crimes he writes about. He also wants us to stop and think – and then become so morally outraged that we act. He wants to help us cultivate, in Jesse Prinz's words, an "intellectual recognition of our common humanity" and to combine this recognition "with a keen sense that human suffering is out-

46 Thomas Borstelmann, *The 1970s: A New Global History from Civil Rights to Economic Inequality* (Princeton, NJ: 2011).
47 Sullivan, "Interview: Elliot Perlman."
48 Sullivan, "Interview: Elliot Perlman."
49 Sullivan, "Interview: Elliot Perlman."

rageous."[50] Commiserating with victims is not enough – there is an important normative dimension to human rights which should not be reduced to compassion. Empathy is a first and important step, but it is not until we combine empathy with reason and moral argument that we can help prevent human suffering. Or, as Steven Pinker puts it:

> *Empathy* (particularly in the sense of sympathetic concern) prompts us to feel the pain of others and to align their interests with our own [...] And the faculty of *reason* allows us to extricate ourselves from our own parochial vantage points, to reflect on the ways in which we live our lives, to deduce ways in which we could be better off, and to guide the application of the other better angels of our nature.[51]

---

50 Prinz, "Is Empathy Necessary for Morality?," 18.
51 Pinker, *The Better Angels of Our Nature*, xxv.

Richard Mullender
Privacy, Blighted Lives, and a Blindspot in British Law

[T]he mode of conceptual representation insinuates itself all too easily into every kind of human experience.
Martin Heidegger, *On The Way to Language*

1 Introduction

In 1997, Britain's Lord Chancellor, Lord Irvine, piloted the Human Rights Bill through Parliament. On becoming law, this statute would give effect (in British law) to the qualified right to privacy and the other fundamental protections enunciated in the European Convention on Human Rights (ECHR).[1] As the Bill made its way through the legislature, Lord Irvine looked forward to a dramatic change in the contours of British law. For he described his fellow judges as "pen-poised [...] to develop a right to privacy."[2] Bold as this statement sounds, it was something of an admission of failure. For the Lord Chancellor was acknowledging the fact that the British had put surprisingly little effort into securing their privacy-related interests by legal means.[3] While, for example, the equitable doctrine of confidence, various

---

1 See Jane Wright, *Tort Law and Human Rights* (Oxford: Hart Publishing, 2001), 10 (noting that the Human Rights Act gives "further effect" to Convention rights on the plane of domestic law).
2 HL Deb, November 24, 1997, Col 785.
3 Curiously, writers on Britain's most populous constituent nation, England, often emphasise a long-standing commitment to respect for privacy as a feature of practical life. See, for example, George Orwell, *The Lion and the Unicorn: Socialism and the English Genius* [1941] (Harmondsworth: Penguin Books, 1981), 39 ("on the privateness of the English life"), Jeremy Paxman, *The English* (London: Penguin Books, 1998), 134 (on "this English obsession with privacy"), and Roger Scruton, *England: an Elegy* (London: Pimlico, 2001), 51 (arguing that the English have (histori-cally) "value[d] privacy more than any other good.") While a body of law relating specifically to privacy is a recent arrival on the British legal scene, a commitment to protecting privacy-related interests through the use of property law was plain to see in England between the early seven-teenth and mid-nineteenth centuries. See Patrick O'Callaghan, *Refining Privacy in Tort Law* (London: Springer, 2013), 75–76 (discussing a stream of authority from *Semayne's Case* (1604) 5 Coke Reports 91a ("[the] house of everyone is his castle" (Sir Edward Coke)) to *Jones v Tapling* (1865) 11 HLC 290 ("privacy is not a right" and "[i]ntrusion on it is no wrong or cause of action" (Baron Bramwell)).

heads of liability in tort, and the law relating to data protection provided privacy-related protections, British law lacked a free-standing right to privacy.[4] At the time the Lord Chancellor made his statement, "privacy" was certainly becoming a more prominent practical concern in Britain.[5] Judges were, for example, taking steps to expand the doctrine of confidence.[6] But the process of change in which they were engaging was piecemeal and did not dispel the impression that the protection of privacy was not a matter of pressing legal concern for the British.

In the decade-and-a-half since Lord Irvine made his statement, it has taken on an overblown appearance. The expansion of the doctrine of confidence that was underway when he spoke continued into the new century. In 2004, a senior judge, Lord Nicholls, declared that the form of harmful wrongdoing that the doctrine of confidence addresses is not equitable but tortious. Lord Nicholls also gave this form of wrongdoing a new name: "misuse of private information."[7] Moreover, he recognised (in passing) that privacy "can [...] be invaded in ways not involving publication of information."[8] This remark has not been a spur to development in the cases on which we will focus. However, another judge, Sir Michael Tugendhat, has recognised that he and his colleagues could elaborate privacy-related protections in ways that provide protection against "intrusion."[9]

---

4 See, for example, *Attorney-General v Guardian Newspapers (No 2)* [1990] 1 AC 109 (doctrine of confidence), *Bernstein of Leigh v Skyviews & General Ltd* [1978] QB 478 (trespass to land in tort), and the Data Protection Act 1984 and the the Access to Personal Files Act 1987.

5 Concern with the protection of privacy-related interests by legal means intensified greatly in the late 1980s when a Home Office committee, headed by Sir David Calcutt, investigated the newspaper industry. The Calcutt Committee published its report in 1990 and recommended that self-regulation by the Press Council should give way to a semi-independent alternative under the aegis of a new body, the Press Complaints Commission. See Alwyn Turner, *A Classless Society: Britain in the 1990s* (London: Aurum Press, 2013), 87.

6 See, for example, *Her Royal Highness Princess of Wales v MGN Newspapers Ltd and Ors* (transcript, Association of Official Shorthandwriters, November 8, 1993), and *Hellewell v Chief Constable of Derbyshire* [1995] 1 WLR 804, 807, *per* Laws J.

7 *Campbell v Mirror Group Newspapers* [2004] 2 AC 457, 464–465. Lord Nicholls' decision to characterise the action for misuse of private information as tortious gave rise to a controversy that rumbles on. See J. Steele, *Tort Law: Text, Cases and Materials* (Oxford: Oxford University Press, 2nd edn), 807 (stating that "[i]t is not clear whether [misuse of private information] is a tort"), and *Vidal-Hall v Google Inc* [2014] EWHC 13 (QB), [66]-[70], *per* Tugendhat J (recognising tortious misuse of private information and the equitable doctrine of confidence as distinct features of the legal landscape).

8 *Campbell v Mirror Group Newspapers*, 465.

9 *Goodwin v NGN Ltd* [2011] EWHC 1437 (QB), [85]-[87] and [113]-[130], *per* Tugendhat J. See also Kirsty Hughes, "A Behavioural Understanding of Privacy and Its Implications for Privacy Law," *Modern Law Review* 75 (2012): 806–836, 823, n. 58.

As we will see, development of the law in this area could provide protection against the forms of harmful wrongdoing that will be our central concern.

As the rather limited process of development that began in the 1990s has unfolded, judges, lawyers, and academics have dwelt on the systemic relationship between lower-order private law (e.g., the doctrine of confidence and tort) and higher-order public law (the Human Rights Act 1998 and the ECHR).[10] Moreover, they have found in the developments we have noted evidence of the onward march of human rights.[11] This view has some merit. However, the cases on which we will focus in this essay reveal a glaring imbalance in the protection British law gives to privacy. These cases concern people who have suffered gross forms of abuse. As we will see, British law has not secured their interests in "home" and/or "family life" (two of the goods that the right to privacy in Article 8(1) of the ECHR protects). Worse still, these cases reveal failures of the imagination on the part of those concerned with the law's operations: e.g., the lawyers seeking to secure the relevant individuals' interests. With the aim of gaining analytic purchase on these imaginative failures, we will draw on a contribution to law and literature scholarship made by Martha Nussbaum. In *Poetic Justice*, Nussbaum contributes to the strand of law and literature concerned with the human capacity to engage empathetically with others.[12] As we will see, she throws much light on failures of imagination of the sort that concern us. However, we will seek to build on her analysis. To this end, we will draw on two further sources of academic guidance that have relevance to the cases we will examine. They are the account of "ruthlessness" set out by the analytic philosopher Thomas Nagel, and the analysis of the human brain's operations offered by the psychiatrist Iain McGilchrist. But before turning to these matters, we must look in some detail at the cases that

---

10 Among other things, they have dwelt on the emergence of a doctrine of wide indirect horizontality according to which judges should elaborate private-law-based protections of privacy in conformity with higher-order public law norms (most obviously, the right to privacy in the ECHR). See, for example, Gavin Phillipson and Alexander Williams, "Horizontal Effect and the Constitutional Constraint," *Modern Law Review* 74 (2011): 878–910.

11 See, for example, Helen Fenwick and Gavin Phillipson, *Media Freedom Under the Human Rights Act* (Oxford: Oxford University Press, 2006), pt IV; *cf* Patrick O'Callaghan, "Monologism and Dialogism in Private Law," *The Journal Jurisprudence* 7 (2010): 405–440, 423, *et seq*.

12 Martha Nussbaum, *Poetic Justice: The Literary Imagination and Public Life* (Boston: Beacon Press, 1995). See also Jane Baron, "Law, Literature, and the Problems of Interdisciplinarity," *Yale Law Journal* 108 (1999): 1059–1085, 1063–1066 (identifying the law and literature movement as embracing three broad "strands": the "humanist" strand (concerned with the "promot[ion]" of identification and empathy in legal contexts), the "hermeneutic" strand (involving the application to law of interpretive methodologies borrowed from literary theory), and a "narrative" strand (that deals with "storytelling in law")).

are our central concern. We will also look at the doctrinal and historical context in which judges, lawyers, and public bodies have made their far from adequate responses to these cases.

2 A Blindspot in British Law

2.1 Bleak Housing and Blighted Lives

In July 2001, James Drummond, a tenant in a flat he rented from Glasgow City Council made a fatal attack on his neighbour, James Mitchell. Like Drummond, Mitchell rented his property from the Council. The two men had been neighbours since the 1980s. In 1994, Mitchell complained about Drummond's decision to play loud music in the early hours of the morning. This prompted Drummond to batter on Mitchell's door with an iron bar and threaten to kill him. Subsequently, Drummond made numerous threats to kill Mitchell. In 1995, Council officials warned Drummond that, if he continued to threaten Mitchell, they would take action to recover possession of his flat. However, Drummond made further threats to kill Mitchell (sometimes at the rate of one a month). In 2001, a local resident provided the Council with a signed statement confirming that she had heard Drummond threaten to kill Mitchell. The Council also had a video tape showing Drummond behaving in a threatening way towards Mitchell. This led the Council to serve a notice for recovery of possession of its property. But Drummond remained in occupation of the flat and continued to threaten Mitchell. As a result, Council officials told Drummond in a meeting with him that they would serve a further notice of proceedings to recover possession and that continued anti-social behaviour would result in eviction. At this meeting (which took place on July 31, 2001), Drummond lost his temper and became abusive before apologising. Following the meeting, Drummond returned to his home and, shortly thereafter, inflicted on Mitchell the injuries that led to his death.

Following Drummond's conviction for culpable homicide, Mitchell's widow and daughter sought compensation from Glasgow City Council. They mounted a negligence claim, arguing that the Council was duty-bound to warn Mitchell of the "real and immediate" threat to his physical safety posed by Drummond after the meeting of July 31.[13] They also argued that the Council had breached Mitch-

---

[13] The European Court of Human Rights has recognised that where a "real and immediate" threat to life exists, public bodies may have to take positive steps to secure the right to life established by Article 2 of the ECHR. See *Osman v United Kingdom* (1998) 29 EHRR 245, para 115.

ell's right to life (within Article 2(1) of the ECHR). Having made two unsuccessful attempts to assert their claims before the Scottish courts, Mitchell's relatives made a further and unavailing attempt to secure redress in the House of Lords.[14] In its response to this claim, the House pursued the theme that to impose a duty on the Council would be to deflect it from its primary concern.[15] On the House's account, this was to promote the public interest by delivering housing provision.[16]

At no point did the lawyers or judges involved in this case canvass the possibility that, prior to his death, Mitchell had suffered a gross and extended invasion of privacy: the inability to enjoy a secure and reasonably peaceful home life. Given the character of the assault on home life we are considering, this is surprising. It is also surprising in light of the fact that counsel in the case did invoke an ECHR-based human right: the right to life. To have made a further leap to Article 8 of the Convention would not have involved a great feat of imagination.

We see the same failure of imagination when we turn to the case of *X and Y v Hounslow LBC*. X and Y were a couple with learning difficulties who (with their children) occupied a council flat. The couple (who were vulnerable to exploitation) befriended some youths and, as a result, saw their home turned into a sordid den. The youths used the flat as a place where they could take drugs, have sex, and store stolen goods. The couple's social worker, on becoming aware of these developments, urged the Council to relocate them. But before the Council had considered what to do, the youths physically and sexually abused the couple in their home.

X and Y sued the Council in negligence. The trial judge decided in their favour. The couple, he concluded, had suffered reasonably foreseeable harm while in a proximate relationship with the Council. Moreover, he took the view that a finding in the couple's favour would not "open the gates to a flood of future claims that would not otherwise have been brought."[17] However, the Council appealed successfully to the Court of Appeal. The Court supported its decision by reference to doctrinal considerations: e.g., the claim fell outside existing categories of case in which judges have imposed liability; the defendant had not assumed responsibility for the claimants' welfare. Alongside these considerations, the Appeal Court judges set two points that are highly relevant to our concerns. They described the Council as having sought (at the time the couple suffered harm) to carry out its statutory functions "and nothing more." In light of

---

14 For the decisions in the Scots courts, see 2005 SLT 1100 and 2008 SC 351.

15 *Mitchell v Glasgow City Council* [2009] 1 AC 874.

16 *Mitchell v Glasgow City Council*, 889–890, *per* Lord Hope, 900–901, *per* Lord Rodger, and 905, *per* Baroness Hale.

17 *X and Y v Hounslow LBC* [2008] EWHC 1168 (QB), [119].

this point, they declined to accept the trial judge's conclusion that it would be "fair, just and reasonable" to impose liability.[18] The phrase "fair, just and reasonable" (which appears in the general duty of care test applied by judges in negligence law) refers obliquely to what judges usually call "policy."[19] This term embraces public interest-related considerations that tell against the imposition of liability: e.g., ensuring that new liability rules do not deflect public bodies from their central concerns.[20] "Policy" thus carries us onto the ground we traversed when we examined the House of Lords' decision in *Mitchell*. As in *Mitchell*, we see public considerations bulking large in the branch of private law we are considering. Likewise, we see the same failure to take account of the couple's privacy-related interests in a secure and reasonably peaceful home and family life.

These decisions confront us with a blindspot in British law.[21] This blindspot is apparent in a case that predates *Mitchell*, *X and Y*, and the coming into force of the Human Rights Act 1998. In *Hussain v Lancaster City Council*, the claimant was the owner of a shop and residential property situated in a local authority housing estate. He suffered forms of abuse that were (according to one member of the Court of Appeal) "atrocious by any standard."[22] Residents on the estate subjected Hussain and his family to harassment and intimidation. Among other things, they engaged in racist abuse, kicked footballs against the family's doors and windows, threw stones and bricks at their property, and mounted arson attacks.[23] In response to this abuse, Hussain sued Lancaster City Council in negligence and in

---

18 *X and Y v Hounslow LBC* [2009] EWCA Civ 286, [90]-[91].
19 For the general duty of care test applied by English judges in negligence actions, see *Caparo Industries plc v Dickman* [1990] 2 AC 605, 616–617, *per* Lord Bridge.
20 John Bell, *Policy Arguments in Judicial Decisions* (Oxford: Clarendon Press, 1983), 22–23, 45–46, and 69–70.
21 Following the Court of Appeal's decision in *X and Y v Hounslow LBC*, the claimants made an application to the European Court of Human Rights, asking it to determine whether (in circumstances of the sort they endured) a local authority is under a duty to prevent violations of home and family life ([a]pplication *no 32666/10 by X, Y & Z v UK*). See Equality and Human Rights Commission, *Human Rights at Home: Guidance for Social Housing Providers*, 25, http://www.equalityhumanrights.com/human-rights/human-rights-practical-guidance/guidance-from-the-commission/human-rights-at-home/ (January 31, 2014). Having made this application, the claimants reached an out-of-court settlement with the defendant local authority. See Giles Peaker, "X & Y v UK settled without a hearing," http://nearlylegal.co.uk/blog/2011/07/x-y-v-uk-settled-without-hearing/ (January 31, 2014).
22 *Hussain v Lancaster City Council* [1999] 4 All ER 125, 129, *per* Hirst LJ. See also 148 (where Hirst LJ identifies the Hussain family as victims of "appalling" racial abuse).
23 *Hussain v Lancaster City Council*, 128–129, *per* Hirst LJ (where the judge also records that the Hussain family's complaints related to "several hundred alleged incidents [...] involving no less than 106 alleged culprits.")

private nuisance. He argued that the Council was responsible for the harms that he had endured since it had failed to control those (local authority tenants) who had abused him. His claims failed. While giving doctrinal reasons for its decision to reject them, the Court of Appeal emphasised the undesirability of deflecting the defendant council from its public functions.[24]

As in *Mitchell* and *X and Y*, *Hussain* confronts us with an assault on home life. Violations of this sort are a commonly encountered feature of life in Britain's less prepossessing neighbourhoods.[25] This grim reality became a matter of wide concern following another sustained and glaringly obvious violation of home and family life. Following a decade-long campaign of abuse by neighbours, Fiona Pilkington (having sought assistance from the police on over thirty occasions) took her own life and that of her learning-disabled daughter. Unlike Mitchell's death, a private law action did not follow these deaths.[26] But as with *Mitchell* and the other cases we have considered, they bring sharply into focus the blindspot in British law we have been considering (see Table 1, below).

We can better understand why this blindspot exists by examining relevant doctrine, historical context, and the rough-and ready-philosophy that seems to inform the law and the practice of public bodies in Britain.

---

24 *Hussain v Lancaster City Council*, 144–145, *per* Hirst LJ. See also see *Mowan v Wandsworth London Borough Council* [2001] EGCS 133 (rejecting an argument for a positive obligation on the part of the defendant local authority to protect the claimant). As with *Hussain*, the claim in *Mowan* arose prior to the Human Rights Act 1998 coming into force. *Cf Donnelly v Northern Ireland Housing Executive* [2003] NICA 55. In this case, a neighbour of the Donnelly family subjected them to persecution on religious grounds. The neighbour (like Donnelly) was a tenant of the Northern Ireland Housing Executive. Donnelly invited the Housing Executive to take action against the neighbour (e.g., commencing proceedings for possession of the neighbour's property). The Housing Executive declined to do so. Thereafter, Donnelly made an application for judicial review in response to which the Northern Ireland Court of Appeal issued a declaration that identified the Housing Executive as having breached Article 8 of the ECHR (by failing to commence possession proceedings).

25 Rosa Monckton, "Living Hell," *The Sunday Times*, October 4, 2009, 1–2 (News Review), and Ben Leach, "Last Desperate Plea of Academic Plagued by Neighbours from Hell," *The Sunday Telegraph*, January 27, 2013, 4.

26 Following the death of Fiona Pilkington and her daughter, the Independent Police Complains Commission found the performance of the relevant police force wanting. See Peter Walker, "Fiona Pilkington case: police face misconduct proceedings," *The Guardian*, May 24, 2011, 10. See also Wesley Johnson, "Fiona Pilkington case 'could happen again,'" *The Daily Telegraph*, March 21, 2013, 18.

2.2 Doctrine, Historical Context, and a Rough-and-Ready Philosophy

The readiness with which senior judges have been able to reject the claims in *Mitchell, Y and Y,* and *Hussain* may surprise those unfamiliar with the body of law we are considering. However, judges have, over an extended period of time, worked up a number of doctrinal devices that shield local authorities and other public bodies (e.g., police forces) from negligence liability in a wide range of circumstances. In the 1860s, the House of Lords took the novel step of indicating that a public body exercising a statutory power could incur negligence liability. However, the House staked out the position that a common law duty could only arise where this was compatible with the relevant statutory scheme.[27] It thus erected a barrier to recovery in negligence that continues to work to the disadvantage of claimants with otherwise good actions.[28]

In the 1940s, the House of Lords placed a further limitation on the ability of claimants to sue public bodies. In *East Suffolk Rivers Catchment Board v Kent*, it decided that claims against public bodies exercising statutory powers could only arise where harm was the result of a positive undertaking. This meant that any damage sustained by a member of the public that resulted from a failure to exercise a statutory power could not ground a claim.[29] More recently, British judges have drawn a distinction between two levels (or types) of activity engaged in by public bodies: one concerned with "policy" and the other with "operational" matters.[30] The "policy" level concerns the exercise of statutory discretion and thus has to do with such matters as politically sensitive resource-allocation decisions.[31] As a result of the introduction of this distinction, it is particularly difficult for claimants to ground negligence claims on decisions made at the policy level. For an action to succeed, the claimant must establish that the imposition of a duty would be compatible with the statutory scheme and that the relevant body has behaved unreasonably in the public law sense.[32] To meet the second of these requirements, a claimant must demonstrate that the decision under scrutiny was so unreasonable that no reasonable decision-maker could

---

27 *Mersey Docks and Harbour Board v Gibbs* (1866) LR 1 HL 93, 107. See also *Geddis v Proprietors of the Bann Reservoir* (1878) 3 App Cas 430, 455–456, *per* Lord Blackburn, and *Stovin v Wise* [1996] AC 923, 946–947, *per* Lord Hoffmann.
28 *Stovin v Wise*, 935, *per* Lord Nicholls.
29 *East Suffolk Rivers Catchment Board v Kent* [1941] AC 74, 102, *per* Lord Romer.
30 The policy-operational distinction derives from American law. See, for example, *Dalehite v US*, 346 US 15 (1953).
31 See *Anns v Merton LBC* [1978] AC 728, 754, *per* Lord Wilberforce.
32 *Stovin v Wise*, 953, *per* Lord Hoffmann.

have taken it.[33] Moreover, judges who address this question must go about their business deferentially. They should not second-guess the decisions of those upon whom Parliament has conferred the power to exercise a statutory discretion.[34] Likewise, they should be alive to the fact that the matters addressed by those wielding statutory powers are typically polycentric and thus lie at the outer limit of the justiciable.[35]

The doctrinal developments we have been examining follow (indeed, seem (albeit slowly) to track) changes in the character of the British state over the last century-and-a-half. As we will see below, these changes in the state's character throw considerable light on the body of law we have been scrutinising (and help to explain the privacy blindspot we detected earlier). During the nineteenth century, the British state greatly increased the range of its domestic activities – a process of development that prompted Frederic Maitland to describe Britain as having become "much-governed."[36] Many of these activities were concerned with promoting the public interest (understood in broadly egalitarian terms as a good or state of affairs that secures the interests of or redounds to the benefit of members of society generally).[37] For example, in the second half of the nineteenth century, the state took on the task of delivering elementary education to all children.[38] As it embraced ambitious tasks such as this, influential political groups (e.g., the Fabians and the New Liberals) detected signs of a commitment to the pursuit of an egalitarian end-state, which gained the name "New Jerusalem."[39] In the Twentieth Century, enthusiasm for the pursuit of this end-state grew and increasingly found expression in talk of a "welfare state." Moreover, commitment to the agenda summed up in phrases like "New Jerusalem" and "welfare state" assumed concrete form in an increased range of activities undertaken by public bodies: e.g., the provision of

---

33 *Anns v Merton LBC*, 754, *per* Lord Wilberforce.

34 *X (Minors) v Bedfordshire County Council* [1995] 2 AC 633, 736, *per* Lord Browne-Wilkinson.

35 Keith Stanton, Paul Skidmore, Michael Harris, and Jane Wright, *Statutory Torts* (London: Sweet & Maxwell, 2003), 76.

36 See Frederic Maitland, *The Constitutional History of England* [1908] (Cambridge: Cambridge University Press, 1974), 501. See also William Greenleaf, *The British Political Tradition*, Vol III, *A Much Governed Nation*, Pt 1 (London: Methuen, 1987), 1.

37 See Brian Barry, *Political Argument* (London: Harvester Wheatsheaf, 1990, revised edition), 190.

38 On William Forster's Education Act 1870, see Ian Bradley, *The Strange Rebirth of Liberal Britain* (Chatto & Windus: London, 1985), 47–48.

39 See Martin Loughlin, *Public Law and Political Philosophy* (Oxford: Clarendon Press, 1992), 116–123, and Corelli Barnett, *The Lost Victory: British Dreams, British Realities 1945–50* (London: Macmillan, 1995) 123.

social (or council) housing.[40] The range of activities embraced by the state continued to increase after the Second World War. Clement Attlee's Labour administration embarked upon new welfare initiatives (most obviously the creation of the National Health Service) and strengthened existing ones (e.g., the provision of council housing).[41] While prominent political figures have sought to limit Britain's commitment to the delivery of "welfare" on the model exemplified by Attlee's government (e.g., Margaret Thatcher), it has remained a prominent feature of British life. In 1997, its place in the public imagination found expression in New Labour's resounding general election victory.[42]

We can draw out of the history we have been surveying a connecting thread that is highly relevant to the privacy blindspot we detected earlier. This is the emergence of a rough-and-ready philosophy that informs governmental activity of the sort we have been examining. This philosophy assumes the state to be an agent of benign social change. More precisely, those who embrace this view of the state's role assume that it can, and should, pursue generally beneficial outcomes. These are outcomes that, in the great majority of cases, serve the interests of those who receive the relevant goods (education, housing, health care, etc.).[43] In seeking to benefit members of society in this way, the state makes apparent its

---

40 See Peter Hennessey, *Never Again: Britain 1945–51* (London: Penguin Books, 2006), 167 (on the Housing and Town Planning Act 1919).

41 David Kynaston, *Austerity Britain, 1945–51* (London: Bloomsbury, 2007), 154–158. See also Robert Colls, *Identity of England* (Oxford: Oxford University Press, 2002), 183, and Greenleaf, *The British Political Tradition*, Vol III, *A Much Governed Nation*, 448, and David Marquand, *The Unprincipled Society: New Demands and Old Politics* (London: Fontana Press, 1988), ch. 1.

42 Paul Addison, *No Turning Back: The Peacetime Revolutions of Post-War Britain* (Oxford: Oxford University Press, 2010), 408 (noting that "New Labour retained a fervent belief in the welfare state.")

43 The assumption that the British state could successfully pursue such outcomes strengthened in the second half of the nineteenth century and the early years of the twentieth. See Arthur Venn Dicey, *Lectures on the Relation Between Law and Public Opinion in England During the Nineteenth Century* [1914] (Indianapolis, Indiana: Liberty Fund, 2008), 99 (on the assumption that "[t]o determine [...] the general conditions which conduce to the prosperity of the millions who make up a State is a comparatively simple matter.") See also Robert Colls, *George Orwell: English Rebel* (Oxford: Oxford University Press, 2013), 223 (on the mid-Twentieth Century view that "life could be made better for more people more of the time by the intelligent intervention of the state.") On one analysis (concerned with processes of state formation), the pursuit of generally beneficial outcomes is a central concern of the nation-state. See Philip Bobbitt, *The Shield of Achilles: War, Peace and the Course of History* (London: Penguin Books, 2003), 370 (on the assumption that the nation-state's "first duty" is "to benefit the mass of its people.") See also 175 (identifying the nation's state's readiness to put itself "in the service of its people" as a source of its claim to legitimacy).

commitment to egalitarianism. But the way in which this commitment finds expression is open to objection in egalitarian terms. For an outcome that is "generally" beneficial fails to conform to the universal impulse at work in strong forms of egalitarianism: i.e., the aim of securing the interests of all relevant people (rather than the great majority of them).[44]

In this feature of the rather rough-and-ready philosophy we are considering, we find a family resemblance to the utilitarian maximum happiness principle, which tells us to seek the greatest good of the greatest number.[45] While this resemblance may come as a surprise to proponents of egalitarianism who have not closely scrutinised British practice, commentators who are familiar with the relevant history have drawn attention to it. For example, Dicey notes that the body of nineteenth century thought that gave currency to the idea of a welfarist end-state owed a debt to the utilitarianism of Jeremy Bentham.[46] On the assumption that Dicey's point is correct, it seems apt to call the philosophy we have been considering "welfare consequentialism."

In light of this brief survey of changes in the British state over two centuries, we are in a position to grasp more adequately the significance of the doctrinal developments we considered earlier. They reveal the judiciary to have made efforts to accommodate the expanding, outcome-focused, state by fashioning doctrines that would enable those working within it to get on with the business of generally beneficial delivery. This is a state of affairs on which public lawyers throw light when they talk of a "green light" understanding of administrative law. Law understood in this way is supposed to facilitate the pursuit of the state's goals (rather than impeding them by operating as a bridle for Leviathan).[47] This outlook finds expression in the doctrines we examined earlier (most obviously the policy-limb of the policy-operational distinction, which embraces an understanding of "unreasonableness" that derives from (green light-informed) administrative law).

While there are many good reasons for judges having accommodated negligence law to the state's welfare consequentialism, this politico-legal state of

---

44 See David Kynaston, *Modernity Britain: Opening the Box, 1957–1959* (London: Bloomsbury, 2013), 237 (discussing Raymond Williams' argument that "the principle of common betterment [...] ought to be an absolute value.")

45 Will Kymlicka, *Contemporary Political Philosophy: An Introduction* (Oxford: Oxford University Press, 2002, 2nd ed.), 50, n. 1.

46 See Dicey, *Lectures on the Relation Between Law and Public Opinion in England During the Nineteenth Century*, Lecture IX.

47 See Carol Harlow and Richard Rawlings, *Law and Administration* (Cambridge: Cambridge University Press, 2009, 3rd ed.), ch. 1.

affairs provides a basis on which to explain the privacy blindspot we detected earlier. In order to make apparent why this is so, we will turn to the writings of Nussbaum, Nagel, and McGilchrist.

3 Martha Nussbaum

3.1 Nussbaum on Law and Literature

Martha Nussbaum argues in *Poetic Justice* that literature, and particularly the genre of the novel, has "the potential to make a distinctive contribution to our public life." For "the literary imagination" is, on Nussbaum's view, "an essential ingredient of an ethical stance that asks us to concern ourselves with the good of [...] people whose lives are distant from our own." She adds that the imaginative capacities that literature serves to foster provide a means by which to counter "refusals of compassion" that arise as a consequence of human sympathies being cultivated "narrowly and unequally." This means that literature can provide guidance concerning the "construction" of institutions, including law, and the training of institutional actors (e.g., judges) who "embody, and by institutional firmness protect, the insights of the compassionate imagination." Drawing on Henry James, Nussbaum argues that this guidance will assist judges in their efforts "to imagine [...] the honourable, the producible case."[48]

Nussbaum has much to say on the subject of imagination. She tells us that this faculty manifests itself in the ability "to see one thing in another." Likewise, it finds expression in the ability "to endow a perceived form with a complex life" and in the capacity to conjure up "non-existent possibilities" in the mind's eye. Moreover, she identifies people as exercising imagination when they recognise that distant strangers are much like themselves. Nussbaum illustrates this point by reference to a novel on which she draws extensively: Charles Dickens' *Hard Times*. She notes how one of the novel's central characters, Louisa Gradgrind, grasps, through the exercise of imagination, that the working people in her midst are, like herself, individuals and not mere factors of production. Nussbaum argues that imaginative breakthroughs of this sort constitute "bridge[s] to social justice." She also argues that, where such breakthroughs occur, they give expression to object-focused "rational emotions" (most obviously compassion).

---

48 Nussbaum, *Poetic Justice*, xvi, xviii (including the quotation from Henry James, "Art of the Novel" (New York: 1907), 223–224), and 2.

Nussbaum claims that if we integrate such emotions into processes of practical deliberation, we can improve the quality of the principles on which we act. However, her readiness to embrace the rational emotions is qualified. For she argues that we need a "filtering device" to separate out useful emotional inputs (e. g., compassion) from those that are unhelpful.[49] She finds such a device in Adam Smith's "judicious spectator."[50] This hypothetical figure's approach to practical deliberation involves the assumption of two perspectives. The judicious spectator adopts the first of these perspectives when he puts himself (so far as imagination will allow) in the situation of those upon whom a particular course of conduct will impact.[51] At this point in his deliberations, the judicious spectator seeks to gain "vivid" insights into the emotion-informed perceptions of those who are the objects of his attention.[52] Thereafter, the judicious spectator engages in "external assessment." This involves evaluating the reasonableness of the conduct under scrutiny, and the reactions of those it affects, from a standpoint that is at once alive to and detached from their emotions. Nussbaum sees deliberation along these lines as a means by which to ensure that those wielding power do so in ways that are sensitive to the viewpoint and interests of those upon whom it bears.

More generally, Nussbaum identifies "realist" Anglo-American fiction as commonly calling into question modes of thought that stultify the imagination and that, as a consequence, fail to provide morally attractive principles of public rationality. This is a point for which she finds support in Dickens' *Hard Times*. She notes that, at the novel's commencement, Thomas Gradgrind (Louisa's father) is a utilitarian ideologue. For he is convinced that he can reduce the organization of society to "a case of simple arithmetic."[53] With the aim of proving that this is the case, he establishes a school that is a threat to the imaginative capacities of the children who have the misfortune to attend it (who include his own daughter). Nussbaum follows Dickens in concluding that Gradgrind subscribes to a philosophy that blinds him to the complexity of others and that turns him into a public menace.

---

49 Nussbaum *Poetic Justice*, xviii, 4, 32–36, and 53–74.
50 Adam Smith, *A Theory of Moral Sentiments* (Indianapolis, Indiana: Liberty Fund, 1984).
51 Nussbaum, *Poetic Justice*, 73.
52 Nussbaum, *Poetic Justice*, 68. See also 74 (on "vivid imagining.") (Nussbaum notes Smith's use of the term "sympathy" when describing the judicious spectator's imaginative responses to the circumstances of the persons in whose shoes he seeks to stand. However, she prefers to talk of "empathetic participation" (see, for example, 73). Presumably, this is because "empathy," unlike "sympathy," does not connote condescension.)
53 Nussbaum, *Poetic Justice*, 20, 66, and 73.

Nussbaum argues that contemporary exponents of rational-choice economic theory exhibit blindness of the sort that afflicts Gradgrind.[54] She also identifies rational-choice theorists as sharing with Gradgrind a determination to aggregate data about individual lives, with the aim of "arriving at a picture of total or average utility." This is an approach to practical questions that effaces qualitative differences between and the separateness of persons. Individuals thus become "drops in an undemarcated ocean." While blind to these considerations, rational-choice theorists and Gradgrind assume that they have at their disposal precise solutions to all practical problems.[55] We thus have grounds for seeing them as being in the grip of hubris – a point Dickens drives home when he describes Gradgrind as surveying social questions from a windowless observatory:

> In this charmed apartment, the most complicated social questions were cast up, got into exact totals, and finally settled – if those concerned could only have been brought to know it. As if an astronomical observatory should be made without any windows, and the astronomer inside should arrange the starry universe solely by pen, ink and paper, so Mr Gradgrind in *his* Observatory (and there are many like it), had no need to cast an eye upon the teeming myriads of human beings around him, but could settle their destinies on a slate.[56]

The hubris on display in Gradgrind's "charmed apartment" provides a basis on which to explain the lack of compassion that Nussbaum associates with his utilitarianism and rational-choice economic theory. This is a point that has (as we will see later) relevance to *Mitchell, X and Y*, and the other cases we considered earlier.

3.2 Applying Nussbaum's Insights

In our examination of *Mitchell* and the other cases that reveal a privacy-related blindspot in British law, we focused on judicial decisions that seek to secure the public interest (by facilitating the delivery of generally beneficial outcomes). The judges who made these decisions exhibited attenuated concern for victims of wrongfully inflicted harm. This is a state of affairs in which it makes sense to take our cues from Nussbaum and talk (*vis-à-vis* each of the decisions) of a "refusal of

---

54 Nussbaum, *Poetic Justice*, ch. 2. See also George Orwell, "Charles Dickens," in *Decline of the English Murder and Other Essays* [1946] (Harmondsworth, Middlesex: Penguin Books, 1965), 84 (describing Gradgrind as "morally blinded.")
55 Nussbaum, *Poetic Justice*, 21 and 23.
56 Charles Dickens, *Hard Times* (Harmondsworth: Penguin Books, 1969 [1854]), 131–132.

compassion." However, we might also talk of an absence of compassion. For the privacy-related interests of claimants have gone unnoticed by lawyers and judges in cases such as *Mitchell*. Moreover, the lack of concern with these interests contrasts sharply with that on display in cases that have to do with the misuse of private information. In this latter area, English private law has developed rapidly in response to actions mounted by claimants who are, in many instances, wealthy.[57] When we juxtapose the law's operations in this area with its non-response to the violations of privacy in cases such as *Mitchell*, we find not just a legal blindspot but also evidence of a distributively unjust imbalance.[58]

This is a state of affairs that we can usefully scrutinise from the standpoints taken up by Smith's judicious spectator. Exercising his imaginative capacities, the judicious spectator would recognise that people in circumstances of the sort endured by claimants in cases such as *X and Y* have good reason to feel aggrieved. The law is inattentive to the violations of home and family life that they suffer, while being highly responsive to other (and in many instances less pressing) interferences with privacy. He could thus see that the people we are considering are not just the victims of abuse but of a distributively unjust imbalance in the law. But at the same time, the judicious spectator would also be alive to the public interest-related considerations that prompt judges not to impose negligence liability on local authorities in cases such as *Mitchell*. This is a matter that we could expect Smith's spectator (committed as he is to making a reasonable assessment of the conduct under scrutiny) to probe further. He might detect a commitment to welfare consequentialism at work in the law and conclude that the pursuit of generally beneficial outcomes necessitates a refusal to secure the interests of claimants such as *Mitchell*. He might also draw the conclusion that the subset of claimants we are considering occupy marginal social positions and are particularly vulnerable to refusals or absences of compassion.[59]

In light of these points, Nussbaum's approach to law and literature clearly has relevance to invasions of privacy in the circumstances we are considering.

---

57 See Richard Mullender, "Privacy, Imbalance and the Legal Imagination," *Tort Law Review* 19 (2011): 109–115. See also Simon Jenkins, "Angry celebrities, come to Britain: our judges are suckers for a glamour trial," *The Guardian*, May 4, 2007, 36.

58 Mullender, "Privacy, Imbalance and the Legal Imagination," 109 and 111. (The ideal of distributive justice enjoins those who embrace it to strive to fashion social institutions that defensibly accommodate the interests of all relevant people. See John Rawls, *A Theory of Justice* (Oxford: Oxford University Press, 1971), 4, *et seq.*)

59 See Lynsey Hanley, *Estates: An Intimate History* (London: Granta Books, 2007), 174 (noting that those who live in council housing are often viewed with "disgust and suspicion.") See also 49 and 181, and Owen Jones, *Chavs: The Demonization of the Working Class* (London: Verso, 2011), 34–35.

However, we can sharpen our analysis of the law's operations by drawing on Thomas Nagel's account of ruthlessness in public life.

4 Thomas Nagel

4.1 Nagel on Ruthlessness in Public Life

In "Ruthlessness in Public Life," Nagel distinguishes between two types of practical impulse that Nussbaum (while much concerned with principles of public rationality) tends to elide. For he draws a number of distinctions between "private" (or "individual") morality and "public morality."[60] Nagel identifies private morality as having to do with close interaction between individuals.[61] By contrast, he associates public morality with "institutions that are designed to serve purposes larger than those of particular individuals or families." In light of these points, he describes public morality as exhibiting a "discontinuity" from the private variant. Nagel develops this point by arguing that those who work within public institutions exhibit "a heightened concern for results." He adds that they typically focus impartially on the means by which to achieve "the best results overall" rather than on individuals who may be adversely affected by their decisions. This leads him to identify public morality as strongly consequentialist in orientation. This feature of public morality has a corollary that is highly relevant to this discussion. When compared with private morality, public morality exhibits reduced concern with "action-centred constraints": i.e., those constraints that limit the means that public institutions may employ to pursue their ends.[62] Insofar as public bodies and public officials enjoy some measure of insulation from these constraints, Nagel concludes that public morality "licenses ruthlessness."[63]

---

60 Thomas Nagel, *Mortal Questions* (Cambridge: Cambridge University Press, 1979) ch. 6. (While Nagel draws the distinction noted in the text, he nonetheless states that "public and private morality may share a common basis without one being derived from the other.")

61 Nagel, *Mortal Questions*, 78 and 83 (associating private morality with interaction between individuals and in families).

62 Nagel, *Mortal Questions*, 78 and 82–85.

63 Nagel, *Mortal Questions*, 82. See also 76 (on the "moral insulation" that, on Nagel's analysis, attaches to public bodies and roles). (The impartiality that Nagel identifies as a feature of public morality provides a basis on which to distinguish his use of "ruthlessness" from another sense of the term (commonly – and rather crudely – associated with the political philosophy of Niccolò Machiavelli). "Ruthlessness" (in the sense associated with Machiavelli) is partial. This is because it has to do with employing whatever means are necessary in order to secure or advance one's own

4.2 Applying Nagel's Insights

Nagel's account of ruthlessness in public life throws light, in a variety of ways, on the area of law we are considering. In their response to the claims in *Mitchell* and *X and Y*, we see judges attaching priority to public concerns: the ability of public bodies to focus on their core functions (pursuing generally beneficial outcomes). Moreover, the body of doctrine they apply when making these responses gives, as we noted earlier, expression to the assumption that public bodies will, in most circumstances, deliver outcomes that serve the public interest. In light of these points, we have grounds for concluding that public morality occupies a place of prominence in the branch of tort we are considering. We can press this point further and in ways that support the conclusion that ruthlessness on the model Nagel describes is at work in the law. In placing emphasis on the pursuit of generally beneficial outcomes, judges exhibit a concern with "the best results overall" – which is, as Nagel notes, a feature of ruthlessness.

There are reasons for drawing the same conclusion *vis-à-vis* another aspect of the judicial response to the cases we have examined. We find the judges in *Mitchell* and *X and Y* downplaying the significance of corrective justice. This feature of these cases merits close examination. This is because judges and commentators typically identify the impulse to do corrective justice as the normative core of negligence law (and tort more generally).[64] This ideal of justice specifies that those who have wrongfully inflicted harm on others while in a close relationship with them should make them whole. In placing this emphasis on wrongful harm-infliction in the context of close relationships, corrective justice and the body of tort law it informs give expression to a practical outlook that bears obvious resemblances to private morality as Nagel describes it. However, in the cases we have considered, corrective justice does not occupy a central place in the law's operations. This marks a shift away from those concerns that are the stuff of private morality. In light of these points we can see that Nagel enables us to gain greater analytic purchase on an issues that Nussbaum addresses (forms of public morality that underwrite the sacrifice of individuals' interests).

---

interests. See Niccolò Machiavelli, *The Prince* (Cambridge: Cambridge University Press, 1988, Quentin Skinner and Russell Price, eds), 62 and 104.)

64 See, for example, *X (Minors) v Bedfordshire County Council*, 633, *per* Lord Browne-Wilkinson (stating that corrective justice should have "first claim" on the "loyalty" of judges in negligence law), and Peter Cane, *Atiyah's Accidents, Compensation and the Law* (Cambridge: Cambridge University Press, 2013, 8th ed.), 416–417. Corrective justice yields the central justification for the incremental elaboration of new liability rules in tort. See Richard Mullender, "Tort, Human Rights, and Common Law Culture," *Oxford Journal of Legal Studies* 23 (2003): 301–318, 308.

Nagel's analysis is also relevant to the distinction we drew earlier between a refusal of compassion and an absence of compassion. Ruthlessness as he describes it provides a clear example of a refusal of compassion. Those who pursue "the best results overall" in ways that require departures from "action-oriented constraints" understand that they are sacrificing some in ways that redound to the benefit of (a great many) others. In such circumstances, it makes sense to talk of a refusal of compassion. For "refusal" predicates appreciation of what is at stake: gains that serve the public interest and associated (individual) losses. Moreover, we can draw a distinction between such appreciation and blindness to the plight of those who suffer in circumstances where a public body acts in ways that yield generally beneficial outcomes. In helping us to bring this distinction into focus Nagel is, again, a valuable adjunct to Nussbaum. However, she appears alive to a consideration that is absent from his analysis of ruthlessness and that is highly relevant to our concerns. In, for example, her account of Dickens' character Thomas Gradgrind, she dwells on a form of dogmatism that is pathological (and that finds expression in the blindness of the utilitarian ideologue in his windowless observatory). We find nothing of this sort in Nagel. If we want to gain a better understanding of the blindness that afflicts Gradgrind, Nagel will not assist us. However, there are, as we will see, reasons for thinking that Nussbaum's concern with pathological blindness intersects with that of Iain McGilchrist.

5 Iain McGilchrist

5.1 McGilchrist on the Divided Human Brain

Iain McGilchrist is a psychiatrist and medical researcher (in the field of neuroimaging). He has also taught English and, in *Against Criticism*, has written on literature's limitations as a response to human experience.[65] In a more recent book, *The Master and his Emissary: The Divided Brian and the Making of the Western World*, McGilchrist pursues some very large ambitions that have relevance to the privacy blindspot we are considering. He offers an account of each of the human brain's hemispheres and their relationship with one another. Moreover, he analyses the ways in which the relationship between the two hemispheres has changed in the Western world over the last three millennia. As he examines this relationship, McGilchrist's aim is to "tell [...] a story about ourselves and the world, and about

---

65 Iain McGilchrist, *Against Criticism* (London: Faber & Faber, 1982).

how we got to be where we are now."[66] This story concerns the relationship between the brain's operations and the ways in which we have and can organize our practical affairs (as individuals and as members of particular societies).

With the aim of helping his readers to grasp "where we are now," McGilchrist sets out an idealised account of the relationship between the brain's right and left hemispheres. As he unfolds this account, he places emphasis on the broad category of "attention." He notes that each of the hemispheres is "responsible" for distinct forms of attention. We owe our capacity for alertness and, likewise, vigilance and sustained attention to the right hemisphere.[67] McGilchrist adds that it is the right hemisphere that grasps what is, so to speak, "out there" in the world and thus exhibits wide vigilance.[68] Moreover, he states that the right hemisphere "deals preferentially with actually-existing things" and that it is "attuned to the apprehension of anything new."[69] This, he adds, is why "much of the spirit of empiricism comes from this side of the brain."[70] These are features of the right hemisphere's mode of operation that McGilchrist dwells on at length. They explain why he describes the right hemisphere as engaging in "presencing," by which he means its capacity to apprehend the complex flux of material that impinges on a human being's consciousness. McGilchrist explains that "presencing" makes it possible for the right hemisphere to grasp "things [while they] are still 'present' in their newness as individually existing entities."[71] He also argues that the right hemisphere equips us to act on Heraclitus's injunction to expect the unexpected and to recognise that, when it arrives, it will be "trackless and unexplored."[72]

When he turns to the left hemisphere, McGilchrist tells us that its "narrow focused attentional beam" complements the right's wide vigilance.[73] For having

---

66 Iain McGilchrist, *The Master and His Emissary: The Divided Brain and the Making of the Western World* (New Haven, Connecticut: Yale University Press, 2009), 1.

67 McGilchrist, *The Master and His Emissary*, 39.

68 McGilchrist, *The Master and His Emissary*, 38 and 164. See also 228 (noting that the right hemisphere "tries to take in all the [...] aspects of what it approaches at once.")

69 McGilchrist, *The Master and His Emissary*, 40 and 50. See also 94 (noting that "new experience of any kind [...] engages the right hemisphere") and 198 (on the right hemisphere's "receptive openness to what is.")

70 McGilchrist, *The Master and His Emissary*, 56. See also George Santayana, *Soliloquies in England and Other Soliloquies* (New York: Charles Scribner's Sons, 1922), 111 ("[s]ense is like a lively child always at our elbow, saying, Look, look, what's that?")

71 McGilchrist, *The Master and His Emissary*, 50, 56, and 93.

72 McGilchrist, *The Master and His Emissary*, 163–164. See also Charles Kahn, *The Art and Thought of Heraclitus* (Cambridge: Cambridge University Press, 1979).

73 McGilchrist, *The Master and His Emissary*, 39 and 44.

grasped what is "out there," the right hemisphere transfers the material it has apprehended to the left hemisphere, which engages in close analysis and categorisation.[74] The upshot of this activity is an abstract framework of thought that yields a schematic re-presentation of the larger whole apprehended but not analysed by the right hemisphere.[75] Thus "the left hemisphere's grasp of the world is essentially theoretical and self-referring" (or, to put the point another way, "virtual.")[76] While this is the case, McGilchrist points up the practical significance of the work it does. For it unpacks "primary experience" and pins things down, thus making it possible for people to make sense of their experiences and their environment.[77] While recognising the importance of the work done by the left hemisphere, McGilchrist drives home the point that it serves up its schematic analyses to the right. For the right hemisphere is (on his idealised account of the hemispheres' relationship) the place where judgment on their significance takes place. This is because it "sees things whole" and in context and possesses "greater integrative power" than the left.[78] Hence, the right hemisphere is better equipped to make judgments on the significance of the left hemisphere's schematic responses to what is "out there." As he unfolds this account of the right hemisphere, McGilchrist moves from description to prescription. For he pursues the theme that the right hemisphere should be the seat of ultimate judgment. This is because the right hemisphere, unlike the "processing house" of the left hemisphere, is "specialised in pragmatics, the art of [the] contextual understanding of meaning."

---

74 McGilchrist, *The Master and His Emissary*, 46. See also 38 (where McGilchrist identifies the left hemisphere as "more typically" concerned with the "selectivity" axis of attention and contrasts this with the right (which is concerned with the "intensity" axis of attention), 39 (where he notes that "selective attention may be bilateral"), and 44 (noting that "the right hemisphere has dominance for *exploratory* attentional movements, while the left hemisphere assists focused *grasping* of what has already been prioritised.")
75 McGilchrist, *The Master and His Emissary*, 195–196 and 200. See also David McNeil, *Hand and Mind: What Gestures Reveal about Thought* (Chicago, Illinois: University of Chicago Press, 1992), 248 (noting that thought (in the right hemisphere) is originally "largely imagistic and minimally analytic.")
76 McGilchrist, *The Master and His Emissary*, 164 ("essentially theoretical and self-referring") and 193 ("virtual.")
77 McGilchrist, *The Master and His Emissary*, 199 (unpacking), 135 (clarifying), and 219 ("primary experience.") See also 215 (noting Kant's point that, without concepts, we are effectively blind), and Michael Oakeshott, *On Human Conduct* (Oxford: Clarendon, Press, 1975), 3 ("[i]ntelligibles emerge out of misty intimations [...] when noticings become thoughts and [...] we come to inhabit a world of recognizables.")
78 McGilchrist, *The Master and His Emissary*, 47, 49, 197, and 206.

On McGilchrist's idealised account of the relationship between the hemispheres, we can trace movement from the right hemisphere to the left and back to the right. When we schematise the movement McGilchrist describes ("right → left → right"), the process takes on a rather laboured appearance.[79] This is unfortunate since the left hemisphere is, as McGilchrist notes, "in constant communication with the right hemisphere at the millisecond level."[80] But while this is the case, he goes on to argue that the relationship between the two hemispheres has often been less fruitful than in the account we have been examining. This, he explains, is because the left hemisphere is apt to assume that it has at its disposal solutions to practical problems that are clear and beyond dispute. When this happens, a relationship of "stable dynamic equilibrium" between the hemispheres gives way to one of "inequilibrium." McGilchrist argues that this unbalanced state of affairs reflects, among other things, the left hemisphere's strong tendency to reify the concepts (and associated frameworks) that it works up.[81] This is one among a range of points he makes in the course of contrasting the "experiential worlds" of the two hemispheres and the "widely differing ways of attending to the world" they each yield.[82]

5.2 "Two experiential worlds"

In the case of the left hemisphere, McGilchrist offers an account of the "world" it brings into existence that emphasises the functions it performs.[83] As the hemisphere concerned with analysis and categorisation, the left hemisphere is the

---

79 McGilchrist, *The Master and His Emissary*, 46, 49, and 219.

80 McGilchrist, *The Master and His Emissary*, 188. See also I. McGilchrist, "Top Brain, Bottom Brain: A Reply to Stephen Kosslyn & Wayne Miller," http://www.iainmcgilchrist.com/exchange_of_views.asp#content (January 31, 2014).

81 McGilchrist, *The Master and His Emissary*, 209, 231, and 359. See also 52 (arguing that "[t]he systematic categorising process of the left hemisphere can sometimes begin to have a life of its own") and 53 (noting that the left hemisphere's "categorising drive" is "at work all the time in all of us.") See also Kynaston, *Austerity Britain*, 128 (on the economist Ferdynand Zweig's description of the tendency to treat as "real" "outworn models, textbook patterns and artifice clumsily put together for certain analytical purposes.")

82 McGilchrist, *The Master and His Emissary*, 43 and 132. See also 94 (on "hemisphere differences") and 215 (on "the mutually inconsistent modes of processing adopted by the hemispheres.")

83 While, for our purposes, it is helpful to offer a functional account of the work done by the brain's two hemispheres, McGilchrist "tr[ies] to stand back a bit from the question of which 'functions' [...] the [...] hemispheres are performing, and [to] think of them [...] more globally as [each] having a disposition, or stance, towards the world." See McGilchrist, *The Master and His Emissary*, 92.

"seat" of language and thus has at its disposal "the means of argument."[84] McGilchrist describes how the left hemisphere uses language and systematic thought more generally to build up an abstract frame of reference on a "piece by piece" basis.[85] The upshot is, as we have noted, a re-presentation of the reality that the right hemisphere apprehends and delivers to it. The left hemisphere tends, as we noted earlier, to repose undue confidence in the frames of reference it establishes, finding in them not just a source of guidance but a path to progress. On this point, McGilchrist tells us that "the left hemisphere sees progress as a straight line." For it understands progress to consist in "unidirectional" move-ment – like that of an arrow as it travels "ever onwards and outwards, through a rectilinear, Newtonian space, towards its goal."[86] While recognising that the left hemisphere delivers a picture of reality that generates some sense of certainty and direction, McGilchrist points up a number of frailties that inhere in the "world" it delivers. He tells us that, from the standpoint of the left hemisphere, knowledge acquired through experience takes on a "suspect" appearance.[87] He adds that the left hemisphere exhibits "unwillingness to change track" and associated tenden-cies towards intolerance, inflexibility, and denial and/or "insouciant opti-mism."[88]

The picture that emerges from this account of the left hemisphere's opera-tions is one of path-dependency. For the left hemisphere is unwilling to revise, in

---

84 McGilchrist, *The Master and His Emissary*, 92 and 228. McGilchrist is, however, at pains to point out that the left hemisphere is not the exclusive home of language. See 81 (where he notes that, while the left hemisphere is concerned with denotation, the right hemisphere exhibits "interest in [...] connotation.")

85 McGilchrist, *The Master and His Emissary*, 228. See also 27–28 and 197–198.

86 McGilchrist, *The Master and His Emissary*, 446. See also 447 (noting that "[s]traight lines are prevalent wherever the left hemisphere predominates.") The goal-focused understanding of progress that McGilchrist ascribes to the left hemisphere provides a basis on which to conclude that it is consequentialist in orientation: i.e., it assesses the value of a course of conduct by reference to its outcomes (or anticipated outcomes). McGilchrist lends support to this view. For he describes the left hemisphere's "phenomenological world [as] being one of getting, of utility" (446). However, he also emphasises "the relationship between the left hemisphere and equality" (344). This might suggest that deontological practical impulses (concerned with doing that which is intrinsically right (e.g., treating people equally)) are at work within the left hemisphere. McGilchrist, however, explains the left hemisphere's interest in equality by reference to its determination to override "the recalcitrance of the particular" and to place it within the "Procrus-tean bed of the category it represents" (344).

87 McGilchrist, *The Master and His Emissary*, 429.

88 McGilchrist, *The Master and His Emissary*, 85 (on denial), 237 (on insouciant optimism), and 432 (on intolerance and inflexibility). See also 215 (on the left hemisphere's reluctance to admit ignorance).

the light of experience, the abstract frames of reference it works up. Likewise, it is unwilling to entertain doubts about the reasons for action it identifies such frames of reference as yielding. This leads McGilchrist to talk of the left hemisphere's "stickiness." By this he means that the left hemisphere is "remarkably entrapped in its [own] vision."[89] He also identifies the left hemisphere as afflicted by hubris.[90] Moreover, he describes the costs of this hubris as high. They take the form of a "loss of context" (and the "broader picture.") Thus he draws the conclusion that the left hemisphere is prone to a "Hall of Mirrors" effect.[91] By this he means that it may become "reflexively imprisoned" in an "essentially self-referring [...] world."[92] While McGilchrist points towards hubris as a basis on which to explain the left hemisphere's tendency to become imprisoned in the systems of thought it creates, he also associates it with our consciousness of ourselves. He states that "[t]he left hemisphere point of view inevitably dominates because it is the most accessible: closest to self-aware, self-inspecting intellect."[93]

When McGilchrist turns to the "world" yielded by the right hemisphere, he offers an account that makes it clear why he identifies it as the more fitting seat of practical judgment. He tells us that our capacity for empathy and, likewise, our ability to feel compassion are rooted in the right hemisphere.[94] McGilchrist adds that, where imagination, creativity, and "a moral sense" are concerned, "a large part, and in most cases the principal part, is played by the right hemisphere."[95]

---

89 McGilchrist, *The Master and His Emissary*, 49 and 162. See also 229.

90 McGilchrist, *The Master and His Emissary*, 82 (on the left hemisphere's tendency to insist on its theory at the expense of getting things wrong).

91 McGilchrist, *The Master and His Emissary*, 50, 229, 446, and 448.

92 McGilchrist, *The Master and His Emissary*, 42, 164, and 229–30. See also 426 (on "the left hemisphere [...] cut off from reality, its self-reflections reverberating endlessly around its mirrored walls") and 450 (on "reflexivity send[ing] the mind ever back into itself.")

93 McGilchrist, *The Master and His Emissary*, 228. See also 218–219 (noting that "it is the left hemisphere [...] that is in control at the conscious level [...] of the consistent nature of 'our' experience.")

94 McGilchrist, *The Master and His Emissary*, 57–58 (noting, *inter alia*, that "[w]hen we put ourselves in others' shoes, we are using the right inferior parietal lobe, and the right lateral prefrontal cortex, which is involved in inhibiting the automatic tendency to espouse one's own point of view"), and 86 (noting that "only humans, with their right prefrontal cortex, are capable of compassion.") See also 93 and 128 (where McGilchrist associates the compassionate orientation of the right hemisphere with a "centripetal" tendency that finds expression in empathetic "relationship[s] of 'betweenness'" with others).

95 McGilchrist, *The Master and His Emissary*, 127. But see 216 (noting that our imaginative faculties "appear to depend on the synthesis of the workings of both hemispheres.") However, McGilchrist emphasises that "flexibility of thought" and our ability to "frame shift" are rooted in the right hemisphere. See 40.

Moreover, the right hemisphere is able to engage in the complex mental operation to which the poet John Keats gave the name "negative capability."[96] We exhibit negative capability when we are able to endure "uncertainties, mysteries, and doubts, without an irritable reaching after fact and reason."[97] Negative capability thus enables us to remain poised between a "vision" and facts that fail to conform to it. To the extent that the right hemisphere can do this sort of thing, it is an "anomaly detector."[98] For this reason, the right hemisphere provides, on McGilchrist's analysis, a corrective for the narrowness of vision, path-dependency, and hubris of the left hemisphere. He adds that the right hemisphere's ability to act as a corrective to the left's deficiencies often finds expression in what he terms "aha!" moments.[99] These are the moments in which we grasp that our existing understanding is in some respect deficient and that an alternative view more adequately captures (or, at least, may capture) the object(s) of our attention.

As well as pointing up the right hemisphere's ability to deliver these insights, McGilchrist argues that we inhabit a context in which we are becoming less and less likely to derive benefit from them.[100] This is because "over-reliance on the left hemisphere" has accelerated in the Western world in the last century.[101] As a

---

96 McGilchrist, *The Master and His Emissary*, 173–174. See also 82.

97 John Cuddon, *A Dictionary of Literary Terms* (Harmondsworth, Middlesex: Penguin Books, 1977), 419.

98 McGilchrist, *The Master and His Emissary*, 52 (quoting from Vilayanur Ramachandran, *Phantoms in the Brain: Human Nature and the Architecture of the Mind* (London: HarperCollins, 2005)).

99 McGilchrist, *The Master and His Emissary*, 47.

100 McGilchrist, *The Master and His Emissary*, chs 12 and 13.

101 McGilchrist, *The Master and His Emissary*, 394. (McGilchrist's claims concerning the increasing influence of the left hemisphere in the practical life of the West form part of a detailed historical narrative that we can examine only briefly here. This narrative carries us back to classical antiquity. McGilchrist notes that in the 6th Century BC a new kind of civilization "erupted" (240). He explains this development by reference to "a (relative) disconnection or sundering of the hemispheres, and the origins of hemisphere specialisation as we now know it" (260). He adds that hemisphere specialisation set the scene for the rapid intensification of the left hemisphere's practical influence. This influence found expression in Greek philosophy and went into "overdrive" in Roman times (with the result that codification, rigidity, and insensitivity to context became prominent features of the social scene) (272 (Greek philosophy), and 291 (Rome)). McGilchrist detects the same tendency towards "left hemisphere overdrive" at other points in history: e.g., the Reformation, the scientific revolution of the seventeenth century, and the Enlightenment (chs 9 and 10). In his examination of the Enlightenment, he fastens on John Stuart Mill's critique of Jeremy Bentham. Mill observes that Bentham knew "little of human feelings" and "still less of the influences by which those feelings are formed." Mill adds that this did not deter Bentham from "attempt[ing] to give a rule to *all human conduct*" (339 (emphasis added)). McGilchrist finds in Bentham a very obvious example of the left hemisphere's hubristic practical outlook and contemplates the possibility that we may be unable to escape from this way of organizing society. This is because of the "Hall of

result, the frameworks of thought and the institutions and practices in which the left hemisphere's influence find expression now exert a damaging influence on practical life in countries such as Britain. McGilchrist illustrates this point by reference to the state. He tells us that the state in the democratic West has become an engine of "systematic conformity."[102] On his account, it is a form of "technology" that seeks to categorise and organize society in conformity with a "picture" (an abstract frame of reference).[103] As he unfolds this analysis, McGilchrist invokes Heidegger who declared that "the fact that the world becomes a picture … is what distinguishes the essence of the modern age."[104]

McGilchrist also finds support for his analysis in two of Heidegger's compatriots, Friedrich Nietzsche and Georg W.F. Hegel. From Nietzsche he takes the point that the contemporary West is a context in which "[m]ore and more, the symbolic replaces that which exists."[105] McGilchrist offers a number of explanations for this development. They include the left hemisphere's preference for what is "familiar." Likewise, they embrace its readiness to assume that the frameworks it establishes bring "fixity" to practical life.[106] McGilchrist adds that the upshot of the left hemisphere's influence in the contemporary West is marked insensitivity to "the fluidity of the real."[107] This leads on to his invocation of Hegel. He notes that Hegel, while meditating on nineteenth century Western culture, declared that "the oracles … no longer speak to men."[108] McGilchrist finds in this rather gnomic observation support for the conclusion that we are often in thrall to systems of thought that render us insensitive to the complexity of the world around us. As a

---

Mirrors" effect that we noted earlier. See also Dicey, *Lectures on the Relation Between Law and Public Opinion in England During the Nineteenth Century*, 96 (noting Bentham's expression of the view that he possessed "a genius for legislation.")

102 McGilchrist, *The Master and His Emissary*, 390 (where McGilchrist also describes the state as "an overweening presence.") A phrase from the novelist Don DeLillo captures the thrust of McGilchrist's critique of the state in the contemporary West. See D. DeLillo, *Underworld* (London: Picador, 1997), 465 (on the danger of being "systemed under.")

103 McGilchrist, *The Master and His Emissary*, 390 (organizing and categorising) and 401 (picture).

104 McGilchrist, *The Master and His Emissary*, 401 (quoting from Martin Heidegger, *The Question Concerning Technology and Other Essays* [1949] (New York: Harper & Row, 1977), 129–130).

105 McGilchrist, *The Master and His Emissary*, 418 (quoting from Friedrich Nietzsche, *Human, All Too Human* (Lincoln Nebraska: University of Nebraska Press, 1996, 2nd ed. (revised)), s 217 (129–130).

106 McGilchrist, *The Master and His Emissary*, 387 and 426 ("fixity.")

107 McGilchrist, *The Master and His Emissary*, 426. See also 400 (on the tendency of the left hemisphere to become "unplugged" from the context(s) it seeks to order).

108 McGilchrist, *The Master and His Emissary*, 450 (quoting from Georg W.F. Hegel, *The Phenomenology of Mind*, trans. J.B. Baillie [1807] (London: George Allen & Unwin, 1949), 753–754.

result, we are less well equipped to respond to the problems and opportunities that present themselves to us than we commonly suppose.

5.3 Applying McGilchrist's Analysis

We can use McGilchrist's account of the "left hemisphere world" to gain analytic purchase on the philosophy that, on our earlier analysis, informs the body of law we examined in section 2. "Welfare consequentialism" is an abstract frame of reference within which we find an emphasis on progress through the successful pursuit of generally beneficial outcomes. For it assumes that public bodies (e.g., housing authorities) are in a position to deliver goods that benefit large numbers of people. Thus we find in welfare consequentialism an understanding of "progress" on the model McGilchrist describes in his account of the "world" yielded by the left hemisphere. Welfare consequentialism gives expression to the assumption that public bodies have it in their power to move large numbers of people into a future that is, in material ways, better than the past they have left, or will leave, behind. This is progress in conformity with the "picture" that emerges from the account that politicians, judges, and public bodies typically give of their purposes. Moreover, we might characterise progress understood in this way as unidirectional movement through the rectilinear space mapped by the relevant (welfare consequentialist) picture.

On the assumption that this analysis is broadly correct, it throws light on the law's response to cases such as *Mitchell* and *X and Y*. As we have noted, these are cases in which judges have concluded that the imposition of duties of care in negligence would deflect public bodies from their core aims and thus be socially damaging. In these responses, we find an emphasis on the pursuit of progress (as the left hemisphere understands it) that is strong enough to exclude countervailing considerations as reasons for action. In this aspect of the law's operations, we also find judges treating an abstract frame of reference (welfare consequentialism) as an adequate basis on which to organize practical life through the elaboration and use of doctrine.

But, more importantly, for our purposes, the "picture" that judges "see" when they respond to claims such as *Mitchell* seems to exert a wider influence. The officials within public bodies and, likewise, the lawyers who become involved in these cases fail to address the issue of privacy.[109] This is, to be sure, a feature of

---

109 *Cf* Equality and Human Rights Commission, *Human Rights at Home*, 25 (noting that "[w]hile there is no human right to expect a social housing provider to keep a resident safe and free from

these cases that we might explain by reference to considerations other than those raised by McGilchrist. We might draw the conclusion that the violations of home and family life we have been considering could be addressed by bodies of law other than that relating to privacy: e.g., the law on anti-social behaviour.[110] We could also point to a long-standing and strong reluctance on the part of judges to impose negligence liability on defendants for the voluntary conduct of third parties.[111] We might also detect in the law's response to the cases we have been examining a lack of urgency that suggests a view of those involved as something of a lost cause (victims as much as perpetrators).[112] But the blindspot we are

---

nuisance at all times, a failure to address or tackle the reported experience of anti-social behaviour may well amount to a failure to respect the private or family life of a victim or an infringement of his or her right to respect for home.")

110 See Susan Bright, "Liability for the Bad Behaviour of Others," *Oxford Journal of Legal Studies* 21 (2001): 311–330, 318. See also *Mitchell v Glasgow City Council*, 889, *per* Lord Hope, and 905, *per* Baroness Hale (identifying the neighbour who killed Mitchell as having persistently engaged in anti-social behaviour prior to turning homicidal).

111 See, for example, *Dorset Yacht Co v Home Office* [1970] AC 1004, 1030, *per* Lord Reid (stating that an act of a third party "must have been something very likely to happen if it is not to be regarded as a *novus actus interveniens* breaking the chain of causation.")

112 Hanley, *Estates*, 44. See also *Mitchell v Glasgow City Council*, 889, *per* Lord Hope (on "the many behavioural problems that arise in local authority estates.") Hegel's account of *der Pöbel* (the rabble) is relevant to the point made in the text. See Allen W. Wood, *Hegel's Ethical Thought* (Cambridge: Cambridge University Press, 1990), 250–255 (on Hegel's conclusion that, throughout history, a subset of people have acquired the status of *der Pöbel* and have, as a result, occupied marginal social positions). A murder in Bristol in 2013 (that arose from circumstances that bear clear similarities to those with which we are concerned) lends support to the view that public bodies tend to regard people who live on local authority estates or in social housing as socially marginal. Bijan Ebrahimi (who had learning difficulties) lived alone in a local authority flat. Children, at the prompting of their father, Lee James, vandalised the hanging baskets outside Ebrahimi's home. Ebrahimi took pictures of the children, with the aim of gathering evidence as to what had happened. Lee James thereafter accused Ebrahimi of being a paedophile. An angry crowd soon gathered outside Ebrahimi's home and chanted "paedo, paedo." Fearing for his safety, Ebrahimi called the police. When the police visited Ebrahimi's home, they saw Lee James trying to attack him. But having assessed the situation, the police arrested Ebrahimi. The next day, they released him without charge. Two days later, Lee James attacked Ebrahimi in his home and gave him a beating that may have been the cause of his death. (Factual accounts of this murder do not provide a clear answer to the question as to whether the beating Lee James gave Ebrahimi was the cause of his death. This is because James, having beaten Ebrahimi, doused him in white spirit and burnt his body.) The decision to return Ebrahimi to his home is now the subject of an Independent Police Complaints Commission investigation. A witness has reportedly described the police as having "delivered [Ebrahimi] back" into a situation where he was under siege. See Matthew Parris, "Our need to hate creates another victim," *The Times*, November 2, 2013, 29. See also Kevin Dowling and James Gillespie, "Burn the Paedo," *The Sunday Times*, November 3, 2013,

considering is so obvious (and the repeated non-responses to it so egregious) as to suggest a problem more fundamental than entrenched prejudice. This gives McGilchrist his *entrée*. His account of the left hemisphere's operations, and (more particularly) its experiential world, seems highly relevant to the failure to establish a cause of action in the area of law we have been examining. A welfare consequentialist picture may blind those in its grip to the plight of people such as Mitchell, X and Y, and Fiona Pilkington and her daughter. While it is natural to respond to such blindness by talking of a lack of imagination, McGilchrist affords a basis on which to deepen our understanding of the way in which this problem can arise.

6 McGilchrist, Nussbaum, and Nagel

Just as we can use McGilchrist's analysis to make sense of the law's failings, so too we can use it to refine our understanding of the analyses of Nussbaum and Nagel (as commentators whose writings are relevant to our concerns). As we noted, Nussbaum finds in the bodies of consequentialist thought she criticises, a basis on which to explain "refusals of compassion." However, we also noted that she appears, on occasion, to be concerned with absences of compassion. There are reasons for thinking that McGilchrist throws light on each of these conditions (refusals and absences). As those who embrace an abstract frame of reference become more invested in it, we might expect to see signs of the "stickiness" and hubris that McGilchrist identifies as features of the left hemisphere "world." Moreover, these features of the left hemisphere's outlook may (over time) become more prominent in practical contexts. Thus we may be able to trace a process of development along a timeline in which refusals of compassion turn, by degrees, into absences. In such circumstances, we have grounds for concluding that (in Hegel's phrase) "the oracles [...] no longer speak to men." While McGilchrist takes the view that this sort of thing is happening in our culture, we might draw a less gloomy conclusion from Nagel's account of ruthlessness. We could read it as supporting the view that those who act ruthlessly in public life require (to use Nagel's term) insulation in order to pursue the best results overall. If this is the case, it suggests that ruthless public officials possess a clear grasp of what is

---

29 (noting, *inter alia*, that the solicitor representing Ebrahimi's family has described him as being the victim of "harassment [...] over a number of years"), and "Bijan Ebrahimi murder: Police 'let vulnerable man down,'" http://www.bbc.co.uk/news/uk-england-bristol-25122280 (noting that the Chief Constable of Avon and Somerset Police, Nick Gargan, has identified "agencies and authorities" as having "failed Mr Ebrahimi") (January 31, 2014).

going on "out there" as a result of their actions. In light of these points, we might find support for the conclusion that we are less likely to fall victim to absences (if not refusals) of compassion than McGilchrist appears to suggest.

The process of doctrinal development in negligence law that we considered earlier may also lend support to this view. As judges have elaborated doctrines that have shielded public bodies from compensation claims, we might see them as engaging in refusals of compassion. For they have developed the law in ways that mark a retreat from corrective justice. The retreat from this ideal in the context we are considering is one to which judges are alive and about which they have, on occasion, sounded notes of (none too convincing) concern.[113] This is not, however, a development that appears to trouble those directly concerned with the delivery of the goods promised by welfare consequentialism (ministers, councillors, civil servants, and other public officials). In their case, talk of an absence of compassion appears to have more traction. The notion of an absence of compassion also has relevance when we turn to the elaboration of privacy doctrine. Judges and lawyers have wasted no time in identifying the development of the doctrine of misuse of private information as a milestone on the road of human rights-related protection. However, privacy and the interests in home and family life protected by Article 8(1) of the ECHR have not loomed into view as salient concerns in cases such as *Mitchell*.

The resulting failure to develop privacy law suggests a profound lack of imagination – the faculty we use when we (among other things) work over and explore the implications (in new contexts) of what we remember.[114] To the extent that British lawyers are failing to do this sort of thing in cases such as *Mitchell* and *X and Y*, it brings us back to one of Nussbaum's central concerns: the exercise of imagination in pursuit of social (or distributive) justice. However, there are reasons for thinking that we can forge links between the law's deficiencies and three understandings of imagination that do not feature in *Poetic Justice*. The first of these understandings is the legal imagination, which has to do with identifying

---

113 *X (Minors) v Bedfordshire County Council*, 663, *per* Lord Browne-Wilkinson (stating that, in the field of negligence law, corrective should have "first claim" on the "loyalty" of judges).
114 Alberto Manguel, *Homer's The Iliad and the Odyssey: A Biography* (London: Atlantic Books, 2007), 151 (drawing on James Joyce's understanding of imagination). The Joycean understanding of imagination intersects with Michael Oakeshott's account of "the pursuit of intimations." The pursuit of intimations is an interpretative practice that involves the identification of and reflection on the practical significance of normative impulses within particular institutions and models of human association (and is thus a precondition of immanent critique). See Michael Oakeshott, *The Voice of Liberal Learning* (New Haven, Connecticut: Yale University Press, 1989), 185–188.

unrealised possibilities for development in the law.[115] The second is the socio-logical imagination. We exercise this faculty when we grasp the relationship between the personal "troubles" of individuals and "issues" of social structure from which they arise.[116] The third understanding relevant to this discussion is the moral imagination. This imaginative capacity has, for reasons we will explore shortly, particular relevance to our concerns. Those who exercise the moral imagi-nation do not, on the account offered by Edmund Burke, assume that they are able to give expression to insights yielded by a "conquering empire of light and reason."[117] Rather, they reflect on the institutions and practices that shape their practical world in the light of the continuous stream of experience that confronts them as they move through life. Their aim in doing this is to refine their institutions and practices in ways that will "raise [them] [...] in [their] own estimation."[118]

When we apply the first of these understandings to the privacy blindspot we have been considering, we can immediately identify a failure on the part of lawyers to exercise the legal imagination. Likewise, we can see in welfare con-sequentialism a body of thought that, in focusing attention ruthlessly on "the best results overall," is anything but a spur to the exercise of the sociological imagina-tion.[119] While each of these understandings of imagination throws light on the problem we have been examining, the moral imagination points towards some-thing of a solution. If we are to exercise this faculty, we must exhibit the wide vigilance that McGilchrist locates in the right hemisphere (as it engages in its presencing operations). This is a point to which Edmund Burke (on whose account of the moral imagination we are drawing) lends force. While recognising that we can inject a significant measure of order into our lives by relying on "general propositions" (rooted in "long experience"), Burke sounds a note of caution. He tells us that we must expect to encounter "exceptions" to the proposi-tions on which we act.[120] He adds that our ability to identify these exceptions will

---

115 See, for example, Scott Brewer, "Exemplary Reasoning: Semantics, Pragmatics, and the Rational Force Of Legal Argument By Analogy," *Harvard Law Review* 109 (1996): 923–1028, 954 (on the uncodifiable imaginative moment in which lawyers identify relevant similarities (of the sort that support arguments for the development of existing doctrine)).

116 Charles Wright Mills, *The Sociological Imagination* [1959] (Harmondsworth: Penguin Books, 1970), 14–15 and 17.

117 Edmund Burke, *Reflections on the Revolution in France* [1790], ed. Conor Cruise O'Brien (London: Penguin Books, 1968), 171. See also Gertrude Himmelfarb, *The Moral Imagination: From Edmund Burke to Lionel Trilling* (London: Souvenir Press, 2006), 11.

118 Burke, *Reflections on the Revolution in France*, 171 and 180.

119 See Nagel, *Mortal Questions*, 82 (on the "moral impersonality" of ruthless public action).

120 Burke, *Reflections on the Revolution in France*, 139 ("general propositions" and "circum-stances") and 148 ("long experience.")

be greatly enhanced if we pay close attention to "circumstances." If we are to do this, we must, according to Burke, exhibit "ever-waking vigilance" and cultivate our capacity for "attentive observation." He also argues that, by adopting this approach, we can avoid becoming intoxicated by theory.[121]

In light of these points, Burke appears to be offering a solution to the problems of the left hemisphere world described by McGilchrist. However, we must be cautious about talk of a solution. The tendency to assume the adequacy of the abstract frameworks that the left hemisphere enables us to work up will not disappear simply because we are alive to it. But we can, at least, recognise that these frameworks do not bring an "all conquering empire of light and reason" into existence. Having grasped this point, we can seek to be attentive to what is out there. To act in this way would mark an effort to move in the direction of the idealised relationship between the brain's hemispheres that McGilchrist describes.[122] This, however, may sound like a tall order in the context of McGilchrist's "left hemisphere world." So it is worth keeping in mind that attentiveness to circumstances is something on which the common law (of which tort is a part) has long placed and continues to place emphasis.[123] Thus we find Karl Llewellyn describing the common law as an institutional context in which opportunities arise for judges to make just responses to novel problems. Moreover, he finds

---

121 Burke, *Reflections on the Revolution in France*, 90, 94, 143, 180, and 205. See also 155 (where Burke associates theory with "pride and intoxication.")

122 While we cannot pursue the point in detail here, the practical outlook Burke argues for has affinities with McGilchrist's idealised account of the relationship between the brain's two hemispheres. To the extent that "general propositions" are the fruit of "long experience," we can see a sustained pattern of movement from the right hemisphere to the left. Moreover, to the extent that Burke's general propositions come under scrutiny in the light of "circumstances," we have grounds for concluding that judgment on their value takes place in the right hemisphere. Though Burke does not talk in the terms used by McGilchrist, he seems to be alive to the problem of "over-reliance on the left hemisphere." See Burke, *Reflections on the Revolution in France*, 133 ("when men are too much confined to professional and faculty habits, and, as it were, inveterate in the recurrent employment of that narrow circle, they are rather disabled than qualified for whatever depends on the knowledge of mankind, on experience in mixed affairs, on a comprehensive connected view of the various complicated external and internal interests which go to the formation of that multifarious thing called a state.")

123 See, for example, *Woodland v Essex County Council* [2013] UKSC 66, [28] [emphasis added], *per* Lady Hale: "[t]he common law is a dynamic instrument. It develops and adapts to meet new situations *as they arise*." See also Gerald Postema, *Bentham and the Common Law Tradition* (Oxford: Clarendon Press, 1986), 66–68 (on Burke's contribution to "classical common law theory"), and Peter Stanlis, *Edmund Burke and the Natural Law* [1958] (New Brunswick, NJ: Transaction Publishers, 2003), 35 (noting that Burke argued that law can render those who study it "acute, inquisitive, dexterous" and (sounding a rather hubristic note) "full of resources.")

ample evidence of judicial willingness to make such responses. This leads him to eulogise the common law as a body of "slow-growing wisdom."[124] This is not, though, a description that we can apply to the cases we have examined. However, Lord Nicholls' statement that privacy-related protections in tort could extend beyond the misuse of private information is worth contemplating from a Burkean standpoint. Judges might treat this statement (when suitable circumstances arise) as opening up the opportunity to revisit the "general propositions" that give the law its current shape. If they were to do this, they would immediately come face-to-face with tort's long-lived commitment to the pursuit of corrective justice in circumstances where a defendant has wrongfully inflicted harm on a claimant's significant interests. "Home" and "family life" provide two such interests. More-over, judges working along the lines contemplated here might act on Tugendhat J's suggestion that the law should provide protection against intrusion. For intrusion is a concept commodious enough to embrace the harmful forms of wrong-doing on which we have focused (see Table 1, below).[125] To act in this way would be to demonstrate the "ever-waking vigilance" of which Burke speaks.

Before drawing this essay to a close, the relationship between "ever-waking vigilance," the common law as a source of "slow-growing wisdom," and McGilchrist's account of the right hemisphere merits further analysis. McGilchrist (as we have noted) indicates that the right hemisphere is not the source of our sense of ourselves as "self-aware, self-inspecting" agents. On his account, the right hemisphere (as well as being the source of the inputs that result from its "presencing" operations) yields what we might describe as deliverances: insights that arrive quite unexpectedly and in "aha!" moments.[126] These insights may be a

---

124 Karl Llewellyn, *The Bramble Bush* (New York: Oceana, 1930) 43. See also O'Callaghan, *Refining Privacy in Tort Law*, 149–152 (on the refinement of privacy-related protections in tort).

125 See William Prosser, "Privacy," *California Law Review* 48 (1960): 383–423, 389–390 and 392 (on instances of intrusion that relate to "home" life). The association between home (or, at least a home-like refuge) and freedom from intrusion is strong in George Orwell, *Nineteen Eighty-Four* [1949] (Harmondsworth: Penguin Books, 1954), 112–113 (where, through a minor character (Mr Charrington), Orwell makes it plain that he is appealing to the notion of privacy that he discusses in *The Lion and the Unicorn*).

126 While it is useful, for analytical purposes to distinguish between the right hemisphere's presencing operations and its capacity to yield insights in "aha!" moments, we should treat this distinction with caution. Many of the insights (or deliverances) of interest to lawyers may derive from the right hemisphere's ability to draw significance from a (social) background that resists but is not wholly unamenable to articulation. Since the right hemisphere alone engages directly with the world we experience, the background falls within its purview. Moreover, the detection of stimuli outside the focus of conscious processing is "strongly lateralised" to this side of the brain. See McGilchrist, *The Master and His Emissary*, 187.

spur to the reflective processes described by Nussbaum in her account of the imagination. Likewise, they may prompt us to exercise our imaginative capacities in their legal, sociological, and moral forms. When we have these stabs of insight, our thought processes are not under conscious control and we are apt to experience a sense of "shakenness" in their aftermath.[127] We may, for example, find ourselves poised between an existing picture of our practical affairs and a new and inchoate alternative – a state of affairs to which Keats's account of negative capability has clear relevance.[128] As we contemplate such an alternative, we are likely to use accustomed (and ordered) modes of thought to think through its implications. For example, we might exercise the sociological imagination by exploring the relationship between the problems of individuals and features of the social structure that may (in light of the new and inchoate view) require reform. To do this sort of thing is to reflect critically on a picture of practical life that does not seem adequate to the relevant reality. In such circumstances, we find ourselves considering how to reconfigure a left hemisphere world that, in the absence of critical reflection and reworking, threatens (for the reasons McGilchrist gives) to make us its prisoner.[129] But, at the same time, the left hemisphere, at once challenged and active, is involved in the process of reordering the "world" it offers us.

If these points concerning critical reflection are broadly correct, a prior process (outside our control) precedes the exercise of imagination. This is a point on which George Santayana has dwelt. For he has described "cloud-like thoughts" that "know nothing of whence they came" or "how they will fall out." Likewise, he has described an "obscure [mental but not reflective] operation" that

---

127 McGilchrist, *The Master and His Emissary*, 173 and 490, n 163 (drawing on the Czech philosophical phenomenologist Jan Patočka). See also Hanif Kureishi, "What they don't teach at creative writing school," *The Daily Telegraph*, January 25, 2014, 22 (Review) (observing that "[o]nce you start thinking about [...] where [the imagination] might take you [...] you're in useful trouble.")

128 See also Mary Midgley, *Science and Poetry* (London: Routledge, 2006), 31 ("imaginative visions [...] involve changes in our larger world-pictures") and 33 ("originating visions are [...] necessarily vague.")

129 See, for example, Philip Bobbitt, *The Garments of Court and Palace: Machiavelli and the World that He Made* (London: Atlantic Books, 2013), 59–61 (identifying Niccolò Machiavelli as "the first philosopher of the modern state" since he "saw in the events around him" the outlines of the princely state while others "were still captivated and ensnared by the old structures" of feudalism), and 103 (arguing that Machiavelli grasped that "in the very heart of Italy there lay the inchoate realm of the first, truly modern, non-feudal state.") See also Oakeshott, *On Human Conduct*, 4 (on "educated imagination" – a capacity we exercise when we use "experiences [...] to serve inferences.")

sets the scene for the exercise of imagination.[130] However, thoughts such as these are in danger of enjoying only a brief and fugitive existence. This is because they are goads to reflection (and in some circumstances action) that may slip away from us unless we pin them down and begin to explore their significance.[131] If we are to do this, we must "want[] to acquire [...] a grasp of something that is *not yet within reach.*"[132] In contemplating this task, we come close to the core of a problem that exercises McGilchrist. If we assume that we have an adequate picture of the world around us, insights that unexpectedly arrive in "aha!" moments are likely to slip away from us. In the common law, we have an institutional means of countering this problem. But it does not promise to provide immediate solutions to our problems. In order for these problems to come into focus, we must be attentive to experience.[133] We must also recognise that we cannot rely on ourselves to grasp its significance immediately. For this reason, it

---

130 George Santayana, *Soliloquies in England and Other Soliloquies*, 123.

131 See Charles Wright Mills, *The Sociological Imagination*, 216–217 (on the way in which "fringe thoughts" and experience act as drivers of "original intellectual work" and keep one's "inner world awake.") The "original intellectual work" to which Mills refers may involve abduction: an ampliative (and rather loose) reflective process in which we treat the insights with which we are grappling as postulates and explore their implications. On abduction, see Cheryl Misak, *The American Pragmatists* (Oxford: Oxford University Press, 2013), 47–49.

132 Gilbert Ryle, *Collected Papers Volume 2: Collected Essays 1929–1968* (London: Routledge, 2009), 506 [emphasis added.] Ryle's use of the verb "grasp" has obvious affinities with McGilchrist's description of the left hemisphere's ability to assist focused grasping of material that the right hemisphere has prioritised. See also Kureishi, "What they don't teach at creative writing school," 22 (noting (in his examination of the imagination) that "[m]ost people have good ideas all the time, [but] they just prefer not to notice them.")

133 In our efforts to be attentive to experience, we might treat George Orwell's "belly to earth" approach to writing as a model. Orwell used the phrase "belly to earth" to express his determination to focus on the material that presented itself to him and to use language that would capture it. See Robert Colls, *George Orwell*, 33 and 45, and William Cain, "Orwell's Essays as a Literary Experience," ch. 6 in *The Cambridge Companion to George Orwell*, ed. John Rodden (Cambridge: Cambridge University Press, 2007), 76. See also George Orwell, *Inside the Whale and Other Essays* [1957] (Harmondsworth: Penguin Books, 1962), 156 [emphasis added] ("[w]hen you think of a concrete object, *you think wordlessly*, and then, if you want to describe the thing you have been visualizing you probably hunt about till you find the exact words that seem to fit it.") The sequence of mental operations in Orwell's "belly to earth" approach bears obvious similarities to that in McGilchrist's idealised account of the relationship between the brain's hemispheres. For Orwell moves from a "concrete object" to "hunt[ing] about" for words, before making a judgment on which of the relevant terms "fit it" most adequately. In going about his business in this way, Orwell's approach (and, indeed, that of McGilchrist) is nominalist in orientation. See Terry Eagleton, *The Event of Literature* (New Haven, Massachusetts: Yale University Press, 2012), 1 and 8 (describing nominalists as determined to use language in ways that cling to "the textures of phenomena.") The nominalist orientation of McGilchrist's thinking is apparent in, for example,

is incumbent on us to attend closely to shards of insight when they race through our minds. For these insights may open the way to imaginative and ultimately critical reflection on the law and its limitations. This sounds rather laborious. So it is. But, then, we are limited creatures and slow-growing wisdom is typically the only sort available to us in practical contexts.

7 Conclusions

Cases such as *Mitchell* and *X and Y*, and the deaths of Fiona Pilkington and her daughter, reveal a blindspot in the British law relating to privacy. This blindspot is a singularly unattractive fact of politico-legal life in Britain. Its existence is as remarkable as it is depressing. Human rights have loomed to prominence in Britain in the last decade-and-a-half and have spurred a process of rapid doctrinal development in private law (the elaboration of the doctrine of misuse of private information). Hence, we might have expected a vigorous response, on the part of judges, public bodies, etc, to the violations of home and family life that we have considered. But there has been no such response. We have found a basis on which to explain its absence in Britain's form of politico-legal life: a context in which a commitment to welfare consequentialism occupies a prominent place. Viewed from the standpoint of this philosophy, claims such as those mounted by James Mitchell's relatives threaten to deflect local authorities and other public bodies from the pursuit of their central aim. This is the delivery of goods that, in most instances, benefit those who receive them. Moreover, we have detected the influence of welfare consequentialism in judicial elaboration of doctrines that shield public bodies from negligence claims.

The upshot is a state of practical affairs on which Nussbaum, Nagel, and McGilchrist each throw light. While Nussbaum (with her emphasis on imagination as a guide to action) is a source of valuable insights, Nagel and McGilchrist each augment her analysis in significant ways (see Table 2, below). In his account of ruthlessness in public life, Nagel brings into focus considerations that do not feature in *Poetic Justice*. They are the distinction between "private" and "public" morality and the readiness in the latter system to insulate public bodies and officials from criticism in circumstances where they act ruthlessly. In offering this account of ruthlessness in the public sphere, Nagel enables us to grasp the complexity of the "refusals of compassion" that Nussbaum describes. These

---

the emphasis he places on the way in which the brain's right hemisphere is able to grasp "things [while they] are still 'present' in their newness as individually existing entities."

refusals are mental operations in which officials recognise that people will suffer as a result of their opting to privilege the pursuit of socially valuable outcomes. When we turn to McGilchrist, we find that he adds something to Nussbaum's analysis by throwing light on the distinct "experiential" (or "phenomenological") world yielded by the brain's left hemisphere. In his account of the deficiencies of this practical standpoint (including "stickiness," hubris, and reluctance to respond to experience), we have a more adequate basis on which to explain the dogmatism that finds expression in Gradgrind's utilitarianism and consequentialism more generally. Moreover, Dickens' account of Gradgrind's observatory provides an example of the way in which an abstract frame of reference may blind those who embrace it to the complexities of the contexts they seek to regulate. Where this problem manifests itself, it becomes easy to see how (in Hegel's phrase) "the oracles [...] no longer speak to [people]" (see Table 2, below).

Having made use, in this discussion, of law and literature, political philosophy, and McGilchrist's account of the brain's two hemispheres, some reflections on interdisciplinarity seem apt. Each of the thinkers on whom we have drawn engages with a broad problem that has both a political and a perceptual or, at least, perspectival dimension. The problem concerns the use of political power in ways that are properly attentive to the interests of all those affected by its exercise. The political dimension of this problem has to do with efforts to approximate and departures from the ideal of distributive justice: e.g., when seeking to secure privacy-related interests in home and family life. The problem's perceptual or perspectival dimension concerns the adoption of, or failures to adopt, a standpoint that makes it possible to grasp the requirements of distributive justice. Nussbaum grapples with the two dimensions of this problem when she identifies consequentialist thought as yielding standpoints that encourage refusals of compassion (arising from, for example, insensitivity to the separateness of persons). Nagel offers an analytically more precise variation on the same theme. For those who focus on "the best results overall" may do so having adopted a standpoint that removes the claims of private morality from their field of vision. McGilchrist's concerns, while broader than those of Nussbaum and Nagel, nonetheless intersect with them. He roots the impulse to embrace an abstract body of thought such as welfare consequentialism in the brain's left hemisphere. Moreover, he identifies the modern state as a form of "technology" that facilitates highly focused pursuit of the ends that find expression in consequentialism and other abstract frames of reference. As McGilchrist develops these points, we can see how the political and perceptual or perspectival dimensions of the problem that he, Nussbaum, and Nagel each address can meld together in ways that stymie the pursuit of distributive justice. This may happen where those in the "Hall of

Mirrors" McGilchrist describes wrongly assume (just as Gradgrind assumes in his windowless observatory) that they are equipped to deliver just outcomes.

In the cases we have examined, something of this sort appears to be going on. If we are to grasp the significance of these cases, we must (on our earlier analysis) be attentive to a wide range of concerns. They include the ideal of distributive justice, the ruthlessness that can find a home in public morality, and the operations of the human brain's two hemispheres. When faced with such a congeries of concerns, the appeal of interdisciplinarity is obvious. It seems likelier to yield an adequate response to the complexity that confronts us than the insights yielded by a single discipline. Hence our use of Nussbaum, Nagel, and McGilchrist. However, we should recognise that others have traversed the territory through which we have moved in this essay and have offered analyses that bear similarities to those in Nussbaum, Nagel, and McGilchrist. This is true, for example, of Milan Kundera. In his *The Art of the Novel*, Kundera argues that, in the seventeenth century, Descartes elevated humankind to the status of "master and proprietor of nature." Kundera adds that this rather hubristic view has found expression in technology and in politics and has had the effect of reducing "man" to "a mere thing." Moreover, he echoes Husserl and Heidegger on the point that a lack of attention to "man's concrete being, his 'world of life' (*die Lebenswelt*)" has accompanied the adoption of the Cartesian worldview.[134] Thus abstraction and large ambitions (humankind as master and proprietor of nature) sit alongside narrowness of vision (insensitivity to "man's concrete being.")[135] Here we find a

---

134 Milan Kundera, *The Art of the Novel* (London: Faber & Faber, 1986), 4. We might see Hegel as having reflected, in one of his earliest writings, on the close relationship between the two matters on which Kundera focuses. See Georg W.F. Hegel, "The Oldest System-Programme of German Idealism" (1796) (arguing that every state inevitably treats people as "mechanical cogs") (discussed in Georg W. F. Hegel *Natural Law: The Scientific Way of Treating Natural Law, Its Place in Moral Philosophy, and Its Relation to the Positive Science of Law* (Philadelphia, PA: University of Pennsylvania Press, 1975), 12–13). The full text of "The Oldest System-Programme of German Idealism" appears in Simon Critchley, *Continental Philosophy: A Very Short Introduction* (Oxford: Oxford University Press, 2001), 129–131 (with the translator using the term '"machinery" rather than "mechanical cogs.")

135 While we cannot pursue the point in detail here, we might see the narrowness of vision Kundera describes as encouraging in politico-legal contexts a practical outlook to which we can apply the label "the regulatory imagination." Those who exercise this limited imaginative capacity tend to view the law's addressees not as people but as objects: pieces in the social jigsaw that they contemplate assembling. We find something of this sort in, for example, Mill's account of Bentham's determination "to give a rule to all human conduct." Mill adds that Bentham knew "little of human feelings" and "still less of the influences by which those feelings are formed." Rather, he "measured" people by "one standard": "their capability to take correct views of utility." He thus focused exclusively on the task of bringing into existence a society (indeed, a world) of

state of affairs that bears obvious resemblances to those on which Nussbaum, Nagel, and McGilchrist have written. This is unsurprising. Their respective contributions have a relevance that extends far beyond the violations of privacy on which we have focused. These contributions embrace complex forms of life in which we find that refusals of compassion, ruthlessness, and unwillingness to learn from experience mock one of society's largest ambitions: to do distributive justice. If we are to fashion institutions that approximate this ideal more adequately, we must look beyond the frames of reference (or pictures) that are our guides to its pursuit. These sources of guidance are far from perfect. But they insinuate themselves all too easily into our thinking and impede our efforts "to imagine [...] the honourable, the producible case" – as the responses to *Mitchell* and *X and Y* make clear.

---

rule-governed utility-maximizers. George Orwell captures a broadly similar practical outlook when he describes a "hypertrophied sense of order" that encourages those in its grip to "reduce the world to something resembling a chess board." See George Orwell, *The Road to Wigan Pier* [1937] (London: Penguin Books, 1989), 166. See also Kynaston, *Austerity Britain*, 136 (on Douglas Jay's maxim that "the gentleman in Whitehall really does know better what is good for people than the people know themselves"), and Peter Weiler, *Ernest Bevin* (Manchester: Manchester University Press, 1993), 74 (on Herbert Morrison's description of the "achievement of tidiness" as a goal of government).

Table 1

The Privacy Blindspot

1 Negligence claims have made this blindspot apparent.

2 The blindspot concerns an interest that negligence law does not protect: privacy (home and family life, within ECHR, Art 8(1)).

3 A response to the blindspot problem: a cause of action in tort for invasion of privacy (or, more particularly, for "intrusion" as a form of invasion of privacy).

Negligence Actions Against Local Authorities

1 In *Mitchell*, and *X and Y*, the claimants suffered invasions of privacy.

2 Judges and counsel in these cases did not address the issue of privacy.

3 Judges rejected the negligence claims on the ground that to accept them would be contrary to the public interest in generally beneficial service delivery: e.g., the provision of council/social housing.

Emphasis on the Public Interest

1 In *Mitchell* and *X and Y*, the public interest is the central concern.

2 Relevant doctrines that shield councils and other public bodies from liability.

3 These doctrines facilitate the pursuit of a "welfare consequentialist" agenda (concerned with benefiting the overwhelming majority of those in receipt of the services delivered by councils).

Addressing the Privacy Blindspot

1 Judicial recognition of "intrusion" as harmful wrongdoing.

2 The elaboration of new (common law) privacy-related liability rules.

3 The common law as a body of "slow-growing wisdom" (Karl Llewellyn) able to respond to intrusion as a form of harmful wrongdoing (that can impact on home and family life within ECHR, Art 8 (1)).

Table 2

An Explanation of the Privacy Blindspot

1 The existence of this blindspot yields evidence of a failure of imagination (to which Nussbaum's *Poetic Justice* is relevant).

2 We can explain the existence of the privacy blindspot by reference to Nagel's account of ruthlessness and McGilchrist's account of the way in which the left hemisphere of the brain operates.

Nussbaum

1 Concern with people whose lives are "distant from our own."

2 The "literary imagination" as a basis on which to counter refusals of compassion.

3 Nussbaum's critique of consequentialism (e.g., Thomas Gradgrind's utilitarianism) intersects with Nagel's analytically more precise account of ruthlessness.

Nagel

1 Nagel draws a sharp distinction between public and private morality.

2 Ruthlessness and a focus on "the best results overall" as features of public morality.

3 While Nagel's account of ruthlessness helps us to understand refusals of compassion, we can find in McGilchrist a basis on which to explain absences of compassion.

McGilchrist

1 The "experiential world" of the brain's left hemisphere.

2 The schematic (and virtual) representations of reality worked up by the brain's left hemisphere.

3 Such an abstract frame of reference (e.g., that of welfare consequentialism) may become a "Hall of Mirrors" in which we become inattentive to the world we seek to regulate.

Maria Aristodemou

A Squeamishness about Existing: Fernando Pessoa's Quiet Rejection of the Human in *The Book of Disquiet*

1 The death of God

If we are not to slit our throats by the time we finish reading Pessoa's *Book of Disquiet*[1] we must be prepared to read it for laughs. Laughter, as Freud knew, is a serious matter and it is the deadly seriousness of extreme hilarity that is called for in addressing this dark text. Line after line, paragraph after paragraph, page after page Pessoa moans and bemoans what has been translated, in a generous understatement, as "disquiet." We will keep this term even though closer fits would have been anxiety, angst, despair, if not suicidal depression.

What is the source of Pessoa's anxiety? His greatest complaint, I will argue, is man's murder of God. He is furious our modernist parents killed God and in the process took away what he claims God would have given him as a present, that is, a "divine toy": the toy of believing in something, even if that something is an illusion. For Pessoa our modernist parents had a decadent party celebrating God's departure and we are left with the hangover and the task of cleaning up the mess of their enjoyment. He uses his diary to examine, reject, and often ridicule, the way modern subjects have responded to the so-called death of God and the substitute objects they have tried to put in its place. These cures, or placebos as they turn out to be, have ranged from law, to reason, to human rights, to work, to sex, to shopping, to love, and finally to literature. This paper will focus on Pessoa's rejection of human rights as a concept capable of filling the gap left by the death of God; this rejection is a natural extension, I suggest, of Pessoa's far from enthusiastic, yet nevertheless accurately grim depiction of the human subject. It is an understanding of the human subject that I suggest is shared by psychoanalysis and most notably by Lacan's reading of Freud. For Pessoa himself, as we will see, only literature comes close to filling the endemic lack in the subject and in the symbolic order but that does not mean that we should not kill ourselves.

---

1 Fernando Pessoa, *The Book of Disquiet* (London: Penguin, 2001), trans. Richard Zenith: further references in the text, abbreviated as *BD*.

In an early essay on Nietzsche, Gilles Deleuze asks, "Did we kill God when we put man in his place and kept the most important thing, which is the place?"[2] For Deleuze, as for Pessoa, God's murder has not been accompanied with the abolition of this place; instead the place is still very much present, indeed all the more glaringly and loudly present, for having been left spectacularly empty. God as we know performs many functions, and fulfils many fantasies. More obviously and uncontroversially, religion provided rules and principles for the good life vis-à-vis oneself and vis-à-vis others, enabling us to coexist a little less painfully or chaotically than might otherwise be the case. The concept of an all-powerful Being that provides vertical links of protection by the One, and guidelines for horizontal ties between subjects, is not only useful but extremely reassuring. Religious ideas, as Freud famously suggested, have their origin in our vulnerable psyches. They are, he says, "illusions, fulfilments of the oldest, strongest wishes of mankind" catering for our longing to be loved and protected, allaying our curiosity about out origins, and assuring us of a future after-life.[3] As Freud hints here, and as Slavoj Žižek has discussed in more detail recently, collective belief also guards against our perennial fear of loneliness.[4] To believe means, first and foremost, to belong: to a community of believers, no doubt, but the belonging in this case is as important as the believing. So much so that the belief does not even need to be that of the believer: the priest, or pope, or nun, or monk, can do the believing for us so that attending mass, going on a pilgrimage, or confessing our sins, is sufficient to qualify us for membership of the faith and render us believers.

---

2 Gilles Deleuze *Pure Immanence: Essays on a Life* (New York: Zone Books 2001), 71.

3 Sigmund Freud, "The Future of an Illusion" in *The Standard Edition of the Complete Psychological Works of Sigmund Freud* Volume XXI 1927–1931, trans. James Strachey (London Vintage 2001), 30: religious ideas "are illusions, fulfilments of the oldest, strongest and most urgent wishes of mankind. The secret of their strength lies in the strength of those wishes. As we already know, the terrifying impression of helplessness in childhood aroused the need for protection – for protection through love – which was provided by the father; and the recognition that this helplessness lasts throughout life made it necessary to cling to the existence of a father, but this time a more powerful one. Thus the benevolent rule of a divine Providence allays our fear of the dangers of life; the establishment of a moral world order ensures the fulfilment of the demands of justice, which have so often remained unfulfilled in human civilization; and the prolongation of earthly existence in a future life provides the local and temporal framework in which these wish-fulfilments shall take place. Answers to the riddles that tempt the curiosity of man, such as how the universe began or what the relation is between body and mind, are developed in conformity with the underlying assumptions of this system. It is an enormous relief to the individual psyche if the conflicts of its childhood arising from the father complex – conflicts which it has never wholly overcome – are removed from it and brought to a solution which is universally accepted."

4 Slavoj Žižek, *On Belief* (London: Routledge 2001).

The problem with killing God is that we no longer know how to address, redress or even repress our desires for protection, for reassurance, and for belonging. This much we know. Pessoa's tragedy is that he knows not only that these reassurances are no longer available to us but further that God was a placebo all along: in other words he knows that God was an illusion but he continues to want it, furious that our predecessors' antics have deprived us of this comforting illusion. He is immersed, therefore, in a hopeless self-sabotage: demanding something he cannot have from someone who does not have it; indeed from someone he knows does not exist and who would not give it to him even if he did exist and even if he did have it. "Where is God," he pleads, "even if he does not exist. I want to cry and to weep" (*BD*, § 88).

2 The empty place

Pessoa's tragedy is that he knows that the desires for someone who could perform these functions were there *ab initio* because every subject, and every system, is plagued by a lack at its centre. Like Deleuze, he knows that the death of God revealed the emptiness at the heart of the symbolic order and at the heart of each subject more glaringly than ever before, but the death of God did not *create* the emptiness because the emptiness was there from the start:

> When Christianity passed over souls like a storm that rages all night until morning, the havoc it had invisibly wreaked could be felt, but only after it had passed did the actual damage become clear. Some thought that the damage resulted from Christianity's departure, but this was just what revealed the damage, not what caused it. (*BD*, § 53)

That religion was a remedy, or placebo, in response to this pre-existing emptiness is not news to psychoanalysis: for psychoanalysis it is not just the modernist house we inherited from our parents but every house that is cracked, the building housing each subject just as the building housing each system. The only building, the only system that does not have cracks, because it does not have an unconscious, is God's building – heaven. Only angels do not have an unconscious, because they do not speak.

Since no system is complete without an arch signifier, every system ends up inventing a fictional closure. This arbitrary limit, whether it is God or the *Grundnorm*, has neither origins, nor content: it is not true or false, powerful or weak, just or unjust, but simply necessary: necessary for closing off the system just like a circumference is necessary to close off a circle. Pessoa recognises this arbitrary and nonsensical limit also applies to the human subject: "I am the centre that exists only because the geometry of the abyss demands it; I am the nothing around which all this spins, I exist so that it can spin, I am a centre that exists only because every circle has one" (*BD, § 262*).

If God was a, if not *the*, solution to the perennial search for closure in the system, how can the revelation of an illusion, the lifting of the veil of a fantasy, wreak such havoc when it was, after all, just a fancy, a hypothesis? The short answer is that what matters about fantasies is not their *content*, which is invariably nonsensical and needless to say embarrassing, but the *place* they occupy in the subject's psychic structure. The fantasy of a Father, a God, a Master may, and all too often is, silly and fanciful but its function is priceless: it fills the place of the *lack* in the structure, that is, the lack in the subject but just as importantly the lack in the symbolic order.

How has modern woman coped with the newly revealed but nevertheless always already present emptiness? Lacan's answer is that God may have been killed, but rather than dead, God became unconscious.[5] So from the subject's point of view, God may be dead but instead of disappearing from our view, our language or our laws and practices, he has become unconscious. The void may be acknowledged consciously, as is the impossibility of filling it by believing anew in God, but the unconscious persists in denying the emptiness and dreaming of substitute replacements. One such (un)likely replacement has been the cult of Reason. What the leap from God to reason did not appreciate however, let alone resolve, is that the impossibility of believing in God did not entail an acceptance of this impossibility: especially someone like Pessoa who behaves like a weeping spoiled child.

> While the sloppy criticism of our fathers bequeathed us the impossibility of being Christians it didn't bequeath us the acceptance of the impossibility; while it bequeathed us a disbelief in established moral codes, it didn't bequeath us an indifference to morality and the rules for peaceful coexistence; while it left the thorny problem of politics in doubt, it didn't leave our minds unconcerned about how to solve it. (*BD, § 175*)

3 The birth of humanity

One of the babies human reason quickly created was faith in the human itself: in other words, human reason reasoned that the human is loveable, and self-love of the human also translated and expanded to love of all humans. Pessoa describes

---

5 Jacques Lacan, *The Four Fundamental Concepts of Psychoanalysis* (London: Penguin 1979), trans Alan Sheridan, 59: "the true formula of atheism is not, God is dead. The true formula of atheism is God is unconscious."

the move from loving God to loving Humanity while letting us know that he certainly shares no such loves:

> most of these young people chose Humanity to replace God. I, however [...] didn't give up God as completely as they did, and I never accepted Humanity. I reasoned that God, while improbable, might exist, in which case he should be worshipped; whereas Humanity, being a mere biological idea and signifying nothing more than the animal species we belong to, was no more deserving of worship than any other animal species. The cult of Humanity, with its rites of Freedom and Equality, always struck me as a revival of those ancient cults in which gods were like animals or had animal heads. (*BD*, § 1)

Pessoa's contempt for humanity, starting with the animal called Pessoa, is not only based on the fact that we are basically a bunch of animals. Pessoa has an intimation, more clearly spelled out by Lacan, that not only are we animals, but we are actually not good enough animals. Even in our animalhood we are lacking. What renders us lacking in particular is the alienation wreaked by our entry into language. Although we are animals, unlike our sisters in the jungle, we are sick animals, alienated even from our own animality. As Pessoa puts it "we are all inferior animals, speaking and thinking are merely new instincts, less dependable than others precisely because they're new" (*BD*, § 254).

This less than enthusiastic appreciation of the human capacity to speak is echoed by Lacan: for Lacan we become sick as soon as we start talking, as soon as we start heeding the signifiers we are bombarded with by others and in turn seek to decipher and respond to them. We are dragged into language by other people's insistence to address us as capable of understanding their mutterings and by our foolhardy attempts to respond in kind. By entering language we suffer a loss psychoanalysis refers to as castration. For Lacan castration is wrought less by a vicious father than by the law of language. For Lacan, as for Hegel, "the word is the murder of the thing," that is, every signifier kills the thing signified, making our communications woefully inadequate to the task of depicting the real, that is, when they do not misfire altogether.[6] Pessoa echoes the same lack of faith in human speech: "Every spoken word double-crosses us. The only tolerable form of

---

6 Friedrich Hegel, *System of Ethical Life and First Philosophy of Spirit* [1803–4], ed. and trans. Henry S. Harris & Thomas M. Knox (Albany, New York: 1979), 221: "The first act by which Adam established his lordship over the animals is this, that he gave them a name, i.e., he nullified them as beings on their own account." Lacan continues this theme: "The symbol manifests itself first of all as the murder of the thing, and this death constitutes in the subject the eternalization of his desire." ("Function and Field of Speech" in *Ecrits: A Selection* (London and New York: Routledge, 1977), trans. Alan Sheridan, 104).

communication is the written word, since it isn't a stone in a bridge between souls but a ray of light between stars" (*BD*, § 209).

4 The aborted animal

Pessoa's tragedy is that he recognizes all too well that death lurks at the constitution of the human subject and of the symbolic order: "everything participates in death and is death" (*BD*, § 178). Before and without Lacan, he describes himself as "an abortion that survived" (*BD*, § 427) and wonders loudly, "What in me dies when I am?" (*BD*, § 63). To answer Pessoa in Lacanese: what dies in you when you are, is the object petit a. Every subject, every system, every God is plagued by a lack at its centre so the making of our subjectivity revolves around losing an object which we are thereafter and forever in search of. No wonder, as Pessoa describes it, "we're hollow on the inside as well as on the outside, pariahs in our expectations and in our realizations" (*BD*, § 169).

Pessoa aptly and clearly anticipated Lacan's formulation of the subject as an incomplete, lacking, pathetic organism that is always looking for its missing bit. That missing bit, that gap is actually the subject itself. "I'm like someone searching at random," he writes, "not knowing what object he's looking for nor where it was hidden" (*BD*, § 63). The subject is tormented by the thought that if only he had the object, he or she would be complete. As Pessoa knows however, the fact that the object never existed does not stop us searching for it, nor from hurting at its loss: "Ah, no nostalgia hurts as much as nostalgia for things that never existed!" (*BD*, § 92).

In other words, the search for an always already lost object condemns the subject to the status of a perennial loser: Pessoa is painfully honest about his loser status: "I was the runner who led the race until he fell down, right before the finishing line" (*BD*, § 290). And in another, of his more "positive" metaphors, he describes the subject as separated from what is most precious to it like a castle from the world beyond its moat:

> it's as if the drawbridge has been raised over the moat of the soul's castle, such that we can only gaze at the lands around the castle, without ever being able to set foot on them. There's something in us that isolates us from ourselves, and the separating element is as stagnant as we are, a ditch of filthy water around our self-alienation. (*BD*, §§ 263)

5 In place of divided subjects: I is another

How come then, that despite our pathetic incompleteness, our separation from what is most precious to us we manage to give an appearance of some functioning, albeit imperfect mechanism? The answer for psychoanalysis is our successful imitation and incorporation of bits of other people; we imitate, or identify, with others so we are no more than simulacra, or semblances, of other people starting with the big others in our lives.

While Lacan was fond of repeating Arthur Rimbaud's famous line "I is another" to depict this condition, Pessoa bemoans his lack of authenticity in an array of colourful and of course depressing metaphors: "I was never more than my own vestige or simulacrum" (*BD, § 456*) he tells us. Recognising that one is a fiction is not bad enough though for Pessoa: we must also recognise that we are not even our own fiction: It is "other people's rubbish" that pile up in the rain in the courtyard that we take or *mis*take for our selves. Although it is grim enough to realise we are "shadows of gestures performed by someone else" (*BD, § 133*), with Pessoa we must go further and recognise that even our shadowy existence is not shadowy enough: it is not our own shadow that we follow, but that of the other. Pessoa's recognition of his own alienation is repeated with an insistence that is obsessively comical: "I'm so isolated I can feel the distance between me and my suit" (*BD, § 83*). Or, "I'm an abyss"; but not just one but two abysses: "We never know self-realization. We are two abysses – a well staring at the sky" (*BD, § 11*). Or again, "My soul is impatient with itself, as with a bothersome child [...] I'm two and both keep their distance – Siamese twins that aren't attached" (*BD, § 16*).

While Christianity presumed to convince us that we are made in God's image, the human subject is at pains to find an image for itself that s/he is happy with and convinced by. For Pessoa, however, the search is painfully futile; identity is a metaphor we spend our whole life constructing, with hopes alias known as lies, that our slippery beings might be anchored at last on a more secure foundation than is warranted by our meagre efforts, unsure methods and forever incomplete results. There is a gap in our making as subjects, a gap that we attempt to plug up with our search for objects that are already lost and by constructing fantasies of complete others whose desires are both transparent and realizable. The absolute coincidence between the self and its image, the unification between a subject and its object petit a, can be found only in death. Because we only coincide with ourselves, with our image, only once, that is, in death: the death mask ensures there is a final print.

"I seek and don't find myself" (*BD, § 134*), "I'm never where I feel I am, and if I seek myself, I don't know who's seeking me" (*BD, § 182*). "I live off impressions that aren't mine. I'm a squanderer of renunciations someone else in the way I'm

I" (*BD*, § 93). Even my dreams "exist apart from me" (*BD*, § 3). "To live is to crochet according to a pattern we were given" (*BD*, § 12); "My life happens to me from the outside" (*BD*, § 100);

> It's never I who thinks, speaks or acts. It's always one of my dreams, which I momentarily embody, that thinks, speaks and acts for me. I open my mouth but it's I-another who speaks. The only thing I feel to be really mine is a huge incapacity, a vast emptiness, an incompetence for everything that is life. (*BD*, § 215)

And finally, in awe: "How many we are!" (*BD*, § 95).

In short, not only are we other people, but the only thing that is truly ours is the gap, the empty place. Pessoa does not hide his contempt for what is left of the human soul, starting with his own: "If a soul were able to reveal itself truthfully, if its shame and modesty didn't run deeper than all its known and named ignominies, then it would be – as is said of truth – a well, but sinister well full of murky echoes and inhabited by abhorrent creatures, slimy non-beings, lifeless slugs, the snot of subjectivity" (*BD*, § 242). "I suddenly felt like one of those damp rags used for house-cleaning that are taken to the window to dry but are forgotten, balled up, on the sill where they slowly leave a stain" (*BD*, § 29).

If, as Lacan insists, and as most of us resist, "It is at this point of lack that the subject has to recognize himself"[7] then Pessoa is like the subject in a perpetual state of recognizing his lack. That is, he is in a perpetual state of subjective destitution; of what Lacan calls, *des-être*. While human beings will do everything possible not to admit the gap in their own making, Pessoa perpetually puts himself in the position of losing and not finding himself.

6 In place of the object: humanity

If the human being only becomes a subject on losing an already lost object, in other words if, as Lacan suggests, "The essence of the object is failure,"[8] we are left with the question, what takes the place of the lost object? The short answer, of course, is fantasy. Pessoa quickly rejects the capacity of reason and science to fill the gap in our subjectivity. Rather than accepting the castration wrought by our entry into language, the emptiness and our inability to understand or to fill it, the cult of reason presumed an inhuman, unreasonable, insane even, ability to

---

7 Lacan, *Four Fundamental Concepts*, 270.

8 Jacques Lacan, *Encore, Book XX; On Feminine Sexuality, The Limits of Love and Knowledge*, ed. Jacques-Alain Miller, trans. Bruce Fink (New York and London: W. W. Norton, 1998), 58.

understand: "Reason is faith in what can be understood without faith, but it's still a faith, since to understand presupposes that there's something understandable" (*BD*, § 176).[9]

The possibility that there is something beyond our understanding, beyond our conscious knowledge, and in particular beyond our capacities of representation was dismissed or at least ignored. For psychoanalysis, this realm beyond our comprehension and beyond representation is, of course, the Real. Yet Reason shrinks from contemplating, let alone acknowledging, that there are also things we do not know that we do know: things that our unconscious knows and that are, albeit with difficulty, accessible to consciousness. This truth, "in its profound horror of our never being able to know it" (*BD*, § 45) is the part that Reason cannot reach.

If the emptiness cannot be filled with rules, if formal law cannot be guaranteed to protect us from pathological, even evil, ends then what do we do? Do we devote ourselves to helping other people? Another unlikely replacement in current vogue, has been the cult of humanity: otherwise known as Human Rights. If divine law prompted and promoted faith in a tradition of natural law, following the death of God the cult of humanity provided a tradition of natural rights as human rights.

Pessoa is not convinced: the problem, he suggests, is not, or not only, that we are too many and too varied to be able to co-exist peacefully, but also, depressingly, that we are irredeemably and unavoidably isolated. In place of the autonomous subject celebrated by modernity, what Pessoa finds is not joyfully independent agents in charge of their destinies but isolated, indeed miserable, atoms. Our ineradicable alienation from ourselves means that we are not only unable to "disembark from ourselves" as Pessoa puts it, it also means that we are fated to be unable to reach other people, however much we may pretend otherwise: "Whoever has crossed all the seas has crossed only the monotony of himself" (*BD*, § 13).

Psychoanalysts are not convinced either. For Freud in his pessimistic late work *Civilization and Its Discontents*, the injunction to love one's neighbour is Christianity's ultimate delusion: "not merely is this stranger not worthy of my love," he protests. "I must honestly confess that he has more claim to my hostility and even my hatred."[10] Freud appreciated that solidarity within the community is only ever achieved at the expense of those outside the group; in that sense, Jews, he presciently claimed, rendered "most useful services" by being the target of

---

9 Reason, he adds, is "the inn half-way between faith and criticism" (*BD*, 176).
10 Sigmund Freud, "Civilization and Its Discontents" in *The Standard Edition*, Vol. XXI (1929), 110.

hatred and thus promoting community spirit among Christians.[11] The rise of nationalism and fundamentalism in the last few decades suggests that, despite the rhetoric of tolerance and multiculturalism accompanying human rights discourse, such rhetoric has not matched the reality. Indeed, as Lacan and Pessoa appreciate, closer co-existence can breed, not more respect and cooperation but more intolerance and hostility. Pessoa confirms that the rush to celebrate our common humanity is a delusion, masking our inevitable distance and strangeness from the other:

> The other doesn't exist for us. Even less so the supposed collective other. No one, I suppose, genuinely admits the real existence of another person... they're like chunks of meat displayed in the window of a butcher's, dead things bleeding as if they were alive, shanks and cutlets of destiny... No, others don't exist. (BD, § 165, 317)

The message of the second half of the twentieth century, a time when an array of human rights international treaties and domestic legislation were passed and sought to be enforced is, unfortunately, not as salient as it promises: indeed the proliferation of human rights documents seems in inverse proportion to their enforcement. Both in domestic and in international fora, it seems the neighbour is only tolerated, respected and celebrated when she is far away from us; when she threatens to come too close, next door or, god forbid, in our own back yard, the rhetoric of toleration, as the plight of refugees and illegal immigrants betrays only too well, shows its limits. Freud and Lacan shared this pessimistic analysis of the limits of human generosity and neighbourly love: altruism, as Lacan pointed out, does not cost much, and indeed it protects, rather than detracts from our egoism, since we only help those who are in our own image. It seems that the other whom we do not recognize as being in our own image, is left to the wiles not of our humanity, but of a God that we profess to have killed.

So the function of Human Rights law may not be to protect, let alone bring the legal subject close to her neighbour, but to keep the other who is not in our image at a proper distance: that is, the underlying focus of the law is not to enjoin us to "care" for our neighbour but to regulate the relationship between us so that the neighbour does not get too close to us.[12] So the charade of political correctness and celebration of multi-culturalism arise not from love of one's neighbour but

---

11 Freud, "Civilization and Its Discontents," 110–11. For further discussion of this point see Kenneth Reinhard "Freud, My Neighbour," *American Imago* 54.2 (1997), 165–195 and again in Slavoj Zizek, Eric L. Santner, Kenneth Reinhard, *The Neighbour: Three Enquiries in Political Theology* (Chicago: University of Chicago Press, 2005).
12 See for example Slavoj Žižek's "Love My Neighbour? No Thanks!" in *Violence* (London: Profile Books 2008).

from the fear of encountering real others; that is, others who are not quite like "us" and the fear of the inevitable violence such encounters entail.

7 My neighbour the extimate

I discussed above Pessoa's frustration and despair at the limitations of the human being, including his disgust at what he perceives to be our inalienable ugly core: the "snot of subjectivity" was one of the moderate terms he uses to describe it. Lacan also has a name for the inassimilable ugly core of human subjectivity, the bit we do not dare approach but is so intrinsically ours that we have hidden safely and secretly in the interior: intimating the closeness of something intimate, and the fact that it is included only in order to be excluded, indeed excluded in the interior, the term Lacan uses is the "extimate." It is the bit in ourselves that we do not dare approach, the unassimilable core, or, as Lacan often described it, the Thing, the un-decaffeinated neighbour exemplifies this radical core. "Freud," Lacan understands,

> recoils in horror at the commandment to love one's neighbour because of the evil that dwells in the neighbour and therefore also in oneself. And what is it that we don't dare go near to? Our jouissance – that which prevents us from crossing a frontier at the limit of the Thing.[13]

Pessoa is more explicit about his disgust with himself as well as with his fellow humans: "Everyone who talks to me, each face whose eyes gaze at me, hits me like an insult or a piece of filth. I brim with disgust at the whole lot. I get dizzy from feeling myself feel them" (*BD*, § 311).

The alien, traumatic kernel, the unbearable Thing, we do not dare approach, except from the safe distance of decaffeinated tolerance and multiculturalism, is the neighbour. The neighbour who has not had the caffeine subtracted from her is the neighbour we do not dare approach and find it harder to love. Pessoa similarly recognises that the only reason we are able to co-exist and have a modicum of understanding between human beings is precisely because we do not know each other: "If there's one thing we should thank the gods is not knowing ourselves and not knowing each other. No one knows anyone else and it's just as well, for if he did, he would discover – in his very own mother, wife or son – his inveterate, metaphysical enemy. We get along because we're strangers at heart" (*BD*, § 255).

---

13 Jacques Lacan, *Seminar VII: The Ethics of Psychoanalysis*, ed. Jacques-Alain Miller, trans. Denis Porter (New York and London: W. W. Norton, 1997), 186.

The problem with human rights rhetoric, as Jacques Alain Miller discusses, is that it seeks to abolish something that is ineradicable, that is, extimacy. "The Christian injunction to love one's neighbour," he says, is to "nullify extimacy."[14] Lawyers and human rights lawyers in particular are used to addressing the symbolic register, the register where one subject can superficially look like another. However, law and the symbolic order generally cannot get rid of the extimate. Human rights discourse may try to reduce the disturbing and unassimilable core of the other to what is common, to the universal, to what conforms to the norm. As Miller puts it, "On the level of the signifier, on the level of form, there is equality, substitutability, peace." But what makes the other *other*, their alterity, their difference, their particularity, is not on the level of the signifier, of the symbolic, but on the level of the Real, of the extimate. At that level, the other is irreducibly different: at that level, as Miller says, "there is war."[15]

This is why, Miller suggests, none of the generous and universal discourses on the theme of "we are all fellow-beings" in legal and political discourse have been effective. Because racism, he continues,

> calls into play a hatred which goes precisely toward what grounds the Other's alterity, in other words its *jouissance*. If no decision, no will, no amount of reasoning is sufficient to wipe out racism, it is because racism is founded on the point of extimacy of the Other. Racism is founded on what one imagines about the Other's *jouissance*; it is hatred of the particular way, of the Other's own way of experiencing *jouissance*. We may well think that racism exists because our Islamic neighbour is too noisy when he has parties; nevertheless it is a fact that what is really at stake is that he takes his *jouissance* in a way different from ours. The Other's proximity exacerbates racism: as soon as there is closeness, there is a confrontation of incompatible modes of *jouissance*. For it is simple to love one's neighbor when he is distant, but it is a different matter in proximity. Racist stories are always about the way in which the Other obtains a *plus-de-jouir*: either he does not work enough or he works too much, or he is useless or a little too useful, but whatever the case may be, he is always endowed with a part of *jouissance* that he does not deserve.[16]

Intolerance, in short, is intolerance of the other's enjoyment. We can now make sense of Kierkegaard's dramatic claim, often repeated by Žižek, that the only good neighbour is a dead neighbour.[17] If the extimate is the neighbour's disturbing jouissance then Kierkegaard is right that the only good neighbour is a dead neighbour: because a dead body can no longer enjoy.

---

14 Jacques Alain Miller, "Extimity," *The Symptom* 9 (June 2008), available at http://www.lacan.com/symptom/?p=36 (September 23, 2013).
15 Miller, *Extimity*.
16 Miller, *Extimity*.
17 Soren Kierkegaard, *Works of Love*, trans. Howard Hong (New York: Harper, 1974), 75.

If what really bothers us about the other is their enjoyment, the fear that they may be getting more than us, then can any law, including human rights legislation, address let alone resolve conflicts when two enjoyments collide? Lawyers might prefer not to remember that the root of the problem with legislating enjoyment is that enjoyment, unlike material goods or wealth, is not like the proverbial manna from heaven that can be counted out and distributed equally or unequally to mere mortals below. As Freud started exploring, the dialectic of pleasure and unpleasure cannot be quantified, let alone resolved, by economic formulas as he had initially assumed: unpleasure is not necessarily the presence of tension, nor pleasure the lack of tension since some tensions can be pleasurable while a state of zero tension is not necessarily pleasant. Criminal sentencing, civil damages, declaring a contract null and void or issuing an injunction may appear important and satisfy the subject at the symbolic level, but the excess enjoyment that bothers us vis a vis the other cannot be legislated let alone eradicated to satisfy the racist or sexist or homophobic subject, however many laws granting our human rights in the spheres of sex, and race, and gender our governments pass. We can now understand why Pessoa declares: "I have a very simple morality. Not to do good or evil to anyone" (*BD, § 208*).

8 The divine toy: losing the belief, and the disbelief too

At the root of Pessoa's dissatisfaction, or disquiet as he calls it, is, as I discuss at the start of this paper, our parents' inconsiderate attempt to kill God without, as he realises, providing anything equally fulfilling in its place. The attempt to insert humanity and human rights as an object worthy of filling that empty place is consistently ridiculed by Pessoa who expresses nothing but disgust at the nature of humanity, starting with himself: time and again he reminds us of the "nausea of commonplace humanity which is the only kind there is [...] a monstrous and vile animal created in the chaos of dreams, out of desires' soggy crusts, out of sensations' chewed-up leftovers" (*BD, § 62*).

So what, if anything, would have remedied this constant disgust? Pessoa's suggestion is that what we lack is the divine toy of belief. Once upon a time, belief consisted of a belief in God (or Gods in the plural), but it has not been possible to inspire, let alone sustain such belief in "humanity":

> Perhaps, deep down is the soul's dissatisfaction because we didn't give it a belief, the disappointment of the sad child (who we are on the inside) because we didn't buy it the divine toy [...] Those who have Gods don't have tedium. Tedium is the lack of a mythology

> [...] tedium is the loss of the soul's capacity for self-delusion; it is the mind's lack of the non-existent ladder by which it might firmly ascend to truth. (*BD*, § 263)

Furthermore, the only way we can sustain a *lack* of belief is if we already believed: that is, what makes dis-belief possible is a strong belief. Conversely, lack of belief makes dis-belief impossible: that is, what has died in modern man and woman, is not only the capacity to believe, but further the capacity *not* to believe: "For people without beliefs, even doubt is impossible, even their scepticism will lack the strength to question" (*BD*, § 263).[18]

For one of the very few real atheists like Lacan, it could not be more simple: "God has all the perfections except one: he doesn't exist."[19] Pessoa is not convinced it is as easy as all that. For a poet who is constantly experiencing and re-experiencing the "humiliation of knowing oneself," relinquishing the hope of an all-knowing Other is not that simple. "Where is God even if he doesn't exist?" he pleads. "I want to pray and to weep, to repent of crimes I didn't commit to enjoy the feeling of forgiveness like a caress that's more than maternal" (*BD*, § 88).

That is why his foremost demand is not to ask for anything: "I only ask the gods to grant me / That I ask nothing of them."[20] Lacan suggests that the desire to desire nothing, to be beyond hope and beyond demand, is indeed the proper ethical aspiration. In his seminar on the ethics of psychoanalysis he praises Antigone for her capacity to occupy "a place of desire in as much as it is the desire for nothing, the relationship of man with his lack of being."[21] But this is a hard task and Pessoa, while recognising this ethical duty, also never manages to go beyond demand; he is always asking for something, even if he claims it to be very little and of course he insists this very little was denied him:

> I asked for very little from life, and even this was denied me [...] not to feel oppressed by the knowledge that I exist, not to demand anything from others and not to have others demand anything from me – this was denied me, like the spare change we might deny a beggar not because we're mean-hearted but because we don't feel like unbuttoning our coat. (*BD*, § 6)

Of course gods are too cunning to grant that wish. And the subject is too much of a cunning moaner to want them to grant it in the first place; thus perpetuating

---

18 So there are two stages to our play with belief, Pessoa suggests: "in the first stage we dogmatically doubt ourselves and every superior man arrives there. In the second stage we come to doubt not only ourselves but our own doubt" (*BD*, 149). So even our doubt is doubtful.

19 Slavoj Žižek, *The Sublime Object of Ideology* (London: Verso, 1989), 163.

20 Fernando Pessoa, *Selected Poems*, trans. Jonathan Griffin (London: Penguin, 2000), 145; and still he asks: "All I asked of life is that it ask nothing of me" (*BD*, 133).

21 Lacan, *Ethics of Psychoanalysis*, 345.

gods' existence, and his own incessant moaning. "Whether or not they exist, we are slaves to the gods" (*BD, § 21*).

9 The anxiety of freedom

Why is Pessoa so desperate to hold on to the illusion of God? Why does he persist in appealing to Him even while acknowledging his own delusion and his own slavery? My suggestion is that Pessoa realises that such slavery is preferable to the experience of real freedom; that being weighed down by the responsibility of being one's own master and legislator is more oppressive for Pessoa than being someone's slave. He recognises that the substitutes we have put in God's place, including the creed and cult of humanity, and the attendant discourse of human rights cannot fill the gap of human subjectivity, nor bridge the gap between one subjectivity and another. He recognises further that to reject God as well as humanity would leave him with the terrible experience of freedom. Freedom unsupported by fantasies is, as few people like Pessoa recognise, an intolerable burden. Pessoa recognizes that letting go of the God fantasy would mean encountering his own nothingness, the anagnorisis that he is, like all of us, "Nothing, nothing, just part of the night and the silence and of whatever emptiness, negativity and inconstancy I share with them, the space that exists between me and me, a thing mislaid by some god" (*BD, § 262*).

That terrible opening when the subject lets go of his comforting fantasies, when he does not know what the other wants, that uncertainty is freedom. Lacan is clear this is the price, and the prize, of a good analysis and Pessoa describes it in similar terms: "Creeds, ideals, a woman, a profession – all are prisons and shackles. To be is to be free" (*BD, § 236*). Freedom then is the capacity to detach oneself from comforting illusions, fictions, from other people and cults: "freedom is the possibility of isolation. You are free if you can withdraw from people, not having to seek them out for the sake of money, company, love, curiosity [...] If you can't live alone, you were born a slave" (*BD, § 283*).

Such an experience of freedom, however, when and if it happens, is shattering. It is the experience of dis-being that Lacan describes as accompanying the end of analysis and it is not pretty. When Pessoa experiences this state he recognises its import and is in a hurry to chase it away:

All of a sudden, as if a surgical hand of destiny had operated on a long-standing blindness with immediate and sensational results, I lift my gaze from my anonymous life to the clear recognition of how I live. And I see that everything I've done, thought or been is a species of delusion or madness [...] I look at my past life as at a field lit up by the sun when it breaks through the clouds and I noted with metaphysical astonishment how my most deliberate acts, my clearest ideas and most logical intentions were after all no more than congenital drunkenness, inherent madness and huge ignorance. I didn't act anything out. I was the role that got acted. At most, I was the actor's motions. (*BD, § §39*)

The experience of true freedom however is hardly welcome for the subject; being free from the fictions making up our reality also means being lost. Pessoa experiences this freedom as a prison sentence and is keen to overturn it: "The sudden awareness of my true being, weighs on me like an untold sentence to serve [...] and so, I wait for the truth to go away and let me return to being fictitious and non-existent, intelligent and natural" (*BD, § 39*). As the discourse of human rights, just like the discourse of God, is one of those comforting non-existent fictions, we can assume that Pessoa returns, like all of us, to them to avoid the much more terrible state of experiencing true freedom. To paraphrase him: "We arrive at Human Rights but not at a conclusion" (*BD, § 16*).

Riccardo Baldissone

I and *Another*: Rethinking the Subject of Human Rights with Dostoyevsky, Bakhtin and Simondon

The subject of human rights is the result of a threefold operation, which began to take place in the seventeenth century. At that time, natural philosophers from Descartes to Leibniz constructed what we now call the modern individual as an entity both enclosed and undivided. The third operation occurred when the declarations of the eighteenth century generalised the synecdochical substitution of the male, Western, adult, able-bodied and well-off individual for the whole humanity. In the nineteenth century, literary inscriptions began challenging the enclosure and the unity of the self, from the astonishing Rimbaudian statement "je est un autre" to Dostoyevsky's "I and another," as described by Bakhtin. However, despite the psychoanalytical opening towards human multiplicity, legal inscriptions seem still unable to keep the pace of literary inscriptions. This is hardly surprising, if we consider that the dissolution not only of the individual, but also of other metaphysical concepts, had to be elaborated first in the narrative register, before gaining access to philosophical inscriptions such as Simondon's texts. If human rights discourse would follow the path towards the overcoming of the metaphysics of the individual, it would find consonance with literary narrations. The rapprochement to the narrative register could also reactivate genealogical resonances from within legal thought, which, at least in its Roman cradle, was not born conceptual.

Dostoyevsky has not yet become Dostoyevsky, he is still becoming him.
Mikhail Bakhtin

If we accept that human rights discourse did not immediately take shape with the 1948 Universal Declaration of Human Rights,[1] and that it harks back to the legal tradition of natural law, we will notice that in relatively recent times the definition of the very subject of rights changed from man to human. In particular, when in the 1948 Declaration the phrase "human rights" replaced the "rights of man" of the 1789 *Déclaration des Droits de l'Homme et du Citoyen* [Declaration of the Rights of Men and the Citizen], this substitution erased the trace – even if not the practice – of the effort required by women to adjust to a historically gendered legal order. The rewording of the subject accompanied a momentous acknowl-

---

1 *Universal Declaration of Human Rights* [hereinafter UDHR], UN General Assembly Resolution A/RES/217 (III) (1948).

edgement of the discrimination of human females, who at least were no longer represented by a male definition.[2]

As synecdoche is the definition of a rhetorical substitution of the whole with a part, we may say that the shift to the word "human" overcame the gender synecdoche that represented the whole humanity with its male part.[3] And yet, this synecdoche was just one in a series of rhetorical substitutions, with which Western modern thought boasted to define humankind in its totality. Stepping back in time, the male ("man") and urban ("citizen") subject explicitly named in the 1789 French Declaration already erased, at least in his definition, most French inhabitants, let alone the black slaves of the colonies.

In turn, the subject of the French Declaration was the heir of the individual subject as defined by seventeenth-century political, legal and philosophical texts. Though seventeenth-century natural philosophers described their newly devised individual with the generic definition of "man," they implicitly construed him as a Western male, adult, well-off and able-bodied representative of humankind. This ideal model took the various shapes of the Cartesian thinking subject, of the object of Lockean observation and of the kaleidoscopic Leibnizian monad. However, the most striking depiction of the isolation of the modern subject was Daniel Defoe's fictional castaway Robinson Crusoe.[4] The background of a desert island perfectly justified Robinson's absolute dis-embeddedness from his context on which he could thus operate at ease.

It is not surprising, then, that later Marx exemplified economic disembeddedness with Defoe's Robinson and the popular genre of eighteenth-century Robinsonade of which he was the model. More than that, Marx mercilessly exposed each isolated producer in Adam Smith and Ricardo's economic texts as "one of the unimaginative fantasies of 18th century romances à la Robinson Crusoe."[5] A

---

2 See Riccardo Baldissone, "A Contribution to a Western Genealogy of the Rights of Men, and Incidentally, of Women," *Australian Feminist Law Journal* 34 (2011): 91–117.

3 See Riccardo Baldissone, "Beyond the Modern Synecdoche: Towards a Non Fundamentalist Framework for Human Rights Discourse" in *Activating Human Rights and Peace: Theories, Practices and Contexts*, eds. Rob Garbutt, Bee Chen Goh and Baden Offord (London: Ashgate Press, 2012).

4 Daniel Defoe's novel *Robinson Crusoe* was originally published in 1719 with the rather explanatory title *The Life and Strange Surprizing Adventures of Robinson Crusoe, of York, Mariner: Who lived Eight and Twenty Years, all alone in an un-inhabited Island on the Coast of America, near the Mouth of the Great River of Oroonoque; Having been cast on Shore by Shipwreck, wherein all the Men perished but himself. With An Account how he was at last as strangely deliver'd by Pirates.*

5 Karl Marx, "Introduction to A Contribution to a Critique of Political Economy" [1957], in Karl Marx, *A Contribution to a Critique of Political Economy*, ed. Maurice Dobb (New York: International Publishers, 1970), 188.

dazzling insight flashes through this otherwise dry outline: just one textual fiction fits all genres.

Whilst geographical isolation could play the role, as it were, of the objective correlative to the outer severance of the modern individual from his context, the inner character of the new subject could not be represented as easily. This new modern self firstly resulted from the Cartesian replacement of "the medieval philosophers' divisions between higher and lower parts of the soul with the dichotomy between mind and body."[6] Descartes' bold displacement of the sensitive parts of the soul outside of the domain of the mind and within that of the body realised an *ethic* cleansing that no medieval scholar could even imagine. Leibniz then derived the simplicity of his undivided self from the Scholastic identity of being and oneness, which through his work was to influence Herbart, Lotze and scientific psychology in general, as it took shape in the nineteenth century.

Since the modern homogeneous and undivided self was devised in the seventeenth century, its unity was only threatened by the traditional Christian dichotomy of good versus evil. In the late nineteenth century, Stevenson made visible this inner strife through the extraordinary psychological and physical duplication of one of his best known literary characters, who was alternatively either Doctor Jekyll or Mister Hyde.[7] However, as Stevenson was not pursuing a moral agenda, we may also understand Doctor Jekyll's failed attempt to gain some moral freedom as the expression of his desire to acknowledge other sides of his self.

A similar duplication had already taken place forty years before in the pages of Двойник [*Dvoinik*], *The Double*, the second novel written by Dostoyevsky.[8] This duplication was not an alternation of identities, as in the case of Jekyll and Hyde's splitting, but it appeared to the replicated character Goliadkin as a terrifying *doppelgänger*. However, in the course of the narration this double was never completely defined as an external occurrence, because Dostoyevsky only allowed us readers to observe it through the eyes of his main character, the duplicated Goliadkin. As Bakhtin remarked, already in his Gogolian period Dostoyevsky produced a small-scale Copernican revolution by turning the authorial perspective into an aspect of the hero's self-definition.[9]

---

6 Genevieve Lloyd, *The Man of Reason: "Male" and "Female" in Western Philosophy* (London: Methuen, 1984), 45.

7 Robert Louis Stevenson's novella *Strange Case of Dr Jekyll and Mr Hyde* was first published in 1886.

8 Fyodor Dostoyevsky' novella *The Double* first appeared in print in 1846 on the literary magazine Отечественные записки [*Otechestvennye Zapiski*], Annals of the Fatherland.

9 Bakhtin, *Problems*, 49.

Hence, it is not surprising that twenty years later, and with the gulag experience in between, Dostoyevsky had the fictional narrator of his *Записки из подполья* [*Zapiski iz podpol'ia*], *Notes from the Underground*,[10] shifting the issue of multiplicity from the outside to the inside of the self. However, just as in *The Double*, Dostoyevsky never ultimately presented the doppelgänger as a state of fact. He instead only let us detect the inner multiplicity of the Underground Man through the latter's own words.

It is worth underlining that the reversal of the authorial perspective into the characters' gaze was not simply a technical literary device. On the contrary, Dostoyevsky's small Copernican revolution allowed the human subjects of his narrations to remain subjects rather than being reduced to objects of observation. The characters could speak with their different voices, whose juxtaposition produced a polyphony[11] that Bakhtin pitted against the monological narrative of author-centred novels.[12]

Moreover, the self-definition of Dostoyevsky's characters was never exhaustive, so that their identity was always described in a state of becoming. In Bakhtin's words, these characters remained unfinalized, because they were always granted a potential further development.[13] We may compare the ability of Dostoyevsky's subjects to become other than themselves to Rimbaud's claim of *being* other that himself. "*Je est un autre*," "I is another," affirmed the very young Rimbaud in his two famous letters to his teacher and mentor Georges Izambard (May 13, 1871) and to his friend Paul Demeny (May 15, 1871).

We may say that inner otherness erupted through the rendering of both Dostoyevsky's characters and Rimbaud's self as construed in his letters, which he wrote just seven years after the publication of Dostoyevsky's *Notes*. Both the Underground Man and Rimbaud clearly acknowledge their uncontrollable inner multiplicity. However, whilst the Russian unnamed narrator is at pains to convince us that he somewhat enjoys his own contradictory and even counterproductive behaviour,[14] Rimbaud seems to accept his self-estrangement as a painful price to be paid by the poet in order to become a *voyant*, that is a seer, and reach the unknown.[15]

---

10 Fyodor Dostoyevsky' novella *Notes from the Underground* was published in 1864.

11 Bakhtin, *Problems*, 3.

12 Bakhtin, *Problems*, 27.

13 Bakhtin, *Problems*, 86.

14 "Let me explain: the pleasure came precisely from being too clearly aware of your own degradation; from the feeling of having gone to the uttermost limits," Fyodor Dostoyevsky, *Notes from the Underground and The Double*, ed. and trans. Jessie Coulson (Harmondsworth: Penguin, 1976), 19.

15 Letter to Izambard, May 13 1871, in Arthur Rimbaud, *Œuvres Completes* (Paris: Hachette, 1999), 237.

As underlined by Bakhtin, in Dostoyevsky's characters the acknowledgement of the inner otherness does not exclude the self, which, as it were, does coexist with her other. More precisely, Bakhtin underlines that in the characters of Dostoyevsky coexist both *я и другой* [*ya i drugoi*], the I and *another*.[16] This dynamic structure keeps personal identity unfinalized. In a note on the expression "*ya i drugoi*," Caryl Emerson, the English translator of Bakhtin's *Проблемы поэтики Достоевского* [*Problemy poetiki Dostoyevskogo*], *Problems of Dostoyevsky's Poetics*, writes:

> Russian distinguishes between *drugoi* (another, other person) and *chuzhoi* (alien, strange; also, the other). The English pair "I/other," with its intonations of alienations and opposition, has specifically been avoided here. The another Bakhtin has in mind is not hostile to the I but a necessary component of it, a friendly other, a living factor in the attempts of the I toward self-definition.[17]

We might well integrate these observations with a note by Svetlana Boym, who remarks:

> in Russian there are two words for "other" (*drugoi* and *inoi*), just as there are two words for "truth." [...] *Drugoi*, the word used in the translation of Western philosophical texts and the one favoured by Mikhail Bakhtin, is related to *drug*, "friend," and originally denotes some form of proximity to the other, either spatial adjacency or temporal sequence. Thus *drugoi* could mean "the next" or "the second," someone close to, rather than different from, oneself.[18]

Though the close vicinity of this internal other does not always make him a friendly presence, it does not necessarily turn him into a hostile antagonist. Moreover, both inner dialogue and confrontation never happen in isolation. This inner dynamism can only be enacted together with the outer relations. As Bakhtin underscores, "the important thing in Dostoyevsky's polyphony is precisely what happens *between various consciousnesses*, that is, their interaction and interdependence."[19]

Hence, if we follow Bakhtin's interpretation, in Dostoyevsky's characters inner and outer dialogue are intertwined, to the point of being sometimes indistinguishable. This relative indistinction transcend the limits of the modern isolated and self-consistent individual. In modern times, the substantial unity of the

---

16 Bakhtin, *Problems*, 293.
17 Bakhtin, *Problems*, 302, note 15.
18 Svetlana Boym, *Another Freedom: The Alternative History of an Idea* (Chicago: University of Chicago Press, 2010), 312, note 13.
19 Bakhtin, *Problems*, 36.

self as a philosophical concept was notably challenged by Hume,[20] historicized by Hegel,[21] emptied by Stirner,[22] dissolved by Marx into the network of social relations,[23] and finally mocked by Nietzsche.[24] And yet, it is in the literary field that for the first time Dostoyevsky gave expression to inner and outer multiplicities and to the reciprocal articulation of their components. Following in his footsteps, Freud first in the epistemic realm put forth an alternative model to the modern self-identical self. He also emphasized the necessity of an ongoing negotiation between the various psychological components. Nevertheless, Freud confined the multiplicities that refused to converge towards a unified will to the field of psychosis, that is a pathological realm that exceeded the reach of psycho-analytical treatment.[25]

In the 1930s, whilst engaging with the psychosocial otherness of New Guinean highlanders, Bateson had the insight that the meaningfulness of the behaviour of irreconcilably fragmented identities could be restored by relocating these identities back to their context and its demands.[26] Two decades later, he generalised this insight as a relation between so-called schizophrenic behaviour and absolutely contradictory injunctions.[27] According to Bateson, these injunctions subjected the weakest link in a troubled relational chain to a double bind, which this weakest subject felt she could only face by splitting herself.

---

20 In the introduction to his *Treatise of Human Nature*, Hume sardonically remarked that human beings, "setting aside some metaphysicians [...] are nothing but a bundle or collection of different perceptions, which succeed each other with an inconceivable rapidity, and are in a perpetual flux and movement."

21 See Georg Wilhelm Friedrich Hegel, *Phenomenology of Spirit*, ed. J. N. Findlay, trans. Arnold V Miller (Oxford: Clarendon Press, 1977).

22 See Max Stirner, *The Ego and Its Own*, ed. David Leopold, rev. trans. Steve Biyngton (Cambridge: Cambridge University Press, 2000).

23 Young Marx argued in his sixth thesis on Feuerbach that human nature "in seiner Wirklichkeit ist es das Ensemble der gesellschaftlichen Verhältnisse," [in its reality is the ensemble of human relations.]

24 For example, Nietzsche wrote in the *Genealogy of Morality*, I-13: "But there is no such substratum, there is no 'being' behind doing, working, becoming; 'the doer' is a mere appanage to the action."

25 Despite his various investigations and hypotheses on the aetiology of psychoses, Freud tellingly described psychoanalysis' understanding of psychosis as "a glimpse beyond the wall," in 1925d [1924] "An Autobiographical Study", in *The Standard Edition of the Complete Works of Sigmund Freud*, 20, 1–74, 61.

26 See Gregory Bateson, "Double Bind" in *Steps to an Ecology of the Mind: A Revolutionary Approach to Man's Understanding of Himself* [1969] (Chicago: University of Chicago Press, 1972).

27 Gregory Bateson et al., "Toward a Theory of Schizophrenia," *Behavioral Sciences* 4.1 (1956): 251–264.

In the 1960s, Bateson's conception oriented the therapeutic practices of psychiatrists such as Cooper, Laing and Esterson among others. As the analytical key of double bind re-legitimated the so-called schizophrenics as meaningful social agents, their dissociation could be trusted as an attempt to work out an individual solution (albeit impossible) to familiar conflicts that were even reproduced through several generations.[28] The so-called anti-psychiatrists argued that in a different and supportive context, this attempt to work out an existential solution could be taken further as a veritable trip across and beyond psychosis.

However extraordinarily moving and effective, the approach of British anti-psychiatry necessarily focused on multiplicities mostly as extreme pathologies, though it radically challenged the very boundary between pathology and so-called normality. Deleuze and Guattari instead claimed the condition of diverging multiplicities as the general condition of becoming, which was thus not subjected to the modern necessary convergence towards unified reason and will.[29] Of course, Deleuze and Guattari also intended to remove the stigma of madness from dissociation in general, but above all they understood the extreme edge of dissociation as an entry point to the long denied non-pathological complexity of the human self.

However, the very concept of self still betrays modern thought's attitude of containment, which since the seventeenth century produced the individual as a mutilated abstraction from a larger subjectivating field. Dostoyevsky appealed to a similar more-than-individual network, which included a double multiplicity, namely the inner multiplicity of each "I and another," and the outer multiplicity of the various interacting "I and another."

There is a striking resemblance between these inner and outer co-implications and the joint processes of individuation and co-individuation as construed by Gilbert Simondon in the late 1950s.[30] Simondon argued that individuals are

---

28 Ronald Laing and Aron Esterson, *Sanity, Madness and the Family: Families of Schizophrenics* (London: Tavistock, 1964).

29 See Gilles Deleuze and Félix Guattari, *Anti-Œdipus: Capitalism and Schizophrenia*, trans. Robert Hurley, Mark Seem and Helen Lane (Minneapolis: University of Minnesota Press, 1983).

30 Simondon's most relevant texts are his two doctoral theses, which he discussed in 1958. The complementary thesis, *Du Mode d'Existence des Objets Techniques* (*On the mode of existence of technical objects*) was published by Aubier in 1958. The main thesis, *L'individuation à la lumière des notions de Forme et d'Information* (*Individuation in the light of the notions of Form and Information*), was published later on and in two parts, the first in 1964 under the title *L'Individu et Sa Génèse Physico-Biologique* (*Individuation and its physico-biological genesis*) at the *Presses Universitaires de France*, and the second, *L'individuation Psychique et Collective* (*Psychic and collective individuation*) in 1989 at Aubier. Simondon's work had a deep influence on Gilles Deleuze and, more recently, on Bruno Latour and Bernard Stiegler.

never completely determined (or individuated), but they always still carry the residues of their pre-individual or natural stage. In order to define this residual potential for further individuations, Simondon recovered the Greek term *ápeiron* or not-yet-determined.[31] This term first appeared in the most famous fragment that is attributed to the sixth-century BCE Greek philosopher Anaximander.

The so-called Anaximander fragment, which is often considered to be the first written Western philosophical statement, is actually part of a text written by Simplicius in the sixth century CE, more than a thousand years after Anaximander. Let's examine its core sentences: "Ἀναξίμανδρος...ἀρχήν...εἴρηκε... τῶν ὄντων τὸ ἄπειρον" [*Anaxímandros...archḕn...éireke...tṓn óntōn tó ápeiron*], "Anaximander... said [that] the principle...of things [is] the non-determined," "ἐξ ὧν δὲ ἡ γένεσίς ἐστι τοῖς οὖσι, καὶ τὴν φθορὰν εἰς ταῦτα γίνεσθαι κατὰ τὸ χρεών" [*ex ṓn dè ē génesís esti tóis oúsi, kài tḕn phthoràn eis táuta gínesthai katà tò kreón*], "whence things have their origin, they also have they ending as it is due," "διδόναι γὰρ αὐτὰ δίκην καὶ τίσιν ἀλλήλοις τῆς ἀδικίας κατὰ τὴν τοῦ χρόνου τάξιν" [*didónai gàr autà díkēn kài tísin allḗlois tḕs adikías katà tḕn tóu chrónou táxin*], "because they pay each other justice and the penalty of injustice according to the order of time."[32]

Following Aristotle, the fragment was generally understood as a cosmological account, which describes a cycle of determination and indetermination charged with ethical and even religious overtones. And yet, this interpretation may have been influenced by the very conditions of transmission of the text.

Simplicius did not directly quote Anaximander, but he referred to a quotation from a text written by Theophrastus eight hundred years before, in the fourth century BCE. Theophrastus was a pupil of Aristotle and he succeeded him as the head of the *Peripatos*, Aristotle's philosophy school. We may reasonably doubt whether Simplicius' quotation of a quotation is a literal rendering of Anaximander or a paraphrase. In particular, Havelock suggests the possibility that Theophrastus, following the systematizing approach of his master Aristotle, could have turned the adjective ἄπειρος [*ápeiros*], or "non-determined" (some-

---

31 The word *ápeiron* is variously translated into English as "limitless," "infinite," "formless" or "indefinite." In the translation of Anaximander's fragment I prefer the expression "non-determined," which keeps the semantic link with the operation of testing (*peiráein*, "to test") and the determination of the limit, *péras*. However, considering Simondon's extended use of the word, in his text I render it as "not-yet-determined."

32 Hermann Diels and Walter Kranz have edited the doxography (A) and the existing texts (B) of the Presocratic philosophers in *Die Fragmente der Vorsokratiker*, Berlin 1951–1952. The so-called Anaximander fragment is n. 12 B1.

thing), into the nominalised neuter form ἄπειρον [*ápeiron*], or "*the* non-determined."[33]

This transformation of an adjective into an abstract noun would fit Aristotle's construction of previous thinkers as being mainly concerned with the definition of ἀρχαί [*archái*], or "principles."[34] Regardless of whether Anaximander himself or Theophrastus operated such a linguistic and theoretical turn, the word *ápeiron* bears witness of a more general transformation, which began after the composition of the Homeric poems.

On the linguistic side, this long process entailed the construction of Greek alphabetic written language. In the course of this process, Greek writers also turned oral poetic narrations of sequences of actions rendered with verbs, into written texts ordered around the theme of an enquiry upon reality, which was mostly described with nouns, and in particular with abstract nouns.[35] On the theoretical side, the linguistic derivation of nouns from verbs was reversed into the logical and ontological priority of these abstract nouns (which we now call concepts) over their specific instantiations.[36] We may well consider as part of this process the Platonic construction of ψυχή [*pschê*] or soul,[37] which combined a series of previous Greek notions.

Since Homeric times, the Greek human body was centred on its middle region, from the navel to the chest.[38] In the sixth century BCE, Empedocles still located the centre of what we now call consciousness in the blood surrounding the heart. Alcmaeon of Croton, experimenting on living animals, seemed instead to have placed this centre in the brain. Though the authors of the Hippocratic corpus were either cardiocentric or cephalocentric, the latter claimed Hippocrates on their side. Plato attributed different functions to different centres, probably in

---

33 See Eric A. Havelock, "The Linguistic Task of the Presocratics" in Kevin Robb ed. *Language and Thought in Early Greek Philosophy* (LaSalle: The Hegeler Institute, 1983), 7–82.

34 See Aristotle, *Metaphysics*, trans. Christopher Kirwan (Oxford: Clarendon Press, 1993); *Physics*, ed. David Bostock, trans. Robin Waterfield (Oxford: Oxford University Press, 1999).

35 See Eric A. Havelock, *Preface to Plato* (Cambridge MA: Harvard University Press, 1963).

36 A famous example is in the Platonic dialogue *Euthyphro*. In this dialogue, the character Socrates surreptitiously sets the subordination of the adjective ὅσιος [*ósios*], "pious," to its substantivated form τὸ ὅσιον [*tó ósion*], "piety," because he searches αὐτὸ τὸ εἶδος [*autó tó éidos*], "the very idea," ᾧ πάντα τὰ ὅσια ὅσιά ἐστιν [*ô pánta tá ósia ósia estin*], "by which all pious actions are pious" (6d).

37 Homer uses the word *pschê* with the meaning of life (for example, Od.1.1).

38 In Homer, the word *thýmos* is variously deployed to name the heart (Il.14.156), the agent of thought (Il.1.193), the seat of anger (Il.1.429), of will (Il.15.710), of courage (Il.20.174), and of the appetite for food (Il.4.263).

order to accommodate these different views.³⁹ In particular, the λογιστικόν [logistikon] or "rational soul"⁴⁰ in the head was to control the other two parts: the Homeric chest-soul θύμος [thýmos], which Plato renamed as θυμοειδές [thymoeidés], and the ἐπιθυμετικόν [epithymetikón], "the desirous soul" set in the abdomen. However, as the leading rational soul was in the head, Plato definitively moved upward the centre of the self.

The previous brief genealogical sketch helps us to understand Plato's decisive intervention on the issue of human identity. Plato domesticated, so to speak, the Greek traditional conception of human psychological plurality, which he accepted only inasmuch as he could reorganize it as a hierarchical structure. The Platonic theoretical bottleneck was a decisive step in the path that was to lead to the construction of the modern isolated individual and her self-consistent self.

Anaximander's supposed ápeiron appeared well before Plato's construction of human identity as centred on the soul. However, Simondon's recovery of the notion of ápeiron from within his theory of individuation extended, as it were, the presence of ápeiron to each individual. Moreover, Simondon's return to Anaximander iterated the modern recasting of classical thought, which in turn repeated the pattern established by early Christian apologists. The Church Fathers broke the classical construction of cyclical time and conceived of history as a linear progression,⁴¹ which moved from creation towards salvation. A thousand years later, Aquinas still followed this pattern whilst adapting the work of Aristotle to the linear Christian progression. Modern authors added to this Christian theme of historical progression the variation of an open-ended linear history. In line with this modern variation, Simondon opened up and transformed Anaximander's circle of individuation and de-individuation into an open multiphasic process.

As previously noted, Simondon constructed individuated beings as bearers of some remnants of their pre-individual or not-yet-determined condition. The persistence of some residual ápeiron within each individual would allow her relation with other individuals as a call for a further individuation, which thus would be

39 See Christopher Collins, *Authority Figures: Metaphors of Mastery from the Iliad to the Apocalypse* (Lanham, MD: Rowman & Littlefield, 1996); Theodore Tracy, "Plato, Galen and the Centre of Consciousness," *Illinois Classical Studies* 1 (1976): 43–52.
40 In the *Republic*, Plato uses the word *logistikón* first in its usual sense of "calculator" (340d), and then to define the rational soul (439d), of which he suggests thus the ability to calculate, that is to rationally evaluate reality.
41 See Karl Löwith, *Meaning in History: The Theological Implications of the Philosophy of History* (Chicago: University of Chicago Press, 1949). I suggested elsewhere that we should take further back Löwith's retrograde movement through history until Eusebius and his of Christian (and synoptic) chronology.

at once transindividual.[42] According to Simondon, the *ápeiron* precedes the series of individuated phases. Hence, the *ápeiron* plays the role of an unlimited reservoir for things to happen.[43] Moreover, this reservoir does not contain forms, which in Simondon's view are individuated entities and belong to the actual, but potentials. These potentials can be actualized through the operation of disparation, which he defined as the construction of a previously non-existent link between two different series of occurrences.[44]

Simondon took sexuality as an example of the non-determination of individuals, and of their ongoing attempt to transcend their own limits.[45] More generally, this residual pre-individual or natural stage is expressed by the emotions. Emotions make emerge the incompleteness of the individual, and they call for her ongoing reorganization. Moreover, because according to Simondon the reorganization of the individual takes place in the relation with other individuals on the basis of the common human incompleteness, individuations always involves a transindividual dimension.

---

42 "The individual has not individuated the preceding being without remainder; it has not been totally resolved in the individual and the milieu; the individual has conserved the preindividual within itself, and all individual ensembles have thus a sort of non-structured ground from which a new individuation can be produced. The psycho-social is the transindividual: it is this reality that the individuated being transports with itself, this load of being for future individuations," unpublished translation by Taylor Adkins from Gilbert Simondon, *L'Individu et Sa Genèse Physico-Biologique* (Paris: PUF, 1964), 193, available at http://fractalontology.wordpress.com/2007/11/28/a-short-list-of-gilbert-simondons-vocabulary/ (July 12, 2013).

43 "Forms interact not with forms but with their ground, which is the system of all forms or, better still, the common reservoir of the tendencies of forms, even before they exist separately or are constituted as a specific system. The participative relationship connecting forms to ground is a relationship that spans the present and disseminates an influence of the future on the present, of the virtual on the actual. The ground is the system of potentialities, of potentials, of progressive forces, whereas forms are the system of the actual. Invention is a taking charge of the system of actuality by the system of potentialities, the creation of a single system from those two systems," Gilbert Simondon, *On the Mode of Existence of Technical Objects*, unpublished translation by Ninian Mellamphy, Dan Mellamphy and Nandita Biswas Mellamphy, available at http://www.mediafire.com/view/?57kscj7yhq7c627 (July 12, 2013).

44 "There is disparation when two twin sets that cannot be entirely superimposed, such as the left retinal image and the right retinal image, are grasped together as a system, allowing for the formation of a single set of a higher degree which integrates their elements thanks to a new dimension," unpublished translation by Taylor Adkins of footnote 15 in Simondon, *L'Individu et Sa Genèse Physico-Biologique*, 203, available at http://fractalontology.wordpress.com/2007/11/28/a-short-list-of-gilbert-simondons-vocabulary/ (July 12, 2013).

45 See Gilbert Simondon, *L'Individuation Psychique et Collective à la Lumière des Notions de Forme, Information, Potentiel et Métastabilité* (Paris: Aubier, 1989).

In Bakhtin's reading of Dostoyevsky, the external perspective of the others' glance grants at the same time the non-determination of individuals and their individuation, albeit unfinalized. In order to better define this external perspective, Bakhtin coined a new Russian word. He contracted the Russian phrase *находиться вне* [*nakhodit'sja vne*], which expresses the condition of being located or situated outside the bounds of someone or something, into the neologism *вненаходимость* [*vnenakhodimost'*], which defines with a single noun the state of being situated outside the bounds.[46] Todorov constructed with Greek roots the French coinage *exotopie*, or, in English, "exotopy," as a literal rendering of the Russian term *vnenakhodimost'*.[47]

In Todorov's translation of a quote from Bakhtin's 1961 notes for the revision of the Dostoyevsky book, the notion of exotopy plays a fundamental double role in constructing the individual and in maintaining her unfinalized. The parallel with Simondon is striking, especially in regard to the consideration of love:

> No fusion with the other but the preservation of his [sic] *exotopic* position and of his *excess* of vision and comprehension, that is its correlative. But the question arises as to how Dostoevsky uses this surplus. Not for objectivation of completion. The most important moment of this surplus is love (one cannot love oneself, it is a coordinated relation); then, confession, forgiveness (the conversation between Stavrogin and Tikhon), finally, simply an active understanding (that does not reduplicate), watchful listening [*uslyshannost'*].[48]

In the same text, Bakhtin synthesizes his and (supposedly) Dostoyevsky's relational approach in a lapidary formula: "*To be* means to *communicate*."[49] In turn, communication practices always involve a multiplicity of languages. This multiplicity emerges in Bakhtin's parable-like depiction of the illiterate Russian peasant:

> he prayed to God in one language (Church Slavonic), sang songs in another, spoke to the family in a third, and, when starting to dictate a petition for the district authority to someone who could write, tried to speak in a fourth (the official-written language of documents).[50]

---

46 See note 28 by Vadim Liapunov in Mikhail Bakhtin, *Art and Answerability: Early Philosophical Essays*, eds. Michael Holquist and Vadim Liapunov, trans. Vadim Liapunov (Austin: University of Texas Press, 1990), 235.

47 Tzvetan Todorov, *Mikhail Bakhtin: The Dialogical Principle*, trans. Wlad Godzich (Minneapolis: University of Minnesota Press, 1984), 99.

48 Todorov, *Mikhail Bakhtin: The Dialogical Principle*, 106.

49 Bakhtin, *Problems*, 287.

50 Mikhail Bakhtin, *The Dialogical Imagination: Four Essays*, Michael Holquist ed. (Austin: University of Texas Press, 1981), 295.

Regardless of its actual accuracy, this vivid sketch hints at the irreducible multiplicity of language registers that traverse, as it were, each individual. In the attempt to grasp this multiplicity Bakhtin produced a triad of compound words: *разноречие* [*raznorečie*], *разноязыкие* [*raznojazyčie*] and *разноголосье* [*raznogolosie*]. Todorov translated them into French as *hétérologie*, *hétéroglossie* and *hétérophonie* respectively: in English, they could be rendered as heterology, or the multiplicity of different discourses; heteroglossia, or the multiplicity of different languages; and heterophony, or the multiplicity of different voices.[51]

If we are to follow Dostoyevsky and Simondon, and their inner and outer shifting human multiplicities, we would also need to follow Bakhtin in the search for a new vocabulary. For example, we could talk of trajectories[52] of subjectivation rather than individual subjects, and of temporary transindividual sharing rather than collective subjects.

I would admit that these replacements are quite awkward. And yet, their awkwardness also reveals our habit of dealing with multiplicities and transformations just as properties of already defined entities. In other words, we are used to conceptualize first an entity whatsoever, and then its relations and transformations. Whilst this intellectual habit was strongly reaffirmed in modern times, it may be traced back to the process of transformation of Greek language that I previously recalled, and which culminated with Plato's writings. Hence, we may call this approach Platonism, metaphysics, logic of identity or language of being. I argue that Dostoyevsky showed through the polyphonic interaction of his literary characters that this approach, however defined, fails to address the complexity of us humans and of our own continuous interactive reproduction.

I already recalled how human rights discourse followed modern trends and entrapped, so to speak, human complexity within the two conceptual categories of the individual and of the immediate totality of humankind. Nevertheless, the more recent declarations of the rights of women, children and indigenous peoples

---

51 Todorov, *Mikhail Bakhtin: The Dialogical Principle*, 56.
52 Latour and Lowe described objects of art as trajectories, in order not to lose the transformations of the object in time. See Bruno Latour and Adam Lowe, "The Migration of the Aura, or How to Explore the Original through its Facsimiles" in Thomas Bartscherer and Roderick Coover eds., *Switching Codes* (Chicago: University of Chicago Press, 2011), 275–297. I followed Latour and Lowe also to show that the apparently same object can belong to multiple trajectories, as construed by different human perspectives. For example, in the Iranian Murghab plain the apparently same object is at once the tomb of Cyrus the great and the tomb of the mother of Solomon. See my "The Costs of Paradise: Temporalisations of Place in Pasargadae" in Ali Mozaffari ed., *World Heritage in Iran: Perspectives on Pasargadae* (London: Ashgate, forthcoming 2014).

introduced into international law some embodied subjects.[53] More important, the statement of the rights of indigenous peoples acknowledged the primal embeddedness at least of indigenous subjects. Though we are yet to produce human rights that address both human embeddedness and human inner multiplicity, we are in the way of reconsidering the very notion of individual, on which rely civil, political and social human rights.

Reconsideration of the individual in the last fifty years may be described as a theoretical shift of focus from subjects to processes of subjectification. Such a change of approach was heralded in the late 1950s by Simondon's shift from the individual to the process of individuation. The shift then clearly emerged during the 1960s, when it notably took the shape of a series of enquiries conducted by Foucault on the history of the techniques of *assujettissement*, that is the construction at once of subjects and of their subjugation.[54] Later on, Foucault also underscored as *subjectivation*, or subjectification as productive care of the self, a more positive and proactive approach to subjectivity-building.[55] However, in both cases his work emphasised the processual aspect of the construction of subjectivities, as opposed to the various ontologies of the subject as an entity. More importantly, Foucault produced his genealogical inquiries in the double political perspective of *désassujettissement*,[56] or desubjugation from authoritarian constructions of subjectivities, and *subjectivation*, or subjectification as reconstruction of non-authoritarian subjectivities, rather than as descriptive historical representations. Foucault shared the refusal of representation with Deleuze, who expressed this rejection as a heartfelt invitation: "never interpret, experiment!"[57]

---

53 *Declaration of the Rights of the Child*, United Nations General Assembly Resolution 1386 (XIV), 20 November 1959; *Convention on the Elimination of All Forms of Discrimination Against Women*, United Nation General Assembly Resolution 34/180, 18 December 1979; *United Nations Declaration on the Rights of Indigenous Peoples*, United Nations General Assembly Resolution 61/295, 13 September 2007.

54 Michel Foucault, *Madness and Civilization: A History of Insanity in the Age of Reason* [1961], trans. Richard Howard (London: Routledge, 2001); *The Birth of the Clinic: An Archaeology of Medical Perception* [1963], trans. Alan Sheridan (New York: Vintage Books, 1975); *Discipline and Punish: The Birth of the Prison* [1975], trans. Alan Sheridan (New York: Vintage Books, 1979).

55 Michel Foucault, *The History of Sexuality Volume 1: An Introduction* [1976], trans. Robert Hurley (London: Allen Lane, 1978).

56 Michel Foucault, "The Subject and Power" in *Michel Foucault: Beyond Structuralism and Hermeneutics*, Hubert Dreyfus and Paul Rabinow eds. (Chicago: University of Chicago Press, 1982), 208–226, 211.

57 Deleuze's original sentence is "*expérimentez, n'interprétez jamais,*" in Gilles Deleuze and Claire Parnet, *Dialogues* (Paris: Flammarion, 1977), 60.

Though the collective practices of experimentation of the long sixties were abruptly put to an end by the neoliberal revolution, the theoretical attempt to replace subjects and entities in general with processes did not subside. On the contrary, this paradigmatic shift spread through the various disciplines, and it was even claimed to be a general narrative turn. Moreover, the questioning of representation did not spare the traditional modern stronghold of description, economics and the natural sciences. The new field of Science and Technology Studies spearheaded a radical reconsideration of the scientific endeavour, which may well be epitomized in Callon's remarkable statement "all science is performative."[58]

The revaluation of narrations and the renewed attention on the performative power of texts – even in the scientific domain – may set in a new light the very role of literature. The performative ability of literary texts (which all along modern times have been quarried as a rhetorical pit) might at last be openly acknowledged as a resource for non-fiction texts too. In turn, the production of non-fiction texts might no longer rely on the absolute priority of conceptual expressions as the straight path to reality.

These possible perspectives would exert a wide influence on the construction of human subjects. In particular, we may well hope that the definition of humans as essentially conceptual beings – who are endowed with likewise conceptual characteristics, from reason to conscience, and from will to freedom – would in the end appear simply to be an enduring narrative; one which since Plato has belittled narrations,[59] though it had to keep recurring to narrations to establish itself. Inasmuch as we acknowledge and expand the role of narrations in our ongoing processes of humanization, we would rather construct ourselves as narrative beings in the various senses of listeners, performers and producers of stories.

This construction would surely help us to deal with the multiplicity of our engagements, as the experience of Bakhtin's fictional illiterate peasant is shared by billions of real human beings who negotiate daily with a variety of roles and

---

58 Michel Callon, "What Does It Mean to Say That Economics Is Performative?," *CSI Working Papers Series* (Paris: Centre de Sociologie de l'Innovation, 2006).

59 Plato conceived of *eidē*, or forms as the grounding for a cultural alternative to Homeric poetry. He did not attack narrations as such, but only inasmuch they conveyed the traditional Greek education, which was his actual target. Hence, he did not question traditional narrations' truthfulness, but rather their educational content, which he deemed as often poor, contradictory and sometimes counterproductive. This is why he could also adopt within his dialogues the narrative register of so-called mythological stories, whose mimetic power he brilliantly exploited to better illustrate his views.

languages. All these various modalities of communication are also veritable degrees of otherness that traverse, so to speak, each individual in her relation with herself and others, and which cannot be reduced to simplistic dichotomies such as I/other, inner/outer and friend/foe. This multiplicity not only challenges the modern closure of individual subjects, but also of collective ones.

Participants to recent political practices such as the *Indignados* and the Occupy movement accepted this challenge by declining to shape their collective individuation as a fusion into a single common identity. On the contrary, they acknowledged and claimed both the continuous osmotic interchange that produced an indistinction between the inside and the outside of the movements, as well as the ongoing transformation of the roles of participants. Instead of a concept, a multiplicity of narrations would better fit these flowing practices and their various sub- and trans-individual processes.

The *Indignados* and the participants to the Occupy movement challenged a long standing political common sense, which understands participating in a political activity as the endorsement of an established blueprint. Instead they turned the blueprint into a task rather than a precondition of political action. More generally, we may argue that these political practices defined the political common and, more in general, human commonalities, as the eventual result of political interactions rather than their prerequisite.

If we translate these practices into the language of human rights discourse, we would have to replace the narrative of the declaration of human rights as natural endowments with that one of the production of human rights as fully political and historical constructions. This replacement implies a shift of focus from the conceptual definition of human rights to the narration of their processes of production, claim and exercise. In turn, such retrospective genealogical reconsideration of human rights discourse opens towards the production, claim and exercise of further rights. Hence, from within this perspective, all human beings are acknowledged not simply as bearers, but as *producers* of human rights.

This shift of focus in human rights discourse from entitlement to production was hinted at by Upendra Baxi and proposed by Boaventura de Sousa.[60] My legal genealogies upheld a similar proposal by narrating the production of human rights entitlement as a step towards the redistribution of this very production.[61] Hence, rather than claiming the universal right to have rights, as proposed by

---

60 See Boaventura de Sousa Santos, "Human Rights as an Emancipatory Script? Cultural and Political Conditions" in *Another Knowledge is Possible: Beyond Northern Epistemologies*, Boaventura de Sousa Santos ed. (London: Verso, 2007), 3.

61 See Riccardo Baldissone, "Human Rights: A Lingua Franca for the Multiverse," *The International Journal of Human Rights* 17.7 (2010): 1117–1137.

Hannah Arendt, I preferred to facilitate the claim to produce rights.[62] This claim would give a normative expression to the spreading demand of human beings to participate in the ongoing construction of their various realities.

And yet, a participative construction of human rights could hardly find expression through a merely conceptual language, which was conceived of precisely to make both historicity and participation redundant. The language of narrations could instead immediately give voice to all human producers of rights. Of course, here I am not attributing a natural character to narrations, as opposed to the cultural construction of conceptual language. I am rather taking into account both the dissemination of narrations as a widespread human cultural technology, and the ability of narrations to construct subjectification paths that do not reduce human beings to fixed entities.

Dostoyevsky exploited with unmatched virtuosity the ability of narrations to produce unfinalized human characters. These characters literally take shape as long as their inner and outer dialogical relations develop in the course of the narration, which unfolds performatively as a veritable subjectivating field. In this sense, Dostoyevsky shows how narrations can construct human subjects as trajectories rather than entities. At the same time, Dostoyevsky presents us with trajectories that only emerge in relation to an inner and an outer multiplicity, so that their path is always at once individual and transindividual.

We may compare Dostoyevsky's characters with the individual subject as construed in the article two of the Universal Declaration of Human Rights. The article rejects "distinction of any kind, such as race, colour, sex, language, religion, political or other opinion, national or social origin, property, birth or other status."[63] That which is left after the cleansing of all human specificities is a disembodied and disembedded virtual entity, which at least should prevent any possible discrimination. And yet, the problem with this human simulacrum is not its excessive abstraction. On the contrary, this larval entity is far too specific as it only inhabits Western modern legal, philosophical and political texts. It is a merely conceptual being, which only as a virtual human enjoys the negative freedom from interference by other subjects. This unhappy monster only shares the satisfaction at its isolation with a similar opprobrium, the greedy individual that populates the wasteland of neoliberal texts.

The disembodied and disembedded subject of the Universal Declaration unfortunately inherited a common feature of conceptual abstractions, which are often

---

62 Baldissone, "A Contribution to a Western Genealogy of the Rights of Men, and Incidentally, of Women," 116.
63 UDHR, art. 2.

amnestic of the circumstances of their production. Of course, we use concepts *as if* they were not the result of a specific production, so that we can extend their field of application. We may even say that in order to fully exploit concepts' ability to be applied, we must temporarily forget their process of production. And yet, if we forget this forgetfulness we may easily turn the application of concepts into an imposition on the basis of these concepts' supposed objectivity.[64]

In this case, the very fact that the concept of the human subject of the Universal Declaration is isolated and abstract – that is devoid of any specificity – reveals instead this subject as the result of a specific cultural and historical context, namely Western culture in its modern stage. Obviously, this legacy as such is *not* a stigma: that which is problematic is rather its obliteration. In other words, we should worry about both the surreptitious erasure of the cultural and historical specificity of this human representation and its smuggling as an immediately universal model.

As previously noted, subsequent declarations integrated the abstract (and synecdochical) universality of the subject of human rights by addressing specific subsets of the human family such as children, women and indigenous peoples. If human rights discourse would continue following the path towards the overcoming of the metaphysics of the individual, the language of narrations could easily support with human flesh the bony abstractions of conceptual language.

Dostoyevsky's narrations exemplify the construction of human subjects as trajectories instead of entities deprived of context and history, and they make room for human multiplicities both within and outside the individual. This precious example could help reorienting the ongoing construction of the human subject of rights. The rapprochement of human rights inscriptions to the language of narrations could also reactivate genealogical resonances from within legal thought, which, at least in its Roman cradle, was not born conceptual.

---

64 The recovery from the oblivion of the processes of construction of concepts may be traced back at least to Geulincx's exposure of the linguistic derivation of classical ontological categories in his *Metaphysica ad Mentem Peripateticam*; the erasure of the construction of theological concepts is an Enlightenment *topos* since Spinoza's *Tractatus Theologico-Politicus*; the analogous erasing of the construction of scientific concepts came instead under theoretical scrutiny only in recent decades. See, for example, "Classical Empiricism" in Paul K. Feyerabend, *Philosophical Papers*, John Preston ed. (Cambridge: Cambridge University Press, 1981), and Bruno Latour and Steve Woolgar, *Laboratory Life: The Social Construction of Scientific Facts* (Beverly Hills: Sage, 1979). However, all these recoveries let emerge a kind of shared path in three movements. The first two movements generally occur at once, and they are the production of conceptual objects and the erasure of the traces of this production – so that the produced objects would appear as being autonomous entities. The third movement involves the appeal to these entities as legitimating authorities. In Nietzschean terms, this path may well be defined as the core process of production of metaphysics.

Daniela Carpi
Dehumanizing the Enemy: How to Avoid Human Rights

> The modern doctrine of the just war provides the conceptual machinery for dehumanizing the enemy and thus for mass killing on a scale unknown to earlier periods.
> Carl Schmitt

One of the many ways the Nazis used to eliminate unwanted people was to dehumanize them: they deprived them of the status of "legal personae", thus paving the way for their elimination. No law protected them any more as they were no longer an acknowledged part of society.

> As soon as Jews were legally denied any rights as individuals and became second-class citizens deprived of the most basic freedoms [...] the destruction process had started, through humiliation pushed to its worst extremes, through atrocious discrimination.[1]

The term "dehumanize" is defined in the Oxford Concise Dictionary as the "act of depriving of positive human qualities." The dehumanizing intent is the essence of the crime of genocide: it embodies the elimination of the victims, but it also orchestrates the cancellation of the social memory of these victims.

This topic, which explodes in the twentieth century with the Nazi persecution of the Jews, is anticipated by previous literary works that patently present the violation of the most common human rights, as they were described in the 1948 Declaration. It can be argued that Shakespeare's Shylock is the most outstanding example of a theatrical figure which, five centuries before the open assessment of the existence of human rights, can be re-read from this perspective. Even more, the exemplary fascination of such a problematic figure has triggered a host of literary re-adaptations, including those of Marowitz and Wesker in the twentieth century.

The aim of my essay is that of comparing Shakespeare's, Wesker's and Marowitz's interpretations of Shylock, in so doing demonstrating how the original text and its re-readings mark the evolution/anticipation of the concept of human rights from the Renaissance to the age of the true birth of the Human Rights

---

1 Caroline Fournet, *The Crime of Destruction and the Law of Genocide. Their Impact on Collective Memory* (Aldershot: Ashgate, 1988), 21.

Declaration: "It is often claimed that the Human Rights Act 1948 has brought about a legal revolution. [...] [T]he human rights era marks a substantial shift in the way in which law and religion interact."[2]

The elements in the Declaration's first column are the best-known human rights: they concern in fact rights to life, liberty, and personal security; bans on slavery and torture; rights to legal recognition, equality before the law, and effective remedies for violation of fundamental rights; freedom from arbitrary arrest and detention; guarantees of fair criminal procedures, the presumption of innocence.[3] This group of provisions, aimed at subjecting the exercise of power to legal rules, protecting individuals from aggression, and assuring fair procedures, marks the unequal treatment to which Shylock is subjected; especially in Shakespeare. He is constantly presented as a devil, as less than human, not worthy of belonging to Venetian society, an inferior being who cannot partake of the common rights of men. On the contrary, Wesker emphasizes Shylock's marked superiority to the rest of the characters: his superior education, his loyalty to his tribe, his friendship for Antonio that goes even against the law and his equitable attitude opposed to rigorous justice, demonstrate Wesker's will to reconduct him within a human rights legislation and the will to stress the unjust anti-racial attitude towards the Jew. Even more than this, we may say paradoxically that Wesker emphasizes the difference of Shylock from the other characters because of his marked superiority. Once more Shylock is not equal to the rest but for opposite reasons.

The third column of the Declaration comprises a list of freedoms that can be considered as "political": freedom of religion and belief; freedom of opinion, expression, and communication; freedom of assembly and association. The violation of all these elements is discernible in Shakespeare's Shylock; something which makes him a literary forerunner of debates on human dignity.

> Art 18: Everyone has the right to freedom of thought, conscience and religion; this right includes freedom to change his religion or belief, and freedom, either alone or in community with others, and in public or private, to manifest his religion or belief in teaching, practice, worship and observance.
> Art. 19: Everyone has the right to freedom of opinion and expression; this right includes freedom to hold opinions without interference and to seek, receive and impart information and ideas through any media and regardless of frontiers.

---

2 Austin Sarat, Lawrence Douglas and Martha Merrill Umphrey eds., *Law and the Sacred* (Stanford: Stanford University Press, 2007), 81.
3 Mary Ann Glendon, "The Rule of Law in the Universal Declaration of Human Rights," *Northwestern Journal of International Human Rights* 2 (2004): 1–18, 6.

Art. 20: (1) Everyone has the right to freedom of peaceful assembly and association. (2) No one may be compelled to belong to an association.

The idea of human dignity precedes and qualifies reliance on human rights: it appears to be the groundwork for a human rights declaration. Human rights are in fact based on human dignity as empowerment and on the idea of individual autonomy: it implies

> not only a duty to respect the dignity of others but also the duty not to compromise our own dignity as well as to act in a way that is compatible with respect for the vision of human dignity that gives a particular community its distinctive cultural identity.[4]

We observe two conceptions of human dignity: human dignity as empowerment and human dignity as constraint.

> Intrinsic human dignity is a seminal idea that acts as the background justification for the recognition of human rights and as the source of the fundamental freedoms to which all humans (*qua* human) are entitled. In this context human dignity as empowerment (specifically, the empowerment that comes with the right to respect for one's dignity as a human, the right to the conditions in which human dignity can flourish) is the ruling conception.[5]

Human dignity as constraint implies the limits imposed on biomedicine and reflects the rules that medicine should respect in "a shared vision of human dignity that reaches beyond the individual,"[6] therefore it does not directly impinge on my critical perspective in this essay.

The idea of human dignity is at the basis of the concept of human rights: the notion of a right to dignity has been used by moral and political philosophers. Spiegelberg asserts that *"Human dignity* [...] refers to the minimum dignity which belongs to every human *qua* human. It does not admit of any degrees. It is equal for all humans. It cannot be gained or lost."[7] At the centre of the philosophical debate we have Kant who claims in his *Metaphysics of Morals* that humanity is the only thing having dignity.

---

4 Deryck Beyleveld and Roger Brownsword, *Human Dignity in Bioethics and Biolaw* (Oxford: Oxford University Press, 2004), 1.
5 Beyleveld and Brownsword, *Human Dignity in Bioethics and Biolaw*, 11.
6 Beyleveld and Brownsword, *Human Dignity in Bioethics and Biolaw*, 29.
7 Herbert Spiegelberg, "Human Dignity: a challenge to contemporary philosophy" in *Human Dignity: This Century and the Next*, eds. Rubin Gotesky and Ervin Laszlo (New York: Gordon and Breach, 1970), 55–60.

Every human being has a legitimate claim from his fellow human beings and is *in turn* bound to respect every other. Humanity itself is a dignity: for a human being cannot be used merely as a means by any human being [...] but must always be used at the same time as an end. It is just in this that his dignity (personality) consists, by which he raises himself above all other beings in the world that are not human beings and yet can be used, and so over all *things*. But just as he cannot give himself away for any price (this would conflict with his duty or self-esteem), so neither can he act contrary to the equally necessary self-esteem of others, as human beings, that is, he is under obligation to acknowledge, in a practical way, the dignity of humanity in every other human being, hence there rests on him a duty regarding the respect that must be shown to every other human being.[8]

In his work *Groundwork of the Metaphysics of Morals*, Kant had already stated that "the dignity of man consists precisely in his capacity to make universal [moral] laws, although only on condition of being himself also subject to the law he makes."[9] According to Kant, we find human dignity in man's capacity to reason and keep within the moral law. Victims of dignity violation are often described as having lost their humanity.

Shylock's human dignity is violated from the very start: Shakespeare's reading insists on his being as human as the rest of the Venetian citizens. His famous speech centred on "Has not a Jew eyes?" is focused on stressing identical somatic characteristics that should put Shylock and the other citizens on the same level.

Hath not a Jew eyes? hath not a Jew hands, organs, dimensions, senses, affections, passions? Fed with the same food, hurt with the same weapons, subject to the same diseases, healed by the same means, warmed and cooled by the same winter and summer, as a Christian is? If you prick us, do we not bleed? If you tickle us, do we not laugh? If you poison us, do we not die? And if you wrong us, shall we not revenge?[10]

Nevertheless, throughout the play the other characters stigmatize Shylock by calling him dog, cur, devil, monster, which has the effect of making him less than human so as to make him not worthy of respect.

Animals are used as metaphors for criminalizing human beings:

The animal is treated exclusively as a stand in for the bad human in its juxtaposition with the criminal. [...] animal images are used in negative metaphorical representations of hu-

---

8 Immanuel Kant, *The Metaphysics of Morals* [1797], trans. and ed. Mary Gregor (Cambridge: Cambridge University Press, 1991), 209.

9 Immanuel Kant, *Groundwork of the Metaphysics of Morals* [1785], transl. and ed. H. J. Paton (London: Hutchinson, 1948), 101.

10 William Shakespeare, *The Merchant of Venice*, ed. J. Dover Wilson (Cambridge: Cambridge University Press, 1969), 3.1.54–61.

mans in order to stress the radical alterity of the person or persons being portrayed by them.[11]

Calling criminals "beasts" has political implications in that they are degraded as human beings to a lower step in the great chain of beings. Animal metaphors contributed to ideological justifications for the punitive treatment of criminals and demonstrated that prejudices about criminals being animal-like, innately different, and marked are long-standing ones with far reaching cultural implications. In the case of Shylock the animal imagery serves the function of dehumanizing the Jew so as to make his classification as a monster easy. His animal-like characteristics and his visible "otherness" in his enemies' eyes mark him as the alien in society and help dehumanize him: being less than human he cannot be included in the protection of the law and he can be easily victimized. The use of animal imagery has ideological implications: the Jew comes to epitomize the fear of social instability.

This instability is much more emphasized in Wesker's re-reading, because the Jew refuses to conform to Venetian law and decides to privilege friendship over the legal system. His operation is particularly subversive because he influences Antonio's action in his wake: the Jew and the Christian unite in order to baffle the law of contract. But once the law is called into question its reaction cannot be contained and the result escapes Shylock's and Antonio's control.

> Shylock: I will not bend the law.
> Antonio: I understand.
> Shylock: I must not set a precedent.
> [...]
> Antonio: The court must understand.
> Shylock: Understanding is beyond them.[12]

In both Shakespeare's and Wesker's texts the central point is the loyalty to one's group or race. In both texts Shylock shows a strong loyalty towards his tribe. Article 29 of the Declaration says: "Everyone has duties to the community in which alone the free and full development of his personality is possible." This loyalty is evident only in the Jewish community because Antonio is not supported by his fellow citizens when in need. As a result of this characteristic, Shylock's

---

11 Greta Olson, "Introduction: Rediscovering the Criminal Animal The Persistent Image of the Criminal Animal" in 'Criminal Animals' from Shakespeare to Dickens: The History of a Prejudice (Berlin/Boston: De Gruyter, 2013), 11.
12 Arnold Wesker, Shylock and Other Plays (Harmondsworth: Penguin, 1974), 1.3: further references in the text, abbreviated as S.

racial community outshines Antonio's, but notwithstanding this it is the Venetian group that predominates.

However we must distinguish between Shakespeare's and Wesker's play. In Wesker the anti-Jewish prejudices are stressed by Bassanio's surprise when he meets Shylock: "and *that* is a Jew?" (*S*, 1.4) His astonishment marks the fact that Jews had been generally represented as monsters, and he did not expect to find a man. Antonio reprimands: "*He* is a Jew." Bassanio's "that" reduces Shylock to a thing, something not even to be named, while Antonio brings Shylock's identity back to humanity: "*He* is a Jew," and he adds: "Have you never met one before?" Bassanio demonstrates by his answer that he had lived on prejudice so far: "Talked of, described, imagined, but…". At this point Antonio asserts "Shylock is my special friend," thus reconducting him within the category of mankind and citizenship and Bassanio is forced to reconfigure him finally as a man: "Then, sir, he must be a special man."

In other words, so far Jews seem to have been legendary figures of horror, not belonging to the human race. Finally meeting a Jew face to face forces Christians to view him as a human being, with feelings and a capacity for decision. The attempt to dehumanize Jews so as to free humankind from responsibility pertaining to their welfare is evident here. However, another element is quite patent in Wesker's Shylock: his sense of responsibility towards his fellow-beings; once the bond is signed and made public in fact, he feels tied to respect its letter because otherwise he would damage his tribe. His sister Rivka acts as his conscience: whose party should Shylock take, his poor friend Antonio's (impoverished by the sea storm and not backed by his people who do not trust him anymore) or his poor people's ("the Ghetto is drained. The last tax emptied every purse," *S*, 2.3)? Shylock's sense of duty is thus divided between two contrasting loyalties.

> Rivka: You've mocked their law
> Shylock: Which mocked at us.
> Rivka: […] Can't you see what you have done?
> Shylock: Asserted dignity, that's what I have done.
> Rivka: To assert the dignity of your mocked people you have chained your friend's life to a mocking bond.
> […]
> Rivka: Shylock! Go and find the money! Knock on every Ghetto door […] before it is too late.
> Shylock: The Ghetto is drained. The last tax emptied every purse.
> Rivka: Then let him borrow from his friends.
> Shylock: They don't trust his future now.
> Rivka: Then plead with the court to bend the law and relieve you of your bond. (*S*, 2.3)

In Wesker's interpretation the idea of responsible behaviour underlines the notion of dignity, and Shylock's and Antonio's mocking of the law stems from a will to assert their own dignity: if a law is senseless one has to assert one's independence from it. Dignity is perceived as a virtue that paves the way for responsible and rational agency. What emerges here is the violence of the law, which curbs reason to rule. Derrida speaks of the "enforceability of the law or contract." "The law is always an authorized force, a force that justifies itself or is justified in applying itself, even if this justification may be judged from elsewhere to be unjust or unjustifiable."[13] That is to say that Shylock and Antonio are forced to obey the law of contract even if they consider it unjust or unreasonable.

The central element in Wesker's play is the different perspective from which the problem of the bond is represented. Here Shylock and Antonio's relationship is based on mutual alliance, respect and deep friendship: this is why Shylock does not want to have recourse to a written contract to lend Antonio the required money. Friendship does not need such assurances, but Antonio insists that the law of Venice needs such a contract. "The contract Shylock. We must draw up a bond" (*S* 1.4). Antonio thus demonstrates that he is less subversive than Shylock and more aware of the legal duties required of a citizen: if one wants to live in the state of Venice one must adhere to its legal system.

> Shylock: A bond? Between friends? What nonsense are you talking, Antonio?
> Antonio: The law demands it: no dealings may be made with Jews unless covered by a legal bond.
> Shylock: That law was made for enemies, not friends.
> Antonio: Shylock! The law says, in these very words: 'It is forbidden to enter into dealings with a Jew without sign and sealing of a bond, which bond must name the sum borrowed, specify the collateral, name the day. The hour to be paid, and –
> Together: – and be witnessed by three Venetians, two patricians and one citizen, and then registered. (*S*, 1.4)

In Wesker's view the real enemy in this situation is the law: it is the law that thrusts people into conflict with each other, it is the law that prevents different races from peacefully coexisting with one another, and it is the law that forbids equitable behaviour because of the rigorous rules that it sets which cannot be bypassed. The law is also defined as jealous of its power: Jews go on being despised because of the law that sets borders and separations. The law appears to be a Moloch that requires human sacrifices: "We are a nervous Empire with a

---

13 Jacques Derrida, "Force of Law: the Mystical Foundation of Authority" in *Deconstruction and the Possibility of Justice*, eds. Drucilla Cornell, Michel Rosenfeld and David Gray Carlson (New York and London: Routledge, 1992), 3–67, 5.

jealous law" (*S*, 1.5). The law threatens and divides, classifies and separates, is inimical to equity and mercy and causes conflicts rather than stifles them.

Law and religion are set at variance and compared: there is Venetian law, which is sacrosanct and "The city's reputation thrives on its laws being trusted" (*S*, 1.5), and the Deuteronomic code that says: "Thou shalt not lend upon usury to thy brother" (*S*, 1.5). In both cases, state law and religious law, the law divides people, establishes borderlines where people cannot be equal, where each person is forced into loyalty to his tribe. On the other hand, Shylock and Antonio stand for a more humane view of the law that abolishes confines and differences and where each person can choose his own "brother" and spread out his loyalty.

In order to make human dignity prevail upon legal constraint Shylock and Antonio decide to baffle the law by imposing a mock contract. However, once the contract is written down and signed it must run its own legal course and it cannot be stopped. Therefore legal rigour wins against human dignity and human rights are subjected to the letter of the law. "Shylock: A lovely, loving nonsense bind. To mock the law" (*S*, 1.5). "Antonio: Barbaric laws? Barbaric bonds!" What is interesting in this quotation is the contraposition between the law seen as barbaric and friendship seen as something transcendental that can overcome racial divisions. Friendship is intended to be a sort of lay religion that transcends human limitations and transports people towards a collective, ecumenical existence where a new kind of coexistence beyond racial divisions is admitted.

However, precisely because the two friends decide to force the law into subjection, both of them fall into the sin of disrespect of one's human dignity. Shylock in fact by asking for the famous pound of flesh reduces Antonio to cattle, to a lower place in the great chain of beings. Antonio is no longer a human being but becomes an object that can be cut into pieces, an animal in a slaughter-house. In other words, the law is superior to any attempt at overcoming it and, if challenged, it strikes back.

This is an important point that distinguishes Shakespeare's Shylock from Wesker's. In Shakespeare Shylock is a vengeful character in that he wants to pay Antonio back for having humiliated him: Antonio called him dog and cur and spit on his gabardine. Then he will have to repay him with his flesh: humiliation for humiliation. In the case of Wesker Antonio and Shylock are friends, so Shylock's asking for a mock payment of a pound of flesh is after all a violation of Antonio's human dignity, because this reduces Antonio to an animal to be weighed and cut. In Wesker's play it is the law that forces human beings to behave inhumanely.

In Wesker's play the non-equality of Jews and Christians is stressed, in that Jews cannot reside any place except inside the Ghetto. UDHR, article 13 asserts: "Everyone has the right to freedom of movement and residence within the borders of each state"; Shylock, however, is deprived of this.

Wesker's Shylock is described as a cultured character surrounded by books: his main occupation is reading and studying.

> Human rights defined the modern person in a manner that mirrors the *Bildungsroman*'s focus on individual formation. Moreover, both human rights discourse and the *Bildungsroman* argue for the individual's inclusion in the nation-state. Such "incorporation" of the individual is the source of the human rights "plot," a narrative pattern that undergirds the shape of human rights law. The oft-quoted phrase from Article 26 of the UDHR that links the right to education to "the full development of the human personality" implies an understanding of *Bildung* that [...] was at play in the creation of the law.[14]

In this case Shylock's *Bildung* becomes a way to stress his human dignity and his existence as a human being worthy of respect. His knowledge is far superior to the Christians'. If the Human Rights Charter openly speaks of the right to education which helps a human being be incorporated within the law and gives him shape as a human being, Shylock epitomizes such a right.

In Shakespeare's Shylock, however, the violation of the Jew's dignity is more patent. His basic human rights are crushed by his being forced to abjure and renounce all property rights. Shakespeare's Shylock anticipates the twentieth century debate on human rights in many points: for instance, art.7 of the 1948 Universal Declaration of Human Rights asserts: "All are equal before the law and are entitled without any discrimination to equal protection of the law." Shylock is a victim of the Foreigners' Edict which states that any foreign citizen who puts the life of a Venetian citizen at risk is subjected to capital punishment. The sort of punishment a Venetian citizen must face for the same crime is far more lenient than the one that awaits the Jew. Apart from the fact that the Alien Statute legally defined those who were to be considered "citizens," it also assessed a hierarchy among citizens who were not equal before the law. In this way everybody's "natural rights" were violated. The obligation to abjure imposed on Shylock is probably the most shocking element. Before this time no general explicit freedom of religion provision was to be found in English law. In the Renaissance there was a passive tolerance of religious difference, but after the Human Rights Declaration we witness a prescriptive regulation and active promotion of religious liberty as a right. This allows us to re-read the figure of Shakespeare's Shylock in this new light. The central article of the Declaration is article n. 9, which provides "a positive right to both the freedom of thought, conscience, and religion (known as

---

14 Eleni Coundouriotis and Lauren M. E. Goodlad, "Comparative Human Rights: Literature, Art, Politics," *Journal of Human Rights* 9 (2010): 121–126, 123.

the *forum internum*) and the manifestation of one's religion and belief (the *forum externum*)."[15]

The UK Equality Act of 2010 protects religion and belief alongside other characteristics, such as age, disability, gender reassignment, race, sex and sexual orientation. This Act also outlaws religious discrimination and all victimization and harassment, as UDHR art.18 asserts. Shylock is forced to abjure his religion in Shakespeare's text, which constitutes the supreme moral violence against the Jew.

> Harassment occurs where A engages in an unwanted conduct related to religion or belief which has the purpose or effect of violating B's dignity or creating an intimidating, hostile, degrading, humiliating or offensive environment.[16]

Another important point entailed at the end of Shakespeare's play is property: Shylock is deprived of all his properties thus leaving him without any means of subsistence. UDHR, article 17 declares: "1) Everyone has the right to own property alone as well as in association with others; 2) No one shall be arbitrarily deprived of his property."

Marowitz's re-reading of *The Merchant of Venice* lacks Wesker's pro-Jewish stance. It is a disturbing and controversial text which solicits in the audience a reaction against both the calculating and subversive Jewish community and the hypocritical and coercive Christian one.[17] The play opens with an introductory "character," which is the typical structure of many Elizabethan plays and which is represented here by a voice over. An attack against King David Hotel in Jerusalem has taken place. There are 91 dead, 47 injured and 43 missing. The Jewish Underground Terrorist organization, Irgun, has claimed responsibility for the attack. The setting is contemporary, plunging the audience into the violent epicenter of today's Israel.

> When the *Variations* were first performed in 1977, the precarious balance of power in the Middle East was as potentially explosive as it is today [...] Substitute Palestinian terrorists for Zionists, and the Israeli government for the British military force, and the political dynamics might look uncomfortably similar.[18]

In Wesker's play the non-equality of Jews and Christians is stressed in that Jews cannot reside anywhere except the Ghetto. UDHR, article 13 asserts: "Everyone

---

15 Sarat, Douglas, Merrill eds., *Law and the Sacred*, 82.
16 Sarat, Douglas, Merrill eds., *Law and the Sacred* , 104.
17 See Martha Tuck Rozett, *Talking Back to Shakespeare* (Newark: University of Delaware Press, 1994).
18 Rozett, *Talking Back to Shakespeare*, 64.

has the right to freedom of movement and residence within the borders of each state"; Shylock is again thus deprived of such freedoms of movement and residence.

The unsympathetic way in which Marowitz portrays Shylock shrouds him in the same defects and violation of human dignity which we have above lamented in the analysis of Shakespeare's and Wesker's portrayal of the Christians' attitude towards the Jew. While in Shakespeare the Christians presented deeply racist characteristics, in Marowitz's text Shylock teaches Jessica (who in this play sides with her father and acts according to his orders) to cheat and baffle Christians, who are deemed to be nothing but heretics.

> Shylock (impatiently): It's no sin to deceive a Christian
> For they themselves hold it a principle,
> Faith is not to be held with heretics,
> But all are heretics that are not Jews.[19]

Shylock's anti-heretical attitude and racist behaviour equals that of the Christians in the previous plays.

In Marowitz's play Jessica determines to hold to standards of equitable behaviour and resists the idea of debasing their "ancient faith" by violating their vows, while Shylock stubbornly insists on repaying the Christians for their oppression. Mercy is stifled: Shylock even solicits Jessica not to have any pity for Christians because they have dealt with Jews pitilessly for centuries. For most of the play Shylock violates Antonio's human dignity by considering him as a mere pound of flesh, as if he were "a mutton, a beef or a goat": "A pound of man's flesh, taken from a man, / Is not so estimable, profitable neither, / As flesh of muttons, beefs, or goats" (*V*, 241). Many characters follow the pattern of disrespect for each other's human dignity. We can also consider Jessica's case. When Gratiano speaks to her he gives vent to his hatred and openly declares that she has no hope of redemption because she is tainted with Jewishness, notwithstanding her conversion. Only if she had not been begot by her father could she vaguely hope in redemption. Gratiano would oblige Jessica to renounce her origins, her tradition and forefathers, which she will not do.

> Gratiano: Yes, truly, for look you, the sins of the father are to be laid upon the children – therefore, I promise you, I fear you. For truly I think you are damned. There is but one hope in it that can do you any good [...] you may partly hope that your father got you not, that you are not the Jew's daughter. (*V*, 254)

---

19 Charles Marowitz, *Variations on The Merchant of Venice* [1977] in *The Marowitz Shakespeare* (New York and London: Marion Boyars, 1990), 229: further references in the text, abbreviated as *V*.

Shakespeare's declaration that "the world is still deceived with ornament" in Marowitz's text is uttered by a disembodied "Voice on wireless." The disembodied voice becomes a sort of metaphysical comment on what is taking place: only somebody or something not belonging to society can comment upon such a corrupt world, where everyone is tainted.

> Voice on wireless: The world is still deceived with ornament.
> In law, what a plea so tainted and corrupt,
> But, being seasoned with a gracious voice,
> Obscures the show of evil? In religion,
> What damned error, but some sober brow
> Will bless it, and approve it with a text,
> Hiding the grossness with fair ornament?
> [...] Thus ornament is but the guiled shore
> To a dangerous sea. (*V*, 261)

But in the end what makes the play a lamentation on how Jews have been treated in history is the quotation of Shakespeare's famous speech "Hath not a Jew eyes?" articulated at the very end. It is as if to say: the Jews in the play behave dishonestly, they are violent and revengeful, but it is the persecutions and humiliations they have suffered for thousands of years that have made them such. Therefore we are once more thrust in the middle of the debate on human dignity: once humanity and humanness are violated, they are lost forever. The reappearance of the voice off makes us understand that the whole plot is a flashback, which serves to explain why riots burst out and why Shylock has been turned into such an inhuman character.

Human rights, as we have seen in the various characterizations of the figure of Shylock, represent a framework through which we can consider the complex relation between art and power, culture and the state. "The poet's function is to describe, not the things that have happened, but a kind of things that *might* happen," stated Aristotle in his *Poetics* more than two thousand years ago.[20] Although he was referring to poetry's objective, this basic intuition is embedded in the minds of any enlightened writer, as it is in any enlightened reader. Widening its scope, this statement can be applied to literature in its entirety, as the description of one of its paramount benefits to human understanding, as one of its essential functions indeed. I am referring to its ability to *see* critical hidden social tendencies in advance, to anticipate problematic cultural conflicts, to recognise menacing elements that might become destructive in the future – and consequently, to wonder, to unveil, to warn.

---

20 Aristotle, *Poetics*, ca. 350 BC. [Italics mine].

Patrizia Nerozzi Bellman
Am I not a man and a brother?

Notes on the Representation of Slavery in Eighteenth Century English Art and Literature

> Consider slavery – what it is – how bitter a draught, and how many millions have been made to drink of it; – which if it can poison all earthly happiness when exercised barely upon our bodies, what must it be, when it comprehends both the slavery of body and mind?
> Laurence Sterne, *Sermon* X.

Taking as a starting point the preceptive statement that the condition of slavery signals grade zero on the scale of human rights, since it turns a *persona* into an object of private property, it must be noted that in the eighteenth century the kidnapped negro slaves were regarded both in law and by the vast majority of their captors and masters merely as property. In fact in the so-called long century of equality and constitutionality, they were neither deserving of nor entitled to any human rights whatsoever.[1] However, in England attitudes towards slavery shifted as the century progressed. In the early decades, the lucrative trade in African slaves and the highly profitable businesses – such as sugar production – to which it was linked, were generally considered as part and parcel of the commercial economy, a built-in institutionalized practice in the colonial system which ensured Britain's greatness. By the end of the century, Enlightenment figures such as the "friends" of the so called Lunar Society[2] conducted the chorus of castigating voices, appalled as they were by the savage slave laws. The "Somersett case," in which the English Court of the King's Bench ruled that

---

1 Terence Brady and Evan Jones, *The Fight Against Slavery* (London: British Broadcasting Corporation, 1975), 7.

2 The Lunar Society of Birmingham was a dinner club and informal learned society of prominent Midlands industrialists, scientists, natural philosophers, artists and intellectuals who met together regularly between 1765 and 1813. The name of the society arose because the group met each month during the full moon when the extra light would make the journey home easier and safer. The members of the Lunar Society were all prominent in British society. Amongst those who regularly attended the meetings were Matthew Boulton, Erasmus Darwin (grandfather of Charles), Josiah Wedgwood, James Watt and James Keir. Less regular attendees and correspondents of the Society included Sir Richard Arkwright, James Wyatt, John Smeaton, Thomas Jefferson and even Benjamin Franklin. Most of them were low churchmen, non conformists or disbelievers like Erasmus Darwin himself. See Jenny Uglow, *The Lunar Men, Five Friends Whose Curiosity Changed the World* (London: Chatto & Windus, 2003).

slavery was unsupported by existing law in England and Wales, neither abolished the slave trade nor made the possession of slaves in either England or the colonies illegal. It nevertheless did awaken public opinion, contributing to the growing culture of English antislavery, strongly influenced by the dissenting religious movements. The abolition of the "horrid trade" gradually came to be felt to be the the duty of all Englishmen.

Figure 1: William Turner, *Slave Ship. Slaver throwing overboard the Dead and the Dying. Typhoon coming on.* (Oil on canvas, Museum of Fine Arts, Boston), retrieved from http://en.wikipedia.org/wiki/File:Slave-ship.jpg. Public domain (October 9, 2013).

Within this frame, this essay directs our attention towards a limited but significant number of representations of slavery and slaves, showing an array of passages and images, literary and artistic highlights rather than following a chronological sequence. The great visual impact of one of William Turner's most spectacular paintings provides us with an introduction to the dramatic relevance of the condition of slavery, bridging the gap with the shocking renderings of today's new media. The canvas was exhibited at the Royal Academy in 1840. John Ruskin bought it only to sell it a little later, as he could not bear to look at such a scene of atrocity. In the background a tempest-tossed ship is sailing away in a stormy sea. This is the slave ship itself though it is not the focal point of the scene. The visual impact of the red sunset actually carries the eye in the opposite direction, to the steely raging waves in the forefront. The surface of the water appears littered, scattered over with the barely recognizable black limbs of dismembered bodies, surrounded by menacing fish. Waiting gulls circle above. The bodies, or what remains of them, emerge from the water like damned sinners from a hellish pit, tossed up by the force of tide and gale (the scene brings to mind a seeming anticipation of Gustave Doré's illustrations of Dante's *Hell*).

Figure 2: William Turner, *Slave Ship* (Detail)

A human leg emerges from the water as if denouncing the condition of slavery: those fighting for their lives were weighed down with irons. William Turner had always been fascinated by the destructive power of natural phenomena, by storms, thunderbolts, shipwrecks, fires, but I do not know of any other of his paintings (perhaps only *The Shipwreck of the Minotaur* can stand the comparison) where the presence of human beings is so dramatically represented, a memento of what had happened sixty years earlier, in 1783.The subject of the painting is the so-called "Zong incident" or "Zong massacre." In 1783 the *Zong*, a British slave ship bound for Jamaica and owned by a syndicate of Liverpool merchants, had been hit by an epidemic. The *Zong* had taken on more slaves than it could safely transport and the number of the dead and dying increased daily. Afraid that his stock of water was running low and knowing that the insurance policy did not cover slaves who died either onshore, or of a "natural death" at sea or perished as a result of unhealthy conditions on board, Captain Collingwood feared that if he arrived in Kingston with half his cargo dead and most of the others sickly, he would not only be blamed but would also lose his percentage of the profit. Conversely, if some slaves were jettisoned in order to save the rest of the cargo, and even the ship iself, then a claim could be made under the notion of "general average." The ship's insurance covered the loss of slaves at £30 a head. Consequently he decided to throw one hundred and thirty-five (or one hundred and thirty-two, according to other sources) sick slaves overboard into the sea, starting with women and children. Realising what was going to happen to them, the last thirty-six resisted. The captain gave instructions for them to be shackled and then thrown overboard. Ten of the slaves struggled free and jumped into the sea as a final desperate gesture of free will.[3]

Back in England, Captain Collingwood justified his action by arguing that this was less cruel than "to suffer them to ginger out a few days under the disorders to which they were afflicted." In due course the case came up for trial in London (in March 1783, at the Guilhall Sessions), not as a murder case, but as an insurance dispute brought to court by the ship-owners seeking compensation from the insurers for the slave-traders' lost cargo, since the underwriters had refused to pay the thirty pounds per capita claimed by the owners of the *Zong* for the jettisoned slaves. The decision went against them, the jury finding "that the case of slaves was the same as if horses had been thrown overboard."[4]

The case was brought to the attention of Granville Sharp, possibly by Oulaudah Equiano, a famous freed slave. Sharp was considered after the "Strong case" as the "Defender of the Negro."[5] He persuaded the underwriters to appeal to a higher court against the decision, and the appeal was heard some months later in

---

3 See Linda Colley, *Britons. Forging the Nation 1707–1837* (London: Vintage, 1996), 370–381.

4 For quotations and references on this subject see Brady and Jones, *The Fight Against Slavery*, 63–64.

5 In 1769 Sharp published *A Representation of the injustice and dangerous tendency of admitting the least claim of private property in the persons of men, in England, etc*, the first major work of anti-slavery by a British author. The book, besides including his legal researches on the subject, specifically refutes the ruling made by Yorke and Talbot in 1729 that slaves remain the property of their owners in England as well as in the colonies. Adding practical action to his legal resources Sharp made his reputation as the defender of slaves kidnapped in England and forcibly put aboard ships bound for the colonies. It 1772 in delivering the judgment of the Court of King's Bench in the case of the slave James Somersett Lord Chief Justice Mansfield made his ruling according to which "no master was ever allowed here to take a slave by force to be sold abroad because he deserted from his service, or for any other reason whatever."

the Court of the King's Bench, with Sharp's old adversary Lord Mansfield, the Chief Justice of the King's Bench, once more presiding. The Solicitor General for England and Wales, John Lee, utterly rejected any appeal to the "pretended feelings of humanity," asserting the "unquestionable right of the Master of the vessel to throw overboard as many living slaves as he pleased, providing he exhibited a powerful reason for doing so." He personally affirmed that there could be no charge of impropriety brought against the captain of the *Zong*.

> What is all this vast declamation about human people being thrown overboard? The question is, was it voluntary or an act of necessity? This is a case of chattels or goods. It is the case of throwing over goods. For to this purpose, and for the purpose of the insurance they are goods and property. This property, human creatures if you will, has been thrown overboard whether or not for the presevation of the rest, that is the real question. Whether right or wrong we have nothing to do with it [...]. The Question is whether there was an Absolute Necessity for throwing them over board to save the rest [...] and the Jury were of opinion there was.[6]

The case established that the deliberate killing of slaves could in some circumstances be considered legal. The only immediate result of the case was a new law, protecting insurance companies against any further claims for slaves thrown overboard.

In 1840, the year of Turner's painting, London was to host the first International Anti-Slavery Convention. A few more dates are contextually suggestive. In 1807 the English Parliament had abolished the slave trade as far as Britain was concerned. But the Act of Abolition was a dead letter in the colonies. Life on the plantations was to remain virtually unchanged for another twenty years. In 1823 the London Society for the Mitigation and Gradual Abolition of Slavery was founded; the Abolition Act of 1833 provided for the emancipation of three-quarters of a million slaves in the West Indian colonies. Five years later, it completed their liberation. It is interesting to note, if briefly, that the antislavery campaign supplied the British with a powerful legitimation for their claims to be the arbiters of the civilised and the uncivilised world, associating the abolition with a sense of progress. A significant remark on the question can be found in a letter by Lord Palmerston. Being informed of slave-trade atrocities in Zanzibar, he wrote to the local British consul asking him "to take every opportunity of impressing upon the Arabs that the nations of Europe are destined to put an end to the African slave trade and that Great Britain is the main instrument in the hands of Providence for the accomplishment of this purpose."[7]

---

6 Brady and Jones, *The Fight Against Slavery*, 63–64.
7 Quoted in Colley, *Britons. Forging the Nation 1707–1837*, 380.

However, the enormous contribution of the transatlantic slave trade to Britain's economy in the eighteenth century remains indisputabile. In some cases the huge profits made in the West Indies were employed to raise the economic and consequently the social status of an English family. Money was turned into landed property where the building of luxurious stately mansions was an imperative.

Harewood House in West Yorkshire has been the home to the Lascelles family ever since the mid-eighteenth century. Edwin Lascelles (1713–1795) commissioned the building with the money his father Henry had made in the slave trade. The house was designed by John Carr with interiors and plaster work ceilings by Robert Adam. The grounds were planned by "Capability" Brown, the oustanding landscape gardener of the day. Thomas Chippendale produced some of his most elegant furniture for Harewood. The best names on the market had joined to complete the house in 1772. At the invitation of Edward Lascelles, William Turner himself painted a watercolour of the property.[8] His work, together with Thomas Girtin's, form the nucleus of Harewood House's remarkable watercolour collection. Harewood is a fine example of how in due course the riches of trade could be transformed into the impeccable taste of a great country house, how they could acquire a title for the owner, the Earl of Harewood, and leave a significant contribution to the National Heritage.

The eighteenth century was an age of mixed feelings, of even paradoxical contradictions as to the justifiability of the slave trade which, however much condemned from the religious and humanitarian point of view, remained a widely accepted expedient to increase the national wealth, proving both profitable and necessary for the well-being of the colonies. At the beginning of the century, with that self-consciousness so typical of his prose, Addison wrote an appeal to "common sense" against the exploitation of Negro slaves and American Indians in the American colonies:

> What colour of excuse can there be for the contempt with which we treat this part of our species; that we should not put them upon the common foot of humanity, that we should only set an insignificant fine upon the man who murders them; nay, that we should, as much as in us lies, cut them off from the prospects of happiness in another world as well as in this and deny them that which we look upon as the proper means for attaining it?[9]

In 1711 Steele's love story of Inkle and Yaricoo published in the *Spectator* firmly denies all "prospects of happiness" to the couple, denouncing the ungrateful

---

8 For Turner's painting, see http://www.jamessmithnoelcollection.org/images/harewood%20house.jpg (October 9, 2013).

9 *Spectator*, 215 in Edward A. Bloom and Lillian D. Bloom, *Joseph Addison's Sociable Animal. In the Market Place, on the Hustings, in the Pulpit* (Providence: Brown University Press, 1971), 50.

English merchant who sells his native American lover into slavery.[10] However, less than two years later Addison himself published *The Trial of Count Tariff*, a short pamphlet against the "Assento," the Tory-negotiated agreement between England and Spain signed in March 1713 which granted an English company a thirty-year slave trading monopoly, empowering English merchants to transport forty-eight hundred African slaves annually and sell them in the Spanish West Indies. The agreement is denounced as a restriction on the unlimited transportation of slaves in British ships from Africa to Spanish America.

"The Man is not Rich because he is Honest, but he is Honest because he is Rich [...] distress removes from the Soul, all Relation, Affection, Sense of Justice, and all the Obligations, either moral or Religious, that secure one man against another..."[11] The wonders of the New World were proving a mine of human and economic opportunities, of wealth and consequently respectability as "riches" were deemed to help make an honest man. Since the first law of nature is self-preservation, freedom from necessity means freedom from crime. This is a recurring theme in Defoe's writings and it left him open to repeated attacks as to the ambiguity and masked colonialism embedded in the "natural" benevolence of Friday and his iconic act of submission to his new Master. "At last he lays His Head flat upon the Ground, close to my Foot, and sets my other Foot upon his Head, as he had done before; and after this, made all the Signs to me of Subjection, Servitude, and Submission imaginable, to let me know, how he would serve me as long as he liv'd."[12] In *The Life, Adventures and Piracies of the Famous Captain Singleton* (1720) young Singleton and a group of sailors are marooned on Madagascar after they attempt a mutiny. Captain Singleton relates his journey across Africa which is rich in documentary descriptions of reality, overfurnished with "useful" information, as ever in Defoe's writings. Singleton discovers hospitable countries and kind "civil" natives. He is mostly "surprized to see the Folly of the poor People. For a little Bit of Silver cut out in the Shape of a Bird, we had two Cows [...] For one of the Bracelets made of Chain-work, we had as much Provision of several Sorts, as would fairly have been worth in England, Fifteen or Sixteen Pounds..."[13]

> We conversed with some of the Natives of the Country who were friendly enough. What Tongue they spoke, I do not yet pretend to know. We talked as far as we could make them

---

10 *Inkle and Yaricoo* is also the title of a three act comic opera by George Colman the Younger.
11 Daniel Defoe, *The Review*, 15 (September, 1711).
12 Daniel Defoe, *Robinson Crusoe*, ed. Michael Shinagel (New York and London: W. W. Norton & Company Inc., 1975), 161
13 Daniel Defoe, *The Life, Adventures and Piracies of the Famous Captain Singleton* (London: Everyman's Library, 1963), 34. Further references in the text abbreviated as *SN*.

> understand us, not only about our Provisions, but also about our Undertaking [...] They told us [...] there were People to be found of one Sort or other every where; that there were many great Rivers, many Lions and Tygers, Elephants, and furious wild Cats... (*SN*, 59)

However, even in such a land of wonders, good English common sense is bound to prevail:

> We enquired in the Country, and found there was no Beast of Burthen known among them [...] At last I proposed a Method for them, which after some Consideration, they found very convenient; and this was to quarrel with some of the Negro Natives, take ten or twelve of them Prisoners, and binding the men Slaves, cause them to travel with us, and make them carry our Baggage; which I alledged would be convenient and useful in many ways, as well to shew us the Way, as to converse with other Natives for us. (*SN*, 63)

A local leader is shortly found and submitted to the white man's enterprise: "the Black Prince" was "to assure us of the Fidelity of the Men in this March [...] he ordered them to be tied two and two by the Wrist, as we handcuff Prisoners in England" (*SN*, 75–78). The Negro "Prisoners" soon become "our Negroes" and even William the Quaker, the voice of benevolent dissent, after admitting that "the Negroes had really the highest Injustice done them, to be sold for Slaves without their Consent" (*SN*, 191) and warning his friends in bibilical terms "thou wilt not punish the poor Men because they cannot speak English" (*SN*, 195), at the end of the story provides a farcical example of "fair" dealing: "William sold all his Negroes, and at last sold the Ship itself" (*SN*, 201).

In the *Life of Colonel Jacques* (1722) the protagonist's humane treatment of the Negro slaves marks a significant step in his advancement as a prosperous planter in Maryland where he is able to live "without that wretched thing, called stealing"[14] and, in due time, rise to the enviable status of an English gentleman. When reflecting on his own past experiences he acknowledges that the condition of the slave must be considered a state of punishment: "I was brought into this miserable Condition of a Slave by some strange directing Power, as a Punishment for the Wickedness of my younger Years" (*CJ*, 119). However, when confronted with the "Negro slaves," he feels bound to exonerate the English from cruelty by laying the blame on the "Negroes" who are by nature brutal and bestial:

> [...] the Cruelty, so much talked of Used in Virginia and Barbadoes, and other Colonies, in Whipping the Negro Slaves, was not so much owing to the Tyranny, and Passion, and

---

14 Daniel Defoe, *The History and Remarkable Life of the Truly Honourable Col. Jacques, Commonly Call'd Col. Jack* (London, Oxford, New York: Oxford University Press, 1970), 117. Further references in the text abbreviated as *CJ*.

Cruelty of the English, as had been reported; the English not being accounted to be of a Cruel Disposition, and really are not so: But that is owing to the Brutality and obstinate Temper of the Negroes, who cannot be mannag'd by Kindness, and Courtisy; but must be rul'd with a Rod of Iron, beaten with Scorpions, as the Scripture calls it; and must be used as they do use them, or they would Rise and Murher all their Masters, which with their Numbers consider'd, would not be hard for them to do, if they had Arms and Ammunition suitable to the Rage and Cruelty of their Nature. But I began to see at the same time, that this Brutal temper of the Negroes was not rightly manag'd; that they did not take the best Corse with them, to make them sensibile, either of Mercy, or Punishment; and it was Evident to me, that even the worst of those tempers might be brought to a Compliance, without the Lash, or at least without so much of it, as they generally Inflicted. (*CJ*, 128–129)

When the good English master is confronted with the "brutal temper of the Negroes," cruel treatment proves wrong only "in Respect of Interest" (*CJ*, 145). Reason works even with Negroes and, what is more, produces better results: "It appeared that Negroes were to be reason'd into things as well as other People, and it was by thus managing their Reason, that most of the Work was done" (*CJ*, 149) "in our Plantation they were us'd like Men, in the other like Dogs." The moral foundation of this is be found not in "the uneasiness of Conscience" but in "meer Reasonings" (*CJ*, 156) "my Negroes [...] serv'd me chearfully, and by Consequence, Faithfully, and Diligently" (*CJ*, 159) following "the Sense of their own Interest" (*CJ*, 160). "Interest" is the key word: humanitarian treatment even though motivated by self-interest can improve the differing pecularities implanted by Nature in different races.

Leaving the colonies and moving on to urban culture, following the route of young Negro slaves transported to London, we arrive at Southwark Fair.

In *Southwark Fair* (1733), amidst that "profuse variety of shapes" so typical of William Hogarth's art, the gallant black boy playing the trumpet at the forefront accompanies the crowd's disordered parade, as if performing on a theatrical stage. *Southwark Fair* is the great fair held in Southwark every September, but it is also "the *Theatrum Mundi*, or Theatre of the World, revealing the wholespectrum of human vices and illusions, with all ages and conditions represented."[15] It is a stage for all contemporary theatrical genres presenting theatrical troupes, street performers, puppet shows and carnival characters, a troupe of players tumbling down from a collapsing stage and also theatrical productions of more "elevated" matter, from the fall of Troy to the biblical fall of Adam and Eve. In London's theatres at the time the figure of the black "slave servant" assumed an important

---

15 David Bindman, *Hogarth and his Times* (London: British Museum Press in association with the Parnassus Foundation, 1997), 127.

Figure 3: William Hogarth, *Southwark Fair* (1733) Engraving, The British Museum, retrieved from
http://commons.wikimedia.org/wiki/File:Hogarth-Southwark-Fair-1734.jpeg. Public domain
(October 9, 2013)

role in the comic/sentimental handling of his traits,[16] as in the case of Mungo, the
black slave servant protagonist of Isaac Bickerstaff's comic opera *The Padlock*
(1768). The "comic Negro" was to become a central presence in the drama of the
second half of the century, already clearly destined to acquire the grotesque traits
of a stereotype whereas the fiction of idyllic plantation life that appears as a
prevailing topos in the last fifteen years of the eighteenth century typifies power
relations in the benevolent planter/grateful slave binary set. This pattern consti-
tues a colonial mirror image of the metropolitan good master/faithful black slave-
servant relation. Good Masters indicatively named Heartwell, Goodwin, Heartfree
appear in both plantations and urban settings, along with devoted slaves and
slave-servants.[17]

---

16 See Franca Dellarosa, *Slavery on Stage. Representations of Slavery in British Theatre,*
1760–1830s (Bari: Edizioni dal Sud, 2009).
17 Dellarosa, *Slavery on Stage*, 15–17.

Figure 4: William Hogarth, A *Harlot's Progress*, Plate 4 (1732), The British Museum, retrieved from http://en.wikipedia.org/wiki/File:Hogarth-Harlot-2.png. Public domain (October 9, 2013).

In William Hogarth's "modern history paintings," young African slave servants are present in side roles which, nevertheless, mark their presence as emblems of London fashionable culture. The series of *A Harlot's Progress* which Hogarth engraved from his own paintings,[18] focusing on the life and career of a fictional London prostitute, Moll Hackabout, was issued in April 1732. The series consists of six plates that depict a young woman's arrival in London, her descent into prostitution, and eventual death. The second plate mimicks an aristocratic toilette. Moll has been transformed from fresh country girl to "kept miss"[19] of a Jewish merchant. She has adopted the manners and way of life of a grand lady, showing off the pretentious façade of contemporary "high life."[20] As Mark Hallet writes:

---

18 The paintings were destroyed by fire later in the Eighteenth century.
19 "The Kept Miss" is the title of a popular story published in 1723.
20 See also William Hogarth's engraving, "Taste in High Life."

> She is surrounded by [...] a maid and an exotically dressed black servant, an elaborately decorated tea table, a curtained bed and the paintings and portraits that hang on the wall [...] the mask that lies nearby suggests [...] her participation in one of the most controversial urban entertainments of the period the masquerade which was regularly critized for its blurring of class distinctions and its incitement to promiscuity.[21]

Moll has become addicted to masquerades, owns a pet monkey and a turbaned black pageboy, the suitable playthings for a fashionable lady, common products of the African continent. The taste for fashionable objects gained increasingly negative connotations in the eighteenth century.[22] In 1710 Steele wrote a parody of the growing practice of slave-owning as part of the fashion for pets, printing in the *Spectator* a fake letter from an enslaved black boy who begrudged his mistress for esteeming a parrot "from our country" as much as him. In this parlour scene Moll is kicking over the small table to create a diversion and let her young lover sneak out. He is making an obscene gesture at the bewigged Jewish merchant who is satyrically seen as trying to imitate the British ways of life such as drinking tea as implied by the tea pot carried by the turbaned page boy.[23]

But what exactly happened to the young African boys transported to London before they were admitted as fashionable objects to high class interiors?

> Lord Montague himself buy me and I praise God for the room pack with men with red faces and wild looks as if they come to eat me, a fattened calf or suckling pig. I am on a platform where all can examine what I resemeble. My coat and shirt are stripped from me to show off my neck and chest and waist and arms. The agent open my mouth and run a finger along my gums to prove to them that I have all my teeth. He run his finger along Captain Thistlewood's crosses on my forehead to prove that I am tamed and trained. They shout out money and the agent write in his book 15, 20, 30, 35, 40 guineas, I can hear his heart thump and see his hand shake or in sweat struggle to grip the pen as he write down the prices, for the bidding is higher than the hope. The men grow in rage, some even stand on their chairs and wave their hands at the agent in case he miss their offer. Only Lord Montague is calm. He stay in his chair. His hand rest on the gold top of his cane. He is the best of all of them in dress. His coat is rich with gold trim and buttons [...] He place a bag of money on the agent's desk without a word. The agent don't even open the bag. He bang the desk with his hammer and that is the end of everything. He bang so hard that

---

21 Mark Hallet, *Hogarth* (London: Phaidon Press, 2000), 84.

22 See Erin Macie, *Market à la Mode: Fashion, Commodity, and Gender in* The Tatler *and* The Spectator (Baltimore: The Johns Hopkins University Press, 1997).

23 The series made its creator a lot of money. "The engravings were sold by subscription, at a guinea a set, which prospective purchasers having looked at the paintings paid half in advance and half on receiving the six prints [...] After a sustained campaign of lobbying and petitioning at Parliament, an act protecting the copyrights of engravers was finally passed into law in the summer of 1735. This act, although it resulted from a collective sense of grievance among London engravers has understandably come to be known as Hogarth's Act, and it was to have a powerful and lasting effect on the artist's own career and fortune" in Hallet, *Hogarth*, 95–96.

the ink pot jump off the table and pour on the floor, and his pen too. When the men go, some step in the ink and leave footprints on the floor [...] Lord Montague lead me kindly by the hand like a father and put me in the coach to sit next to him and a picture he buy [...] When we enter the house, people appear from everywhere, one to take Lord Montague's stick, another his hat, another his coat, another the picture, another bags from the back-standing man, another me, and all the time the first man in red watch them coming and going with such ease [...] Later I get to know all their names – Valet, Butler, Steward, Footmam, Groom and the Women-Servants of the kitchen, the pantry, the still-room and the spinning-wheel [...] And best of all, no one even look at me or say anything, for I am as unseen as Lord Montague. The rich are like spirits who you feed and worship and tend to, though you can't see them.[24]

David Dabydeen's[25] novel, *A Harlot's Progress* (1999) reinvents the story of William Hogarth's prints giving Hogarth's young slave the role of the protagonist and narrator. Mungo, now the oldest black man in London, is urged by a Mr Pringle of the Abolition Committee to tell him the story of his life as a slave in exchange for charity.[26]

In any case, life as a fashionable presence in London was much better than working on the fields in the colonies.

The *Marriage A-la-Mode* is the story of the *mésaillance* between a rich merchant's daughter and the debauched son of an extravagant aristocrat. In *The Toilette* (1745), an exotically dressed African page is sitting in a corner pulling a small figure of Actaeon out of a basket. His pointing at the horns sets up a mythical counterpart to the satirical narrative of the dissolute new earl as a cuckolded husband. The scene represents the alderman's daughter, now dignified by the title of Countess Squander thanks to the old earl's recent death, rapidly progressing in the vices typical of her newly acquired aristocratic rank. Following the French custom of receiving visitors at her levée, she is in her bedroom, surrounded by visitors and hired hands: an Italian castrato singer, an effeminate French dancing master, a dozing country squire, his wife in raptures over the music. A young African servant is offering the company drinking chocolate with an amused expression. Her ladyship's morning levée is crammed with exotic and French allusions. A copy of the French erotic novel *Le Sopha* by Crébillon lies next to the

---

24 David Dabydeen, *A Harlot's Progress* (London: Jonathan Cape, 1999), 173–175.

25 Academic, novelist and poet the Carebbean David Dabydeen also has a scholarly knowledge of colonialism and slavery. Among his academic texts: *The Blacks in English Literature* (1985) and *Hogarth's Blacks: Images of Blacks in Eighteenth Century English Art* (Manchester, Manchester University Press, 1987). More recently in 2002 Dabydeen published *Turner* a long, moving poem written in response to M. W. Turner's painting *Slave Ship*.

26 Mungo is also the name of the black slave-servant protagonist of Isaac Bickerstaff's comic opera *The Padlock* which was greatly successful at the time.

Figure 5: William Hogarth, Marriage *A-la-Mode, The Toilette*, Plate 4 (1745), The British Museum, retrieved from http://en.wikipedia.org/wiki/File:William_Hogarth_042.jpg. (October 9, 2013) *The reproduction is part of a collection of reproductions compiled by The Yorck Project. The compilation copyright is held by Zenodot Verlagsgesellschaft mbH and licensed under the GNU Free Documentation License*

flirting lawyer Silvertongue with whom she is betraying her husband. In Hogarth's satires lawyers are grasping and deceitful, exhibiting the vices associated with their profession. The African page is significantly placed next to the mock antiquities which are littered round on the floor. As may be seen by the labels still attached to them, they have only recently seen purchased and represent specimens of newly acquired false taste. The black page, that desirable object of acquisition and exchange. He is winking at the audience, showing what is happening behind the scenes. The reference to Actaeon's myth acts as a prelude to the following tableau where the earl discovers the adulterous couple in a bagnio.[27]

---

27 The term "bagnio" originally meant a public bathhouse in Turkey or Italy. In England it was used to name coffee houses which offered Turkish baths, but by 1740 it signified a place where rooms could be hired by clandestine couples.

In classical mythology Actaeon surprises Diana while she bathes in secret. His punishment is to be transformed into a stag and killed by Diana's pack of dogs. The *Marriage A-la-Mode* frames a tragedy of decline and fall where the repudiation of both the protagonists' social class leads inevitably to the ultimate catastrophe. In Hogarth's vision those who seek to move out of their own social class by any other means than hard work and virtuous behaviour, like the "Industrious Apprentice" of the homonymous series, are bound to come to a bad end. Aristocrats whose irresponsible extravagance forces them to sell out to the middle classes are damned in the same way as the merchants who offer up their wealth in the vain attempt to acquire the prerogatives of birth and manners. The *Marriage A-la-Mode* is also an attack on fashionable extravagance, on the fashion for foreign goods, foreign art, music, clothes and foreign servants.

Figure 6: William Hogarth, *Captain Lord George Graham in his Cabin* (1745), oil painting, Royal Museums Greenwich, retrived from http://en.wikipedia.org/wiki/File: Captain_Lord_George_Graham,_1715–47,_in_his_Cabin.jpg (October 9, 2013) Public domain.

In *Captain Lord George Graham in his Cabin* (1745), a conversation piece of convivial merriment, one of the ship's crew sings a song to the drum music played by the most elegantly dressed black servant standing on the right.

The liveried black slave became a "hallmark" of eighteenth-century English urban life, a sought-after possession and a motif in contemporary paintings, textiles, prints, porcelain, and poetry. Meanwhile, some free blacks became a source of English pride [...] examples of the civilizing capacity of English culture."[28]

Life on the West Indian plantations, far away from the bustle of London, can be the subject of idyllic representations but slavery remained "Britain's foulest stain" in the words of an abolitionist poet like Edward Rushton. In the words of Erasmus Darwin, trading in slaves should not be called trade at all as it is an affront to British notions of philosophy, art and religion: "Hear, oh, BRITANNIA! potent Queen of ideas,/On whom fair Art, and meek Religion smiles,/How AFRIC's coasts thy craftier sons invade/With murder, rapine, theft, – and call it Trade."[29]

When the Quaker-led *Society for Effecting the Abolition of the Slave Trade*, founded in that year by Thomas Clarkson, met in London, in 1787, three members were asked to develop a design which could serve as the Society's seal. An image, depicting an "African in Chains in a Supplicating Posture" was selected. "AM I NOT A MAN AND A BROTHER?" were the words placed around him.[30] No one knows for sure who designed and engraved the seal, but historians attribute the design to either William Hackwood or Henry Webber who both worked at Wedgwood's factory where the jasperware medallion was manufactured by the thousand. Joshia Wedgwood was then a Society member and the medallions show that interwining of neoclassical models and contemporary suggestions so typical of the great potter. The medallions were an immediate success with the fashionable set, worn on bracelets and as hair ornaments, and inlaid with gold as ornaments for snuff boxes. The design was also used in printed form on plates, enamel boxes for patches, as well as on tea caddies. In February 1788 a consignment of the cameos was shipped to Benjamin Franklin in Philadelphia, where the medallions became a fashion statement for abolitionists and anti-slavery sympathizers. Thomas Clarkson, who had published his *Essay on the Slavery and Commerce of the Human Species* in 1786, wrote of the great success the medallions had in United States:

---

28 Catherine Molineux, "Hogarth's Fashionable Slaves: Moral Corruption in Eighteenth-Century London," *ELH*, Baltimore 72.2 (Summer 2005): 495–520.
29 Quoted in Roy Porter *Enlightenment. Britain and the Creation of the Modern World*, (London: Allen Lane The Penguin Press, 2000), 359.
30 An anti-slavery medallion by Josiah Wedgwood can be found under http://www.britishmuseum.org/explore/highlights/highlight_image.aspx?image=ps357430.jpg&retpage=20496 (October 9, 2013).

Some had them inlaid in gold on the lid of their snuff-boxes. Of the ladies, several wore them in bracelets, and others had them fitted up in an ornamental manner as pins for their hair. At length the taste for wearing them became general, and thus fashion [...] was seen for once in the honourable office of promoting the cause of justice, humanity and freedom.[31]

It was 1788. Among the mix of authors who joined the journey into print, Ignatius Sancho, "the extraordinary Negro" as he came to be called, former slave and servant of the Duke of Montague, published poems, two plays and a tract on musical theory, *Theory of Music*. His portrait was painted by Thomas Gainsborough (1768). The two-volume collection of his letters was posthumously published in 1782 under the title of *The Letters of the Late Ignatius Sancho* for his family's benefit. No wonder the book sold well with London's fashionable élite. The autobiography of Olaudah Equiano, explorer, writer and merchant, a prominent figure among British abolitionists, was published as *The Interesting Narrative of the Life of Oulaudah Equiano or Gustavus Vassa* in 1789, the year the Bastille fell; it rapidly went through several editions. The abolitionists believed their moment had arrived. Thomas Paine's *The Rights of Man* had become compulsory reading for the middle classes. But rather than hastening the advent of the age of freedom, equality and brotherhood, the French Revolution had a negative influence on the cause of liberalism in England for forty years. The English took their distance from the horrors of the revolution, also fearing revolts in the colonies. The final blow came with the French declaration of war in 1793. Without going into historical details but in order to show the mixed feelings of contemporary opinion regarding the English colonial system, Lord Nelson's declaration in 1805, the year of the battle of Trafalgar, may be considered exemplary:

I ever have been and shall be a firm friend to our present colonial system. I was bred in the good old school and taught to appreciate the value of our West Indian possessions, and neither in the field nor in the Senate shall their just rights be infringed whilst I have an arm to fight in their defence or a tongue to launch my voice against the damnable, cruel doctrine of Wilberforce and his hypocritical allies; and I hope my berth in heaven will be as exalted as his who would certainly cause the murder of all our friends and fellow-subjects in the colonies.[32]

These words can be set against what Thomas Walker, the Manchester cotton manufacturer, Dissenter and political activist, wrote in 1794:

---

31 Thomas Clarkson, *The History of the Rise, Progress and Accomplishment of the Abolition of the Slave-Trade by the British Parliament*. (New York: John S. Taylor, 1836), 297.
32 Brady and Jones, *The Fight Against Slavery*, 93.

"[We do not seek] an equality of wealth and possessions.The equality insisted on by the friends of Reform is AN EQUALITY OF RIGHTS [...] that every person may be equally entitled to the protection and benefit of society; may equally have a voice in the election of those persons who make the laws [...] and may have a fair opportunity of exerting to advantage any talents he may possess. The rule is not to 'let all mankind be perpetually equal' – God and nature have forbidden it – but to 'let all mankind start fair in the Race of life.'"

At the turn of the century, *Obi*, John Fawcett's pantomime draws in the unsettling shadow of slave revolt, possibly influenced by the insurrection of St Domingo.[33]

In the last decades of the eighteenth century the attraction exerted by exotic people living on fictional island paradises was becoming a distinct feature in the late Enlightenment culture. In poems like *The Injured Islanders* (1779) the English discoverer, a Captain Wallis is implored to leave the island by the mythical local queen: "Canst thou forget, how cheerful, how content/ Taheitee's Sons their Days of Pleasure Spent." *Humanity* (1788) by Courtney Melmoth proclaims the natives' right to be left "peaceful and blest where rich Bananas grew." The titles of the poems speak for themselves.[34] After all it must be recognized that however primitive the natives look to our civilized eyes they are "human beings from the hand of the same almighty Creator." But there is more to it than that, "they are the natural, and in a strict sense, the legal owners of the various territories they inhabit," wrote Lord Morton to Captain Cook.[35]

The portrait of the young Polynesian Omai (c.1753–79?), painted by Joshua Reynolds in classical robes, still proclaims an utopian well-wisher's view of the exotic "noble savage." Prince Omai had been brought to London by Captain Cook to be positively 'improved' by the cultural achievements and 'civilized' virtues of the West End élite. He soon became a celebrity, more as an object of curiosity than of the announced scientific experiment aimed at celebrating the power of culture over nature by transforming a "natural" man into an educated individual adoptable by contemporary society. Reynolds wanted to add his portrait to his gallery of celebrities in fashionable London. It was exhibited at the Royal Academy not long after Omai's return in 1776 to the South Sea islands where he died a few years later.

The portrait, not one of Reynold's best, shows a very interesting fusion of differing and contrasting influences. Omai's robe intends to demonstrate his rank as a prince in his country, though the Roman toga gives him the general effect of a classical model. The tattoos on his hands and arms show that he belongs to a

33 Dellarosa, *Slavery on Stage*, 17.
34 See Roy Porter, *Enlightenment: Britain and the Creation of the Modern World* (London: Allen Lane, The Penguin Press, 2000), 363.
35 Porter, *Enlightenment*, 362.

different world, but his gestures call to mind the statues of the saints in Catholic churches that Reynolds had possibly visited in Rome.

The Tahitian prince's portrait reveals a mixture of the various cultural influences constructing the utopian belief in the transformation of the child of nature into the "civilized man." As a result he looks pathetically out of place, transformed and misunderstood by a typically Eurocentric artistic discourse. In some way, this painting could be held up as an iconic demonstration of the Europeans' almost total failure to know others on any terms other than purely European ones. For all its cherished formulas regarding the development and transformation of human kind through politics and science, the new-found freedoms, and consequently the new-found human rights, Eighteenth century British culture here shows its highly conservative albeit idealized side.

Reynold's portrait brings to the fore the profound cultural anxiety which, following different paths, goes through the so-called "great century" of the slave-trade. In literature and in the arts, dramatic and satirical, tragic and even comic or agiographic representations of slaves and slavery, interweave the aesthetic perspective with philosophical, moral, economic and social issues. The sequence

Figure 7: Joshua Reynolds, *Omai*, c.1776, oil on canvas, Private Collection, retrieved from http://en.wikipedia.org/wiki/File: Joshua_Reynolds_-_Portrait_of_Omai.jpg (October 9, 2013) Public domain.

illustrates the crucial debate regarding the rights and "natural" equality of man. It also suggests that progress was variable and fluid as the century developed. In 1792 Edward Gibbon wrote a letter to Lord Sheffield to express his approval of the vote against the slave trade in the House of Commons: "If it proceeded only from an impulse of humanity, I cannot be displeased [...] But in this rage against slavery, in the numerous petitions against the slave trade, was there no leaven of new democratical principles? No wild ideas of the rights and natural equality of man? It is these I fear."[36] The echoes of the French Revolution cast a frightening shadow over whatever demand for freedom, marking the boundary between a humanitarian disposition and the acknowledgment of the individual's universal and inalienable human rights.

---

36 Norman Hampson, *The Enlightenment* (London: Penguin Books 1968), 153.

Chiara Battisti
Mental Illness and Human Rights in Patrick McGrath's *Asylum*

> Madness constitutes a right, as it were, to treat people as vermin.
> Lord Shaftesbury

In his analysis of the phenomenology of historical and social madness, Michel Foucault not only investigates the social function and the autonomous existence of the mad, but also that "strange proximity between madness and literature",[1] which leads madness itself to being a "prodigious reserve of meaning. [...], a figure that contains and suspends meaning, which furnishes a void where all that is proposed is the still unaccomplished possibility that a certain meaning might appear there."[2] Madness is thus the excluded language which manages to escape the furrow ploughed by reason; and mental institutions, the places of madness, have proved through the centuries to be a fertile resource of the fantastic that acts as silent memory.

Since the meanings of a literary text can only be gathered *in toto* within the correlation between the text itself and the codes of the cultural system from which it stemmed, facing the "dormant world of monsters, supposedly engulfed in the darkness of Hieronymus Bosch which had spewed them forth"[3] implies an analysis of the modalities through which "madness" shapes itself as a phenomenon that belongs to a particular cultural system, as well as an investigation on the limits of that very system. Such analysis therefore implies the necessity to write a "history of limits" which, according to Foucault, are

> those obscure gestures, necessarily forgotten as soon as they are accomplished, through which a culture rejects something which for it will be the Exterior; and throughout its history, this hollowed void, this white space by means of which it isolates itself, identifies it as clearly as its values.[...] To interrogate a culture about its limit-experiences is to question it at the confines of history about a tear that is something like the very birth of history.[4]

---

1 Michel Foucault, "Madness, the absence of an oeuvre" in Michel Foucault, *History of Madness* (London and New York: Routledge, 2006), Appendix I of 1972 edition, 548.
2 Foucault, "Madness, the absence of an oeuvre," 547.
3 Michel Foucault, *Madness and Civilization: A History of Insanity in the Age of Reason* (New York: Vintage, 1988), 209.
4 Michel Foucault, "Preface to the 1961 edition" in Foucault, *History of Madness*, XXIX.

The fantastic literature of madness and horror, evoked by Foucault, finds its own emblematic exemplification in the Gothic, a peculiar and elusive literary genre which developed within the speculative and scientific frame of the late eighteenth century. The gothic narrative questions such speculative perspective, revealing its limits as well as the inner contextual transformations of the cultural system itself. Such models, which mirror a culture of innovation and radical transformations, translate themselves into a sought-after emphasis on the psychological dimension; an emphasis that relies on the readers' imagination, leading them to recognise the contradictions raised by the impossibility for such thinking to suit the limits set by rationalism.

Imagination, which had always been considered to be beyond rational control, contaminates the rationalistic world and jeopardises it. The rigid constraints of rationalism are to be bypassed, and the exasperated urge to overcome the limits imposed by such a contradicted system leads to an investigation of those anomalous and irrational areas of the human, alluding to the liminal condition of man in the nineteenth century; the symbolic expression of the division that denies any possible balance and resolution between man and world, nature and culture. Such bipartition in the vision of the world and the impossibility of merging the different aspects of existence find their paradigmatic representation in privileged figurative places: the disturbing and deceptive spaces of the gothic novel. Castles, convents, abbeys, the under-grounds become an expression of an intense anguish which gathers the ancestral fears of all humanity. The Gothic in fact "involves confrontation between us and the uncanny, between us and the other. [...] All literature may ultimately be about defeat, but few genres stress it as the Gothic does, so often dwelling on our grand strivings and hopes all wickedly moving in reverse."[5]

Patrick McGrath, author of *Asylum*, attributes to Edgar Allan Poe the capability to leave such gothic spaces, where the direct confrontation between "us and uncanny" is never settled. Such spaces are in themselves the metaphor of the "going under", and lead to the unknown and unsettling realm of the irrational. Poe explicitly directs his interest to the psyche and the unconscious, analysing the extreme states of psychological disturbance.

> It is with Poe that we first see the Gothic shifting away from an emphasis on props and sets – dark forests and lugubrious caverns, skeletons and thunderstorms – and towards a particular sensibility characterized by transgressive tendencies and extreme distortions of perception and affect. Poe's genius lies in his recognition of the sorts of structural analogies

---

5 Daniel Olson ed., *21st Century Gothic: Great Gothic Novels since 2000* (Plymouth: Rowman and Littlefield Publishing Group, 2011), XXVI.

possible between the trappings and the sensibility, then in the deftness with which he splices them together.[6]

Once the classically gothic paraphernalia have been abandoned, Poe's neo-Gothic acknowledges the fascinating features of the gothic tradition, and draws an intertextual connection with it, rewrites it and revises it, in order to create tales that are "no longer shackled by the conventional props of the genre, but [which] nonetheless strongly manifest the Gothic sensibility."[7]

Today, the gothic reconfigures itself, with the further help of the media, and gives new life to one of the most powerful genres inherited from eighteenth/nineteenth century imagination. If, according to Nina Auerbach, every age embraces the gothic it needs[8], the metaphors introduced by the classical gothic tradition to voice eighteenth-and-nineteenth-century political, social, and psychological conflicts are taken up again, reproduced and displayed in neo-Gothic with richer nuances and new shades of meaning which relate to more specific contemporary concerns and needs, such as relations of power and alienation, attitudes toward illness, and which can be interpreted from critical perspectives which bring together different discursive fields, including ethnography, anthropology, medicine, criminality, early modes of feminism, psychoanalysis, psychosexuality and economy. This continuing transformation and evolution of the gothic over the centuries and its powerful grip on our imagination can be traced back to its metaphorical value, to the actual capacity of this literary genre to be, in any given generation, the expression of individual problems (going deeper within the Self, and in the unknown area of the unsettling and the irrational) and social issues.

Although reluctant to accept labels and categories, Patrick McGrath acknowledges his own parodic engagement with the gothic tradition; his "first impulse was to play with its [of the Gothic genre] very well established conventions."[9] However, he gradually increases his distance from the parodic reprise of such conventions, in order to approach a rewriting "whose strongest, most dominant themes are transgression and decay, but which does not necessarily use the furniture of the Old Gothic [...] the castle and the forest and the stormy night and

---

6 Patrick McGrath, "Afterword: the New Gothic," *Conjunctions* 14 (Spring 1990), available at http://www.conjunctions.com/archives/c14-pm.htm (June 27, 2013).

7 Bradford Morrow, Patrick McGrath eds., *The New Gothic: A Collection of Contemporary Gothic Fiction* (New York: Random House, 1991), XIV.

8 Nina Auerbach, *Our Vampires, Ourselves* (Chicago and London: The University of Chicago Press, 1995), 145.

9 Gilles Menegaldo "Interview to Patrick McGrath," *Sources* 5 (November 1998): 109–127, 111.

the dungeon and so on... Transgression and decay cover a lot of territory a lot of human behaviour [...] especially madness. "[10] The Gothic/neo-Gothic in the novel *Asylum* – and more generally in his 1990s trilogy, *Spider* (1990), *Dr Haggard's Disease* (1993), and *Asylum* (1996) – can first and foremost be seen in the engaging narration that accompanies the readers through a problematic path that leads to transgression of social norms, and destabilises the limits of the Self in the complicated realm of human behaviour to which McGrath alluded, one ruled by the language of madness.

In a reflection on the role of the writer, McGrath merges the two figures of writer and psychiatrist, which in his perspective share the interest in the analysis of the relationship between one culture and its contradictory and ambiguous side, which is constantly rediscovered in madness. This is the obscure relationship between men and his ghosts. Madness, the lyrical aura of illness, and literature, the transgressing side of language, merge in the common ground "of the exploration of human dysfunction. The writer wants to create forms of entertainment and to give pleasure, the psychiatrist is engaged in a therapeutic task. But [they] are both essentially engaged in the exploration of human nature."[11] In particular, McGrath's literary exploration often implies a blurring of the line between "normality" and "madness," inviting the readers of his novel "to sit next to the madman [...] and to look through his eyes."[12]

In McGrath's writing, the madman's foreign body and mind therefore become monstrous texts which announce (de-monstrate) themselves as the place of resurfacing repression:

> The body that scares and appals changes over time, as do the individual characteristics that add up to monstrosity, as do the preferred interpretations of that monstrosity. Within the traits that make a body monstrous- that is, frightening or ugly, abnormal or disgusting- we may read the difference between an other and a self, a pervert and a normal person, a foreigner and a native.[13]

In Western culture, the madman is often described as deviant and insane, who with his diversity disturbs the social bodies and, as such, is unrecognized by the "sane" mind, *alias* the intellectual class which creates the culture. Thus, it is not

---

10 Magali Falco ed., *A Collection of Interviews with Patrick McGrath* (Paris: Publibook, 2007), 19.
11 Interview with Nicholas Wroe, *Guardian*, July 12, 2008, available at http://www.guardian.co.uk/books/2008/jul/12/ saturdayreviewsfeatres.guardianreview19 (June 27, 2013).
12 Magali Falco "Patrick Mc Grath's Case Histories or the Ruin(s) of Psychoanalysis," *Anglofonia: French Journal of English Studies* 15 (2004): 94–104, 98.
13 Judith Halberstam, *Skin Shows: Gothic Horror and the Technology of Monsters* (Durham: Duke University Press, 2000), 8.

by chance that the first-person narrator of *Asylum* is a psychiatrist, the *par excellence* symbol of that intellectual class that both creates and controls culture and society. Doctor Cleave, to be seen as "the greatest of [Poe's] followers, the psychologist Freud"[14] shapes his narration in the attempt to trace a path through darkness. Thanks to a prosaic writing that is neat and elegant he provides a description of one of the saddest "catastrophic love affair[s] characterized by sexual obsession."[15] Freudian psychoanalysis becomes therefore a provocative pretext for McGrath's narration, and at the same time psychoanalysis is read in the light of the neo-Gothic. McGrath highlights the encounter between psychoanalysis and the novel at a literary level, and the seminal idea that Freud could be one of Poe's followers (thus consequently making his case studies, in fact, gothic narrations) can historically be drawn to the fact that gothic novels, which contained the "tropes" of psychoanalysis, were often used by Freud; who was himself fascinated by literature and who availed himself of Poe's narrative path, thoroughly exploiting it "in the creation of some of the most inspired tales in the genre, the chillingly macabre case studies."[16] On the other hand, according to Magali Falco, McGrath himself re-uses the "tropes" of psychoanalysis "insofar as

---

14 McGrath, "Afterword: the New Gothic."

15 Patrick McGrath, *Asylum* (New York: Random House, Vintage Books, E-book), Chapter 1: further references in the text, abbreviated as *A*. The novel is set in England in 1959. From a mental institution, a psychiatrist, Dr Peter Cleave, starts reporting, with apparent detachment, the saddest and most disturbing clinical case he has ever had to deal with in his whole career – the lethal passion between Stella Raphael and Edgar Stark. The former is Dr Max Raphael's wife, a psychiatrist who works in the same hospital; the latter is a patient, an ill sculptor who beheaded his wife out of jealousy. Stella is attracted to this man since their first encounter in her garden, where Edgar has been engaged to repair their greenhouse. The inevitable attraction between the two results in an intense liaison. Edgar manages to escape the mental institution thanks to Stella's unwitting help. She will eventually join him, abandoning her family to spend the rest of her life with him in one of London's most squalid neighbourhoods. Stella is torn between her guilt for having abandoned her son, and her totalising passion for Edgar. Edgar's psychic stability becomes increasingly fragile and when madness reappears to the surface Stella is forced to leave. She is eventually found and taken back home. Despite her desire to see Edgar, she cannot but turn to her family, especially her son Charlie, whom she loves, but whose presence is not enough to draw her away from depression. The last part of *Asylum* is set in Wales, where the Raphaels follow Max, who lost his job after the scandal and has found another job in a little hospital. Stella is deeply depressed and Max is resentful towards her. While in Wales, Charlie's painful death occurs. Stella will witness it in a state of trance: she could save Charlie but her absence, even to her own Self, impedes any intervention. She is then accused of murder and interned in the mental institution directed by Peter Cleave, where Edgar has been taken. Within those walls, the story will come to its tragic end.

16 McGrath, "Afterword: the New Gothic."

he imitates the style of Freud's case studies, in the same way as he has integrated into his work his experience of madness and parodied the Gothic Novel."[17]

However, Freud's stories were partly fictional (Freud himself used to warn his readers that he had to "fictionalize" his case studies changing the names of his patients in order to hide their identities and not to give a full account of their cases for social reasons). Similarly, the clinical case narrated by Peter Cleave, which initially shows a clear plot, a psychoanalytical containment that expresses in writing an anomalous and misleading trace – that is the love story between Edgar Stark and Stella Raphael – later becomes a language that steers from the path of linear reasoning.

Peter's narration, which thanks to its evocative immediateness enhanced by symbols and metaphors seems to transform the mind's extreme and traumatic experiences into a rationally conceivable aesthetic matter, reveals how the truth is still hiding somewhere under many textual layers. In other words, McGrath provides his readers with a subverted case study, which shows how the discourse of analysis is often contaminated, even symptomatic. Not only does McGrath incorporate psychoanalysis into his work, but he also ruins, fragments, and metaphorizes it as the gothic is metaphorized by the neo-Gothic:

> As the role of psychoanalysis is to dig out the reasons for mental disturbances and to find a meaning out of fragmented representations of reality, this process is paradoxically reversed in McGrath: the motifs of psychoanalysis are used by the Gothic as an element of the fictional structure in order to operate a reversal within the established order of reality and of the novel.[18]

Patrick McGrath's decision to avail himself of a first-person narrator, Peter Cleave, who at the end of the novel proves to be unreliable, is one of the narrative strategies which are intended to introduce the reader into that liminal space which marks the border between sanity and madness.

This uncanny threshold, hidden within the shadows and shades of madness, is thus the product of paranoid narration, in which the reader participates in the doubts and uncertainties created by the narration itself without being able to choose a true reality. This aspect leads one to reflect upon the logic of a madness which becomes literary word and keystone of the artistic creation:

> In identifying irrationality or pathological disturbance in [...this] writing, we admit, even succumb, to the strange "logic" of fictive madness. In defining madness in a [...] text, whose pathology is in question? [...] Traditional psychoanalytic approaches have provided familiar

---

17 Falco "Patrick Mc Grath's Case Histories or the Ruin[s] of Psychoanalysis," 96.
18 Falco "Patrick Mc Grath's Case Histories or the Ruin[s] of Psychoanalysis," 97.

yet problematic answers, accounting for the "madness" on display in literary texts by analyzing the pathology of authors or literary characters. Freud describes the writer as "not far removed from neurosis" and "oppressed by excessively powerful instinctual needs" (Freud, 1973, 423), or as an egotist shaping her/his infantile fantasies into pleasurable aesthetic form (Freud, 1990, 129–41). For classic psychoanalysis, literary madness is an aberration to be exposed or therapeutically tamed, either by interpretative authority or the artist's conscious control; madness may even be harnessed or enlisted for creative or therapeutic purposes. Yet as witnesses to literary madness, can we assume a position safely outside its flickering, enigmatic effects? While the role of the reader attracted little scrutiny from psychoanalytically oriented criticism until the later twentieth century, Freud did emphasize that the analyst, through the effect of transference, is not securely outside the subject or condition he or she analyses. Psychoanalysis dwells in and repeats the symptoms and obsessions exhibited in the analytic encounter, leaving it perilously close to inhabiting the psychic conflicts it treats. Since critical interpretation involves readerly desires, we cannot recognize and diagnose textual madness without implicating our own delusions and anxieties.[19]

In *Asylum* the textual narration brings the notion of insanity back to the character of Edgar (and in this, it is sustained by the *mastering discourse* of psychiatry which labels Edgar as criminally insane) and partially to Stella (whose refusal of patriarchal authority becomes a symptom of neurosis). However, the reader perceives the need to stay out of a narration that, in its unravelling, seems increasingly deranged. During this narration, the reader often has the impression that in telling the story of other people's madness, Cleave the psychiatrist is speaking of himself: "Through the voice[...] of Peter Cleave [...]" asserts Sue Zlosnik "psychiatry is shown to be more deeply involved with its subjects than it would claim – or than the reader finds comfortable."[20]

In trying to assume "a position safely outside the flickering, enigmatic effects" of literary madness and in the (perhaps vain) attempt to establish whether Cleave's narration is a rational narration or a deviant and insane track, the readers themselves are therefore forced to repeat the interpretive and diagnostic act of the first person narrator making insanity "the rhetorical condition of [their] reading."[21]

This playing with madness at textual and meta-textual level, which starts from the fictional narrative of Patrick McGrath – madness in the clinical sense, madness as boundary and beyond everyone's experience – invites the readers to

---

19 Scott Brewster, "Seeing Things: Gothic and the Madness of Interpretation" in *A New Companion to the Gothic*, ed. David Punter (Oxford: Oxford University Press, 2000), 481–482.
20 Sue Zlosnik, *Patrick McGrath* (Cardiff: University of Wales Press, 2011), 10.
21 Shoshana Felman, *Writing and Madness: Literature/Philosophy/Psychoanalysis* (Stanford Palo Alto: Stanford University Press, 2003), 270.

make a judgment about where they stand on the spectrum of mental soundness and gradually leads them to perceiving the varieties of discrimination experienced by the mentally ill, even when made with the most benign intentions within the disciplines of psychiatry and law.

Moreover, the unbearable realisation of the impossibility of standing outside the "mad" narration, the "mad" characters and the "mad" narrator, of the impossibility therefore to situate madness in the "other," enacts a sympathetic reading with which the readers understand how and why people with mental disorders are particularly vulnerable to human rights violations and how the stigma, myths and misconceptions associated with mental disorders, allow the violation of fundamental principles of international human rights discourse.

1 Asylum, madhouses and mental hospitals

The first narrative strategy through which McGrath makes madness the rhetorical condition of the reader's act of reading is the deconstruction of the time-space dimension of the novel's reality. This alienating deconstruction, offered by McGrath's meta-textual engagement with insanity, mirrors a particular phenomenon of dissolution in the flux of time which, according to many psychiatrists and psychoanalysts, is typical of some manifestations of mental illness.[22] Although he describes a clearly recognizable Great Britain in the 1950s, McGrath overlays this description with disturbing and sinister tones that seem to introduce two different, but parallel historical moments: there is a "real" time, that of the narration,

---

22 For instance, psychiatric studies show how psychoses cause the very concept of time to irreparably deteriorate as a consequence of the dissolution of personality (thus confirming the temporal nature of the "I"/the Self). Yet a clear relationship between one's life and one's specific pathologies does not exist. It is the case of the perceived "slowing down of time" in schizophrenia, i.e. the impression of thoughts constantly running at incredible speed. Similarly, depression causes thoughts to be processed at a lower speed or to be impeded altogether. It is also often accompanied by a notable shortening of temporal perspective, as a result of the loss of motivation, and thus equally lends itself to the feeling of the slowing down of time. In conclusion, by considering such anomalies (inability to place oneself and events in the stream of social time, the creation of unreal connections between events and the very duration of one's own existence) and the absence of anomalies regarding the adaptation of behaviour (psychotics are perfectly able to control their actions, commensurate with events happening around them), it does not seem implausible to conclude that mental illnesses concern one's conscious representation of time rather than one's actual experience of it. See Simon Grondin, *Psychology of Time* (Bingley: Emerald Group Publishing, 2008); Claudia Hammond, *Time Warped. Unlocking the Mysteries of Time Perception* (Edinburgh: Canongate Books, 2012).

set in the contemporary period, more precisely the year in which "the Mental Health Act had just been passed into law" (*A*, Ch.1). This is the time of "reason" in which Cleave, Max Raphael, Brenda and everyone who belongs officially to the sane world live and act; this is the time of the proclamation of an act which abolished the distinction between psychiatric and other hospitals and encouraged the development of community care; an act which sought to create a legal framework within which the hospital treatment of mental disorders could approximate as closely as possible that of physical illness. This is the time of an act which excluded promiscuity or other immoral conduct as grounds (alone) for detention.[23]

There is then an alternative "evoked" time, that of the Victorian era, linked to the figure of Stella and, marginally, to that of Edgar Stark. This is the time of that Victorian age which "saw the transformation of the madhouse into the asylum [and then] into the mental hospital,"[24] and in which moral therapy emerged as the primary source of treatment. From the first pages, Cleave's narration clarifies the time of the story's action – "It was the summer of 1959" (*A*, Ch. 1) – the reader, however, feels transported into the claustrophobia of the Victorian era with a perception of a time parallel to the action. This perception becomes stronger and stronger as the narration proceeds, notwithstanding the repeated emission of realistic data (such as, for example, the model of Max's car) which brings us back to the second half of the 1900s. The world which imprisons and protects Stella is Victorian: the greenhouse that Edgar restores at Max's request is Victorian, the type of masculine power exerted is Victorian[25], the structure of the insane asylum itself is Victorian.

The mental hospital is the *Asylum* of the title, whose etymological meaning indicates a closed institution, a protected place and, at the same time, a prison:

> It is maximum-security, a walled city that rises from a high ridge to dominate the surrounding country […]. It is built on the standard Victorian linear model, with wings radiating off the main blocks so that all the wards have an obstructed view across the terraces to the open country beyond the Wall. This is a moral architecture, it embodies regularity, discipline, and organization. (*A*, Ch. 1)

---

23 Section 4 (5) of the 1959 Act says: "Nothing in this section shall be construed as implying that a person may be dealt with under this Act as suffering from mental disorder […] by reason only of promiscuity or other immoral conduct."

24 Andrew Scull, "Psychiatry in the Victorian Era" in *Madhouses, Mad-Doctors and Madmen*, ed. Andrew Scull (London: The Athlone Press, 1981), 6.

25 Peter, alluding to the possibility of becoming director of the mental hospital, brings to light the pleasant possibility of being able to exercise the power of Victorian paternalism: "To exercise Victorian paternalism on the grand scale." (*A*, Ch. 3)

This building, constructed using the linear models of Victorian architecture, represents the continuity of the social morality in which the laws in force, officially recognized and upheld, are those of family and work. It is exactly this place of containment that concentrates Stella's tensions as a social creature, alluding, with its greatness, to the gigantic power structure in which the doctor, moral and legal guarantor, is an essential figure. It is the doctor who, with absolute power, establishes the rules and procedures which, by determining what is considered normal or rational, can silence what is excluded. As Stella's thoughts reveal, a person cannot speak or behave without obeying a tacit and unexpressed archive of rules and restrictions, on penalty of condemnation to insanity or silence:

> Their power is absolute, and suspicion alone is quite enough to seal a man's fate; they can stall him indefinitely on the basis of suspicion [...] It was the raw bare face of institutional power she was seeing on the back lawn that night, she was hearing the voice of the master. It hurt her cruelly, hurt her as though her child were being taken from her, and what was worse was that that voice would not be contradicted, because Edgar had no voice; he was silent, just as she was now silent. (A, Ch. 3)

Silence thus becomes a further allusion to the social repression expressed in the "different" in order to exorcise the power of its mysterious otherness, and force it to be inarticulate, formless, in other words, powerless. Cleave subsequently becomes the sick, psychotic incarnation of psychiatric power, exemplifying its total, all-encompassing character.[26] This totally absorbing feature is symbolized in the impediment to social exchange and the impossibility of escape towards the outside world, and is firmly embedded in the description of the psychiatrist as he who possesses the keys and can close the door of the institution:

> Peter Cleave is jealous and possessive in a much more sophisticated way, and a much more successful way. He is able to possess because he runs the asylum, he has the key, he can lock the door, he has them under his control, and his possessions are human beings.[27]

Peter's possessiveness explains the social situation which the psychiatrist enjoys as holder of an institutional authority, that allows him to offer an official version of reality that puts the patients "under his control," that makes them, even if "human beings," objects of his power. The reason why psychiatric power is

---

26 On the total institution see: Erving Goffman, *Asylums: Essays on the Social Situation of Mental Patients and Other Inmates* (New York: Doubleday Broadway Publishing Group, Random House, 1961).

27 Falco ed., *A Collection of Interviews with Patrick McGrath*, 26.

deployed in such an all-encompassing way depends, according to Foucault, on the fact that at the heart of the mental hospital's space there is a problem to overcome; as Foucault affirms, "before the problem being one of knowledge, or rather, for the problem to be able to be one of knowledge, of the truth of the illness, and of its cure, it must first of all be one of victory. So what is organized in the asylum is actually a battlefield."[28] Taking up this image of the mental hospital as a "battlefield," in *Asylum* the description of the psychiatric practice of control is complementary to the recognition of the struggle of resistance for identity on the part of the patients. "What is involved is the confrontation of two wills, that of the doctor and those who represent him on one hand, and then, that of the patient. What is established, therefore, is a battle, a relationship of force."[29]

The world of total institutions is also represented by the capacity of the patients to "resist" the habitual practices of possession and dispossession. The patients' answer to an institution's totalitarian demands is to create communicative channels that are alternative to the official ones, to create solidarity networks. Let us consider, for instance, Edgar's proud claims of his belonging to a very exclusive club whose members are all mad – "He told her that at times he felt he had joined a superior gentlemen's club, for he knew bankers, solicitors, army officers, and stockbrokers; old Etonians as well as men from lower depths" (*A*, Ch. 1) – or the instructions given by Edgar to Stella in order to allow her to recognise and, thus, defend herself from the institution's totalising mechanisms.

> Vigilance. There was nothing Jack said that Edgar hadn't already told her he'd say. [...] She was uncomfortably aware of how persuasive the superintendent was, of how easy it would be to succumb to the warm, paternal tone he employed as he offered her his understanding and support. I required vigilance, and more than vigilance, it required a deliberate act of will to keep in the foreground of consciousness that it was Jack Straffen who was attempting to manipulate her, not Edgar. (*A*, Ch. 4)

The dual chronological reality of *Asylum* thus draws what can be defined as the institutional question of psychiatry, and introduces what has up to now been considered the core agenda in addressing human rights and mental health, that is the necessity to move from paternalistic, controlling responses (in this perspective, the emphasis on the superintendent's persuasiveness, of his hypothetical support, understanding and warm paternal tone in the above mentioned passage are noteworthy) towards emancipatory ones, to recognize the validity of the lived

---

28 Michel Foucault, *Psychiatric Power, Lectures at the College de France 1973–74* (Basingstoke: Palgrave Macmillan, 2006), 6–7.
29 Foucault, *Psychiatric Power, Lectures at the College de France 1973–74*, 10.

experience of sufferers and promote rights-based practices in mental health. Contemporary reflection in fact underlines how the prerequisite conditions of mental health and psychosocial well being are precisely those that support the promotion of human dignity, which is the essence of the concept of human rights.

2 Mental illness, identity and stigma

The alienating deconstruction of reality evoked by McGrath acquires further importance since it draws a connection to these key terms and issues in contemporary reflections on human rights and mental illness. The Mental Health Act[30] of 1959 and the description of the Asylum as "a moral architecture" that corresponds to a "Victorian linear model" isolate two key issues prominent in the debates which moved around the contemporary anti-psychiatry movement.

The allusion to Victorian madhouse reality serves to exemplify those total institutions described by Ervin Goffman in the early 1960s as encompassing, and as "symbolized by the barrier to social intercourse with the outside and to departure that is often built right into the physical plant, such as locked doors, high walls, barbed wire, cliffs, water, forests, or moors."[31] The barriers that the institution places between the "inmates" and the outside world dispossess the inmates of roles that are part of their self-determination, a process Goffman defined as the "mortification of the self." Such a process is exacerbated by admissions procedures during which "inmates" are stripped of many of their personal possessions and their full names. Since these things are associated with oneself, their loss involves a curtailment of the self.

The 1959 Mental Health Act was instead characterized by a "more inclusive health care approach where the distinction between mental and physical illness was, to some extent, lessened."[32] Mental health services were incorporated into the rest of the health services. It was envisaged that integration would encourage

---

30 The 1959 Mental Health Act was heralded as a great piece of liberalising legislation, but its reputation became tarnished by concern about failures of services and abuses of professional power. The Act was seen as being deficient in safeguarding the rights of detained patients, and in introducing its subsequent review the Government noted: "The general philosophy behind the proposals is based on the need to strengthen the rights and safeguard the liberties of the mentally disordered, whilst retaining a proper regard for the rights and safety of the general public and of staff" (DHSS et al, 1978, para. vi). DHSS, Home Office, Welsh Office, et al (1978) Review of the Mental Health Act 1959 (Cmnd 7230). London: HMSO.
31 Goffman, Asylums: Essays on the Social Situation of Mental Patients and Other Inmates, 4.
32 Nicola Glover-Thomas, *Reconstructing Mental Health Law and Policy* (East Kilbride: Thomson Litho, 2002), 23.

the adoption of a universally high standard and promote parity between mental and other health services, thereby reducing any residual stigma. In this it failed. Yet the 1959 Act remained important, for "it [was] at that point in the history of mental health legislation that the influence of medicine in defining the nature of learning disability exerted its greatest impact."[33]

This act, the developments in its favour or against it, and a series of other legal procedures together with a new ethical approach to medicine in general granted increasing rights to the mentally ill. The long debate on the relationship between psychiatry and law which took place in the late 1950s and early 1960s was characterised by a contestation of mental institutions, considered unable to provide therapeutic benefits to their patients (a perspective that is symbolically represented in the novel by the Victorian rigidity of the asylum which seems to reduce the sense of self-worth of its inmates and to strip their identity) and by the emphasis on the terms "compassion" and "human dignity" (which were confirmed in the attempt of de-stigmatize in the 1959 Act). The anti-psychiatry movement[34] which evolved during the 1960s and 1970s had a significant role in the development of contemporary mental health care. Disconcerted by what was perceived to be psychiatry's monopoly over the mental health arena, this movement was strongly critical of Western mental health practices for its perceived propensity for trying to control behaviour that deviated from a psychological norm by labelling it as mental illness. Accordingly it further viewed the development of techniques for behavioural control as a threat to individual human rights. During the 1970s, the anti-psychiatry movement became an advocate for psychiatric abuse cases, commonly investing legal representation for the mentally ill. "Before long," as Benoir Lepage points out, "the human rights of the mentally ill [...] became the main focal point of the [...] judicial system[s]."[35] The desire to place limitations on the power of the mainstream psychiatric establishment reflected support for an ideology of equality and for the rights of those labelled as mentally ill.

---

33 Bob Gates, "The Nature of Learning Disabilities" in *Learning Disabilities. Toward Inclusion*, ed. Bob Gates (China: Elsevier, 2007), 6.

34 The *Oxford Dictionary of Sociology* identifies "Anti-psychiatry" as follows: "A term coined in the 1960s for writers who are highly critical of the ideas and practice of psychiatry. Precisely who is included within this group (which is always theoretically and politically heterogeneous). Frequently mentioned are the radical libertarian Thomas Szasz, the more left-wing, existentialist-inclined R. D. Laing and his colleague David Cooper, the Italian mental health reformer Franco Basaglia (all psychiatrists), and two sociologists- the symbolic interactionist Erving Goffman and labeling theorist Thomas Scheff. Sometimes Michel Foucault is also cited in this context." John Scott and Gordon Marshall eds., *A Dictionary of Sociology* (Oxford: Oxford University Press, 2009), *ad vocem*.

35 Benoit Lepage, *The Many Changing Faces of Schizophrenia* (Victoria: Trafford, 2009), 79.

Since then the psychiatric community has reduced its level of criticism, but this period signalled the start of significant changes throughout the fields of mental health and disability rights which *in primis* required a consideration of the individual as a person, rather than as a problem. Hence the insistence on the existence entrusted to community care, with the aim of promoting an uninterrupted dialogic exchange with the individual experience, subtracted to the automatism of the removal of madness, and the segregation of otherness. Hence, the abandonment of contentious methods, the obligation to share space, the depersonalisation, the namelessness, the un-acknowledgment that the mental institution seemed to want to impose. This emphasis on the individuality of those who are affected by mental disorders, while also acknowledging differences in describing their experience of illness, is reflected in Patrick McGrath's rewriting as well as in his personal experience. When telling about his childhood, he recalls its peculiar features, describing a childhood characterised by the fact of living "next door to a large, top-security hospital."[36] A peculiar childhood "made normal by [his] father's teaching [him] that the mentally ill were not monsters," and a childhood in which his "father showed [him] how to understand the work he did, and created in [him] an attitude towards insanity which was one of compassion – the desire to know, and to understand, always to sympathize and never to make moral judgments."[37] McGrath's early experience of mental illness led to his evocation, in *Asylum*, of a correlative concept of stigma and spoiled identity, the definition of so-called madness as mental illness or mental disability, and the idea of the identity of a mental patient as a person.

Let us consider, in this sense, how in the novel "Stella's sense of justice" causes her to consider "incompatible with the care and treatment of the mentally ill [...] the indignities of primitive plumbing, lack of privacy, bullying, boredom, and utter uncertainty about his future" (*A*, Ch. 1). Stella's thought introduces key rights and principles of human rights, such as the right to privacy and individual autonomy and freedom from degrading treatment. It also transmits the fundamental aim of mental health legislation, which is "as the WHO's Resource Book on Mental Health, Human Rights and Legislation makes clear, [... to] protect, promote and improve the lives, well being and rights of citizens suffering from mental disorder, people who are thereby vulnerable to abuse and also stigma."[38] With her words Stella underlines how people with mental disorders are, or can be, particularly vulnerable to abuse and violation of rights and evokes a legisla-

---

36 Falco (ed.), *A Collection of Interviews with Patrick McGrath*, 17.
37 Falco (ed.), *A Collection of Interviews with Patrick McGrath*, 17.
38 Michael Dudley, Derrick Silove, Fran Gale eds., *Mental Health and Human Rights: Vision, Praxis, and Courage* (Oxford: Oxford University Press, 2012), 28.

tion able to protect vulnerable citizens (including people with mental disorders). Such request implies the necessity of defining the legal status of the patient. Nowadays, during recoveries, the classification of patients as either detained patients, voluntary patients or restricted patients influences the amount of control they have over the direction of their care and treatment. In the past, as well as in the time when *Asylum* is set, psychiatric patients have, on the basis of their status, been prevented from holding a variety of rights including property rights, voting rights and access to the courts. It is only with the Mental Health Act 1983 that the above rights were retained for the patient after admission to hospital.

Not only does the role of Stella help us consider the importance of mental health legislation, but it also underlines how the presence of such legislation does not in itself guarantee respect and protection of human rights, particularly when we find ourselves in the presence of patients considered dangerous. In particular, the novel deals with the issue of balancing the rights of the patient with the needs of the wider community; which Nicola Glover Thomas aligns to the legal act mentioned in *Asylum*: "The 1959 Act was supposed to represent a 'new era of enlightened mental health provision,' yet many considered the highly liberal approach threatened public safety. The emphasis upon medical discretion had gone too far with the result that some patients, who in the past would have been considered too dangerous, were being released into the community."[39]

Initially, in fact, much of the mental health legislation drafted was aimed at safeguarding members of the public from "dangerous" patients and isolating them from the public, rather than promoting the rights of persons with mental disorders as people and citizens. As a consequence, in some countries, mental health legislation has resulted in the violation, rather than the promotion, of the human rights of people with mental disorders, whilst the shift to a greater protection of mentally ill patients' rights promoted an unwelcome oscillation between the necessity to protect patients' rights, perceived with increasing urge because by the 1970s rights culture had become truly entrenched in social thinking, and the need to re-introduce strict legal regulation to protect the wider community.

If we go back to the novel to observe how such balancing is resolved on a fictional level: since chapter one, Peter Cleave (the psychiatrist) traces a definite portrait of Edgar Stark: he is "an extroverted man [...] possessed of a certain [...] animal vitality" (*A*, Ch. 1), "a wounded bear" (*A*, Ch. 1), a patient locked up for "five years" and "it looked to me [Cleave] as though he'd be with us another five years at least" (*A.*, Ch I). The linguistic emphasis of Edgar's animal nature, his very reduction from human to wild and uncontrollable animal, implies and

---

39 Glover-Thomas, *Reconstructing Mental Health Law and Policy*, 30.

justifies a necessity to totally deprive such "being" of his own freedom. The image of the animal as a negative metaphorical representation of the human underlines the radical and innate otherness of man-as-beast. This imports certain significant legal implications. Throughout the centuries animal categorization and the use of derogatory animal metaphors have been used to justify exploitation, objectification, slaughter and enslavement. Madness, in particular, was commonly compared with animality, for which reason those deemed to be mad were commonly and intentionally treated as animals. Being less than human, mad people were quite literally treated as outlaws. Dehumanization legitimised abuse: "A particular conception of madness, linked with a set of ideas about animality is bound up with violent power practices acted on the bodies of those classified as mad."[40]

Such dehumanization enhances Cleave's precise attempt to describe Edgar's illness as a grouping of symptoms, as a set of labels bearing mere heuristic value – delirium, obsession, paranoia, psychosis – which become cages to whose immutability the singular experience of the sculptor is added. The psychiatrist's emphasis on the sculptor's psychotic symptoms – Edgar is in fact described as a patient, characterized by "a ghostly resemblance to logic in [his delusional] thinking" (*A.* Ch. III), who "suffered from a paranoid psychosis" and for whom, at the trial "the insanity defence was accepted by the court" (*A.* Ch IV) – and on his potential manifestations of violence – "the room was alive with violence," "proliferating signals that an act of violence was imminent" (*A.*, Ch VII)- reintroduces on a fictional level media stereotypes of people with mental disorders. Such a representation, which "emphasize[s] the high rates of violence among those with mental illness and treat the entire topic with misinformation and even ridicule"[41]; perpetrates the development of stereotypes, equating mental disorders with violence and fosters that stigmatization[42], which, according to David Satcher, is "the most formidable obstacle to future progress in the arena of mental illness and mental health."[43] These depictions shape the attitudes and emotional responses of the general public which, frightened by these perceptions of violence and risk

---

40 Clare Palmer "Madness and Animality in Michel Foucault's *Madness and Civilization*" in *Animal Philosophy*, eds. Matthew Calarco, Peter Atterton (London, New York: Continuum, 2004), 81.
41 Stephen P. Hinshaw, *The Mark of Shame: Stigma of Mental Illness and an Agenda for Change* (Oxford: Oxford University Press, 2007) X.
42 See Heather Sturat, Norman Sartorius, Julio Arboleda Florenz eds., *Paradigms Lost: Fighting Stigma and the Lessons Learned* (Oxford: Oxford University Press, 2012), 108.
43 David Satcher, U.S. Department of Health and Human Services, "Mental Health: A Report of the Surgeon General." Rockville, MD: U.S. Department of Health and Human Services, Substance Abuse and Mental Health Services Administration, Center for Mental Health Services, National Institutes of Health, National Institute of Mental Health, 1999.

of violence, gives its support for coercive treatment, legislative solutions and justifications for social inequities and injustices. An example of this is the intensity of pressure placed on governments to reform Mental Health acts in favour of greater public protection particularly at those moments when the media chooses to emphasise incidents where mentally ill people have committed serious crimes.

It is however interesting to observe how McGrath's decision to invest the characters of the psychiatrists, especially Cleave, with ambiguous, almost psychotic traits, allows the reader to understand how mental health acts could not resolve the difficult balancing issue described above; often leading to individual psychiatrists being placed in situations which might infringe on patients' human rights[44].

Stella's position is diametrically opposed to Peter Cleave's, yet equally intriguing. For Stella, Edgar is "this man," "this artist," "my lover," a person whom "she was starting to doubt [...] was mentally ill" (*A*, Ch. 1), a man who was the object of suspicions "and suspicion alone is quite enough to seal a man's fate; they [the psychiatrists] can stall him indefinitely on the basis of suspicion" (*A*, Ch. 3). In an exasperated and unarguably partial way Stella highlights how the indefinite detention of people militates against the basic principle and spirit of article 5 of the European Convention on Human Rights (Art.5 ECHR), that no one shall be deprived of his/her liberty

In Stella's view, Edgar is so deprived of any freedom that he cannot dispose of his own future; when describing this future, Stella uses terms that underline its

---

44 Wai Ching Leung, in an article on the impact of the Human Rights Act 1998 on medical decision making, highlights the practical implication of this act for psychiatrists: "The power to impose compulsory treatment in the white paper proposal brings much greater responsibility for doctors. When these proposals come into force, doctors face several practical dilemmas. First, doctors may be called upon to manage patients with "social problems" such as intoxication due to illicit drugs or drink. On the one hand, the proposed legislation provides power to detain the patient in order to protect the public. Doctors who fail to use these powers could be held accountable for any adverse consequences to the public. On the other hand, compulsory detention of the patient for such problems might potentially infringe upon the patient's human rights. Until a test case arises, it is impossible to be certain how the European Court of Justice will rule. [...]. Second, doctors (especially psychiatrists) may be called upon to compulsorily detain persons with personality disorders perceived to be dangerous, even when their conditions are considered untreatable. Again, if doctors fail to exercise such power, they might be held accountable for any adverse consequences to the public. However, since the conditions are untreatable, they cannot fulfil their traditional roles as healers. Instead, they are required to act as public protector, a role they have not been trained to excel in. Third, doctors may be under pressure to compulsorily treat and monitor patients with mental health problems who are currently stable and in remission." W.C. Leung, "Human Rights Act 1998 and Mental Health Legislation: Implications for the Management of Mentally Ill Patients," *Postgraduate Medical Journal*, 78.917 (2002): 178–181, 180.

indefinite nature: "utter uncertainty about his future" (*A*, Ch. 1). In her upside-down world ("She said later it felt as though everything had been turned upside down. Instead of her emerging from her full world and reaching out a to solitary, fugitive man, it was he who from the security of his world drew her in" (*A*, Ch. 5)), Edgar's escape becomes a legitimate attempt to gain his own freedom. In fact, as Edgar has committed murder, "he had killed his wife with a hammer, and he had mutilated her corpse" (*A*, Ch. 4), he could for good reason be considered dangerous. Thus McGrath requires the reader to engage the difficult issue of safeguarding the safety of the public without compromising, at the same time, the human rights of the individuals.

Moreover, Stella's emphasis on Edgar's humanity more than his pathology introduces, at the fictional level, another key issue of the topic "mental illness and human rights": the relationship between impairment and disability in the specific case of mental illness. Stella's words and behaviour state that the world does not consist of "normal" and "mentally ill"; it consists of people, all of whom may experience mental and emotional distress at some times in their lives. Stella, in fact, associates her passion for Edgar with a madness-driven momentary salvation – "She told herself it had been a moment of madness, no more than ever" (*A*, Ch. 1) – and she underlines how every person features "abnormal fragments of behaviour, fleeting nuances of expression, certain absences of response of which [the person him/herself] would not be aware" (*A*, Ch. 2).

Stella's provocative accusation directed towards Peter Cleave and Max, her husband, is that it is the creators of the dominant discourses of "mental illness" who accentuate and perpetuate those fragments and that difference through their construction of users of madhouses as Other: "Max seemed to her now a sort of dead man, a bloodless creature who behaved toward human beings like an insect collector, skewering them in glass cases with labels underneath, this one a personality disorder, this one a hysteric" (*A*, Ch. 7). Stella's rejection of dehumanizing "mental illness" labels assigned through arbitrary, unsystematic form of scientific diagnosis translates into her effort "to separate the man from his illness" (*A*, Ch. 8). Even when Edgar's illness worsens, Stella is not afraid of him, but "of the madness that [is] in him" (*A*, Ch. 8), which she describes as a storm which "raged in [Edgar's] benighted mind, but the storm wasn't him! The storm would pass, he would recover, he would be himself again" (*A*, Ch. 8). Stella's attempt to articulate her own understanding of Edgar's experience counterpoises the overarching dominance of medicalized explanations of mental illness which contribute to the increased segregation and stigmatization of people with disabilities in general and mental disabilities in this specific case.

The line between humanity and illness introduced by Stella can be aligned with contemporary attempts to offer an alternative to the dominant psychiatric discourses whose theoretical foundation is to be found in disability studies and which identify a crucial element in the distinction between impairment and disability, the real, psychological condition and the socially constructed or cultural condition. In Great Britain, the Disability Discrimination Act describes a disabled person as "anyone with a physical or mental impairment, which has a substantial and long term adverse effect upon their ability to carry out normal day to day activities."[45] The Act definition asserts something very simple: impairment, whether physical or "of mind", results in and creates disability, which exists at the intersection between the particular demand of a given impairment and society's interpretation of that impairment.

As Lennard Davis explains, impairment is a form of biological, cognitive, sensory or psychological difference and disability is the result of the negative social reaction: "An impairment involves a loss [...] of sight, hearing, mobility, mental ability, and so on. But an impairment only becomes disability when the ambient society creates an environment with barriers- affective, sensory, cognitive, or architectural."[46] Another aspect, which is tightly connected to disability, is the creation of socio-political barriers, and in fact "when categories of citizenship were questioned, challenged, and disrupted, disability was called on to clarify and define who deserved, and who was deservedly excluded from citizenship."[47] Disability thus becomes a human rights issue since "those [...] who happen to have a disability are fed up being treated by the society and [their] fellow citizens as if [they] do not exist or as if [...] they were aliens from outer space. [They] are human beings with equal value, claiming equal rights."[48]

The concept of mental disability denotes the negative aspects of the interaction between an individual (with a health condition) and that individual's contextual factors (environmental and personal factors). Edgar's illness involves a loss – Stella observes that Edgar "was ill and his illness robbed him of responsibility" (*A*, Ch. 7) – "the ambient society", Stella, however, does not create barriers, on the contrary she offers empathy and comprehension – "instead of running for her life, she went back to bed and took him in her arms and held him" (*A*, Ch. 7).

---

45 Disability Discrimination Act 1995, section 1.1, available at http://www.legislation.gov.uk/ukpga/1995/50/contents (September 24, 2013).

46 Lennard J. Davis, *Bending Over Backwards: Disability, Dismodernism and Other Difficult Positions* (New York and London: New York University Press, 2002), 41.

47 Douglas C. Baynton, "Disability and the Justification of Inequality in American History" in *The Disability Studies Reader*, ed. Lennard J. Davis (New York: Routledge, 1997), 17.

48 Speech by Bengst Lindqvist, Special Rapporteur on Disability of the United Nations Commission for Social Development, at the nineteenth Congress of Rehabilitation International, Rio de Janeiro, 25–30 August 2000.

And Edgar's impairment does not become, in Stella's perception, a disability. McGrath underlines how Stella's attitude leads Edgar to exploring his own artistic creativity in order to attempt to control the appearance of the symptoms of paranoid psychosis. The sculpture represents a continuous, never-ending struggle to cure a deep wound, to free himself from a past in which "the pathological manner in which he related to women" has put into motion "the process that had led to murder once already" (*A*, Ch. 2).

The moment when the known world dissolves into the delirious reorganisation of the real and the familiar become fearful. Edgar engages the surrounding world through art, establishing a structuralising relationship and attempting to re-aggregate all perceptive-emotional elements that compose the world itself with a violent projection on the clay of disturbing experiential content. Understanding that his ability to comprehend reality's essence is altered, he tries to work on his perception of the world (significantly represented by Stella) and to transfer that perception onto the clay. Such acts of transference help to give the organisation of experiences some sort of shape, through a modality that lies at the basis of a therapeutic as well as a creative process. Art and artistic form are better able to fill such a structural absence, and it is to this that Edgar aspires; the seriousness of his pathological conditions forbids him to escape the pre-conscious state of shapelessness.

Edgar – considered by Stella to be an individual with his own life experience, wishes, desires and needs – reacts as an individual when he is ill. He fights to defeat his illness. His experience, more broadly, alludes to the possibility that people with mental disorders might be considered not merely recipients of care, but as individuals capable of involvement in their own care and able to articulate their wishes. The Recommendation of the Council of Europe on "Principles Concerning the Legal Protection of Incapable Adults"[49] is of particular relevance here. Consistent with the trends in disability rights, it proposes that mentally ill people "should be involved as reasonably possible in the decisions that affect their lives, and that views of the individual should be taken into account even if that person lack legal capacity"[50] (see, in this sense, Principle 9 – Respect for wishes and feelings of the person concerned). What has been analysed on a fictional level thus demonstrates how the configuration of the impairment-disability system is particularly useful for people in the disability rights movement,

---

49 "Principles Concerning the Legal Protection of Incapable Adults," Recommendation no. R (99) 4, adopted by the Committee of Ministers of the Council of Europe on 23 February 1999, available at https://wcd.coe.int/ViewDoc.jsp?id=407333&Site=COE (September 24, 2013).
50 Peter Bartlett, Oliver Lewis, Oliver Thorold, *Mental Disability and the European Convention of Human Rights* (Leiden: Martinus Nijhoff Publishers, 2007), 25

who hope to combat stigma and to protect the civil rights of people with disabilities: by shifting attention away from the biological (impairment) to the social (disability), one can identify and affect discrimination.

Madness, the lyrical aura of illness, and literature, the transgressing side of language, merge in the mutual grounds of the exploration of human dysfunction. Such dysfunction, far from being deviant and condemned to invisibility, by denouncing the dangers and the violations of rights engages the hegemony of normalcy. This normalcy is, as it has been noticed, constantly enforced in novels and media through images "of individuals with mental illnesses as violent, criminal and dangerous"[51]; no doubt often responding here to the voyeuristic preferences of the readers/spectators themselves which lead in turn to their looking for both identification with the violent madman and a redeeming rejection of him. The lunatic criminal becomes a visual, ghostly representation of an impulse, common among most humans, towards transgression, not only of the law, but also of their own unconscious laws. The distancing effect guaranteed by the act of reading/watching restores an image of us/readers (embodied, precisely, by the criminal lunatic) enriched by the darkest sides, that permits us to experiment with it and to distance ourselves from it as different than ourselves. In this the representation of the individual with mental illness as violent and criminal responds "to our need that the mad be identifiable, different from ourselves."[52]

Differently from many media images and many other novels, however, *Asylum* does not present "mentally ill people as fundamentally different from others." On the contrary, the banality of mental illness comes into conflict with our need for categorizations and, as Sander Gilman points out:

> Our shock is that they are really just like us. This moment, when we say "they are just like us" is most upsetting. Then we no longer know where lies the line that divides our normal, reliable world, a world that minimizes our fears, from that world in which lurks the fearful, the terrifying and the aggressive.[53]

In McGrath's attempt to represent the unstable boundary between the sound mind and madness, in his constructing the madman as both alien and familiar, in his invitation to an empathetic identification which results in an uncanny perception of madness, in his attempt, therefore, to present to a public audience a different image of psychiatric disorders/illnesses and to contribute, therefore, to shaping a different attitude of the public itself, we can identify the writer's struggle against

---

51 Otto Wahl, *Media Madness* (New Jersey: Rutgers University Press, 1995), XV.
52 Sander L. Gilman, *Disease and Representation: Images of Illness from Madness to Aids* (Ithaca and London: Cornell University Press, 1988), 94.
53 Gilman, *Disease and Representation*, 13.

the hidden burden of stigma and discrimination of people with mental disorders. Conscious of the fact that "the way our society presents and treats people with mental illnesses is indeed a human rights issue, not just an issue of mental health care"[54]; McGrath provides an effective tool to make the public aware of the importance of adequate and appropriate care and the protection of the human rights of people with mental disorders, whilst also demonstrating that "human rights retain a critical distance from law and stretch its boundaries and limits."[55]

---

54 Otto Wahl, *Media Madness* (New Jersey: Rutgers University Press, 2003), X.
55 Costas Douzinas, *The End of Human Rights* (Oxford: Hart Publishing, 2000), 344.

Sidia Fiorato

The Role of Forensics in Human Rights Discourse: Kathy Reichs's Crime Fiction and the Rights of the Dead

> Recognition of the inherent dignity and of the equal and inalienable rights of all members of the human family is the foundation of freedom, justice and peace in the world [...]
>
> [T]he peoples of the United Nations have in the Charter reaffirmed their faith in [...] the dignity and worth of the human person.
>
> Preamble to the Universal Declaration of Human Rights

The Preamble to the 1948 Universal Declaration of Human Rights states the recognition of the inherent dignity[1] of human beings, and professes its faith in the dignity and worth of the human person, which it posits as the foundation of freedom, justice and peace in the world. Dignity is presented as "inherent" to human beings, i.e., involved in their constitution or essential character, an intrinsic, permanent or characteristic attribute[2], therefore it is inseparable from human condition. Significantly, the recognition of human dignity is presented as deriving from faith, not from an official act which constitutes or bestows it; moreover, it is associated with worth, which implies a moral or personal aspect "as something which is honorable or of an intrinsic value, and thus calls for unconditioned respect."[3] By stating that "All human beings are born free and equal in dignity and rights,"[4] Article 1 leads to the conclusion that dignity is an

---

1 The terms of "human dignity" and "sanctity of life" have undergone legal institutionalization and enjoy an anchored position in current national and international law. With regard to this, see Kurt Bayertz, "Introduction: Sanctity of Life and Human Dignity" in *Sanctity of Life and Human Dignity*, ed. Kurt Bayertz (Dordrecht: Kluwer Academic Publishers, 1996), xiii.
2 See Roberto Andorno, "Human Dignity and Human Rights as a Common Ground for a Global Bioethics," *Journal of Medicine and Philosophy* 34 (2009), 223–240, 229.
3 Klaus Dicke, "The Founding Function of Human Dignity in the Universal Declaration of Human Rights" in *The Concept of Human Dignity in Human Rights Discourse*, eds. David Kretzmer and Eckart Klein (The Hague: Kluwer Law International, 2002), 111–120, 116.
4 Article 1 reads: "All human beings are born free and equal in dignity and rights. They are endowed with reason and conscience and should act towards another in a spirit of brotherhood." In this formulation, "'reason and conscience' is regarded as the substance of human nature and thus of dignity." (Dicke, "The Founding Function", 116). There are two more

expression of the unity of humankind. The Declaration does not offer any definition of the concept of dignity, nor does it make reference to any specific philosophical tradition, thus pointing to a non-negotiable, foundational concept, a "transcendental norm" with a legitimizing function for human rights claims. Moreover, the concept develops throughout and engages with the expression of human rights themselves. The intrinsic dignity of every human being is seen "either as synonymous with humanity and hence a starting point for elaborating a theory of rights, or as the ultimate expression of rights realized;"[5] it acts as the foundation for human rights[6] which, conversely, possess a normative force, "their standards and rhetoric implicitly defining the parameters of the human."[7]

In the literary field, the question of man's dignity and its connection to the right to life (stated in Article 3) is addressed by contemporary forensic detective fiction, which usually focusses on victims of violent death. In such novels, the body comes powerfully to the forefront as the *corpus delicti*, the "'material

---

references in the context of social and economic rights. Art. 22 states: "Everyone, as a member of society, has the right to social security and is entitled to realization, through national effort and international cooperation and in accordance with the organization and resources of each State, of the economic, social and cultural rights indispensable for his dignity and the free development of his personality." Article 23, paragraph 3 states: "Everyone who works has the right to just and favourable remuneration ensuring for himself and his family an existence worthy of human dignity, and supplemented, if necessary, by other means of social protection."

5 Adam Rosenblatt, "International Forensic Investigation and the Human Rights of the Dead," *Human Rights Quarterly* 32 (2010): 922–951, 926.

6 See Kretzmer and Klein, "Foreword" to *The Concept of Human Dignity in Human Rights Discourse*, eds. Kretzmer and Klein, v. With regard to this, see also, Elizabeth S. Anker, *Fictions of Dignity: Embodying Human Rights in World Literature* (Ithaca: Cornell University Press, 2012), 3: "the concept of dignity has been central to formulations of human rights since the end of World War II and is widely invoked as essential to both the broad ethos and intellectual coherence of human rights norms, representing something of a constant reconciling the manifold ideals subsumed within their logic. [...] some theorists cite this emphasis on dignity as what fully renders human rights universal, in effect positing that it finds counterparts in virtually all cultures."

7 Anker, *Fictions of Dignity*, 15. The Universal Declaration of Human Rights therefore asserts and at the same time is based upon a conception of humanity which is presented as "the only valid framework of values, norms and principles capable of structuring a meaningful and yet feasible scheme of national and international civilized life." (Yehoshua Arieli, "On the Necessary and Sufficient Conditions for the Emergence of the Doctrine of the Dignity of Man and His Rights" in *The Concept of Human Dignity in Human Rights Discourse*, eds. Kretzmer and Klein, 4).

substance' upon which a crime has been committed."[8] In order to preserve the evidence and to establish the identity of the victim, such a body must be deconstructed. Autopsy entails the disfigurement of a cadaver, as pathologists remove and analyse major organs; in this process the body is literally fragmented, reduced to its component parts, thus "stripping away the safety of the boundary between life and death."[9] In this sense, the reasons to justify such an action come to the forefront and they are usually connected to the quest for truth, that is, for the cause and manner of the dead's decease.[10]

In forensic novels, the investigative and medical quests become parallel processes to a more ethical and humanitarian quest for the victims' identity,[11] entailing a respect for their inherent dignity when dealing with their mortal remains. This in my view highlights how the human body is not depersonalized during forensic examination; on the contrary, the immediacy of the dead body confronts us with the dignity of the cadaver[12] as a former person, demonstrating a still strong connection with its former personhood. The body is not only a biological specimen but a formerly living human being and this underlines its past life more than its present status of death. This perspective can be said to represent the recognition of the victims' rights to the acknowledgement of their status of juridical personae beyond death[13], their right to have such juridical

---

8 Henry Campbell Black, *Law Dictionary*, 1990, quoted in Thomas W. Laqueur, "The Dead Body and Human Rights" in *The Body*, eds. Sean Sweeney, Ian Hodder (Cambridge: Cambridge University Press, 2002), 75.

9 Lucy Kay, "Female Pathology and Anthropology in *Déjà Dead* and *Silent Witness*," *Mortality* 7 (2), 2002: 155–170, 163.

10 David Gareth Jones, Maja I. Whitaker, *Speaking for the Dead: the Human Body in Biology and Medicine* (London: Ashgate, 2009), 80–81.

11 The importance of the establishment of the victim's identity is present from the very beginning of the detective fiction genre. In Poe's story "The Mystery of Marie Rogêt," Dupin underlines the priority of the investigation of the identity over the cause and manner of death: "our first step should be the determination of the identity of the corpse with the Marie Rogêt who is missing," thus anticipating the concerns of forensic fiction. See Edgar Allan Poe, "The Mystery of Marie Rogêt" in *Selected Tales*, ed. David Van Leer (Oxford: Oxford University Press, 2008), 162 and Sidia Fiorato, "L'indagine medico-legale sul corpo umano: da Edgar Alla Poe a Kathy Reichs" in *Medicina e bioetica nella letteratura inglese contemporanea*, ed. Daniela Carpi (Verona: Cierre Grafica, 2012), 121–163.

12 See Gareth Jones, Whitaker, *Speaking for the Dead*, 16.

13 "Frequently it is stated that the identification of dead bodies is related to the rights to identity, understood as the right that a body be identified after death. However, the concept of the right to identity as a protected human right has evolved in a different sense." (Mary Elizabeth Stonaker, ed., *Management of Dead Bodies in Disaster Situations* (Washington DC: PAHO, 2004), 145). "The American Convention on HR does not expressly sanction the right to identity, but this could be

persona restored for a dignified and legally acknowledged and sanctioned conclusion of their life. In the specific case, biolaw is called to defend the dignity of
human life, and to defend the fundamental rights to life and integrity of every
human being at every stage of physical, psychological and social development,
including the end of life.[14] Stripping someone's identity after death and leaving
the body in an unwanted, unchosen place (where it will decompose) is a violation
that haunts the practice of forensic investigation. Such violation, in turn, renders
necessary what is perceived as a further violation through the medico-legal
analysis of the remains. "The identification of the dead is imperative in society;
[...] humanity demands the dignity of identification of its dead"[15] which counter-
acts the indignity caused by the murder. Such deeply ethical activity inserts itself
in the fulfillment of human rights.[16]

These various issues are powerfully addressed in Kathy Reichs's novels,
whose protagonist Temperance Brennan[17], a forensic anthropologist who works
at the Institute of Legal Medicine in Montreal, underlines the role of forensic
anthropology in criminal investigations, in particular in cases of violent death.

Forensic anthropologists are physical anthropologists usually with a spec-
ialization in osteology.[18] Also called "interpreters of the skeleton langua-

---

developed based on the right to recognition as a person before the law (Article 3), personal
integrity (Article 5) and protection of the family (Article 17)." (Stonaker, *Management of Dead
Bodies*, 145, footnote 35).

14 See Laura Palazzani, "Person and Human Being in Bioethics and Biolaw" in *Autonomy and
Human Rights in Health Care: An International Perspective*, eds. David N. Weisstub, Guillermo Diaz
Pintos (Dordrecht: Springer, 2007), 96.

15 William Eckert, *Introduction to Forensic Sciences*, Second Edition (London: CLC Press LLC,
1997), 301.

16 Rosenblatt, "International Forensic Investigation," 928.

17 Kathy Reichs is forensic anthropologist for The Office of the Chief Medical Examiner, State of
North Carolina and for the Laboratoire des Science Judiciaires et de Médecine Légale of Quebec.
She is certified member of the American Board of Forensic Anthropolgy and is often called as
expert witness in criminal trials.

18 Anthropology divides itself into the two fields of physical (or biological) anthropology and
cultural anthropology. Physical anthropology studies the human species both from the biological
and evolutionary point of view, focusing in particular on variations, that is, the biological
analogies and differences among individuals and groups; it includes further disciplines, such as
paleoanthropology, epidemiology, neuro-anthropology, osteology. Cultural anthropology deals
with non biological aspects of human life and society, such as the language, the organization of
families and of the community; it divides itself into further disciplines, such as archaeology,
ethnology, linguistics, ecologic anthropology. (See Rebecca Stefoff, *Forensic Anthropology* (New
York: Benchmark Books, 2011), 14–15). Forensic fiction can be said to unite the concerns of both
disciplines.

ge"[19] or "bone detectives"[20] they collaborate to criminal investigations by analyzing victims' bodies which are reduced to skeletal remains in order to achieve biological and cultural information which can lead to identification.[21] Moreover, they can help to determine "what happened to the remains, especially with regard to the evidence of foul play."[22] As Brennan states,

> As a forensic anthropologist, it is my job to unearth and study the dead. I identify the burned, the mummified, the decomposed, and the skeletonized who might otherwise go to anonymous graves. Sometimes the identifications are generic, Caucasoid female, mid-twenties. Other times I can confirm a suspected ID. In some cases, I figure out how these people died. Or how their corpses were mutilated.[23]

The forensic anthropologist works in close contact with other medical experts such as the forensic pathologist and odontologist, as well as with the detective[24], and contributes to discover the location of the victims, to analyse the crime scene, to transport the body to the institute of legal medicine and to identify the body by analyzing the skeleton in its distinctive characteristics which constitute it as a specific individual. In this way, the victims' bodies powerfully come to the forefront in their anatomical concreteness and detail.

---

19 Clea Koff, *The Bone Woman* (New York: Random House, 2004), 11, quoted in Sarah Dauncey, "Crime, Forensics and Modern Science" in *A Companion to Crime Fiction*, eds. Rzepka Charles, Horsley Lee (Chichester: Wiley Blackwell, 2010), 165.
20 Stefoff, *Forensic Anthropology*, 6.
21 Linda L. Klepinger, "Background Setting for Forensic Anthropology" in *Fundamentals of Forensic Anthropology*, ed. Linda L. Klepinger (Hoboken: John Wiley and sons Inc., 2006), 4. See also Stanley Rhine, *Bone Voyage: A Journey in Forensic Anthropology* (Albuquerque: The University of New Mexico Press, 1998), xv: "They also assist in the recovery of bodies and perform many other tasks having to do with human remains in the interesting intersection between medicine and the law."
22 Douglas H. Ubelaker, "Introduction to Forensic Anthropology," 4. See also Bradley J. Adams, *Forensic Anthropology* (New York: Infobase Publishing, 2006), 6: "A major component of physical anthropology is the study of the human skeleton, or human osteology. Experts in the study of the human skeleton, human osteologists, may apply their skills to the fossilized remains of ancestral humans (paleoanthropology), the study of populations through their dead (biological anthropology or paleodemography), or the analysis of human remains within the medicolegal context (forensic anthropology). Regardless of whether the skeleton is fossilized, prehistoric, historic, or modern, many of the goals of an osteological analysis are the same: to reconstruct as much as possible about a person's life from a thorough examination of his or her bones after death."
23 Kathy Reichs, *Grave Secrets* [2002] (London: Arrow Books, 2008), 3.
24 See Ubelaker, "Introduction to Forensic Anthropology," 10 and Adams, *Forensic Anthropology*, 4.

In the case she is investigating in *Déjà Dead*, Temperance Brennan starts her analysis from the head of the victim; once it has been cleaned, it is photographed and sent to the radiology laboratory. Hair samples are sent to the biology laboratory to undergo microscopic analysis. The victim's remains are subsequently cleaned in order to allow a complete analysis of all the bones at disposal[25] and proceed to an estimation of age based on an examination of skeletal development (bones and teeth).[26] These procedures aim at the establishment of a biological profile, the most important aspect of which is the age estimation at the moment of death in order to narrow the potential matches for identification with missing people.

As she is filling in the form relative to the victim she is examining and which reduces it to a series of numbers and medico-legal jargon[27], Brennan freely expresses her feelings, the rage she had managed to contain up to that moment[28] and gives voice to her humanity in the presence of the consequences of violent death

[I] experienced my usual wave of anger at the arrogant indifference of the system. Violent death allows no privacy. It plunders one's *dignity* as surely as it has taken one's life. The body is handled, scrutinized, and photographed, with a new series of digits allocated at each step. The victim becomes part of the evidence, an exhibit, on display for police, pathologists, forensic specialists, lawyers, and, eventually, jurors. Number it. Photograph it. Take samples. Tag the toe. While I am an active participant, I can never accept the impersonality of the system. It is like looting on the most personal level.[29]

---

25 See also Kathy Reichs, *Bones to Ashes* [2007] (London: Arrow Books, 2008), 97: "There are 206 bones in the adult human skeleton, all varying in size and shape. Singly, they yield few clues about a person's life story. But together, like interlocking puzzle pieces, they say a lot. Age. Sex. Ancestry. Health. Habit. The more bones, the more is revealed."

26 See Sue Black, Eilidh Ferguson, eds, *Forensic Anthropology: 2000–2010*, Oxford, CRC Press (Taylor and Francis), 4: "Skeletal development is a relatively reliable indicator, as the various phases are based on the rather stable and predictable appearance of primary and secondary ossification centres, morphological changes in size and shape and finally the fusion of these centres which results in the attainment of a skeletal adult form."

27 See Kathy Reichs, *Déjà Dead* [2008] (London: Arrow Books, 1998), 20: "Name: *Inconnue.* Unknown. Date of autopsy: June, 3, 1994. Investigators: Luc Claudel, Michel Charbonneau, Section des homicides, CUM. Homicide division, Montreal Urban Community Police. I added the police report number, the morgue number [case #26704], and the Laboratoire de Médecine Légale, or LML, number."

28 In order to manage to focus on her task Brennan had previously asserted: "I filed the outrage in another place and forced myself to concentrate." (Reichs, *Déjà Dead*, 19). See also Reichs, *Grave Secrets*, 12–13: "Focus Brennan. Channel your outrage to uncover evidence."

29 Reichs, *Déjà Dead*, 20 (emphasis added).

The novel powerfully stages the shocking confrontation of the protagonist (who becomes the reader's alter ego) with the reality of medico-legal examination on the victim's body. The human body possesses "a unique system, integrated and organized [...] which intrinsically contains all genetic information, individual as well as specific, teleologically and autonomously oriented to the actualization of the body in its entirety, in the different phases of its continuous, gradual and coordinated development."[30] Such continuity in its development is interrupted by violent death and it is the reality of the body on the autopsy table that makes the people involved in the investigation feel its concrete implications and consequences.

> Everything but the body. [...] Photographs were no threat. The blood and gore were somewhere else. Distant. The murder scene was a clinical exercise. No problem. Dissect it, study it, solve the puzzle. But place a body on an autopsy table and it was a different matter.[31]

In these words we notice how, in a process opposite to the one carried out by Victor Frankenstein, and which provokes a reflected horror, the body, which had previously been a living body, is deconstructed in its anatomical parts, thus violating the modern ontology of corporeal integrity:

> Bodily integrity suggests that the body is a discrete unit that contains the self. Bounded by the skin, the visceral aspects of the body are confined and controlled in a kind of private space of the self, rendered invisible and thus discrete. Bodily integrity is intimately associated with a subject's capacity to exercise sovereignty over her or his body/self.[32]

At the morgue, the victims are displayed on stainless steel tables, their bodies decayed or mutilated, their organs arranged in what appears to be the wreck of the human body. Their self-exposure is evident in the traces on the body or the traces left by it in a sort of "ritual that reclaims the body, reinscribing its violation to serve the law."[33] Science tries to obfuscate the fearsome image of the violated corpse by conceiving the body as a scientific text to be read in order to reconstruct a narrative of crime, as well as a narrative of identity; however the pathologist by presenting the violence of the killing from the perspective of the weapon re-enacts the last moments of the victim's life through empathetic imagination. "This empathy works against the portrayal of the objectified body that is laid out on the autopsy table."[34]

---

30 Laura Palazzani, "Corpo e persona", 133. [My translation].
31 Reichs, *Déjà Dead*, 27.
32 Neil Gerlach, Sheryl N. Hamilton, Rebecca Sullivan, Priscilla L. Walton, *Becoming Biosubjects. Bodies, Systems, Technologies* (Toronto: University of Toronto Press Incorporated, 2011), 8.
33 Ellen Burton Harrington, "Nation, Identity and the Fascination with Forensic Science in Sherlock Holmes and CSI," in *International Journal of Cultural Studies* 10(3): 365–382, 2007, 373.
34 Harrington, "Nation, Identity," 374.

Therefore, in Reichs's forensic detective fiction the victim's body transforms itself and from an inert text, liable to the doctor's and the detective's interpretation, becomes an active communicative agent. As law presumes, it is through the body that man expresses his identity; the body speaks to those who are able to understand its language: "inserted in a communicative logic, the body affirms itself not only in its physical aspect, but also in its identity, thanks to the irreducible multiplicity of its intentional valences."[35] The victim's body becomes a witness, "a subject for the scientist-observer to engage in dialogue."[36] The morgue is not presented just as the clinical context for a medical detached investigation of the bodies but becomes a place for "sympathetic understanding and communion,"[37] where the doctor is characterized by his ability to speak and act for the victims in an act of restitution of narrative authority to their voices which underlines their humanity.

Brennan expresses her own feelings in the following terms:

> Some amount of professional detachment was mandatory in order to do the work, but not to the extent of abandoning all feeling. The deaths of these women had stirred something in me. I ached for their fear, their pain, their helplessness in the face of madness. I felt anger and outrage [...] I felt for these victims, and my response to their deaths was like a lifeline to my feelings. To my own humanity and my celebration of life. I felt, and I was grateful for the feeling.[38]

Discussions on human dignity tend to focus on the sacred nature of human life and do not address the question of dead humans; the dignity celebrated by the UDHR is the human dignity of the living, while forensic experts, both in fiction and in actual cases, powerfully refer to the "dignity of the dead."[39] As a matter of fact, inherent dignity is inseparable from the human condition, it cannot be gained or lost, nor does it allow for any degree.[40] Even the non-living body, as it represents the

---

35 Francesco D'Agostino, *Parole di Bioetica* (Torino: Giappichelli, 2004), 41.

36 Dauncey, "Crime, Forensics, and Modern Science", 165.

37 Dauncey, "Crime, Forensics, and Modern Science", 172.

38 Reichs, *Déjà Dead*, 391–392.

39 Rosenblatt, "International Forensic Investigation," 938. Even if Rosenblatt asserts that the dead do not enjoy human rights in the same universal and inalienable way professed by the declaration and do not possess a universal and inalienable dignity, he then recognizes that they can clearly be the victims of indignity and therefore call for a posthumous dignity. This in my view leads to what can be called posthumous rights. Rosenblatt himself acknowledges a sort of rights or claims of the dead and defines them "far more contingent than those of the living, more fragile." (Rosenblatt, "International Forensic Investigation," 942).

40 See Herbert Spiegelberg, "Human Dignity: A Challenge to Contemporary Philosophy," in *Human Dignity. This Century and the Next*, eds. Rubin Gotesky, and Ervin Laszlo (New York:

memory of lived life and the value of corporeity, maintains its own symbolic dignity as *res sacra*.[41] The victim's body therefore is not considered according to the reductionist materialistic anti-metaphysic perspective, that is to say, as extended matter with specific spatial and temporal coordinates (in fact it occupies a precise space and has a specific continuity over time), but rather according to the personalistic metaphysical perspective, that is to say, as an embodiment of the subject, the seat and manifestation of the person. Therefore it "acquires a value which participates of the dignity of man himself [...] the body is a subjective value which must be respected, preserved and protected, due to its relationship with the person of whose dignity it participates by being its embodiment."[42]

In human rights discourses, corporeal integrity is a "baseline condition that precedes the ascription of dignity and rights to an individual" thus ignoring its vulnerability and decay, and negating the core dimension of embodied experience. This leads to a decorporealized vision of the subject, which remains ambiguous in its quality, as it is built upon contrary images of bodily fragmentation:

> the dignified individual in possession of rights is imagined to inhabit an always already fully integrated and inviolable body: a body that is whole, autonomous and self-enclosed. [...] Yet paradoxically, the dual conceits of human dignity and bodily integrity simultaneously require for their legibility the threat of bodies being violated, broken, and defiled, entailing that human rights discourses and norms are ironically vindicated by inverse images of corporeal unmaking and abuse.[43]

Literature, in particular forensic novels, allows the immediacy and the significance of the fragmented body to emerge.[44] At the morgue the victim's body appears after it has been "dumped, naked and mutilated, stripped of everything that linked it to a life" (*Déjà Dead*, 19). It is reduced to a *soma*; however, the *soma*, the concrete biological body of a person is the means for his self-representation to the world, to the others, as well as the site of his acknowledgement as a person.[45] The *soma* is the embodiment of the *bios*, which refers to the living man in his

---

Gordon and Breach, 1970), 39–62, 55, quoted in Andorno, "Human Dignity and Human Rights," 231.

41 Elio Sgreccia, "Corpo e Persona" in *Questioni di bioetica*, ed. Stefano Rodotà (Roma-Bari: Laterza, 1993),116. See also Palazzani, "Person and Human Being", 95: The presence of a substantial principle makes it possible to recognize the actual status of the person in the human being even in conditions of "potentiality" and "privation."

42 Sgreccia, "Corpo e persona," 113. [My translation].

43 Anker, *Fictions of Dignity*, 4.

44 Anker, *Fictions of* Dignity, 2.

45 See Michele Aramini, *Introduzione alla Bioetica*, Milano, Giuffré, 2003, 95.

empirical individuality. The foundation and the individuality of the *bios* (the life *quam vivimus*) is given by the *psyché*, which opens the *bios* to its actualization. The *bios* and the *psyché* are ontologically linked and it is with reference to the *psyché* that man receives the name the law purports to protect and preserve. It is the name which constitutes the individual as a legal person. The *bios* is the only place where life can manifest itself as *psyché* and acquire value in the world. The law does not pertain to the natural world, but can act only in it. What the law protects is the *psyché*; however, as it cannot reach it, the *bios* acquires juridical relevance as the site of the manifestation of the *psyché*.[46] This embodiment of the *psyché* in the *bios* confers to the juridical person an ontological density: in order to underline the embodied nature (*psyché/bios*) of the person, juridical debates adopt the term "bio-juridical" person.[47] And the *bios*, in turn, is embodied in the *soma*.[48] This is connected to the original Latin term *dignitas homines*, which denoted worthiness and in particular referred to the outer aspect of a person's social role which evokes respect and embodies the esteem presiding in office or personality.

Human dignity is increasingly treated as a legal term, although it is not that; it refers to a pre-juridical dimension, and human rights represent its judicial concretization.[49] In the cases considered, the term broadens to include the victims of violent death to whose remains it is ascribed and it thus opens a liminal space in which "ethics and law touch each other and overla[p]"[50] in a development of the meaning and implications of human rights.

> The term human dignity in its socio-political application is aimed at threats to humanity, human self-determination and self-unfolding, which originate from human action and its social consequences. [...] Protection is thus no longer directed towards the human being as the subject of its own action, but as the object of actions of other human beings.[51]

---

46 See D'Agostino, *Parole di Bioetica*, 28–31.

47 Stéphane Bauzon, *La persona biogiuridica* (Torino: Giappichelli, 2005), 3.

48 See Giorgio Agamben, *Homo Sacer: Sovereign Power and Bare Life* (Stanford: Stanford University Press, (1995) 1998), 75: "Declarations of rights represent the originary figure of the inscription of natural life in the juridico-political order of the nation-state. The same bare life that in the ancient regime was politically neutral and belonged to God as creaturely life and in the classical world was (at least apparently) clearly distinguished as *zoe* from political life (*bios*) now fully enters into the structure of the state and even becomes the earthly foundation of the state's legitimacy and sovereignty."

49 See Martin Hailer and Dietrich Ritschl, "The General Notion of Human Dignity and the Specific Arguments in Medical Ethics" in *Sanctity of Life and Human Dignity*, ed. Bayertz, 93, 99.

50 Hailer and Ritschl, "The General Notion of Human Dignity," 99.

51 Kurt Bayertz, "Human Dignity: Philosophical Origin and Scientific Erosion of an Idea" in *Sanctity of Life and Human Dignity*, ed. Bayertz 80.

The legal order revolves around individual action and responsibility; yet, after death, an "(assumed) annihilation of the person and the cessation of her capacity to experience or be aware of actions to which she is subject"[52] takes place. However, the dead were once persons, "the paradigmatic right-holders;"[53] for this reason they are identifiable by their name, physical look and retained memories. Most importantly, they continue to belong to the moral community of humans: the dead are dead persons and leave behind them a legacy, whether material (property), psychological (memories), or both. They "continue to exist symbolically, in light of what [they] accomplished and the kind of person [they] were"; therefore, "the moral attributes of the dead person [...] make this subject a potential but also an actual right-holder."[54] The rights of the dead configure themselves as more contingent than those of the living and are linked to specific considerations, in particular

[a] right is a justified claim on someone, or on some institution, for something which one is owed. The right-holder, in claiming a right, is asserting that he is entitled to be treated in certain ways by other people and by social institutions. [...] Human rights do not tell us who or what we are; rater, they tell us how we should treat our fellow human beings. Human rights do not describe our nature; rather they prescribe our behavior[55]

This is the condition Reichs's novels address; Brennan's response to the dead raises ethical questions that go to the heart of what it means to be human.[56] The sight of still another victim in the morgue provokes in her contrasting feelings:

The relentless exposure would be a final *indignity*, an assault after death to exceed any she might have endured at the end of life. A part of me wanted to cover her, to wheel her from these sterile strangers to the sanctity of those who had loved her. To allow her family to put what remained of her in a place of peace. But the rational part of me knew better. This victim needed *a name*. Only then could her family bury her. Her bones deserved an opportunity to

---

52 Daniel Sperling, *Posthumous Interests: Legal and Ethical Perspectives* (Cambridge: Cambridge University Press, 2008), 4. See also Stonaker, *Management of Dead Bodies*, 130: "At death, one is no longer considered a person, that is, a subject of the law. Thus, cadavers are regarded, in general, as 'things.' This classification might be deemed inappropriate since cadavers are not subject to common rules about possessions and property, and, for that reason, they are not a 'thing' in the legal sense of the word."
53 Sperling, *Posthumous Interests*, 82.
54 Sperling, *Posthumous Interests*, 83.
55 Brian Orend, *Human Rights: Concept and Context* (Peterborough: Broadview Press, 2002), 17, 19.
56 See Gareth Jones, Whitaker, *Speaking for the Dead*, ix. As one of the forensic protagonists of the series *Bones* based on Reichs's novels asserts, "we are here in the first place – because we treasure human life" (quoted in Steenberg, 88).

speak, to scream silently of the events of her last hours. Only then could the police hope to reconstruct what had befallen her. So we gathered with our forms, our blades, our scales, our calipers, our notebooks, our specimen jars, our cameras.[57]

Although it provokes a deconstruction of the human body to its anatomical components and appears to reify them by constantly handling them and assaulting their integrity, the forensic anthropologist's work configures itself actually as a defense of human dignity, of the bio-juridical dimension of the person which extends itself beyond the limits of life:

> At least I would give this victim a *name*. Death in anonymity would not be added to the list of violations he or she would suffer.[58]

> In my view, death in anonymity is the ultimate insult to *human dignity*. To spend eternity under a Jane Doe plaque. To disappear nameless into an unmarked grave without those who care about you knowing that you have gone. That offends.[59]

Forensic anthropology, by acting upon the body, restores the juridical name to the victim, in a sort of restitution of their juridical status of personae. According to biojuridical reflections, the status of legal person finishes with a person's death: in the case of the novel's victims I would advocate a status of "post-persons" (even if this possibility is usually ruled out in bioethical debates[60]) or rather "persons who were" and who have the right of being acknowledged for their past existence, to have such past existence reconstructed through their memory and the right to conclude it in the dignity of their cultural and familial dimension. Actually Palazzani acknowledges that although there is no duty to protect the human biological body deprived of personal subjectivity, there is the possibility to acknowledge it certain rights, following specific considerations.[61] I would link these considerations to the right to life and to the full development of one's personality in society, rights which are violated by the crime of murder. A

---

57 Reichs, *Grave Secrets*, 167 (emphasis added).
58 Reichs, *Déjà Dead*, 20 (emphasis added).
59 Kathy Reichs, *Break No Bones* [2006] (London: Arrow Books, 2007), 73.
60 See Laura Palazzani, *Introduzione alla Biogiuridica* (Torino: Giappichelli, 2002), 195–195: "there are no post-persons [...] [man] ceases to be a person when he ceases to exist as a living organism." [My translation]. See also Laura Palazzani, "Person and Human Being in Bioethics and Biolaw," 95: "The personal being belongs to the ontological order; the possession of a substantial personal status cannot be acquired or diminished gradually, but is a radical condition (one is not more or less a person, a pre-person or a post-person, but either a person or not a person)."
61 Palazzani, *Introduzione alla Biogiuridica*, 72–73.

victim's body thus becomes a strong juridical alterity, which demands to be acknowledged.[62] The human body is always the body of a human person: body and person are united in the humanity of the being.[63]

The body is the original condition of the individual's being in the world and assumes a fundamental importance in the perspective of the restoration of the identity of the person, which is not a possession, but rather a process. The human being manifests his personal subjectivity in a relational dimension, that is, his identity is based on his own perception of himself as an "I" and on being recognized by the others as a "you."[64] As soon as the victim's identity is individuated, forensic novels in fact proceed to illustrate the victim's interaction with the world, in which the "I" had assumed and formed a world of meanings, values, models, rules of behaviour[65]; the reader is transported into the victim's daily reality through the reconstruction of his life and his personal relations. About the novel's first victim, Isabelle Gagnon, we learn that

> She'd lived with her brother and his lover in St. Edouard, a working class neighbourhood northeast of Centre-ville. She worked in a lover's boutique, a small shop off St. Denis specializing in unisex clothes and paraphernalia. [...] Isabelle disappeared on Friday, April 1. According to the brother, she was a regular at some of the bars on St. Denis and had been out late the night before. He thought he he'd heard her come in around 2 a.m., but didn't check. The two men left for work early the next morning. A neighbor saw her at 1 p.m. Isabelle was expected at the boutique at 4 p.m. She never showed up. Her remains were discovered none weeks later at Le Grand Séminaire. She was twenty-three.[66]

Brennan's reflections in the course of her work underline how "Any death deserves proper attention [...] A person's a person. [...] Every person deserves to be accounted for"[67]; the inherent human dignity of the victims renders them irreplaceable. The main message of Kathy Reichs's novels is that "the destruction of

---

62 Palazzani, *Introduzione alla Biogiuridica*, 96.

63 See Palazzani, *Introduzione alla Biogiuridica*, 39. See also Gareth Jones, Whitaker, *Speaking for the Dead*, 4: "The body is always some body, it is somebody's body."

64 See Laura Palazzani, "Corpo e Persona: I percorsi filosofici della bioetica e della biogiuridica" in *Il corpo de-formato. Nuovi percorsi dell'identità personale*, ed. Francesco D'Agostino (Milano: Giuffré, 2002), 113–148, 138–139 and Francesco D'Agostino, *Bioetica* (Torino: Giappichelli, 1996), 164–165.

65 See Angiola Filipponio, "Il Corpo: principio di identità. Un'introduzione" in *Il corpo de-formato*, ed. D'Agostino, 95. As in the case of the already quoted "The Mystery of Marie Rogêt" by Poe, the investigation opens a painful overview on the everyday life of the victims. (See Fiorato, "L'indagine medico-legale sul corpo umano," 131).

66 Reichs, *Déjà Dead*, 62.

67 Kathy Reichs, *206 Bones* [2009] (London: Arrow Books, 2010), 17–18, 71.

life with no explanations and no consequences"[68] cannot be accepted; "Violence wounds the body and it wounds the soul. Of the predator. Of the prey. Of the mourners. Of collective humanity. It diminishes us all."[69] Brennan's work underlines the human cost of crime[70] and her mission is devoted to the victims, to the dead but also to the living:

> I work *with* the dead, but *for* the living. I work to help families resolve issues of missing members; I testify in court to bring justice if there has been violence.[71]

> The dead have a right to be identified. To have their stories drawn to a close and to take their place in our memories. If they died at the hands of another, they also have a right to have those hands brought to account.[72]

The main aspect which emerges from Brennan's work is not so much the individuation of the culprit, but rather the restoration of the victim's social ties with the community and their restitution to the physical and social worlds from which they were violently torn.[73] Dead bodies cannot be approached in an ethical vacuum; the respect for life is a supreme value because it is the origin for other fundamental human values, such as respect for the human person, its psychic and physical integrity, its body, its belonging, its lifestyle. Respect for life must refer to any stage of human and social life.[74] All that remains of the person is the cadaver, which though no longer a human presence "still reminds us of the presence that once was utterly inseparable from it."[75] The respect for that person, and for the memory of that person, finds expression in the respect for the person's remains, and creates a powerful link which includes human dignity and *pietas*.

Funeral rites express the social persona, they emphasize and remember the identity of the deceased. The tomb perpetuates his/her name through his/her inclusion in the generational continuity of a family[76], for which reason the

---

68 Kathy Reichs, *Fatal Voyage* [2001] (London: Arrow Books, 2008), 276.
69 Reichs, *Break No Bones*, 36.
70 Harrington, "Nation, Identity," 372.
71 Reichs, *Devil Bones*, 2008, 333.
72 Reichs, *Fatal Voyage*, 276.
73 Rosenblatt, "International Forensic Investigation," 950–951.
74 See Mariano Bianca, *Scienza, Etica e Bioetica* (Firenze: Angelo Pontecorboli Editore, 1999), 193–194.
75 William F. May, "Religious Justification for Donating Body Parts," *Hastings Center Report* 15.2 (1985): 38–42, 39, quoted in Gareth Jones, Whitaker, *Speaking for the Dead*, 57.
76 Stonaker, *Management of Dead Bodies*, 85, 97. See also a.o. Michael Parker Pearson, "Mortuary Practices, Society and Ideology: an ethnoarchaeological study" in *Symbolic and Structural Archaeology*, ed. Ian Hodder (Cambridge: Cambridge University Press, 2007).

lettering on a memorial creates a powerful link between the living and the dead. Reichs's protagonist therefore transcends the reality of her work and celebrates the human right of the dead to the full development of their personality even beyond death:

> While I cannot make the dead live again, I can reunite victims with their *names*, and give those left behind some measure of closure. In that way, I help the dead to speak, to say a final goodbye and, sometimes, to say what took their lives. [...] I would not walk away.[77]

Dignity thus becomes "the epitome of everything that the human being represents within this world"[78] and pertains both to Brennan's victims and to herself in the performance of her work.

---

77 Reichs, *Break No Bones*, 73.
78 Kurt Bayertz, "Human Dignity," 74.

Roxanne Barbara Doerr

Rumpole and the Rights of Accused Terrorists

In the aftermath of 9/11 and later attacks in Europe, terrorism entered everyday social and legal discourse in both the global and the local context. The experience has dramatically increased interest in human rights and promoted a number of recent transnational and multidisciplinary studies on "literature, the visual and performing arts, film, and popular culture."[1] In her overview on human rights Amy Zalman points out that not only victims but also the suspected perpetrators of attacks have rights, such as "the right not to be subject to torture or other degrading treatment, the right to be presumed innocent until they are deemed guilty of the crime, and the right to public trial."[2] The defence of these rights promotes the equal treatment of all people before the law. On an international level

> This legal approach [of international texts] responds to demands for the concrete protection of inherent rights, and goes some way to meeting the criticism that we are simply talking about desires and selfishness. The shift to positive law also fixes these rights in an agreed written form.[3]

As a result, when it comes to terrorism, one must approach and face not only a question of whose rights are more important (the defendant's or the general public's) but also which legislation is better equipped to pursue the most appropriate outcome. This has led to philosophical, moral and ethical reflections on the nature, extent and limits of human rights, which are indivisible and universal but must still be adjusted to particular and (often) controversial cases. The clash between national and international procedures highlights the fact that "where and how often one sees justice miscarrying may depend on how one draws the

---

1 Eleni Coundouriotis and Lauren M. E. Goodlad, "Comparative Human Rights: Literature, Arts, Politics," *Journal of Human Rights* 9 (2010): 121–126, 121. For more on the effects of pluralism and multiculturalism in the legal field, see Omid A. Payrow Shabani, ed., *Multiculturalism and the Law: a Critical Debate* (Cardiff: University of Wales Press: 2007).
2 Amy Zalman, "Human Rights & Terrorism: an Overview," available at http://terrorism.about.com/od/humanrights/a/Human_Rights.htm (November 7, 2012).
3 Andrew Clapham, *Human Rights: A Very Short Introduction* (Oxford: Oxford University Press, 2007), 23.

relative boundaries of justice and institutional law."[4] This experience has provided much food for thought in both popular culture and the law. An interesting example is John Mortimer, author of the Rumpole stories.[5] In both the short story *Rumpole and the Rights of Man* (published in 1995 in the collection of short stories *Rumpole and the Angel of Death*) and the novel *Rumpole and the Reign of Terror* (2006) barrister Horace Rumpole defends a person of Middle Eastern origins[6] accused of terrorist activities and arrested under circumstances that call human rights laws into play. These stories engage a series of reflections on his clients' rights to fair treatment and to a fair trial, and although their conclusions are very different, both focus on the difficulties that may arise when dealing with human rights and terrorism in a modern multicultural society.

1 Rumpole and the Rights of Man

From the very beginning of *Rumpole and the Rights of Man*, human rights are described in a very lofty, idealistic way, as is the bond between the nation members of the European Union.[7] In fact, the time in which the story is written is, according to Thomas Buergenthal, one in which "the world underwent dramatic changes to which the human rights revolution contributed significantly and from

---

4 Richard Weisberg, "Margins of Error" in *When Law Fails: Making Sense of Miscarriages of Justice*, eds. Charles J. Ogletree Jr. and Austin Sarat (New York: New York University Press, 2009), 70–111, 71.

5 For more on this, see the interviews "Madeleine Begun Kane profiles John Mortimer," available at http://www.madkane.com/mortimer.html (November 7, 2012); Lucasta Miller, "The Old Devil," *The Guardian*, October 7, 2006, available at http://www.guardian.co.uk/books/2006/oct/07/featuresreviews.guardianreview10 (July 14, 2013) and Colin Murphy, "Remembering John Mortimer," *Prospect Magazine*, January 17, 2009, available at http://www.prospectmagazine.co.uk/magazine/rememberingjohnmortimer/#.UfQUh4Ozhic (July 15, 2013). See also Paul Bergman, "Rumpole's Ethics," *Berkeley Journal of Entertainment and Sports Law* 1.2 (2012): 117–124.

6 The Middle East and its cultural disputes with Western countries on matters of human rights, along with oppositions within the West itself and with East Asia, have raised questions about the cross-cultural validity and international legitimacy of human rights norms. For more on this and on various perspectives on human rights in such contexts see Micheal Ignatieff, "The Attack on Human Rights," *Foreign Affairs* 80.6 (November- December 2001): 102–116.

7 For a detailed inquiry into the way in which human rights have influenced bureaucratic structures, relations between nations and the general public's perception of the standards of a certain country and its legislation, see Anthony D'Amato, "The Concept of Human Rights in International Law," *Columbia Law Review* 82.6 (October 1982): 1110–1159.

which the revolution also benefitted significantly."[8] Although he is hailed as "The defender of human rights,"[9] Rumpole is very sceptical of such legislation, for he does not feel "European" and claims that he defends the underdog simply "for the sake of the rent of the mansion flat and my wife's effort to boost consumer spending every Saturday at Safeway's" (*RM*, 180).

Rumpole's client is the young Iraqi student Amin Hashimi, who is accused of murdering a Netherbank middle manager at an underground station. His opponent in court is Judge Billy Bloxham, famous for being "allergic to any sort of alien. Visitors from what was once our far-flung empire bring him out in a nervous rash" (*RM*, 184). Being set in a time before terrorism figured prominently on the international agenda, the word "terrorist" is never used in the story, yet the accusation and actions taken against Hashimi say otherwise. Judge Bloxham supervises the case in an apparently fair and unbiased manner while court is in session but proves the falsity of his conduct by making decisively racial comments after a rugby match once the case had concluded. These were reported verbatim in the next day's newspaper:

> A great many of these towel-headed gentry come here as so-called students to escape the tough laws of their own countries. No doubt they find a short stretch of community service greatly preferable to losing a hand if they're caught with their fingers in the till. No doubt they prefer our free Health Service to the attentions of the Medicine Man in the Medina. I don't know how much studying they do, but they certainly have time for plenty of extra-curricular activities. They take special courses in drug-dealing and the theft of quality cars. Coming from a part of the world where scraps were always breaking out, they are easily drawn into violence. This is not so bad when they do it to each other, but not, repeat not, when a law-abiding subject of Her Majesty gets shot in the Underground. I have to tell you, gentlemen, that when my jury brought in a guilty verdict on the murderer Hashimi, I had a song in my heart. I retired to my room and invited my dear old usher, ex-Sergeant Major Wrigglesworth of the Blues and the Royals, to join me in a sherry. "Well done, sir," Wrigglesworth said. "You managed to pot the bastard." "One down," I replied, "and thousands left to go." (*RM*, 187)

The revelation of such claims becomes the tenuous basis on which Rumpole may focus and construct an appeal – first to the British Court of Appeal and then to the

---

8 Thomas Burgenthal, "The Normative and Institutional Evolution of International Human Rights," *Human Rights Quarterly* 19.4 (1997): 703–723, 713. For more on the development of human rights in the international scenario since the 1940s, see also Kenneth Cmiel, "The Recent History of Human Rights," *The American Historical Review* 109.1 (2004): 117–135.
9 John Mortimer, "Rumpole and the Rights of Man" in *Rumpole and the Angel of Death* [1995] (New York: Viking Press, 1996), 178–216, 178–179: further references in the text, abbreviated as *RM*.

European Court of Human Rights.[10] It is precarious because although the judge's dislike for foreigners runs deep and is renown, his conduct in court did not appear to betray his true beliefs.[11] However, in order to win an appeal "the defendant has to identify some clear manifestation in trial strategy or mechanics that the conflict produced, and convince the appellate court that this alteration of tactics or choice of mechanisms may have contributed to the bad outcome"[12]; something which did not however emerge during the trial.

In accordance with his inability to feel European, Rumpole is unfamiliar with the workings of international human rights law: after losing in the Court of Appeal[13] it is his current instructing solicitor Peter Fishlock who looks "like a man possessed of a well-kept secret" (*RM*, 189) and suggests appealing to Article Six of the European Convention of Human Rights. Article Six establishes, among other things, that "In the determination of his civil rights and obligations or of any criminal charge against him, everyone is entitled to a fair and public hearing within a reasonable time by an independent and impartial tribunal established by law."[14] Moreover, when talking of taking the case to a higher level, Rumpole first mistakenly thinks of the International Court of Justice in the Hague (which deals with disputes between states and advisory opinions on legal questions submitted by international organs) instead of the European Court of Human Rights (ECHR) in Strasbourg (which judges individual appeals and violations of human rights under the European Convention on Human Rights).[15] Such confusion is partially due to the abstract nature of human rights laws, as opposed to criminal laws and

---

10 For a detailed account on the rights of the accused in international legislation see Salvatore Zappalà, *Human Rights in International Criminal Proceedings* (Oxford: Oxford University Press, 2003).

11 Judicial behaviour and discretion in cases involving other – and sometimes conflicting – cultures has become a very recent and pressing manner, one discussed in detail in ed. Omid A. Payrow Shabani, *Multiculturalism and Law: a Critical Debate* (Cardiff: University of Wales Press: 2007).

12 Weisberg, "Margins of Error," 89.

13 This could also have happened because, as Colin Warbrick points out, "The English Court of Appeal has upheld a central plank of the anti-terrorism legislation allowing for indeterminate detention of non-UK nationals," "The European Response to Terrorism in an Age of Human Rights," *The European Journal of International Law* 15.5 (2004): 989–1018, 995.

14 The content of the Convention for the Protection of Human Rights and Fundamental Freedoms may be found at http://conventions.coe.int/treaty/en/Treaties/Html/005.htm, last access July 15, 2013.

15 For more on this, see Warbrick, "The European Response to Terrorism in an Age of Human Rights." For more on the European Court of Human Right's history, groundbreaking decisions and significant cases, see Michael Goldhaber, *A People's History of the European Court of Human Rights* (New Brunswick, NJ: Rutgers University Press, 2007).

criminal law
natural legal rights?
human rights law

Rumpole and the Rights of Accused Terrorists ━━ **175**

consolidated national legal institutions, as Amartya Sen observes: "Proclama-
tions of human rights [...] are really strong ethical pronouncements as to what
should be done. [...] they are not claims that these human rights are already
established legal rights, enshrined through legislation or common law."[16] This
divergence may be seen in the contrast between the idealistic human rights
principles and international political reality that emerges during a day trip when
some of the people accompanying Rumpole mention the ethnic cleansing in
Bosnia and Saddam Hussein's purchase of Russian nuclear weapons. The realization of how much injustice there truly is leads to "a sudden, strangely uncomfortable silence, as though we had all been brought face to face with the ending of
the world" (*RM*, 199–200).

With such a conflicting state of mind, Rumpole turns to the ECHR but insists
on attaining justice for his client through his own use of rhetoric and the law:
"What I profoundly hoped would stir them out of their international coma would
be the Rumpole address, the rallying cry against injustice, the devastating
destruction of Billy Bloxham with which I expected to win the day" (*RM*, 195).
However, upon arriving to court he is intimidated by its appearance and functioning, which, like its legislation, gives it a very impersonal and disorienting impression compared to the Old Bailey:

> The Court was a long, grey concrete erection beside a river, with two circular towers like
> gasworks sawn off crookedly. Inside, we had wandered, uncertain of the way, in what
> looked like the vast boiler-room of a ship, painted in nursery colours. We went up and down
> steel and wire staircases, and travelled in lifts whose glass sides let you see more of the
> journey than made you entirely comfortable. And then I was standing up at a desk in a huge
> courtroom. Across an expanse of blue carpet, so far away that I could hardly distinguish
> their features, sat the Judges in black gowns under a white ceiling perforated like a giant
> kitchen colander. Human rights, it seemed, like the scientific romances of H. G. Wells, had
> been set in the future and now the future had arrived with a rush and overtaken me before I
> was quite sure how to address it. (*RM*, 206–207)

Rumpole's final eloquent speech is still centred on the English system, starting
from Judge Bloxham's Albion, "the hypocrisy and slyness of a certain class of
Englishman" (*RM*, 208) and expounding on the "perfidious" Court of Appeal,
although he claims he "even touched on the subject of human rights about which
I had heard so much since I went to Europe" (*RM*, 209). He wins but does not
consider it "a famous victory" (*RM*, 210) even before the troubling outcome of the
story. Amin is acquitted a few months later and Rumpole discovers from another

---

16 Amartya Sen, *The Idea of Justice* (London: Penguin Books Ltd, 2010), 357–358 [italics in
original].

source that the student was a member of a weapon trafficking circle along with a Member of the European Parliament and a knowledgeable German lawyer both of whom had so grandly supported Rumpole and heralded the values of equality and human rights. The cry for human rights was therefore only a way to cover activities that disrespect human rights and maliciously exploit international human rights institutions and Rumpole's desire to help the underdog. The efficiency of evoking human rights in court is also underlined by Andrew Clapham as follows:

> Playing the "human rights" card can be persuasive, sometimes even conclusive, in contemporary decision making: this is one aspect of what makes the moral force of human rights so attractive – they help you to win arguments and, sometimes, to change the way things are done.[17]

Far from helping, Rumpole is thus accused of "Peddling human rights. The right to get us all blown up" (*RM*, 213) but his mistake was that of not truly grasping the workings and consequences of a body of law as malleable as human rights legislation. Upon asking himself who is at fault he once again blames Judge Bloxham not for his behaviour but because "he should never have developed a taste for football" (*RM*, 215). In doing so he turns away again from "being a European," bringing the weight of the case full circle back to the familiar English system and its agents, an action which harks back to the beginning of the story, when Rumpole asks himself "Was I European? I supposed so, although I had never thought of it before. If I think about it at all, I suppose I'm English. Not British" (*RM*, 178). This recalls the problem of determining a common standard for all countries when it comes to rights and freedom, which has been and can only be approximately established.[18] In the end, the all-compassing European identity and defence of human rights are still too vague and extensive for Rumpole and for many Europeans.

17 Clampham, *Human Rights: A Very Short Introduction*, 1–2.
18 In fact, according to Tom Bingham, *The Rule of Law* (London: Penguin books, 2010), 68: "there is no universal consensus on the rights and freedoms which are fundamental, even among civilizations. [...] It must be accepted that the outer edges of some fundamental rights are not clear-cut. But within a given society there is ordinarily a large measure of agreement on where the lines are to be drawn at any particular time, even though standards change over time, and in the last resort the courts are there to draw them. It is, I think, possible to identify the rights and freedoms which, in the UK and developed Western or Westernized countries elsewhere, are seen as fundamental, and the rule of law requires that those rights should be protected."

2 Rumpole and the Reign of Terror

While terrorism is never openly mentioned but only alluded to at the end of the story through Hashimi and his companions' criminal activity, in *Rumpole and the Reign of Terror* racial discrimination and terrorism figure prominently. The novel in fact conveys the heated atmosphere following the London bombing in 2005, the transatlantic aircraft plot in 2006, and the enforcement of *Terrorism Act 2006*. In the very beginning, Rumpole's Head of Chambers Samuel Bollard covers the names of the Chamber's barristers in fear of their – and especially his – vulnerability because "blowing up a leading QC and a senior representative of our great legal system such as... [...] Well, for instance, myself, would be a distinct feather in al-Qaeda's cap!" (*RT*, 3–4). Such fear of terrorism pervades the novel and shapes public opinion: "Terrorism and fear of terrorism had increased in the world. Every news bulletin brought details of new explosions, assassinations, religious hatred and wanton death" (*RT*, 155).[19] This is due to terrorism's lack of boundaries, limits or specific targets, for it consists in "politically motivated violence perpetrated against noncombatant targets by subnational groups or clandestine agents, usually intended to influence an audience."[20] The sense of terror that is transmitted by such acts also surpasses the single event or attack, for

---

19 It is impossible not to mention the 9/11 attacks, which brought terroristic activities into the spotlight and made discussions on the definition of terrorist and terrorism necessary. In the American Office of the Coordinator for Counterterrorism's "Patterns of Global Terrorism 2001," the former Secretary of the United States Colin L. Powell describes the delicate situation as follows: "Terrorists respect no limits, geographic or moral. The frontlines are everywhere and the stakes are high. Terrorism not only kills people. It also threatens democratic institutions, undermines economies, and destabilizes regions," quoted in Charles Tilly, "Terror, Terrorism, Terrorists," *Sociological Theory* 22.1 (March 2004): 5–12, 5. In this essay, Tilly also deals with the parallel progression of reports and theories on human rights and global terrorism.
20 C. L. Ruby, "The Definition of Terrorism," quoted in Tilly, "Terror, Terrorism, Terrorists," 7. Tilly sustains that there are four steps to identifying terrorist activity in general: "(1) noticing that a recurrent strategy of intimidation occurs widely in contentious politics and corresponds approximately to what many people mean by terror; (2) recognizing that a wide variety of individuals, groups, and networks sometimes employ that strategy; (3) relating the strategy systematically to other forms of political struggle proceeding in the same settings and populations; and (4) seeing that specialists in coercion ranging from government employees to bandits sometimes deploy terror under certain political circumstances, usually with far more devastating effects than the terror operations of nonspecialists." (Tilly, "Terror, Terrorism, Terrorists," 9). See also Eugenia Dumitriu, "The E.U.'s Definition of Terrorism: The Council Framework Decision on Combatting Terrorism," *German Law Journal* 5.5 (2004): 585–602 and Mahmood Mamdani, "Good Muslim, Bad Muslim: A Political Perspective on Culture and Terrorism," *American Anthropologist* 104.3 (September 2002): 766–775.

"In addition to whatever harm it inflicts directly, it sends signals – signals that the target is vulnerable, that the perpetrators exist, and that the perpetrators have the capacity to strike again."[21] Steve Tsang inserts this reasoning within a vicious cycle bringing together terrorist attacks, citizens' hostility against suspected minorities and the government and intelligence service's subsequent need to focus on pre-emptive intervention in order to avoid further attacks and to reassure the public. Such interventions however are necessarily based on suspicion and infringe many of the accused's rights.[22]

Conversely, human rights resurface under many forms in *Rumpole and the Reign of Terror*, especially when it comes to considering how the accused and his case are treated and how human rights legislation is compelled to step in to remedy injustice. In this case, Horace Rumpole's client, the Pakistani doctor Mahmood Kahn, is arrested and detained although no real terrorist activity had been committed. This contradicts the idea, voiced by David Cole, that "any preventive-detention regime must closely conform to the traditional model of military detention of prisoners of war" instead of "the much more broader and more malleable concept of 'suspected terrorists'" and that such an action "should be authorized only where we are engaged in an ongoing armed conflict."[23] This, according to Lord Bingham, is the result of Britain's long history of dealing with various forms of terrorism, which brought the British government to treat "terrorism as a civil emergency, not a war, and [...] the terrorists [...] as criminals and not as combatants."[24] In addition, Kahn's arrest does not respect any formal procedure, as his wife's testimony confirms:

> They came for Mahmood Kahn when Tiffany was getting their children ready for school and he was about to leave for the hospital. They were three police officers in plain clothes and they refused to explain why he was being arrested or where he was being taken. He, it seemed, was controlled and told her it must be some extraordinary mistake. It was only as they were going out of the house that one of the officers thought to announce that Mahmood

---

21 Tilly, "Terror, Terrorism, Terrorists," 9.
22 Steve Tsang, "Stopping Global Terrorism and Protecting Rights" in *Intelligence and Human Rights in the Era of Global Terrorism*, ed. Steve Tsang (Westport, CT: Praeger Security International, 2007), 1–14, 6. See also the essays by Mark Urban, "The British Quest for Transparency," 17–25 and John N. L. Morrison, "Political Supervision of Intelligence Services in the United Kingdom," 41–53 in the same volume for more on the relation between British politics, intelligence and approach to human rights and terrorism.
23 David Cole, "Out of the Shadows: Preventive Detention, Suspected Terrorists, and War," *California Law Review* 97 (2009): 693–750, 699.
24 Bingham, *The Rule of Law*, 134. Interestingly, Bingham claims that this approach has allowed British authorities to be more successful in their prosecution of terrorists to conviction than their American counterparts, 137.

was being arrested under the Terrorism Act. The last thing she heard him say was that the idea was ridiculous.[25]

The doctor is imprisoned without any charge or trial date in a maximum-security prison which gives Rumpole "the feeling of entering another country, a land in which the principles of justice had been forgotten" (RT, 28) solely on the basis of "some sort of preliminary statement" (RT, 29) devoid of any indication of names, dates, times, places or circumstances. This clearly disregards the European Commission of Justice's guidance on the procedural rights of the suspected and accused, which was proposed precisely because "violations of defence rights, as set in Articles 5 and 6 of the European Committee of Human Rights (ECHR) do occur."[26] Along with an evident infringement of *habeas corpus*, Mahmood Kahn's right to information (enforced starting May 22, 2012), right to communicate with family members (currently being discussed) and the "Green paper" (enforced starting June 2011) were also violated. Because of his situation, he was suddenly taken away from his home and incarcerated in a high security prison without being able to contact his family (it is his wife Tiffany who asks Rumpole to defend him). Moreover Belmarsh prison, where Kahn is confined, is "a maximum-security prison which houses murderers, rapists and major drug barons" (RT, 28) and where living conditions are extremely uncomfortable.

Fortunately, the *Soering* principle of the ECHR,[27] according to which a suspect cannot be deported from a Convention state if the country of destination does not respect human rights, comes to Rumpole's aid and is upheld, as a consequence of Mahmood's alleged plotting and terrorist activities against the Pakistani regime. Such activities consisted of "women's rights and free speech and fair trial and police who didn't do things like strangle a woman's baby to make her confess" (RT, 3), objectives that characterize human rights struggles rather than criminal offences.[28] In contrast with Amin Hashimi, who always upheld his culture of origin, Mahmood wanted his country of origin to enjoy "all the good things you

---

25 John Mortimer, *Rumpole and the Reign of Terror* [2006] (London: Penguin Books, 2006), 16: further references in the text, abbreviated as *RT*.
26 This and more on the rights of suspects, including the "Green paper," concerning pre-trial detention and treatment, may be found at http://ec.europa.eu/justice/criminal/criminal-rights/index_en.htm (July 14, 2013).
27 For more on this, see Warbrick, "The European Response to Terrorism in an Age of Human Rights," 1007–1008. He significantly points out that the United Kingdom's response to terrorism is the most incompatible with human rights legislation compared to that of other EU countries.
28 This recalls Michael Ignatieff's idea that "Human rights have gone global by going local, empowering the powerless, giving voice to the voiceless," "The Attack on Human Rights," 111.

have in England" (*RT*, 30) and considers England not a foreign or hostile country, but rather "my home, my dear, dear country" (*RT*, 31). This alternative approach, as well as the indiscriminate evaluation of both of Rumpole's clients from the outside confirms Michael Ignatieff's claim that "the West has made the mistake of assuming that fundamentalism and Islam are synonymous. But in fact Islam speaks many voices, some more anti-Western or theocratic than others."[29]

Even after the subsequent evaluation of the case by the Special Immigration Appeals Commission, no information on the case against the accused is disclosed. SIAC does not "'do' particulars" (*RT*, 51), for to do so would compel them to reveal the source or sources of their information. Once again, the Court of Human Rights intervenes "against [us] detaining suspects in Belmarsh"[30] (*RT*, 66) and Kahn is placed under house arrest with constant supervision. This leaves him in a legal and professional limbo, for he cannot work or provide for his family, putting the Kahns at financial risk. Rumpole therefore finds himself in the paradoxical situation of actively seeking his client's charge in order to have a trial by jury and thus enter the domain of the English criminal law system; a situation often experienced in many real life cases:

> Now for lawyers, intelligence is tricky stuff: how it is gathered, how it is evaluated, how it is used. This is particularly so where we are concerned with preventive action under special regimes, where the state claims the necessity of interfering with an individual's rights in support of a public interest relying on information which cannot be fully (or at all) revealed, cannot be properly challenged, either regarding its reliability or its probative value. The need to maintain accountability procedures as required by human rights standards as far as possible arises because of the fallibility of intelligence-based reactions to terrorism.[31]

The British legal system has treated the matter in a disproportionate manner, recalling here that "The state may also legitimately prefer preventive detention to prosecution during wartime because of differences in the burden of proof. In criminal cases, including war crimes, the government must prove guilty beyond a

---

29 Ignatieff, "The Attack on Human Rights," 104.

30 This refers to the case of *A and others v Secretary of State for the Home Department* [2004] UKHL 56, also known as the "Belmarsh Prison case" which closely resembles Mahmood Kahn's case. It began with 9 indefinitely detained prisoners in Belmarsh prison under the accusation of threatening national security appealing to the SIAC. During the trial it emerged that section 4 of the *Anti-terrorism, Crime and Security Act 2001*, which had been applied and granted the government the power to detain certain foreign terrorist suspects, was declared incompatible with the European Convention of Human Rights (and more precisely, Article 5) and was therefore modified. For more on this, see Bingham, *The Rule of Law*, 147–149.

31 Warbrick, "The European Response to Terrorism in an Age of Human Rights," 991–992.

reasonable doubt."[32] Such a burden of proof is lacking in Kahn's case but its substitution with terrorist prevention measures makes it easier for the state to secure a conviction in a time when people wanted to feel that terrorists were being duly taken care of. It also credits the idea that terrorists do not deserve trials and that to consent to one is merely and redundantly procedural for "The dominant view has been that clemency or mercy breaks the logical retributive link between crime and deserved punishment."[33] Rumpole's wife Hilda claims that "terrorists don't need defending. What they need is locking up securely, or at least turfing out of the country" (*RT*, 25) and that "we're only going through the motions of a trial to show the world how fair British justice is, even to terrorists" (*RT*, 158).[34]

Her husband, on the other hand, is out to prove how unfair British justice has been. To do so however, he is compelled to turn to alternative means, for "not

---

32 Cole, "Out of the Shadows: Preventive Detention, Suspected Terrorists, and War," 731. Patricia Ewick "The Scale of Injustice," in *When Law Fails: Making Sense of Miscarriages of Justice*, 304–305, explains this delicate balance between justice, injustice and power in particular cases as follows: "In acts of surveillance, confiscation, detention, incarceration, reformation, and execution, the law claims for itself the right to commit acts of violence and transgression that would otherwise be forbidden. Yet its power is not limitless. Within the official discourse, justice demarcates the limits of legal power by defining standards against which that power can be held accountable." The latter statement motivates Rumpole's closing arguments of his final speech during the SIAC hearing, when he tells the judge and jury to "think of what justice is and do it" (*RT*, 56).

33 Weisberg, "Margins of Error," 73.

34 Another example of such thinking may be found in the article by Douglas Murray and Robin Simcox, "Rights of terrorists suspects have now overtaken those of the general public," *Telegraph*, February 3, 2011, available at http://www.telegraph.co.uk/news/uknews/terrorism-in-the-uk/8302100/Rights-of-terrorists-suspects-have-now-overtaken-those-of-the-general-public.html (July 14, 2013). Here they support Lord Carlile's intervention on the Abu Qatada case and his worry that terrorists would be more protected than the public and that it would eventually become impossible to deport any terrorists since "there is no other country in Europe as literal as this one [Britain] in obeying the ECHR." In *Rumpole and the Rights of Man* however, Judge Bloxham and Rumpole mention the relationship between the British and EU government in different terms: while the judge states that "the Euro Judges may not want to upset the British Government" the barrister replies "But the British Government's always upsetting them" (*RM*, 203). Significantly, the above mentioned Qatada case was overturned in 2013, although in the article from Cherie Booth, "We must not withdraw from the European convention on human rights," *The Guardian*, July 12, 2013, available at http://www.guardian.co.uk/commentisfree/2013/jul/12/european-convention-human-rights (July 14, 2013), the author still sustains the European convention on human rights because of the positive and equally important yet less publicized results it managed to attain on the human rights front. She also points out that "Respect for human rights is part of Britain's DNA" recalling Rumpole's references to the Magna Charta, presumption of innocence and Bill of Rights during his final speech at the SIAC as well as other trials, which lead to him being accused of "living in the past" (*RT*, 54). For more on the public's and politicians' perception of terrorists and their rights, see chapter 11 "Terrorism and the Rule of Law" of Bingham's *The Rule of Law*.

only are there several ways of safeguarding and promoting human rights other than legislation, these different routes have considerable complementarity."[35] Rumpole uses these means to the limit, openly confronting the Home Secretary on television and blackmailing him later upon discovering he was part of a terrorist group in the Sixties. As a result, Dr. Mahmood Kahn is "formally charged under the Terrorism Act with conspiring with others to commit acts of terrorism and failing to inform the police when he knew that such acts were planned" (*RT*, 115).[36]

The prosecution's disclosed evidence now consists of letters in Urdu mentioning plots, targets, as well as financial and medical assistance for terrorist groups. These however were attained by the Special Branch by breaking and entering into Kahn's office without a search warrant at night while the doctor was away on Christmas holiday, a procedure which clearly does not follow the provisions specified by *Terrorism Act 2006*.[37] The operation is justified by saying that "If the superintendent had done that [told the hospital authorities beforehand] Dr Kahn would have been warned and might have removed the letters" (*RT*, 165). He was also followed and reported to have been at a place where a terrorist had been arrested but the defence has no right to know the sources.[38] Again, it is only through legally questionable means – using lists, letters and information that had been used as stolen evidence for another of Rumpole's trials in the Kahn case – that he manages to prove that the letters were written, handled and planted by someone else.

Only in the course of the trial through both legal means (cross-examining a witness turned hostile) and by implying to a newly appointed judge that he would

---

35 Sen, *The Idea of Justice*, 366.

36 There are also many questionable points, as previously mentioned, in the conditions in which the doctor's arrest and the search of his office occurred. For more on how the United Nations regulate such procedures, see the Counter-Terrorism Implementation Task Force (CTITF)'s publication on "The Stopping and Searching of Persons" (September 2010), available at http://www.un.org/en/terrorism/ctitf/pdfs/bhrrg_stopping_searching.pdf, last access July 15, 2013.

37 The entire text of *Terrorist Act 2006* is available at http://www.legislation.gov.uk/ukpga/2006/11 (July 14, 2013).

38 Bingham admits that "In this country, the right of those in jeopardy to know the case against them so that they can answer it has perhaps been 'effectively gutted'," *The Rule of Law*, 151. He also writes of the increase of surveillance since 9/11, which resulted in the British becoming "the most closely monitored people of the free world," *The Rule of Law*, 155. Moreover, he claims that while according to early provisions "it was necessary for a warrant to be obtained in advance signed by a secretary of state; the issues of warrants was retrospectively scrutinized by a judge, whether serving or retired," since the *Regulation of Investigatory Powers Act 2000*, more public bodies have been empowered to obtain communications data, *The Rule of Law*, 156.

go to the Court of Appeal if this were not allowed, Kahn's employer and his Pakistani wife are revealed as the true culprits. To get Kahn arrested they had purposely exploited a culturally engendered fear of terrorism and suspicion of Middle Eastern people. As a result, just as human rights were exploited for the cause of terrorism in *Rumpole and the Rights of Man*, anti-terrorism legislation becomes the banner under which human rights are disrespected in *Rumpole and the Reign of Terror*.

3 Conclusions

Although the works take on a playful tone, both cases contain serious critiques about the excesses of current legislation when it comes to evaluating cases concerning terrorism and human rights. The English courts oppose Rumpole, reflecting the legal system and public's fear of terrorism and the perceptions of justice and innocence it entails. In the face of terrorist attacks, democratic governments have been compelled to decide between due process and human rights, for

> due process requires presumption of innocence with a high standard of proofs being produced before anyone is convicted of a crime, whereas preemption implies acting to foil an attack before it happens or acting against an individual or a group of people before a heinous crime is committed.[39]

In both cases it is possible to see the negative effects of an imbalance in favour of one or the other. In *Rumpole and the Rights of Man*, the uncontrolled exaltation of human rights, defense against discrimination, and abstract ideals of international fraternity blind Rumpole to the concrete proof against his client. In *Rumpole and the Reign of Terror* on the other hand, a man's rights are repeatedly and deliberately disrespected in order for those in charge to "save face." Rumpole is therefore compelled to find alternative measures in order to overcome the system's hurdles and insufficiencies, using information and sources that were found outside of the case or courtroom. Such measures enable him to win both of his cases and therefore prevail against a hostile system.

Mortimer's message appears to be twofold. First, it is essential to avoid both the idealisation of human rights, which is not the final solution, but rather "the shared vocabulary from which our arguments can begin, and the bare human minimum from which differing ideas of human flourishing can take root"[40] and

---

39 Tsang, "Stopping Global Terrorism and Protecting Rights," 1.
40 Ignatieff, "The Attack on Human Rights," 116.

the demonization of suspected terrorists when the case against them is not sustained by solid proof. Second, legal systems must ensure that the knowledge and procedures of international and national laws in such matters are well delineated and autonomously functional yet compatible through common general standards so that they may better complement and regulate one another in cases which engage terrorism and human rights.

Carla Dente
Reality, Theatre and Human Rights

The dramatic text constructs possible worlds.[1] Like any other literary text, it does so through more complex codes of expression which bring into play several channels of perception, in which the text is only one of the codes involved, whilst also in performance, using objects from reality to construct its fictional worlds. The tension between reality and fiction is essential to theatre at least in so far as the performance uses a space, a time and real bodies, to predicate a fictional space, time and characters. Moreover, theatre also uses the dynamics of real processes of reception that the play triggers in the audience, in the neurological and psychological dimensions and in that of the intellectual acquisition of knowledge. When theatre constructs or reconstructs worlds which are anyway closely related to reality, it creates an equally close relationship with reception, since the bond with reality can be recognised only by those who can have an awareness of it, because they are experiencing it, have experienced it in the past and remember it, or because they possess cultural references to it. This relationship, therefore, must clearly be included in the context of communication between stage and audience and this implies that reality is hierarchically superior or rather "prior" to what is fictitious.

This is our starting point, from which we can engage in a more general reflection on how we conceptualize the real; the concept of mimesis of the real and its communication, the communicative strategies that the theatre uses and which for the audience refer to a determinate cultural-historical context which places it, in the last resort, in the position of witness. Auslander had considered this process of conceptualization, which led him to formulate the concept of "liveness," the effect of mediated immediacy in the process of performance reception, which might be identified as a species of "mimesis."[2] In like terms, Barthes in *S/Z*[3] spoke of the "effect of reality" which concentrates on the techniques of authentication in the representation of reality. This authentication takes

---

1 See, among others, Umberto Eco, *Trattato di semiotica generale* (Milano: Bompiani, 1975); Keir Elam, *The Semiotics of Theatre and Drama* [1980] (London: Routledge, 2002); Juri Lotman, *La struttura del testo poetico* [1970] (Milano: Mursia, 1976).
2 Philip Auslander, *Liveness. Performance in a Mediatized Culture* (London: Routledege, 1999), 2: "Live performance is the category of cultural production most directly affected by the dominance of media."
3 Roland Barthes, *S/Z* [1970], trans. Richard Miller (London: Jonathan Cape, 1975).

into consideration, in a non-contradictory way, the perceptive and psychological dimensions of the witness and the spectator. Commenting on Auslander, Borowski and Sugiera argue: "[He] claims that eliminating illusion by abandoning all strategies of engendering a fictional, enclosed world and replacing them with self-referential actions and situations was to give the spectators the impression that they can get in touch with an undeniably palpable reality."[4]

The construction of reality implies a constant interrogation not least with questions of perception and validity and with questions of temporality, too. The process of dramatic writing and theatrical staging must do the same. The desire to explore the nature of reality in European theatre particularly in the consideration of marginalized groups, such as the working class, women, ethnic minorities began in the 1960s. Such an engagement leads also to broader cultural responsibilities, as Homi Bhabha has suggested taking issue with Hannah Arendt's original defence of the public sphere as a ground for such mimetic exercises.[5] It is possible here to discern two alternative strategies, a first which is intended to protect human life and health, without distinctions in terms of race, nationality, sex, religious or political beliefs, and a second one, more recent, which evinces a more culturally sensitive approach to humanitarian operations. Modern human – rights discourse operates between the two, and so do modern dramatists.

Realist drama of course seeks to deflect the attention of its audience from mediation, as very obviously does contemporary documentary theatre. It is not a question of trying to distance the perception of the text from reality with irony, but rather of embracing reality conscious of the dimension of the conflict which this has with the subjectivity represented. Recent conceptualizations of hyperrealism suggest an interesting dimension.[6] Donnarumma argues that the "hypermodern, which has abandoned faith in progress, does not completely believe in its promises of happiness. It is a neurotic compulsion which neutralizes its own idols [...] at the very moment that it raises them up."[7] More familiar dramatic strategies, Donnarumma continues, commonly "fail to grip, go haywire, the ferocious fairytales of the age of Reagan and Thatcher long extinguished," for which reason it is possible to assert that "the hypermodern is the answer and in part the conse-

---

4 Mateusz Borowski and Małgorzata Sugiera eds., *Fictional Realities/Real Fictions* (Newcastle: Cambridge Scholars Publishing, 2007), X.

5 Homi Bhabha, *The Location of Culture* (London: Routledge, 1994).

6 See for example Raffaele Donnarumma, "Hypermodernità: ipotesi per un congedo dal postmoderno" in *Allegoria* XXIII. 64 (July/December 2011): 15–50. Donnarumma cites, among others, Gilles Lipovetsky and Sébastien Charles, *Les Temps hypermodernes* (Paris: Grasset, 2004); Nicole Aubert ed., *La Société hypermoderne: ruptures et contradictions* (Paris: L'Harmattan, 2011).

7 See Donnarumma, "Hypermodernità," 19. If not otherwise stated, translations are mine.

quence of the postmodern [...]. The prefix *hyper-* thus spawns every possible celebratory nuance, and reveals its anxiety-inducing and intimidating load: the *hyper-* is the imperative of contemporaneity, its performance obsession."[8]

The social dimension of literature has produced forms of political awareness and activity that are imposing, pervasive and immediate in their effect; critical attitudes of the present nurtured by an ethical imperative, again present in literature and in the theatre, in the first instance in the choice of representative themes which testify to civil participation. Where classical theatre provided moral teaching, contemporary performance reconfirms this imperative in terms of an immediate, dramatic encounter between theatre and audience in the presentation of reciprocal images that are designed to emphasize the split between personal experience (aesthetics, ethics and politics) and perception, which the medium (or the media) makes manifest and for which the spectator takes responsibility.[9] Finally the tension between personal experience and collective perception has memory as its common denominator; memory, which is not just "archive" or "history," but also "function," the capacity to address itself to action and to the needs of the present in motion. Memory is connected with identity, and when collectively connected with the present also has an emotionally significant cohesive force. From this perspective memory can strengthen and stabilize social or collective identity around respective political and ethical frames.[10]

In this context we can turn to a particular species of modern theatre which has found recent expression most obviously on the London stage during the last two decades. In truth this species presents at least two sub-species: documentary theatre and verbatim theatre. The former systematically explores the use of the "document" and emphasizes the relation of the textual and the extra-textual. The second presents a direct word-for-word re-articulation of events, commonly verbal and simulating the presence of the source and a superficially unmediated access to the content, intimate or not, of completely conscious feelings and thoughts. In both cases the question of transparency is pressing, for even at the moment of presenting a "real" fact, neither dramatic form can exclude the role of the dramatist in the selection of materials, their disposition in the economy of the text and the conventions used for scripting and performance; elements which are at the audience's disposal in the process of interpretation. In the case of "verbatim theatre" the prospective distance from reality is even greater, since it involves presenting verbal acts of real people that report events that have actually taken

---

8 See Donnarumma, "Hypermodernità," 19–20.
9 See Hans-T. Lehmann, *Postdramatic Theatre*, trans. K. Jürs-Munby (Oxon: Routledge, 2006).
10 Lotman, *La struttura del testo poetico*.

place, and each of the passages is potentially subject to manipulation, conscious or unconscious. All this seems to obscure the voice of the dramatist in the process of the construction of the text, yet the dramatist remains the residual source for the selection and disposition of materials in the text, the elements that the audience uses to establish its interpretive process. In a long interview with Dan Steward and Will Hammond, Nicolas Kent, artistic director of Tricycle Theatre explained the advantages of addressing current issues with a play rather than with a piece of written journalism:

> [a]ny inquiry is rather like a good courtroom drama, because they always follow the same narrative form: you lay out the circumstances first, then what happened, and the reaction of the authorities to what happened, and then the examination of whether those people reacted correctly or incorrectly; then they come to some form of conclusion within the inquiry before the inquiry report is written [...]. The other thing that lends itself to the theatre is the cross-examination process, because it is often a process of conflict and it is obviously very interesting for people to see someone state something with enormous confidence, and then to see a lawyer disrupt that confidence, or make them reconsider the evidence, or get to the truth.[11]

One of the first examples of modern documentary-theatre broadly conceived was *The Colour of Justice*[12] (1999), which re-enacts a controversial parliamentary enquiry into the investigation of the murder of black teenager Stephen Lawrence. It was first produced in Kent's Tricycle Theatre. Another is *Bloody Sunday*[13] (2005) which revisits one of the most critical episodes in the "Troubles" in Northern Ireland, the killing of 13 Irish Catholics by British soldiers in Belfast in 1972. A number of the most provocative examples of this sub-species of theatre have come from the pen of David Hare, including *The Permanent Way*,[14] a play from 2003 on the crisis of the British railways, and more recently *Stuff Happens*[15] which invited the audience to contemplate the Iraq war.

Another still more recent example is Victoria Brittain and Gillian Slovo's, *Guantánamo: "Honor Bound to Defend Freedom"*[16] (2004), which addressed the

---

11 Interview to Nicolas Kent by Dan Steward and Will Hammond, in *Verbatim* (London: Oberon Books 2008), 139.

12 Richard Norton Taylor ed., *The Colour of Justice* (London: Oberon Books, 1999).

13 Richard Norton Taylor, *Bloody Sunday: Scene from the Saville Inquiry* (London: Oberon Books, 2005).

14 David Hare, *The Permanent Way* (London: Faber and Faber, 2003).

15 David Hare, *Stuff Happens* (London: Faber and Faber, 2005).

16 Victoria Brittain and Gillian Slovo, *Guantánamo "Honor Bound to Defend Freedom"* (London: Oberon Books, 2005): further references in the text, abbreviated as *G*.

internment of terrorism suspects. *Guantánamo* is very obviously a campaigning play with an immediate political agenda, dramatically interrogating the audience in regard to associated questions of public and private "testimony" in the context of international responses to the traumatic events of 9/11. Following 9/11, suspected terrorists captured by allied forces were held at the American naval base of Guantanamo in Cuba. This "solution" to the problem of prisoners constructed the possibility of their indefinite detention without trial in a military base outside the national territory and the jurisdiction of the United States. The jurisprudential incongruity of this situation, together with the secrecy with which all the quasi-juridical procedures had been conceived and executed, clearly lent itself to dramatic expression, something emphasized by the impossibility of monitoring of the conditions of detention and "non-conventional" military protocols of interrogation. The evident breach of international law and convention, including the possibility of collateral breaches of human rights and torture conventions, was subsequently reinvested by documentary record, most obviously in the form of detainee interviews, and interviews with other interested parties, including lawyers and politicians.

Guantanamo and *Guantánamo* ask fundamental questions not just of international and domestic jurisprudence, but of what we mean by "human" rights. In the immediate aftermath of 9/11 President Bush openly, and notoriously, proclaimed that his country was at war.[17] The definition of "proactive war" or "attack" must be contemplated in the context of the Geneva Conventions; which imply the necessity for an adversary to be identifiable. Terrorist acts do not here conform. It is no coincidence that the United Nations Security Council, after examining the facts, approved only a "recommendation" to maintain peace and international security. The US government, however, claimed a right to self-defence and to attack Afghanistan on the grounds that the leader of Al Qaeda was residing in that country; something subsequently confirmed by the Court of the District of Columbia. Among the internees of Guantanamo, therefore, a differentiated regime could be created for those deemed to be combatants and non-combatants. It can however be said that the Geneva Convention, in its third version, in Article 4(A), meticulously lists those who have the right to be considered POWs, while Article 5 extends this right even in cases where the precise

---

17 See George W. Bush, "Statement by the President in His Address to the Nation," September 11, 2001, available at http://www.whitehouse.gov/news/releases/2001/09/20010911-16.html (August 21, 2013); and George W. Bush, "President urges Readiness and Patience," September 15, 2001, available at http://www.whitehouse.gov/news/releases/2001/09/20010915-4.html (August 21, 2013).

categorization of detainees remains judicially unclear.[18] Although the role of "state" is not recognized in the context of Al Qaeda under the terms of the third Geneva Convention, other legal arguments can be applied to protect prisoners. Moreover in Britain the 1988 Human Rights Act obliges public authorities, including courts, to act in compliance with the European Convention. Section 7 permits individuals to challenge alleged acts that are incompatible with the Convention. The fact that five of the Guantanamo detainees were British citizens led to the British Court of Appeal contemplating the breach of the Human Rights Act in November 2002. The simple fact that the Court was willing to confirm jurisdiction is significant. The matter remained rather unsettled, however, in US law, leading many commentators to coin the metaphor of a legal "black hole." Following the decision to accept habeas corpus application in US courts, a Military Commission was set up in August 2004, only to be suspended three months later when a federal judge in Washington judged the Commission to be a violation of the Geneva Conventions. Successive Obama administrations have sought to ameliorate the situation, but with little success. Guantanamo has come to represent something of a diplomatic embarrassment, whilst at the same time promoting much heated consideration amongst lawyers and academics both within and without the US.

It is here that the questioning of the reality/fiction dialectic in *Guantánamo* becomes pertinent. The play is presented as a series of interwoven monologues. But this does not preclude the editorial presence of the writer. Moreover, as Ian Ward points out,[19] terrorism is a subject that resonates with those dramatic images presented in alternative media:

---

18 Geneva Convention III of August 12, 1949, available at http://www.icrc.org/ihl (August 21, 2013). Article 4 specifies that the following can be considered "Prisoners of War": members of the Armed Forces, militias or voluntary bodies that are part of the Armed Forces, resistance movements in the territory or outside the territory which operate under the command of a person in charge, recognisable at a distance, openly equipped with weapons, operational according to recognised warfare techniques; allies. Those assigned to logistical and medical support, journalists, "contractors," and all duly authorized members of the Merchant Navy or civil aviation companies. Civilians who take up arms to defend themselves in the event of invasion of their territory are also covered. It is likewise clear that in all other cases, if an isolated individual, non-combatant, takes an active part in combat, he/she may commit a war crime and face criminal prosecution. This is the situation regarding "unprivileged belligerents," except what is contained in art. 5 which reads: "Should any doubt arise as to whether persons, having committed a belligerent act and having fallen into the hands of the enemy, belong to any of the categories enumerated in Article 4, such persons shall enjoy the protection of the present Convention until such time as their status has been determined by a competent tribunal."
19 Ian Ward, "The Play of Terror" in *Law and Art. Justice, Ethics and Aesthetics*, ed. Oren Ben-Dor (London: Routledge, 2013), 177–187.

The common affinity with spectacle and enchantment binds terrorist and dramatist together. So much was noted by Harold Pinter in his excoriating critique of the "war on terror" articulated in his 2005 Nobel Acceptance Speech. But there is as Pinter noted a critical inversion. Where the politician pretends to "truth" in order to weave a "tapestry of lies," the dramatist seeks recourse to the literary imagination in order to cut through the deception, and to try to retrieve our "moral sensibility."[20]

In this perspective, docu-theatre, based on documents, together with verbatim theatre, which is based on direct testimony, must be reconceived in order to assist in this process of reinvesting moral sensibility. The testimonies reported in *Guantánamo* were collected in the spring of 2004, just a month after the release of the detainees, and presented on stage when popular debate was still urgent and heated amongst a disorientated public. The play was clearly intended to intervene in this debate. The context was moreover ideal for bringing to the stage facts that must appear to be live and immediate rather than otherwise manipulated.[21]

The text of *Guantánamo* begins with Lord Justice Steyn's Mann Lecture given on November 23, 2003, as indicated to the audience on the dot matrix:

LORD JUSTICE STEYN: The most powerful democracy is detaining hundreds of suspected foot soldiers of the Taliban in a legal black hole at the United States naval base at Guantanamo Bay, where they await trial on capital charges by military tribunals. This episode must be put in context. [...]. But it is a recurring theme in history that [...] even liberal democracies adopt measures infringing human rights in ways that are wholly disproportionate to the crisis. Ill-conceived, rushed legislation is passed [...] The purpose of holding the prisoners at Guantanamo Bay was and is to put then beyond the rule of law, beyond the protection of any court [...].

---

20 Ward, "The Play of Terror," 178. Quotation from Harold Pinter, Nobel Prize for Literature, Acceptance Speech, 2005, published by *The Guardian*, December 8, 2005 (9–13), but also his acceptance speech of the Laurea Honoris Causa in Literature and Philosophy, University of Florence, September 8, 2001.

21 Remember in this regard the CNN footage of the landing by U.S. marines on the beaches of Mogadishu on the night of 8 December 1992. "The following night members of 1st Force Reconnaissance Company, 7th Platoon landed in three separate teams to control the beach and port facilities. The team on the beach were surprised to meet members of the news media who made their job difficult with crowds of cameramen using bright lights to get footage of the wet, camouflaged Marines who were now brilliantly lit up in the dark night. Soon however, regular Marines from the 15th Marine Expeditionary Unit arrived and attention shifted to them and the Force Recon Marines were able to finish their original mission of ensuring two anti-aircraft guns spotted on satellite were inoperable and then securing the runway for assault. Four SEALs conducted surf observations and initial terminal guidance for the Marines' landing craft." Report available at www.specialoperations.com/Operations/Restore_Hope/operation1.htm (August 21, 2013).

The regime applicable at Guantanamo Bay was created by a succession of presidential orders. [...]. The military will act as interrogators, prosecutors, defense counsel, judges, and, when death sentences are imposed, as executioners.[...] in all respects subject to decisions of the president as Commander in Chief [...].
As STEYN leaves house light dim. (*G*, 7–8)

The orientation is strong. Later, in the second act, the text introduces a transcription of a long press conference by the U.S. Secretary of Defence, Donald Rumsfeld, interwoven with questions and provocative comments by Gareth Peirce, a British lawyer who specialized in associated miscarriage of justice cases, including earlier cases involving the alleged IRA terrorists, the so-called 'Guildford Four' and 'Birmingham Six'. To quote from the play:

DONALD RUMSFELD *in press conference*
RUMSFELD We were able to capture and detain a large number of people who had been through training camps and had learned a whole host of skills as to how they could kill innocent people. (*G*, 30)

They are not POW's, they will not be determined to be POW's. (*G*, 31)

The play concludes with a quotation from Peirce, alongside that of Major Michael Mori, a military lawyer who was appointed to the defence of an Australian detainee named Hicks, and then Lord Steyn's closing invocation of a sermon given at Lincoln's Inn by the seventeenth century metaphysical poet John Donne. The audience is left with an invitation to Islamic prayer, and a voice over by the director of a press release at the moment of the release of the first five British prisoners which, having identified them individually, goes on to specify that they were part of the 650 prisoners in Guantanamo. In particular: "Most are from countries with even less power than Britain to influence events. They are held indefinitely. / *Exit*" (*G*, 59).

Cleverly the text utilizes strategies of rhythmic scanning found in calls to Islamic prayer, of ritualistic suggestion, and by the juxtaposition of silence and voices, and which contribute to maintaining a marked sense of rituality of the whole. Part of the more general orchestration is also the balance perceived by the audience between the emotionally dominant position of the dramaturgical construction, with its exploration of individual suffering and private injustice which originates from the interviews, and the need to keep the audience involved with an autonomous reflection of the broader context.

In sum then, this theatre of crisis, which is a crisis of the impotence of the law, of the individual right to a trial, and of human rights, but which is also an epistemological crisis, produces forms of alternative civil and literary activity, which can take the shape of campaigns of solidarity or expressions of critical comment. A documentary poetics has very obvious extra-literary practical, moral and civil aspirations. To quote Donnarumma once again:

> Hypermodern documentary poetics are completely distinct from naturalistic poetics: while the naturalists intended to produce a work that was itself, also, a document, hiding and reabsorbing the sources in the fabric of the narration [...], now the source is exhibited in its literalness and in its otherness. The account thus becomes multi-vocal by statute, and tends to multiply the hallmarks of responsibility.[22]

Any question of responsibility can only be applied to subjective mediation; that is to say to those cases in which the "other" text is not a document, but a testimony. This document/testimony substitution is possible because the aim of the testimony is directed at the truth, superordinate to the multiple aims which the document may assume. The document aims at reality, the testimony at the truth. The witness as the source of the story realized on stage is involved directly with this responsibility. An obvious comparator here would be Holocaust literature, where there is considerable focus on the nature of memorial testimony. The witness speaks to affirm the truth, that which is therefore ethically right, to testify to the fact and not the law. Reality pre-exists the testimony of itself, but paradoxically is incapable of establishing itself if it is not certified by it.

The witness incarnates the assumption of truth and takes responsibility for it, and has as an exclusive aim this communication. Testimony is mediation between the world investigated individually and in writing, a transparent mediation that provides a glimpse of an irreducible substance beyond itself, the factual reality that belongs to a world that is bigger than that of the subjects implicated in the story, a world that includes the audience in its own collective failure, and makes it an accessory to the fact. With its mechanisms of documentary realism and testimonial realism it lays bare the distinction and at the same time the permeability between fiction and non-fiction which is indispensable to the interpretive process of the dramaturgical text. As Ian Ward suggests, in the context of *Guantanamo*: "Literature more broadly and drama more closely have a particular capacity for raising [this] responsibility, for making us think rather more deeply not merely about terrorism, but, more importantly, about our response to terrorism."[23]

In fact testimony, directly related to various media genres, is crucial to culture in that it invites collective consideration of individual experience. *Guantánamo* underlines precisely this. Speaking more broadly, Carol Martin suggests:[24]

---

22 Donnarumma, "Hypermodernità," 27.
23 Ward, "The Play of Terror," 187.
24 Carol Martin, "Bodies of Evidence," *TDR* 50.3 (2006): 8–15, 9.

> How events are remembered, written, archived, staged, and performed helps determine the history they become. More than enacting history, although it certainly does that, documentary theatre also has the capacity to stage historiography. [...] It directly intervenes in the creation of history by unsettling the present.

Following this interaction between theatre and recent history, the individual trauma of the characters is shared. It assumes the characteristics and the relevance of a collective cultural trauma. Such a trauma demands that the spectator lives within a real experience insofar as it appeals to his or her obligations in regard to history and culture. Ultimately the change nurtured in the spectator resembles that of an active cultural mobility which admits of no return to the past.

Ian Ward
The Rights and Wrongs of Marriage: Article 16.2 UDHR and the Case of Edith Dombey

Article 16.2 of the United Nations Declaration on Human Rights states that: "Marriage shall be entered into only with the free and full consent of the intending spouses." Articles 16.1 and 16.3 are rather better known. They state respectively that: "Men and women of a full age, without any limitation due to race, nationality or religion, have the right to marry and to found a family. They are entitled to equal rights to marriage, during marriage and its dissolution." And: "The family is the natural and fundamental group unit of society and is entitled to protection by society and the State." Article 16.2 conversely remains relatively obscure. There is no equivalent in the European Convention, for which reason there is no equivalent in the British Human Rights Act either. This is not to say that the sentiment of Article 16.2 does not resonate today. Current debates regarding the efficacy or otherwise of what are variously termed "arranged" or "forced" marriages suggests that the resonance remains strong. The purpose of this essay is not however to engage these more recent debates, or indeed the immediate context within which Article 16.2 was originally drafted. It is rather to reach back precisely one hundred years in order to contemplate a rather different if no less "forced" marriage; that of Edith Dombey. The marriage of Edith Dombey, it might be suggested, was precisely the kind of marriage which Article 16.2 is supposed to prevent; except of course that it is also precisely the same kind of marriage which no amount of well-intentioned jurisprudential rhetoric is, in reality, ever likely to preclude.

Edith Dombey was married in 1848. It was not of course a real marriage. It was a fictional marriage, the collapse of which lay at the heart of what many scholars have suggested is Charles Dickens's first serious novel *Dombey and Son*; serious insofar as it engaged more obviously pressing questions of social justice, of the kind which were less prominent in the more comic tones of *Pickwick* or even *Nicholas Nickleby*. It was certainly the first novel in which Dickens enjoined wider contemporary anxieties regarding the "condition" of the middle class English family; debates which as we shall shortly see ultimately found statutory realisation in the shape of the 1857 Divorce Act, and then in due course a succession of later Matrimonial Causes and Matrimonial Property Acts, along with a series of tangential Infant Custody Acts. The middle decades of the nineteenth century witnessed a revolution in English matrimonial law. What is immediately striking, however, is that these reforms were intended to deal with the consequences of matrimonial breakdown. The problem for Edith Dombey however, as we shall again see, lay in the fact that she felt obliged to marry Paul Dombey, a man she did not love and in time came to loathe and who, more pertinently, she never wished to marry.

1 Wives for Sale

Few mid-Victorian women, middle class or otherwise, craved anything other than to be married. Even Frances Power Cobbe conceded that marriage was "manifestly the Creator's plan for humanity."[1] Once married of course a wife would expect, and be expected, to assume the requisite responsibilities of the "angel of the house."[2] She would bake and breed. Countless domestic manuals confirmed as much, as famously did John Ruskin in his lecture "Of Queen's Gardens." A "true" wife, Ruskin was keen to affirm, should be valued as a "helpmate" rather than a "slave." Where the husband is the "doer, the creator, the discoverer, the speculator," the wife is designed for "sweet ordering, arrangement, and decision."[3] Observe these defining principles of "separate spheres" and domestic harmony should be assured; or so Ruskin's argument ran. By the middle of the century however it was becoming ever more apparent that such fanciful hopes bore little resemblance to the altogether harsher realities of far too many abusive and dysfunctional Victorian marriages. Novel readers had suspected this for some time; the respective journeys taken by the likes of Anne Bronte's Helen Huntingdon and George Eliot's Janet Dempster being only too grimly familiar. After the establishment of the new Divorce Court in 1858 any residual doubts were surely removed. The Court quickly assumed the role of a legal "confessional" a place of "hideous revelations" as Cobbe confirmed.[4] The Victorian home was not, in far too many cases it seemed, a happy one. Two years after its establishment, Queen

---

1 Frances Power Cobbe, "Celibacy v Marriage" in *Criminals, Idiots, Women and Minors: Victorian Writing by Women on Women*, ed. Susan Hamilton (London: Broadview, 1995), 83.
2 The metaphor was most famously articulated in Coventry Patmore's poem "The Angel of the House." Patmore's "angel" was in fact love, or domestic harmony, but it became Victorian cultural shorthand for the ideal housewife.
3 In John Ruskin, *Selected Writings* (Oxford: Oxford University Press, 2004), 158.
4 For Cobbe's comment, see her "Celibacy v Marriage," 82. See also Barbara Leckie, *Culture and Adultery: the Novel, the Newspaper and the Law 1857–1914* (Philadelphia: Pennsylvania University Press, 1999), 67 and Gail Savage, "Erotic Stories and Public Decency: Newspaper Reporting of Divorce Proceedings in England," *Historical Journal* 41 (1998): 511–28, 513–14, quoting Lord Chancellor Campbell's misgivings as regards the establishment of the new Court, that "like Frankenstein, I am afraid of the monster I have called into existence."

Victoria wrote to chastise her Lord Chancellor, observing that "none of the worst French novels" were as likely to prejudice the "public morals of the country" as salacious newspaper reports of proceedings brought before the new Court.[5]

There was moreover a wider context within which discussions as regards the nature of marriage and the reform of matrimonial law evolved. A nascent "question of women" had already begun to take shape in the preceding decades, a variant perhaps of the wider "condition of England" interrogatory. Not everyone was persuaded of the wisdom of framing such a question. George Eliot was famously moved to observe that "There is no question on which I am more inclined to hold my peace and learn, than on the Woman Question."[6] Others were however less discreet. At an extreme could be found those few, like most famously John Stuart Mill, who doubted the very institution of marriage itself. A wife, Mill opined, was the "bond-servant of her husband: no less so, as far as legal obligation goes, than slaves commonly so called." There was, he concluded notoriously, "no legal slaves" left in England "except the mistress of every house."[7] Mill's voice was not quite a lone one. It was joined by those of nascent feminists such as Mona Caird who deployed the same rhetorical trope advanced, in their different ways, by Mill and Ruskin. Writing in 1888, Caird likened the European marriage "market" to the "Mongolian market-place" with its "iron cage, wherein women are held in bondage, suffering moral starvation, while the thoughtless gather round to taunt and to insult their lingering memory."[8] What was distinctive in the critique of the marriage "market" ventured by the likes of Caird and Mill was the focus not on how to end unhappy marriages, but on how to prevent them.

To an extent those who advanced the case for "companionate" marriages shared the same aspiration. Any devotee of Eliot or Gaskell, for example, would have been left in little doubt as to the greater benefits of a "companionate" marriage. Here again however the problem was not perceived to lie in the institution of marriage, but in the practice of making them. It was a view which, as we shall see, would have been similarly discerned by readers of Dickens's *Dombey*. Even as she witnesses the violent fragmentation of her own father's marriage, Florence Dombey desires nothing more than to be married to her beloved Walter, whilst the church beadle Mr Sownds confirms, with a Burkean flourish, "We must

---

5 Quoted in Lawrence Stone, *The Road to Divorce* (Oxford: Oxford University Press, 1990), 295.
6 In Nicola Thompson, *Reviewing Sex: Gender and the Reception of Victorian Novels* (London: Macmillan, 1996), 123.
7 John Stuart Mill, *The Subjection of Women* (New York: Hackett, 1988), 32, 86.
8 Mona Caird, "Marriage" in Hamilton, *Women*, 279.

marry 'em... and keep the country going."[9] Before we embark on a closer reading of *Dombey* and more particularly the marriage of Edith and Paul Dombey, it is worth pausing to note another fictive critique of marital practice, in the opinion of many subsequent critics the most caustic of its generation, William Makepeace Thackeray's *The Newcomes*.

The Newcomes was Thackeray's last great novel, published in serial form between 1853 and 1855.[10] It tells the story of the newly moneyed Newsome family as it tries to climb the social ladder of mid-Victorian England. Central to the realisation of this aspiration is the contracting of strategically suitable marriages. The Newcome "trump" is the beautiful Ethel, who is duly touted before various prospective aristocratic matches. Ethel however is rebellious, in one of the most famous scenes in the novel drawing a comparison between the exhibiting of paintings and the exhibiting of daughters, commenting to her indomitable match-making aunt:

> We young ladies of the world, when we are exhibiting, ought to have little green tickets pinned on our backs, with "Sold" written on them; it would prevent trouble and any future haggling you know. Then at the end of the season the owner would come and carry us home.[11]

Later that evening as the Newsomes assembled for dinner "Ethel appeared with a bright green ticket pinned to the front of her white muslin frock."[12] Ethel manages to avoid the variously gruesome matches proposed by her aunt. Her sister-in-law Clara is however altogether less fortunate; finding herself "sold" to Ethel's abusive brother Barnes. The account of Clara's ultimate flight from Barnes into the arms of her lover Lord Highgate, and its consequences, gave Thackeray the opportunity to inscribe one of the most caustic narratives of a criminal conversation suit in nineteenth century English literature, the case of *Newcome v. Lord Highgate*.

Critics have surmised that Thackeray may have been influenced in his devastating critique of middle-class marital practice by John Boyd Kinnear's notorious essay on the subject. The grotesque narratives written into *The Newcomes* were, as Kinnear confirmed, only too real:

---

9 Charles Dickens, *Dombey and Son* (London: Penguin, 2002), 868: further references in the text, abbreviated as *D*.

10 And his most substantial, the baggiest of the Victorian "baggy monsters," as Henry James put it, whilst also acknowledging that it was very probably Thackeray's masterpiece. See his *The Art of the Novel* (London: Scribner, 1934), 84.

11 William Makepeace Thackeray, *The Newcomes* (London: Dent, 1994), 277.

12 Thackeray, *The Newcomes*, 278.

Frequent the fashionable London drive at the fashionable hour, and there he will see the richest and the most shameful woman-market in the world. Men stand by rails, criticising with perfect impartiality and equal freedom while women drive slowly past, some for hire, some for sale – in marriage – these last with their careful mothers at their side, to reckon the value of the biddings and prevent lots from going off below the reserved price.[13]

As the century progressed the allusion to prostitution would come to replace that of slavery in critical commentary and literature. As we shall shortly see it found a sharp expression in Dickens's *Dombey*.

Once again however, it was the practice of marriage not the idea that generated such contempt. Marriage should be reformed, not abrogated. The legal reforms enacted in the 1857 Act were intended to do this. But their focus was again reactive. The Act was intended to deal with the consequences of matrimonial dissolution, as in large part were supplementary Matrimonial Property and Infant Custody Acts. No one, or at least no one in Westminster, countenanced the idea of legislation written to preserve women like Ethel Newcome or Clara Newcome from the demeaning horrors of the marriage market. The very idea would have been insupportable. The force of law, it would have loudly declaimed, was not to be summoned to interfere with either the course of true love or the entrenchment of familial alliances. The thought that secondary legislation might be written to protect women, and men, from 'forced' marriages might have seemed credible in 1948, if perhaps only just. It was not, despite all the rhetorical support for 'companionate' alternatives, in 1848. But if no one imagined such a law, they did however continue to muse on the consequences of its absence.

2 The Marriage of Edith Dombey

It is, as noted before, a critical commonplace to suggest that *Dombey and Son* was Dickens's first serious novel, at least the first in which he asked serious questions about the "condition" of England.[14] This was certainly the impression of contemporary admirers such as Thackeray and Dickens's first biographer, John Forster. The novel, as the narrator is quick to point out, is about "dark shapes." Perhaps

---

13 From his *The Social Position of Women in the Present Age*, quoted in Mary Shanley, *Feminism, Marriage and the Law: Victorian England 1850–1895* (Princeton, NJ: Princeton University Press, 1989), 62.

14 See, perhaps most influentially, Frank Raymond Leavis and Queenie Leavis*Dickens the Novelist* (London: Penguin, 1994), 22, and Katherine Tillotson, *"Dombey and Son"* in *Dickens: Modern Judgements*, ed. Anthony Dyson (London: Macmillan, 1968), 158–61, 179.

the darkest, certainly the most notorious, of its dark passages is found in chapter forty-seven, when Dombey, infuriated by the behaviour of his second wife Edith, lashes out and strikes his daughter Florence. It is as this point that Dickens famously raises a spectre:

> Oh, for a good spirit who would take the house-tops off, with a more potent and benignant hand that the lame demon in the tale, and show a Christian people what dark shapes issue from amidst their homes, to swell the retinue of the Destroying Angel as he moves forth among them. (*D*, 702)

It is an invocation which resonances with the sentiment found on the preface to Anne Bronte's similar account of marital violence, *The Tenant of Wildfell Hall*; the determination to bring before the Victorian reading public the "truth," no matter how indecorous and distasteful. Thirty thousand readers followed the violent disintegration of Paul Dombey's marriage month by month for the best part of two years between 1848 and 1850.

Edith Granger never wanted to marry Paul Dombey, and it is never really clear why Dombey wanted to marry Edith either. As the narrator observes "Dombey and Son had often dealt in hides, but never in hearts" (*D*, 12). The eager maker of their match is the egregious Mrs Skewton, Edith's mother. The Grangers are broke, their one hope of financial salvation being the conveniently widowed Edith. Dombey conversely is rich, very rich, and persuaded that a man of his standing really ought to have a wife, preferably a respectable and beautiful one, like the only too available Edith Granger who, it is reported, is of good "blood" (*D*, 321). The pair are entirely incompatible, a fact exploited by Dombey's scheming business manager Carker who aspires to seduce Edith. In reality Edith despises Carker almost as much as she comes to despise her husband. But she is fatefully prepared to toy with the possibility if only to torture Dombey. It is when Dombey discovers that Edith has left the marital home, apparently intending to elope with Carker, that he turns to violence and assaults Florence, convinced that she has somehow assisted in his wife's desertion, "since they had always been in league" (*D*, 721).

It is not the first time that Edith has been "bought" by a husband, as she informs her mother. Her first marriage was similarly contracted, her first husband dying rather inconveniently before "his inheritance descended on him" and so leaving Edith penniless:

> There is no slave in the market: there is no horse in a fair: so shown and offered and examined and paraded, Mother, as I have been, for ten shameful years... Is it not so? Have I been made a bye-word of all kinds of men? Have fools, have profligates, have boys, have dotards, dangled after me, and one by one rejected me, and fallen off, because you were too

plain with all your cunning: yes, and too true, with all those false pretences: until we have almost come to be notorious? ... Have I been hawked and vended here and there, until the last grain of self-respect is dead within me, and loathe myself? (*D*, 432)

Edith's complaint is of course precisely that which would be articulated just a few years later by Thackeray's Ethel Newcome. Dickens, moreover, invokes both of the allusions commonly made in contemporary literature. First, Edith identifies herself with the slave-market:

I have been offered and rejected, put up and appraised, until my very soul has sickened. I have not had an accomplishment or grace that might have been a resource to me, but it has been paraded and vended to enhance my value, as if the common crier had called it through the streets... I suffered myself to be sold, as infamously as any woman with a halter round her neck is sold in any market-place. (*D*, 823)

Second, she considers herself to have been prostituted in marriage. To confirm this particular allusion, Dickens aligns the narrative of Edith Dombey with that of Alice Marwood, one of Carker's previous lovers, who is now reduced to selling her body on the streets. Dickens was, of course, famously interested in the fate of "fallen" women, taking a prominent role in governing the rescue which he established with Alice Burdett Coutts at Urania Cottage; at precisely the same time, it might be noted, as he was writing *Dombey*.[15] His commentary on the sad case of Alice Marwood moreover leaves little doubt as regards his contempt for the role of the law in alleviating the condition of such "fallen angels":

There was a criminal called Alice Marwood – a girl still, but deserted and outcast. And she was tried, and she was sentenced. And lord, how the gentlemen in the court talked about it! And how grave the judge was, on her duty, and on her having perverted the gifts of nature – as if he didn't know better than anybody there, that they had been made curses to her! – and how he preached about the strong arm of the Law – so very strong to save her, when she was an innocent and helpless little wretch! (*D*, 531)

The thought that Dickens was a critic of the law or least of the practice of law in mid-nineteenth century England is not new. As he penned the final passages to *Dombey and Son*, he was already sketching out the plot for *Bleak House*. The question however remains as to whether Dickens really thought that legal reform could do that much to save women like Alice Marwood and Edith Dombey from their respective, seemingly rather different but ultimately intimately related, falls.

---

15 See Jenny Hartley, *Charles Dickens and the House of Fallen Women* (London: Methuen, 2009), 10–11, 43.

3 The Limits of Article 16.2

There is of course a necessary conceit in the contemplation of a UDHR right in the context of a mid-Victorian novel. The world had changed rather obviously in the century that lay between the publication of *Dombey* and the enactment of the UDHR. The problem with rights however has not, and the question as to the practical efficacy of an Article such as 16B UDHR retains its pertinence. Critics of rights commonly seize on precisely these kinds of questions. If there had been an equivalent Article in force, either in a universal "declaration" or in domestic implementing legislation, would it have been likely to help Edith Dombey or the thousands of young women, real or fictional, who found themselves caught in the same unenviable position; obliged, by reason of parental pressure or economic necessity to marry a prospectively violent boor such as Paul Dombey? And the answer is most probably no.

In his renowned 1993 lecture on the subject of human rights, Richard Rorty intimated exactly this. In terms which echoed those found in countless essays written by critical legal scholars such as Duncan Kennedy, Allan Hutchinson and Mark Tushnet, Rorty suggested that too great a focus on the idea of rights tends to distract attention from the altogether more important questions as to what it means to be human. The energy of liberal anxiety he suggested would be far better directed at refuting instances of "cruelty" than composing erudite academic theses on human rights or it might be inferred drafting grand human rights statutes. But he also suggested something else, something that imports an especial pertinence in the context of this essay. Where jurisprudence might be an appropriate science with which to analyse the idea of a legal right, literature is much better suited to contemplating what it means to be human. A more literate non-foundational idea of human rights, accordingly, would be shaped as an expression of "consciousness," a response to writing, and reading, "sad and sentimental stories," rather than admiring abstruse collections of juridical rights supposedly rooted in some kind of moral imperative.[16]

It is pleasing to imagine Dickens sat in a comfortable chair somewhere in his beloved Garrick Club musing on the recently established UDHR of 1848, perhaps even chatting with Thackeray on the subject of a natural or civil right; provided of course that they were, at that particular moment, on speaking terms. What might Dickens have ventured, for we can be reasonably sure he would have had an

---

16 Richard Rorty, "Human Rights, Rationality and Sentimentality" in *On Human Rights: The Oxford Amnesty Lectures 1993*, eds. Stephen Shute and Susan Hurley (New York: Basic Books, 1993), 111–34.

opinion and been keen to expound it? Dickens's politics have never been easy to pin down. There is a natural tendency to assume that the author of novels such as *Oliver Twist* or *Hard Times* harboured Radical sympathies. It is less easy however to assume that the author of *Dombey and Son* did. Radicalism to the mid-Victorian gentleman of gently Whiggish inclination, such as Dickens, meant something different from what it does to us today. We are however on rather safer ground if we suppose that Dickens might have been something of a rights-sceptic, perhaps even a Rortian liberal ironist. He was certainly persuaded of the strategic value of narrating "sad and sentimental stories" in the cause of improving the lives of those less fortunate that himself; which in mid-nineteenth century England was the overwhelming majority.

Even so, as he contemplated Article 16 it is reasonable to suppose that there was much in the first clause that would have earned a nod of approval; not just the right to marry, but the right to have that marriage dissolved. The 1857 Act was intended, in its in particular way, to enshrine such a right in English law. And there is no reason to believe that he would have discerned anything objectionable in the third clause. It was rare indeed to find any mid-Victorian, male or female, and no matter how radical, who believed anything other than the fact that the family was indeed the "natural and fundamental group of society." The vast panoply of matrimonial law inherited by the mid-Victoran jurist, meanwhile, was testament to the "protection" which the English "State" was prepared to extend to the hallowed institution of the family; the "supreme object of idolatry," as the prominent contemporary jurist Fitzjames Stephen confirmed.[17] Accordingly it is no surprise to find prominent lawyers proclaiming the importance of law in regulating marital matters. In the word of Lord Brougham:

> There is no one branch of law more important, in any point of view, to the great interests of society, and to the personal comforts of its members, than that which regulates the formation and the dissolution of the nuptial contract. No institution indeed more nearly concerns the very foundation of society, or more distinctly marks by its existence the transition from a rude to a civilized state, than that of marriage.[18]

Dickens was, of course, famously critical of certain legal institutions, and certainly not shy in regard to expressing his concerns on paper. *Bleak House* remains one of the great literary critiques of nineteenth century English legal practice. But there is no evidence that he was critical of the thought that law might serve to

---

17 In Karen Chase and Michael Levenson, *The Spectacle of Intimacy: A Public Life for the Victorian Family* (Princeton NJ, Princeton University Press, 2000), 215–16.
18 Quoted in Stone, *Divorce*, 1.

better regulate matters of matrimony or by implication matters of the heart. In this context it is further tempting to suppose that the man who created the characters of Edith and Paul Dombey might have nodded most vigorously of all when he contemplated the sentiments of Article 16.2. Of course whether the sceptic in Dickens would have been prepared to countenance the idea that statements of jurisprudential good-intentions were, in the final analysis, of sufficient practical use is a different matter.

Paola Carbone
Manju Kapur's *Difficult Daughters* and the Cause of Female Literacy in India

Literate men have literate sons;
literate women have literate children.
Old Kerala Wisdom

Educate one man, you educate one person, but
educate a woman and you educate a whole civilization.
Mahatma Gandhi

The Vedas are the oldest texts in the world and Indians claim that their education system is likewise the oldest in the world. The ideals of Vedic education (2500–1500 BC) lie in the liberation (*moksha*) achieved by controlling the mind to fight ignorance, seen as the cause of all worldly suffering. It follows that knowledge belongs to the whole of humankind, that is to both men and women, and is free from any government or political control. The *Rigveda* states: "if one is greater than the other, that does not mean that he has extra bodily organs, but he is greater because his intellect and mind have become enlightened and completed by real education."[1] But under the pressure of foreign invasion and colonization, even the highest ideals underwent alteration, so that contemporary India is a very different reality. At the end of the nineteenth century, it was this open-minded, ancient, Vedic teaching that reformers called on specifically for women who, in the course of Indian history, have undergone gender discrimination and unequal treatment. The Vedic age encouraged education for women (*Yagnopavatini*), who could openly take part in public discussions, officiate over both public and private sacrifices and be present on the battlefield as equals in status to men. And, as for men, the capacity to refine their *karma* was fully recognized. Although transcendence and immanence still walk side by side, and not a single breath eludes either *dharma* (generally translated into English as law, righteousness, truth, justice, morality, consistency, destiny) or tradition, these days women are mainly asked to be wives and mothers.

---

1 Quoted by Ram Nath Sharma and Rajendra Kumar Sharma, *History Of Education In India* (New Delhi: Atlantic Publisher and Distribution, 2004): 5.

Manju Kapur's novel *Difficult Daughters*,[2] published in 1998, focuses on women's fundamental right to education. Briefly, the story takes place over the span of few decades at the crossroads to Indian Independence. The main character Virmati, the eldest of eleven children, is burdened, against her will but following a strong sense of duty, with the responsibility of caring for her exhausted mother and younger siblings. She attends school, finding a female ideal in her cousin Shakuntala, an independent postgraduate who has chosen to put her education before marriage: "With all this reading-writing, girls are getting married later. [...] What is the need to do a job? A woman's *shaan* is in her home" (*DD*, 15–17).

Shakuntala's disappointed mother continually grumbles. While Kasturi, Virmati's mother, disapprovingly judges:

"She's become like a mem, [...] Study means developing the mind for the benefit of the family. I studied too, but my mother would have killed me if I had dared even to want to dress in anything other than was bought for me."
Virmati listened, [...] drawn to Shakuntala, to one whose responsibilities went beyond a husband and children. (*DD*, 17)

For these older women, a girl should never forget that marriage is her destiny, and so, when the time comes, the family "selects"[3] an "educated and homely" fiancé (*DD*, 23) for Virmati. At first the girl accepts her parents' choice, only to realize immediately afterwards that, on the one hand, she wants to continue studying and, on the other, that she is in love with an older neighbour, a professor of literature – Harish – who returns her love but is the dissatisfied husband of an arranged marriage to an illiterate woman named Ganga. After an attempted suicide, Virmati persuades her parents to let her move to Lahore, like Shakuntala, to become a teacher. She gets her degree and starts working as both principle and teacher at a cutting edge school in Sirmur State, only to give everything up when she eventually marries Harish to become his second wife. But, more than anything else, it is through her education that Virmati chalks up a black mark for the entire community: by studying more than any other girl in the family and marry-

---

2 Manju Kapur, *Difficult Daughters* (London: Faber and Faber, 1998): further references in the text, abbreviated as *DD*.
3 As marriages are generally arranged in India by families, Article 16 of the UDHR is not generally respected: Article 16. (1) Men and women of full age, without any limitation due to race, nationality or religion, have the right to marry and to found a family. They are entitled to equal rights as to marriage, during marriage and at its dissolution. (2) Marriage shall be entered into only with the free and full consent of the intending spouses. (3) The family is the natural and fundamental group unit of society and is entitled to protection by society and the State.

ing for love against the consent of her relatives, she has dared to defy the harmony of the patriarchal tradition and the cosmic primary female role of wife and mother. To fully understand the complexity of the character, it must be said that Kapur places her half way between a Sita and a Ganika, two very different Hindu feminine ideals.

Sita is Rama's wife, the pure wife who does not hesitate to leave the comforts of a royal court to serve as companion and complement to her husband in the forest. But she is also asked to throw herself into the fire to prove her faithfulness to her husband. If at first this act was seen as a refusal to submit femininity and dignity to power, later it came to be seen as a symbol of modesty and submissiveness to man. In patriarchal Hindu society, a woman is envisaged as a modest, decent, faithful, loving, silent wife and mother, while she is supposed to take on different roles such as councillor and playmate to her partner.[4] She should conform to the six criteria listed in the famous *sloka* (verses)

> Karyeshu Mantri, Karaneshu Daasi,
> Rupecha Laksmi, Kshamayaa Dharitri,
> Bhojyeshu Mata, Shayentu Rambha
> Shat karma Yukta, Kulu Dharma Patni (Acharya; 351)

which means that for her husband a woman should work like a servant, advise like a minister, feed like a mother, make love like a nymph, be as beautiful as Goddess Lakshmi and forgiving like the earth.

Clearly, a woman is expected to be an almost divine creature, totally devoted to her family. Her entire life is lived within the confines of her home which, in itself, is the source of her true identity, since she *exists* only in relation to her husband and in-laws.[5] It is her fully committed modesty and dependency which engender her with public respect and dignity, her generally appreciated worthi-

---

4 See Amar Nath Prasad, *New Lights on Indian Women Novelists In English* (New Delhi: Sarup & Sons, 2005): 61.

5 Indians explain the differences between sexes as "natural differences" which legitimise different roles inside the couple. A woman needs protecting and strengthening, and according to *Manava Dharma Shastra* (or Manusmiriti, c. 500 BC) she must be defended by her father during maidenhood, by her husband during covertures, and by her sons in widowhood. As a consequence, women are considered safer at home, and they must live under their husband and in-laws' authority. It is true that many women accept their *purdah*, role and rules, and feel threatened by reformers such as Virmati, who become "difficult daughters." The novel offers several examples of this prototype: Kasturi gets married very young and from that moment on she spends her life procreating beyond even her limits of physical tolerance; similarly Harish's first wife, Ganga, spends her life cooking and believing that bearing her husband's children is her only task in life. When she refuses to study as her husband wishes, she cannot possibly imagine that she will be

ness and public virtue. By accepting the role allotted to her by patriarchal society, a woman demonstrates her ability to control her actions and to conform to what is *right* according to her individual Hindu duty (*svadharma*). It is respect for the law (dharma) and individual duty that safeguard peace and harmony in the cosmic order of the *trailokya* (the three worlds: earth, firmament, sky). A Sita sees her rights and honour granted through her compliance to the rule, not because she possesses them as "natural rights." It serves no purpose to point out that this idea runs counter to the spirit of Art. 1 of the Universal Declaration of Human Rights: "All human beings are born free and equal in dignity and rights. They are endowed with reason and conscience and should act towards one another in a spirit of brotherhood." Yet, "Beggars cannot be choosers!" (*DD*, 141) as Swarna Lata, one of Virmati's feminist girlfriends, repeats when talking about women's dependency on men.

Quite differently, a Ganika is a woman with expertise in the sixty-four arts to be studied with the *Kama Sutra*:

1. Singing.
2. Playing on musical instruments.
3. Dancing.
4. Union of dancing, singing, and playing instrumental music.
5. Writing and drawing.
6. Tattooing.
7. Arraying and adorning an idol with rice and flowers.
8. Spreading and arraying beds or couches of flowers, or flowers upon the ground.
9. Colouring the teeth, garments, hair, nails, and bodies, *i.e.*, staining, dyeing, colouring and painting the same.
10. Fixing stained glass into a floor.
11. The art of making beds, and spreading out carpets and cushions for reclining.
12. Playing on musical glasses filled with water.
13. Storing and accumulating water in aqueducts, cisterns and reservoirs.
14. Picture making, trimming and decorating.
15. Stringing of rosaries, necklaces, garlands and wreaths.
16. Binding of turbans and chaplets, and making crests and top-knots of flowers.
17. Scenic representations. Stage playing.
18. Art of making ear ornaments.
19. Art of preparing perfumes and odours.

"replaced" by Virmati. But when this does happen, her defence is that she "had taken her duties as a wife seriously" (*DD*, 250), using tradition to justify her inadequacy and deficiency.

20. Proper disposition of jewels and decorations, and adornment in dress.
21. Magic or sorcery.
22. Quickness of hand or manual skill.
23. Culinary art, *i.e.*, cooking and cookery.
24. Making lemonades, sherbets, acidulated drinks, and spirituous extracts with proper flavour and colour.
25. Tailor's work and sewing.
26. Making parrots, flowers, tufts, tassels, bunches, bosses, knobs, &c., out of yarn or thread.
27. Solution of riddles, enigmas, covert speeches, verbal puzzles and enigmatical questions.
28. A game, which consisted in repeating verses, and as one person finished, another person had to commence at once, repeating another verse, beginning with the same letter with which the last speaker's verse ended, whoever failed to repeat was considered to have lost, and to be subject to pay a forfeit or stake of some kind.
29. The art of mimicry or imitation.
30. Reading, including chanting and intoning.
31. Study of sentences difficult to pronounce. It is played as a game chiefly by women and children, and consists of a difficult sentence being given, and when repeated quickly, the words are often transposed or badly pronounced.
32. Practice with sword, single stick, quarter staff, and bow and arrow.
33. Drawing inferences, reasoning or inferring.
34. Carpentry, or the work of a carpenter.
35. Architecture, or the art of building.
36. Knowledge about gold and silver coins, and jewels and gems.
37. Chemistry and mineralogy.
38. Colouring jewels, gems and beads.
39. Knowledge of mines and quarries.
40. Gardening; knowledge of treating the diseases of trees and plants, of nourishing them, and determining their ages.
41. Art of cock fighting, quail fighting and ram fighting.
42. Art of teaching parrots and starlings to speak.
43. Art of applying perfumed ointments to the body, and of dressing the hair with unguents and perfumes and braiding it.
44. The art of understanding writing in cypher, and the writing of words in a peculiar way.
45. The art of speaking by changing the forms of words. It is of various kinds. Some speak by changing the beginning and end of words, others by adding unnecessary letters between every syllable of a word, and so on.

46. Knowledge of language and of the vernacular dialects.
47. Art of making flower carriages.
48. Art of framing mystical diagrams, of addressing spells and charms, and binding armlets.
49. Mental exercises, such as completing stanzas or verses on receiving a part of them; or supplying one, two or three lines when the remaining lines are given indiscriminately from different verses, so as to make the whole an entire verse with regard to its meaning; or arranging the words of a verse written irregularly by separating the vowels from the consonants, or leaving them out altogether; or putting into verse or prose sentences represented by signs or symbols. There are many other such exercises.
50. Composing poems.
51. Knowledge of dictionaries and vocabularies.
52. Knowledge of ways of changing and disguising the appearance of persons.
53. Knowledge of the art of changing the appearance of things, such as making cotton to appear as silk, coarse and common things to appear as fine and good.
54. Various ways of gambling.
55. Art of obtaining possession of the property of others by means of mantrasor incantations.
56. Skill in youthful sports.
57. Knowledge of the rules of society, and of how to pay respects and compliments to others.
58. Knowledge of the art of war, of arms, of armies, &/c.
59. Knowledge of gymnastics.
60. Art of knowing the character of a man from his features.
61. Knowledge of scanning or constructing verses.
62. Arithmetical recreations.
63. Making artificial flowers.
64. Making figures and images in clay

It is not easy trying to conjure up a woman with all these accomplishments. A Ganika is a public woman of high quality, endowed with a good disposition and beauty. She sits in an assembly of men, is respected by kings (*raj-ganika*) and praised by learned men. Hindus believe that the duty of a woman (svadharma) lies in her satisfying her husband's *kama*, that is his earthly pleasure and love as codified in the *Kamashastra* and in the *Kama Sutra* by Vatsyayana. In practice, while a woman is generally treated as an extension of her husband, it is as a sexual partner that she becomes complementary to him. Unlike a common courtesan or a wife, the Ganika caters to a man's sexual or sensory satisfaction, but also ensures that his mind, insight and aspirations are fulfilled. She is trained for this special task from her childhood by a thorough education (*shastraprahatabud-dhih*) in writing, reading, arithmetic, music, drawing, architecture, foreign languages, grammar, logic, rhetoric... alongside her training in understanding people's characters and tendencies. Therefore, she lives her life in public spaces, but more than anything else, she is *assertive* of her intellectual power: a Ganika does not *beg*, but *asserts* which means that she creates a cultural system around her.[6] In the past her profession was considered a civilizing activity which could also add lustre to a city, and she was often hired to teach courtly etiquette, poetry and music to the Nawab's sons.

Needless to say, a woman who is brought up to be a wife does not need such a refined education. Moreover, getting married at a very early age leaves her no time for training in the sixty-four arts as the household absorbs all her energies. One of the most striking differences between a Ganika and a Sita is that a courtesan can work for money, while a wife is unable to make a living. In the *Kama Sutra*, Vatsyayana maintains that

> if a wife becomes separated from her husband, and falls into distress, she can support herself easily, even in a foreign country, by means of her knowledge of these arts. Even the bare knowledge of them gives attractiveness to a woman, though the practice of them may be only possible or otherwise according to the circumstances of each case.[7]

In his mentioning of "a wife," Vatsyayana seems to extend this learning experience to all women. Thus, the Ganika is an economic player able to produce wealth and achieve self-realization, even in a gender-based world, by means of her education. While, on the contrary, Sita's social opportunities are more strictly confined and she depends on others for a decent standard of living. It should also be noted that towards the end of the novel, when talking about the Draft Hindu Code Bill,[8] Swarna Lata declares that men do not want family wealth to be divided

---

6 See also John Searle, *Mind, Language and Society. Philosophy in the Real World* (New York: Basic Books, 1998): 135–163.

7 In the *Kama Sutra*, Vatsyayana states that "A man who is versed in these arts, who is loquacious and acquainted with the arts of gallantry, gains very soon the hearts of women, even though he is only acquainted with them for a short time." See *Kama Sutra*, Chapter III § 26 "On the Arts and Sciences To Be Studied."

8 The Hindu Code Bill was presented to the Constituent Assembly on April 9, 1948 in order to replace the body of Hindu personal law with a civil code. After a long debate the Bill was reorganized in four different specialized Acts: the Hindu Marriage Act (1955), Hindu Succession Act (1956), Hindu Minority and Guardianship Act (1956), and Hindu Adoptions and Maintenance Act (1956). It is of interest to us here that polygamy was outlawed and, regarding the inheritance of family property, daughters were finally placed on the same footing as widows and sons.

among women: "The family structure itself would be threatened because sisters and wives would be considered as rivals instead of dependents who have to be nurtured and protected. As a result women would lose their moral position in society!" (*DD*, 251–252).

While tradition and dependency produce inequality, they do assure dignity, a moral position to women and, strangely enough, this occurs within the framework of a legal order: a woman is not allowed to tackle her husband outside the institutional hierarchy, unless she is a Ganika. The latter holds a place of honour among men not only because of her refined intellect, but also because she is not a wife. She is not equal to other women so much as she is not equal to men, but more than anything else she is not a rival: she might not be the "same," but her uniqueness is never destitute of public respect. As we will see later, when Virmati gets her first job, along with her financial independence, she finds her own personal place beyond her "natural" or "social" role: she is finally a person, albeit always within a network of communitarian relationships.

Before dealing more in depth with Virmati, I would like to make a digression in order to underline the strong inverse relationship between the gender gap in literacy and the status of women in contemporary Indian society. As the preamble of the Universal Declaration proclaims, the faith in the dignity and worth of the human person and in the equal rights of men and women are determined "to promote social progress and better standards of life in larger freedom." This point justifies the importance of a novel like *Difficult Daughters*, which tells the story of a right – the right to education – as a precondition for human and social development.

Longevity and health, education and knowledge, and a decent standard of living are the three criteria by which the overall achievement of a country may be evaluated according to the Human Development Index (HDI).[9] The *UN Human Development Report 2011 on Sustainability and Inequality*[10] released in November 2011, which assesses long-term progress in health, education and income indicators, ranks India a low 134 among 187 countries, that is to say far behind scores of economically less developed countries such as Iraq or the Philippines. One of the principal reasons for this low ranking is poor achievement in the social sector and less availability of social opportunities. Considering also that the wealth of a

---

9 See Deepti Gupta, "Disparities in Development, Status of Women and Social Opportunities: Indian Experience," *Journal of Alternative Perspectives in the Social Sciences* 1.3 (2009): 687–719.
10 See "UN Human Development Report 2011: Sustainability and Inequality," available at http://hdr.undp.org/en/reports/global/hdr2011/ (December 4, 2012).

nation lies not in *material resources* but in *human resources*,[11] it is remarkable how the number of poor in India constitute more than half of the population (612 million), according to the UN report.

With reference to education, the *2011 Indian Census*[12] reveals that the literacy rate for the country lies at 74 percent:

Tab. 1: From Statement 6.1 – Literacy rate in India by sex and residence, 1991–2011

	Literacy Rate								
	1991			2001			2011		
	Total	Rural	Urban	Total	Rural	Urban	Total	Rural	Urban
Persons	52.21	44.69	73.08	**64.84**	58.75	79.92	**74.04**	68.91	84.98
Males	64.13	57.87	81.09	**75.26**	70.70	86.27	**82.14**	78.57	89.67
Females	39.29	30.62	64.05	**53.68**	46.14	72.86	**65.46**	58.75	79.92

It is evident that since 1991 the situation has improved, regarding both the urban vs. rural areas rate as also the number of persons who have access to education, which goes from 52 to 74 percent. The above table also indicates that the gender gap in literacy has come down from 24.8 percentage points in 1991 to 16.6 percentage points in 2011, but less than 17 percent of the population means that almost 200 million women are illiterate. Moreover, we must bear in mind that the Indian Union is comprised of 28 States and 7 Union Territories which are characterized by enormous variations in regional experiences and achievements, so it is always necessary to distinguish between these different realities. For example in 2001 "the gender gap in literacy is as low as 6.3 percentage points in Kerala[13] and as high as 32.1 percentage points in Rajasthan." If in 2001 only a few States had a rate of more than 81 percent while the majority fell below the 69 percent level,

---

11 Seema Joshi, "Economic Reforms and Trends in Social Sector Expenditures in India" in *Human Development: Concept and Issues in the Context of Globalisation*, ed. S. K. Pant (New Delhi: Rawat Publications, 2006): 203.

12 See *India Census 2011*, "Status of Literacy," 196, available at http://www.censusindia.gov.in/2011-prov-results/paper2-vol2/data_files/Mizoram/Chapter_6.pdf (December 4, 2012).

13 See Kathryn Ross, "Status of Women in Highly Literate Societies: The Case of Kerala and Finland," *Literacy* 40.3 (November 2006): 172: "This is important because, as was pointed out in a paper on Kerala's development achievements, 'the ratio of men to women in the population is characteristic of a society where there is not a systematic bias against the survival of girls and women in the population' (Ramachandran, 1997, p. 225). In short, the fact that women have consistently out-numbered men is indicative of Kerala's progress in the realm of overall female well-being."

nowadays almost only the BIMARU States (Bihar, Madhya Pradesh, Rajasthan, Uttar Pradesh) and Orissa are below 66 percent, but these are the States in which 40 percent of the country's population live.[14] Furthermore, when we examine the Human Poverty Index (HPI), which is a measure of deprivation, the data from these areas are even more alarming. So, when examining the "Disparities in Performance among the Best and the Worst Performing States in India," we can easily understand how literacy goes hand in hand with deprivation, violence, lack of authority, poor health conditions, and high maternal mortality rates:

Tab. 2: Disparities in Performance: The Best and The Worst Performing States in India[15]

Indicators	Best performer	Worst performer
Human development index (2001) value	Kerala (0 638)	Bihar (0.367)
Total literacy, 2001 (percentage of population)	Kerala (90.9)	Bihar (47.5)
Infant Mortality Rate (per 1000 births), 2001	Kerala (16)	Orissa (98)
Female literacy rate, 2001 (percentage of population)	Kerala (87.9)	Bihar (33.6)
Households with piped drinking water, 2005–06 (percentage)	Tamil Naidu (84.2)	Bihar (4.2)
Households with toilet facility 2005–06 (percentage)	Kerala (96)	Orissa (19.3)
Households with electricity, 2005–06 (percentage)	Himachal Pradesh (98.4)	Blhar (27.7)
Married women who participate in household decisions, 2005–06 (percentage)	Maharashtra (63.8)	West Bengal (38.1)
Women who have ever experienced spousal violence 2005–06 (percentage)	Himachal Pradesh (6.2)	Bihar (59)
Anemie women, 2005–06 (percentage)	Kerala (32.3)	Assam (69)
Maternal Mortality Rate, 2001	Gujarat (28)	Uttar Pradesh (707)

Deepti Gupta offers food for thought:

> Maternal mortality is not merely a health disadvantage, but also a reflection of social and gender injustice. The low social and economic status of girls and women limits their access

---

14 See the website "Education For All In India" and the comment on *India Census 2011*, "Status of Literacy," available at http://www.educationforallinindia.com/chapter6-state-of-literacy-2011-census.pdf (last access December 4, 2012).
15 See Gupta, "Disparities in Development," 691–692.

to education, appropriate nutrition, as well as health and family planning services. All these directly impact on pregnancy outcomes. The overriding causes of the high Maternal Mortality Ratio across India are the absence of a skilled birth attendant at delivery, poor access to emergency obstetric care in case of a complication and no reliable referral system (with easy mobility), to ensure that women who experience complications can reach life-saving emergency obstetric care in time. Any skilled birth attendant, however proficient she may be, also needs the back up of a functioning health system and cannot succeed without drugs, equipment and infrastructure.[16]

The reconsideration of certain unequal traditions such as female seclusion, restricted female property rights, boy preference in fertility decisions, the separation of a woman from her family, plus easier access to education (also) for girls might empower the development of the nation along with social opportunities. Can we assume that shared resources and more human rights – specifically *education* and *literacy* as human rights – will promote the empowerment of the nation? Are fundamental rights a resource to achieving *wealth* or (*human*) *well-being*? What does "(human) well-being" mean for a woman in India? How can svadharma, human rights and human well-being be reconciled?

Whenever we talk about human rights in relation to non-Western countries, and in particular to India, we are told that they originate from the specific historical and cultural circumstances of the western world.[17] That is to say their cultural relativism is discussed in opposition to their supposed universality. Hindus replace Western "natural rights" with "natural duties"[18] which are responsible for and functional to the development of one's own self-consciousness and spiritual awareness, that is purification and self-realization. The main idea is that any living being is part of a wider harmonious whole, and that the "individual's duty is to maintain his 'rights'; it is to find one's place in relation to Society, to the Cosmos, and to the transcendent world."[19] Therefore, all aspects of social life are ruled by dharma as codified in the *Dharmashastra*, the book of the law. Dharma is not concerned "with finding the right of one individual against another

---

16 See Gupta, "Disparities in Development," 696. See also "The 'genocide' of India's daughters: We ask if the patriarchal mindset that runs across castes and class can be changed to prevent foeticide and infanticide," *Al Jazeera*, (January 13, 2013), available at http://www.aljazeera.com/programmes/insidestory/2013/01/20131117433572851.html (January 14, 2013).

17 Among others see Jack Donnelly, "Human Rights and Human Dignity: An Analytic Critique of Non-Western Conceptions of Human Rights," *The American Political Science Review* 76.2 (June 1982): 303–316.

18 About human rights in India see also Paola Carbone, "A White Tiger in the Indian Law Jungle: A Reading of Aravind Adiga's Debut Novel," *Pólemos* 7.1 (2013): 123–142.

19 Raimond Pannikar, "Is the Notion of Human Rights a Western Concept?," *Diogenes* 120 (1982): 97.

or of the individual *vis-à-vis* society, but rather with assaying the *dharmic* [...] or *adharmic* character of a thing or an action within the entire anthropocosmic complex of reality."[20]

This throws light on the way in which the three basic tenets of human rights – *individualism, rights,* and *legalism* – are substituted by *collectivism, duties,* and *reconciliation* and *repentance,* as the primary method for dealing with any violation of duties.[21] Along the same lines, Raimond Pannikar invites us to replace "individual" with "person" since the latter lives in a net of relationships and not as an abstraction separated from society. Rights are not disconnected from duties because *my* right depends on *other people's* rights and duties: svadharma is at the same time a result of and a reaction to the dharma of everyone else.[22] As a consequence, dignity is achieved only in such a perspective, so that while self-realization (moksha, or liberation towards Brahman) should be the life purpose of any human being, self-determinism is bound by the karma as much as by the clan.

Returning to *Difficult Daughters*, it is my opinion that we cannot understand the novel unless we recognize that, rather than asserting her own (human) right to education, the main character struggles to find her own place in the community, with respect to her ambition to be a learned woman, to her family, and to her karmic destiny. Breaking her engagement, Virmati says:

> As far as Inderjit is concerned, I don't think I have done him any wrong. He has got Indu [her sister], who will make him an infinitely better wife. As for me, I know I have failed in my duty and will be punished one day. Nobody can escape their karma. Maybe what is happening to me now is part of it, and there is no use protesting. (*DD*, 92)

Her svadharma is so much an intrinsic part of her that she feels uneasy with herself both when she fights her parents and when she follows her own desires, because she knows she is behaving against her good karman, which is achieved only by acting in conformity with the law (dharma, tradition). Her dilemma becomes reality when her act of rebellion causes the whole community distress and suffering: the narrator underlines the fact that by declining the marriage proposal she is humiliating her grandfather, "who was publicly associated with female education, betraying her father who had allowed her to study further, and spoiling the marriage chances of her sibling" (*DD*, 57). As her mother keeps telling her in a fit of pique, "You are so *educated,* aren't you?" (*DD*, 220). Virmati deserves both unhappiness and her ousting from the community because of her

---

20 Pannikar, "Is the Notion of Human Rights a Western Concept?," 96.

21 Nidhi Gupta, "Women's Human Rights and the Practice of Dowry in India. Adapting a Global Discourse to Local Demands," *Journal of Legal Pluralism* 48 (2003): 87–89.

22 Pannikar, "Is the Notion of Human Rights a Western Concept?," 96.

lust for learning, which is seen as pride, arrogance and self-importance. Virmati is a new Ulysses who dares to endanger her sailors by passing beyond the Pillars of Hercules to gain knowledge of the unknown. Her "individual" right, commonly perceived as a mistake or an individualistic adharmic choice, is dramatically manifested by her ongoing repentance: she will beg her family's pardon throughout her life, and particularly her mother's.

Contrary to what we might suppose, Indian mothers are the most resolute opponents to female schooling. When, in the nineteenth century, movements for women's education arose, such as The Social Reform Movement, the Nationalist Movement and the Arya Samaj[23] mainly thanks to male innovators, women took a passive role in their emancipation as they were treated by social reformers as "subjects to be changed and formed" rather than active partners in the fight. The question was: "how can they be modernized?" instead of "what do women want?," as Geraldine Forbes points out.[24] Needless to say, this attitude recalls the "civilizing mission" of the colonialists. In reality, traditional women perceived their Sita-identity as being under threat. For this reason, in literature it is very common to find mothers and mothers-in-law opposing young girls, while their fathers or fathers-in-law support them. In all probability, mothers see their daughters in a semantic continuity with themselves: a daughter is not *other than* her mother, but tradition becoming form and substance at the same time. A daughter is a *fact* not a *potential happiness* to be. For example, in Kamala Markandaya's *Nectar in a Sieve*,[25] written in the 1950s, the main female character, Ruku, is taught how to read and write by her father, while her mother believes that education is not a priority, especially for rural girls because of their vital domestic role:

---

23 In the novel we are told that Virmati's grandfather is a member of the Arya Samaj, and that is the reason the girl is always backed by her father and grandfather. It is also specified that when Kasturi married and arrived at her husband's home, her father-in-law made sure she had some skills in reading and writing. He thought that only a learned woman could properly hand down the core values of the family to the children. Arya Samaj is a Hindu organization founded in 1875 in Bombay by Dayanad Sarawasati. They preached against animal sacrifice, the cult of the ancestors, a caste system by birth, untouchability, child marriage. Along the same lines they were for girls' education, at least in so far as it could help a woman to be a better companion and mother.

24 See Geraldine Forbes, *Women in Modern India* [1996] (Cambridge: Cambridge University Press, 2004), 12.

25 Kamala Markandaya, *Nectar in a Sieve* [1954] (New York: Signet Classics, 2002): further references in the text, abbreviated as *NS*.

"What use," my mother said, "that a girl should be learned! Much good will it do her when she has lusty sons and a husband to look after. Look at me, am I any worse that I cannot spell my name, so long as I know it? Is not my house clean and sweet, are not my children well fed and cared for?" My father laughed and said, "Indeed they are," and did not pursue the matter, nor did he give up his teaching. (*NS*, 12)

But the father knows that for his daughter education would be "a solace [...] in affliction, a joy amid tranquillity" (*NS*, 12), as well as a good dowry at the proper time. After her marriage, other women are amazed or scornful that Ruku can write but, luckily, her illiterate husband quite simply accepts her accomplishment: "yet not once did he assert his rights and forbid me my pleasure, as lesser men might have done" (*NS*, 13). It was then commonly assumed that a knowledge of letters would facilitate female intrigue, but even worse, there was the irrational belief that a literate girl would soon become a widow after marriage.[26] Women used to live in almost segregated worlds, and learned women usually preferred to keep their knowledge secret, in order to avoid prejudice and superstition.

In the forties, when part of the story takes place, the narrator tells us that "Virmati was seventeen and studying for her FA exams, but since the tail end of her education is in sight, it was felt that missing a little of it to help her mother was quite in order. After all, in a year or so, the girl would be married" (*DD*, 10). Here, the voice is implicitly that of Kasturi, Virmati's mother, who was

the first girl in her family to postpone the arrival of the wedding guests by tentative assault on learning. Her father, uncle and teacher made sure that this step into modernity was prudent and innocuous. Her head remained modestly bent over her work. No question no assertion. She learned reading, writing, balancing household accounts and sewing. [...] During Kasturi's formal schooling it was never forgotten that marriage was her destiny. After she graduated, her education continued in the home. Her mother tried to ensure her future happiness by the impeccable nature of her daughter's qualifications. She was going to please her in-laws. (*DD*, 62)

In Indian society, marriage and education run along parallel lines[27] and a woman is expected to be mainly trained to be a good wife. Even the British approved of this attitude to a certain extent. When in 1882 Sir William Hunter was appointed to the first Indian Education Commission, known as the Hunter Commission, the major recommendations on primary and secondary education were discussed. The Com-

---

26 Forbes, *Women in Modern India*, 32–33.
27 See Urmila Dabir, Shubha Mishra, and Vandana Pathak, *Contemporary Fiction: An Anthology of Female Writers* (New Delhi: Sarup & Sons, 2008), 256.

mission maintained that, considering the different life duties for girls, they needed a special curriculum dedicated to domestic science while literary subjects would be totally useless and were therefore avoided.[28] In the same way, the social reformers at the beginning of the twentieth century also established schools with curricula specifically conceived for women, as Kasturi makes clear in the above quotation. Women were trained to be better wives and mothers, that is as helpmates to their husbands and teachers for their children (like Ruku). Such women were considered to be more desirable than "common" wives, but only rarely were they taught to be self-sufficient. Two reformers who moved against the tide stand out: Ramabai Ranade, one of the first women's rights activists in the nineteenth century, who founded the "Hujurpaga school" in Pune, and Maharshi Karve, the man who set up the "Hingne Stree Shikshan Samstha" school for widows (1896) whose aim it was to make these most ill-fated women able to manage for themselves.

We must keep in mind that even nowadays the lack of interest, poor quality of schooling, and low economic return to education – added to the data considered above regarding living conditions and justice – are responsible for the high rate of female dropouts.[29] A better education for boys is justified by the fact that this is seen as an investment for the entire family, whereas the benefits of a girl's education go to the family she marries into. Education is still considered as part of a woman's dowry: with her education, Virmati would have no difficulty in finding a husband, just like Kasturi before her, and Ruku in Markandaya's novel. Nevertheless, too high an education in a daughter-in-law could be seen as pointless, if not actually a problem, since it might unsettle traditions: what man would marry a Ganika, an independent woman who lives in public spaces, when the perfect wife is a modest, homely, respectable Sita?[30] We read in the novel that

---

28 See Ram Nath Sharma and Rajendra Kumar Sharma, *History Of Education In India*, 120.

29 See Sushrut Desai, "Gender Disparity in Primary Education: The Experience in India," *UN Chronicle* (December 1, 2007): section Archive, "The MDGs: Are we on track?," available at http://www.un.org:80/wcm/content/site/chronicle/home/archive/issues2007/themdgsareweon-track/genderdisparityinprimaryeducationtheexperienceinindia (last access, December 2012). "In a society as deeply stratified as India [...], [f]or scheduled caste and scheduled tribe girls, the gender gap in education is almost 30 per cent at the primary level and 26 per cent at the upper primary stage. In India's most depressed regions, the probability of girls getting primary education is about 42 per cent lower than boys, and it remains so even when other variables, such as religion and caste, are controlled. [...] Sarva Shiksha Abhiyan (SSA) or "Education for All" – places special emphasis on female education and the achievement of gender parity. The question remains, of course, whether this can be attained before the MDGs deadline in 2015." See also Gupta, "Disparities in Development," 699–701.

30 In *Heat and Dust*, questioned about his wife Ritu, Lal "said she was intelligent. Also she had not had much education – his mother had not wanted him to marry a very educated girl; she said

after the protagonist gains her degree in Fine Arts, her fiancé's parents "thought that she was already well qualified to be the wife of their son, the canal engineer. They did not want too much education in their daughter-in-law, even though times were changing. Virmati wept and sulked" (*DD*, 45).

Anguished by her *natural* desire to love and to better herself, Virmati lets her *social* being prevail, in order to appear *right* in the eyes of other people, or according to her *natural* duty or karma. She is so convinced of her social inappropriateness that she claims to be proud of her household knowledge.[31] She wants to be a good housewife for her husband, *but* she is a learned woman who has studied mainly for her own satisfaction, not for her future domestic accomplishment. Even the Ganikas are trained to please men! It is obvious that from this point of view, education is not offered as a way of pursuing human well-being, but as an *individualistic* right, which is culturally-speaking an *unnatural* right when the clan is the basic social unit. This is the reason why Virmati does not deserve public respect, why she has no public dignity. More easily shared access to social opportunities and less social conditioning to take her own needs also into consideration when establishing her priorities in life would have rendered her dilemma less severe and her choice less blameworthy.

Paradoxically, while her father and grandfather are behind her, Virmati's attempt to enlarge her universe is, as she herself says, paralyzed by her husband, the professor of English literature who studied at Oxford. Her love for an older, educated, married man leads her to conform to the Sita ideal, the pure wife. This is her real *faux pas* – *hamartia* – which leads the protagonist into an unhappy marriage. If, before marriage, she avoids all engagement in political activism (that is citizenship) unlike her roommate Swarma, totally focused as she is on her lover, after marriage, she becomes the learned-Ganika rarity to be shown in public for her vain husband.[32] In this way, not only does she deny herself the chance men

---

there was nothing but trouble to be expected from such a quarter. Ritu had been chosen on account of her suitable family background and her fair complexion. His mother had told him she was pretty, but he never could make up his mind about that." Ruth Prawer Jhabvala, *Heat and Dust* [1975] (London: John Murray, 2003): 49.

31 When after college Virmati starts to work, she teaches English literature and Household. "Household was hygiene, nutrition, domestic management, health care, and enough applied maths to balance a budget. The prime minister, [...] publicized the soundness of female education through Household, a traditional subject taught in a scientific way by the principal herself" (*DD*, 184).

32 In chapter XI the narrator tells us that as soon as the marriage is decided, "Kasturi and her mother spent hours alternately crying and preparing the trousseau. [...] A small suitcase contained her clothes – six sets of salwar kameez. A wife was not for show, after all" (*DD*, 66). A woman is supposed to stay home and be modest. Her education should glorify the husband, who can show

are usually given to acquire social status, but she becomes the victim of her own knowledge. Harish loves the learned woman she externalises more than the underlying Virmati herself. Before dying she tells her daughter: "When I die, [...] I want my body donated. My eyes, my heart, my kidneys, any organ that can be of use. That way someone will value me after I have gone" (*DD*, 1).

As a scholar, Harish could find no satisfaction in an illiterate wife like Ganga[33] who had been chosen for him, with whom he had nothing in common and who embarrassed him in front of his friends (*DD*, 209, for example by using a *ghunghat*, a traditional veil on her face). As soon as they get married, when Virmati complains that she cannot take care of him as well as Ganga does – that is as a housewife – he replies: "You are my other self. Let her wash my clothes, if she feels like it. It has nothing to do with me. I don't want a washerwoman. I want a companion" (*DD*, 217). Virmati fulfils his intellectual *côté*, discussing poetry, philosophy and music both at home with him and in public with his friends. But she is also brave enough to behave unexpectedly for a wife, as when she takes a bath in a tank in the garden in summer with other men. On this occasion, Ganga is described as controlling the situation from the kitchen. Virmati is the perfect Ganika, but she is not a courtesan. She is a Ganika with all the disadvantages of a Sita: but unlike Sita she does not possess her supposed purity. Hence, Virmati renounces her status of learned and praised woman to serve her husband[34] and him alone. Her husband does not want her to share her knowledge as civil commitment, as she did before marriage when she had been proud to serve the cause of national literacy by accepting to work at the Sirmau State girls' school (*DD*, 181). Instead he craves to put his possession of her uniqueness on show. Rather than producing prosperity, she satisfies one man's egotism, but that is not the purpose of knowledge and he humiliates her most intimately. She becomes so very unhappy, and also so very unsatisfying for Harish that she is sent away to study again, where she lives as a sort of widow, an ironic variation in the super-stition mentioned above. Wherever she lives, Virmati appears culturally incon-

---

everybody that he can afford a learned wife who takes care of him and his children. Harish's mother has the same opinion when she reminds her son that a wife is not a showpiece (*DD*, 209).

33 Harish tries hard to teach his wife how to read and write, because "he wanted his wife to become a companion quickly" (*DD*, 40). When Virmati hears about this story, before meeting him, she is fascinated and thinks that "it is very noble of the Professor to try and teach his wife. It showed he really cared for women's education, just like her grandfather" (*DD*, 39). She so starts to idealize this man without really knowing him, because she believes that he "respects" women like her ancestor.

34 It is curious how Rama, Sita's husband, is generally referred to as a perfect son, brother and king – "He is a Rama like son, a Rama like brother, or a Rama like king," but it is rare to hear "Rama like husband or son-in-law" as a compliment.

sistent, surviving out of dharma: she might not act wrong with respect to her moral integrity, but she certainly acts wrong with respect to social harmony, that is to that entire anthropocosmic complex of reality Raimon Pannikar talks about.

In her attempt to be as conventional as possible, while at the same time responding to her need for knowledge, she loses dignity, respect and esteem since she is able to assert neither her presence as a human being nor her rights. Poles apart from the Vedic ideals, here education becomes the origin of all Virmati's worldly sufferings. Article 26 of the 1948 Universal Declaration of Human Rights, paragraph 2 states: *"Education shall be directed to the full development of the human personality and to the strengthening of respect for human rights and fundamental freedoms. It shall promote understanding, tolerance and friendship* among all nations, racial or religious groups, and shall further the activities of the United Nations for the maintenance of peace." [My italics]. I wonder whether or not education is also a civil *duty*. Virmati's fight should make all her intellectual pro-activity and civil role manifest, as when she becomes the school principle and is respected[35] as an emancipated woman by everybody. Education, however, has a different effect on Harish: in the eyes of her husband, she is a trophy, instead of being seen as a companion or as representative of civilization, understanding, tolerance and friendship. Respect for people's human value is the foundation of a humanistic culture and equality, but in the novel the Professor plays the role of cultural colonialist who feels superior for his being a man with a British education and civilization. In reality, he is simply suspended in a cultural paradox and will never have the courage to pass beyond the Pillars of Hercules nor to challenge India's male-oriented culture and privileges. He is a low-minded Pygmalion who does not care for his student's ultimate improvement and needs. As the narrator remarks, "Virmati and he had been at their happiest when he had been teaching, and she learning." It was then, according to Harish, that she had had a proper respect for their relationship (*DD*, 247). At this point Virmati should have reminded him of her *human right* to equality and dignity.

Far from doing so, she chooses not to tell him what is really happening with Ganga, with her mother-in-law and with her own family so as not to bother him with the complications of family life. Her silence here is in sharp contrast with the assertive language of Swarma and her activist friends in Lahore as they fought for Independence, khadi-wearing, the Muslim cause, religious identity, and the Hindu Code Bill... Even though, Swarma now talks about that past in the following terms:

---

35 It must be underlined that Virmati is chosen by the forward-looking queen Pratibha both for her highly qualified curriculum and for her impeccable family background (*DD*, 179).

> That was the time when people were very aware of what was happening around them. I got involved with IPTA, we agitated against rising prices, we organized singing squads with songs based on folk songs to arouse awareness, we wanted rationing centres opened, we wanted profiteers punished, we wanted more equality between men and women, and we were against, *totally* against, segregation on religious lines. (*DD*, 137)

Virmati had witnessed this struggle, but had not taken any part in it. It is as if her initial personal fight for education had drained all her energies. Even for a highly educated woman like Virmati, inequality is normative,[36] and yet "Beggars cannot be choosers!" as Swarma used to say (*DD*, 141). Schooling should not unseat tradition, as some people feared it would, but rather the patriarchal system, social injustice, cultural colonialism, and violence. More so than men, women should learn what they deserve, that is respect for their dignity, which is a central concern of both Hinduism and fundamental rights, albeit in different ways. The Preamble to the Universal Declaration states that

> every individual and every organ of society, keeping this Declaration constantly in mind, shall strive by teaching and education to promote respect for these rights and freedoms and by progressive measures, national and international, to secure their universal and effective recognition and observance, both among the peoples of Member States themselves and among the peoples of territories under their jurisdiction.

If a woman believes that her husband has the right to beat her she cannot make a claim for human rights or she cannot expect that her human, family or legal rights will be respected, as Nidhi Gupta points out.[37] A woman should understand first of all that she has the *right to life*, that is not to be a victim of "female foeticide, female infanticide and bride burning," as also not to be discriminated against with respect to health care and food. She needs to be protected from cultural constructs as from domestic violence, sexual abuse, dowry death... Along with a right to education, women need education to their rights in conformity with their cultural context. We should bear in mind that on December 10, 1948, the UN General Assembly had called upon all Member States to publicize

---

36 See Darlene E. Clover, Catherine McGregor, Martha Farrell and Mandakini Pant, "Women Learning Politics and the Politics of Learning: A Feminist Study of Canada and India," *Studies in the Education of Adults* 43.1 (Spring 2011): 8–33, 19. In the novel, when Virmati attends her father's funeral, she is treated like a criminal because her mother believes that she is responsible for her husband's death. On the contrary, Harish is welcomed because he behaves as if he were the most respectable among the men.

37 Gupta, "Women's Human Rights and the Practice of Dowry in India. Adapting a Global Discourse to Local Demands," 101.

the text of the Declaration and "to cause it to be disseminated, displayed, read and expounded principally in schools and other educational institutions, without distinction based on the political status of countries or territories." How can you spread the hermeneutical circulation of these principles among young citizens if they have no access to schooling, literacy or self-awareness? No contradiction should exist between the right to study and the female svadharma, or human rights and Hinduism, because the one does not prevail over the other, as the Indian Government[38] and the "Education for All"[39] project should clearly demonstrate. To understand your rights in depth, you must have access to the language, culture and philosophy[40] which sustain them and this is possible only through education and citizenship, that is through acquiring the theory and practice of these rights.

Culturally speaking, the only traditional way to guarantee Indian girls an economic position, that is to say a net of social relationships which would promote citizenship with social protection (in theory at least, considering the common practice of the Indian police who, more often than not, turn a blind eye on domestic violence) is through the husband. It is through marriage that a woman is admitted to the *polis*. But in India women seem to be only observers rather than players in the social arena. In the recent past, it seems that for his

----

38 As P. Geetha Rani writes: "The Government of India in its preamble in the Constitution under Article 45, made a resolution to provide free and compulsory education up to the age of 14 within a period of 10 years. The National Policy on Education, 1986 and the Programme of Action in 1992 reiterated the Constitutional Directive that free and compulsory education of satisfactory quality be provided to children up to the age of 14 years before the 21st century. Though this target period has been revised time and again, recently the bill on Elementary Education as a Fundamental Right has been passed in the parliament in its 93rd Amendment. Elementary education as a fundamental right underlines the paramount significance of the Central government in achieving universal elementary education." See P. G. Rani, "Growth and Financing of Elementary Education in Uttar Pradesh: A Province in India," *Education Policy Analysis Archives* 12.25 (June 13, 2004): 2, available at http://epaa.asu.edu/epaa/v12n25/(last access November 2012).
The Indian Constitution, Part III. – Fundamental Rights. – Arts. 21A states: Protection of life and personal liberty: "21A. The State shall provide free and compulsory education to all children of the age of six to fourteen years in such manner as the State may, by law, determine."
39 "Education for All" is a project led by UNESCO devoted to developing universal primary education with special emphasis on female education and the achievement of gender parity. The project's deadline is in 2015. For more information see:
http://portal.unesco.org/education/en/ev.php-URL_ID=42579&URL_DO=DO_TOPIC&URL_SEC-TION=201.html (last access November 2012)
40 See also Jacques Derrida, *Negotiations: Inventions and Interviews, 1971–2001* (Stanford: Stanford University Press, 2002): 329–342.

Swadeshi[41] only Gandhi had asked women to participate and be active in society. Although his was a highly conservative idea of women, he did compare India's purity to that of Sita and he advocated that women be allowed to cultivate their strength of soul in order to educate their children (both male and female) to respect and self-respect in a dharmic context. However much Gandhi still followed the lines of the great social reformers, he did extend liberation from socio-political oppression to women. His innovative approach is that he saw women not as objects of reforms and humanitarianism, but as self-conscious arbiters of their own destiny. As with the khadi movement, he succeeded in creating a homogeneous critical mass of persons undifferentiated in terms of class, caste, religion or region. Moreover, he made no separation of male and female roles on purely biological sexual bases. For Gandhi, women had to participate in the making of the nation just like men.

In the Indian Constitution, numerous patriarchal traditions are supported by the "Fundamental right to freedom of religion," which allows religious communities to have their own personal laws such as, for example, the laws governing marriage and inheritance. On this basis, it can come about that legal protection holds women's emancipation in check, as they are subject to moral and cultural determinism: women are not generally considered "the same" (equal) to men but "different" on a purely biological level, that is weaker and in need of protection. This, of course, turns into a pretext which justifies violence and exploitation. We often find that the Indian High and Supreme Courts interpret the law according to moral and culture-specific purviews.[42]

We should consider in a similar light Article 26 Paragraph 3 of the 1948 Universal Declaration of Human Rights: "*Parents have a prior right to choose the kind of education* that shall be given to their children" [my italics], which was extended in the First Protocol to the European Convention on Human Rights 1953, 213 U.N.T.S. 262 as follows: "the State shall respect the rights of parents to ensure such education and teaching in conformity with their own religious and philosophical convictions." Exactly to what extent can parents – that is fathers in a patriarchal society – make decisions about their (male and female) children's schooling and education? So far, we have pointed out some of the difficulties women in India face, the next issue is whether or not women should be seen as a *minority* group in need of human rights to protect them from cultural discrimina-

---

41 Gandhi is often quoted in the novel. In particular, the school Virmati administers was established by Queen Pratibha to allow girls improvement in a changing world, exactly as Gandhi was teaching.

42 Kanchan Sinh, "Indian Women in a Modern State and a Pre-Modern Society," *Gender and Development* 11.3 (November 2003): 19–26.

tion, which in perspective means survival, social opportunities and happiness? As human rights are legal devices, which should be applicable to each and every citizen and not just a part of the population, one may wonder about the eventual consequences of superimposing a right. Probably none at all, since the right might be guaranteed but the problem remains: what is the cultural and ethical value of a right once it becomes law in an unreceptive society? It seems to me that here what is most lacking is a common language to enhance dialogical praxis among different voices. It is also my opinion that such a dialogue should originate from the concept of *duty*, of what is right for the community of citizens, that is from what is dutiful for the citizens. Parents have the right to decide what kind of citizens their children should be, but they also have the duty to ensure this outcome. The civil right of the parents might be in conflict with the social right of the child to education, and this is a central issue in contemporary educational policy debates.

Kapur's novel highlights the fact that, if it is true that a child has the social right to be educated, s/he does not seem to have the right to education. This is like saying that though one deserves a certain opportunity, one has no right to the praxis of achieving it.[43] If schooling should create the citizen-to-be, Virmati puts up a struggle for her right only to relinquish it immediately afterwards because of an opposing cultural humus. She had known since her early childhood what she wanted to be as an adult member of the human family, but she sacrifices her *right to knowledge* on the altar of a patriarchal cultural construct: she gives up the fight because she allows her husband's right to prevail. Human rights are for all, and Virmati is not ready to live as an outsider (adharmic), that is as a "different" citizen or member of the community, unlike Swarma or Shakuntala who find a satisfactory balance between their femininity and their political activism. No matter how right her need to education may be, Virmati's times and personality are not ready for an equal society. As in a tragedy, the novel tells a tale of trampled innocence: we could probably say that as a human being Virmati finds her dignity in respecting the law (dharma), but it appears that it is only through respecting the fundamental rights that her being can be respected. These double perspectives are not in contradiction with one another, but complimentary.

---

43 See Ylva Bergström, "The Universal Right to Education: Freedom, Equality and Fraternity," *Studies in Philosophy & Education* 29 (2010): 167–182. Only the *Convention on the Rights of the Child* (1990) emphasizes the autonomy of the child and the importance of taking the child's views into consideration. Article 12 suggests what child/childhood means: "States Parties shall assure to the child who is capable of forming his or her own views the right to express those views freely in all matters affecting the child, the views of the child being given due weight in accordance with the age and maturity of the child," 173.

Afterword:
Virmati and Harish have a daughter, Ida, who decides to write her mother's story in order to understand that difficult, unhappy and unloving mother. Ida feels herself to be something like a pencil notation on the margins of society (*DD*, 278), because she does not want to behave according to her parents conventions: she "wanted to please herself sometimes, though by the time she grew up she was not sure what self she had to please" (*DD*, 279). Since Ida shows no signs of intellectual brightness, she is educated in classical music, dance and classical literature, which she is expected to discuss intelligently with her father, with the specific purpose of graciously exhibiting her accomplishments in front of her parents' guests. Yet again, knowledge is supposed to provide a woman with a social life of quality rather than a high quality of life: the kind of knowledge Harish and his wife are giving their daughter does not endow her with power, self-realization and liberation in the ancient, noble spirit of the Vedas. Harish pursues his vanity also with respect to his daughter, but by writing her mother's story, that is by sewing together the life of an Indian woman, Ida manages to shore up the fragments of her family's traditions and dilemmas.

Lisa Lanzoni

The Trial of Jomo Kenyatta, by Montagu Slater: Oral Tradition and Fundamental Rights in the Trial

In 1955, the British novelist, poet and playwright Montagu Slater wrote *The Trial of Jomo Kenyatta*, one of the most important and dramatic trials of the twentieth century.[1] In many ways the book emphasized just how fundamental was, and still is, the confrontation between the African tradition and the period of what is called "Colonial Modernity."

There are two parts to the book. The first one is composed of more than 2,000 pages, and reports the trial charged against the first President of Kenya, Jomo Kenyatta. The second part describes the trial having recourse to a "novel perspective," by considering in depth some aspects of Kenyan culture and marking in many ways the confrontation between African tradition and the already mentioned "Colonial Modernity" period.

In this contribution I will consider some passages in the first essentially chronicle part of the *Trial of Jomo Kenyatta*, with particular reference to some points concerning the relationship between African traditional law and Western written law. In particular, I would like to highlight how the protection of fundamental rights could be strictly linked to the oral tradition. As a consequence, a legal system – based on written law and totally inaccessible to oral law – could violate some human rights established in the oral tradition. From this perspective, one of the most important examples is the 1952 trial *Regina v Jomo Kenyatta and five others*, which continues to offer a significant representation of the contradictions between orality and literacy, tradition and modernity in African culture.[2]

As is well known, Jomo Kenyatta was the leader of the Kenya African Union (KAU) – a national movement – and became Kenya's first President following the independence in 1963.[3] In 1952, he was put on trial by the British colonial

---

1 Montagu Slater, *The Trial of Jomo Kenyatta* (London: Secker and Warburg, 1955).

2 For further references see Peter Leman, "African Oral Law and the Critique of Colonial Modernity in *The Trial of Jomo Kenyatta*," *Law and Literature* 23.1 (Spring 2011): 26–47.

3 On Jomo Kenyatta's life and history, see David Anderson, *Histories of the Hanged: The Dirty War in Kenya and the End of the Empire* (New York & London: Norton, 2005), 35–43.

government for leading the militant liberation movement known as Mau Mau.[4] Before looking to the protection of fundamental rights in this case it will be necessary to consider first what it means to say that some African oral traditions are legal.

Many African societies are based on an oral culture, mainly addressed to individuals pertaining to illiterate groups. In these societies, the boundaries that divide law from other forms of cultural expression do not exist. Furthermore, the oral (or "folk") law can be contained in various forms of oral expression. As some Authors have argued, oral laws

> are manifested through a variety of cultural expressions. [...] in proverbial form, e.g., as maxims. [...] They may be explicit in different types of traditional rituals, e.g., ordeals and oaths. They may be exemplified through the use of culturally accepted symbols.[5]

Thus, oral traditions in their various forms (proverbs, songs, oaths, narratives and others) can be used both to fix a sort of "legal wisdom" in the society and to establish legal procedures readily adaptable on a case-by-case approach. In this respect, oral traditions can be thought of as being jurisprudential. Moreover, since they act as a medium, poets or singers can thus be considered *the* "legislators" within these societies.[6]

Writing his thesis[7] on the Kikuyu[8] – the most populous ethnic group in Kenya – the same Jomo Kenyatta described in a paradigmatic way the *itwika* ceremony, which was used by the elders to draft new sets of laws, "constitutional" rules, regulations and procedures. After the elders had agreed about them, "the words of the drafted constitution were put into song-phrases,"[9] and announced through dances in the different districts. Kenyatta highlighted that this ceremony – as well as other similar performances – was "the only way through which the words, phrases and rhythmic movements of the new songs and dances, in which laws and

---

4 In October 1952, Kenya declared the State of Emergency for the violence enacted by the rebel movements.
5 Alison Dundes Rentel and Alan Dundes, *Folk Law: Essays in the Theory and Pratice of Lex Non Scripta*, vol. I (New York and London: Garland Publishing, 1994), 395.
6 On the relationship between law and poetry in Kenya, see Peter Leman, "Singing the Law: *Okot p'Bitek's* Legal Imagination and the Poetics of Traditional Justice," *Research in African Literature* 40.3 (Fall 2009): 109–128, 109.
7 After an early education in a Scottish Mission school, in 1934 Kenyatta enrolled at the University College London and from 1935 studied anthropology at the London School of Economics (LSE); his revised LSE thesis, *Facing Mount Kenya*, was published in 1938. See Jomo Kenyatta, *Facing Mount Kenya. The Tribal Life of the Gikuyu* (New York: Vintage Books, 1965).
8 The Kikuyu was the primary group interested by the Mau Mau conflict.
9 Kenyatta, *Facing Mount Kenya*, 185.

regulations of the *new democratic government* were embodied, could be introduced effectively into the life of the community."[10] The *itwika* ceremony was repeated periodically until 1925, when it was declared illegal by the British Government.[11]

It is evident, however, that the Government could not ban something that was passed within the community from one generation to the next in the oral tradition.[12] In fact, throughout the late colonial period, orality played a crucial role by supporting national and militant movements both to enforce the sense of community within the ethnic groups and to build an alternative authority. At the same time we cannot deny that the protection of human rights provides a strong connection between the African oral law and the Western written one. As described above, traditional oral law can express not only legal procedures, but also "constitutional" laws and rules, directly linked to the tribal and indigenous culture and to the fundamental rights of *equality, identity* and *freedom of speech*. Furthermore, oral law is the only facility for allowing *democratic participation* in the decision-making of illiterate peoples.

We can see all these features in a specific exchange during the trial of Jomo Kenyatta. In 1951–1952, before his arrest, Kenyatta went on a "stump campaign"[13] in central Kenya. He explained to an audience of thousands the aims of KAU, and spoke about the need to fight for the constitutional protection of civil and human rights. As he had reported several times to the press, the majority of his audience was illiterate. As a consequence, he spoke directly in the Kikuyu language, using the traditional expression of "curse." The curse is a performative utterance of Kikuyu society used by the elders to maintain order and bind the hearers. It served the function of a police force. Kenyatta had the acknowledged authority to use the curse in his speech to thousands of illiterate Kikuyus, bounding them "within a mutual obligation"[14] and demonstrating the effectiveness of the oral law.

---

10 Kenyatta, *Facing Mount Kenya*, 186 [italics mine].

11 The British Government described the ceremony as "seditious." Kenyatta, *Facing Mount Kenya*, 189.

12 Jacques Derrida described as a "founding violence" of the law the imposition of writing (and written law) and of a language (such as French and English) in Africa as acts commencing a legal regime. The author considered these as acts of violence and repression that could destroy other social rules, such as those established by the oral tradition. See Jacques Derrida, "Force of Law: 'The Mystical Foundation of Authority'" in *Deconstruction and the Possibility of Justice*, eds. Drucilla Cornell, Michael Rosenfeld and David Gray Carlson (London and New York: Routledge, 1992), 34.

13 Leman, "African Oral Law and the Critique of Colonial Modernity in *The Trial of Jomo Kenyatta*," 37.

14 Leman, "African Oral Law and the Critique of Colonial Modernity in *The Trial of Jomo Kenyatta*," 38.

In several speeches, Kenyatta used the traditional Kikuyu curse to condemn Mau Mau actions. In particular, one of these speeches reported in a Swahili newspaper highlighted that "Kenyatta told Mau Mau to go and be hanged."[15] During the trial the Deputy Public Prosecutor sought to prove that the phrase was coded to incite the Mau Mau movement to continue their fight in hiding. A long series of newspaper reports of Kenyatta's speeches were presented in order to point out they did not contain any explicit denunciation of Mau Mau activity. Kenyatta's Counsel Denis Nowell Pritt responded that this was an absurd interpretation of his client's speech, and that the evidence was inconclusive, circumstantial and contradictory. Furthermore, Kenyatta asked the Court to admit as evidence the magnetic tape on which the debated speech was recorded. At first, the Supreme Court judges granted the petition (and the Defense requested a *subpoena* to obtain the recording), but then they rejected it. The *ratio* represents a crucial instance of the conflict between African orality and written law and a clear violation of human rights and the truth of evidence in the trial. Rejecting Kenyatta's petition, the Supreme Court referred to the *Indian Evidence Act* of 1872, which was in force in Kenya at the time. The Act defined the *documents* admitted as evidence as follows: "'Documents' means any matter expressed or described upon any substance by means of letters, figures or marks or by more than one of those means, intended to be used, or which may be used, for the purpose of recording that matter."

In compliance with this definition, the Act illustrated a list of "documents" (writings, words printed, lithographed or photographed, maps, plans, inscription on a metal plate or stone, caricatures, etc.). For obvious reasons the 1872 Act did not include a magnetic tape as document. But it seemed to be in keeping with the spirit of the law, which aimed to acquire documents as evidence, in order to reconstruct the facts in the trial.

The Crown established that the sound recordings of Kenyatta's speech were not admissible as evidence; in particular, the Supreme Court specified that:

> The nature of the substance with which metal tape was coated having been changed by an electrical impulse. [...] it is at least equally possible that the effect of an electronic impulse on the magnetic tape is not to change the nature of the tape, but rather to vary in some manner its properties; and we are by no means certain that a variation in the properties of a substance necessarily entails a variation in the substance or any marks upon the substance [...]. We do not consider that a sound track is a document within the meaning of the Indian Evidence Act.[16]

---

15 Leman, "African Oral Law and the Critique of Colonial Modernity in *The Trial of Jomo Kenyatta*," 38.

16 Quoted in Montague Slater, *The Trial of Jomo Kenyatta*, 249–250.

In this way it was clear that the Crown not only banned the subversive potential of the oral law expressed by the Kikuyus' traditional performance of curse, but also violated the already mentioned fundamental right of equality, as well as the rights of identity, freedom of speech and democratic participation, strictly connected with the first one.

Kenyatta's case underlined the failure of the British Government to respect the system of "indirect rule" which it had adopted. This system recognized the African customary/traditional oral law but only with specific limits. In this way, African societies were supposed to accept more readily those rules codified by the Crown, because they repeated those customs and traditions that ordered African societies. The difficulty lay in the fact that British administrators often reshaped such traditions to comply with colonial aims, trying to maintain the stability afforded by the so-called *Pax Britannica*, but, in practice, necessarily over-reaching traditional oral law.[17]

We can accordingly see how Kenyatta's trial offered significant insights into the contradictions between the protection of human rights established at the international level and the preservation of the oral tradition and heritage in Africa. In particular, it highlighted the concept of equality in relation to the concept of non-discrimination, as afterwards elaborated in international and regional treaties and documents. Now it is widely accepted that equality and non-discrimination are positive and negative statements of the same principle.[18]

Equality as a principle of non-discrimination was recognized by the Sub-Commission on the Prevention of Discrimination and Protection of Human Rights, created in 1947 by the United Nations specifically to deal with such issues. Early in its first session, the Sub-Commission described the prevention of discrimination as the prevention of any action that denies individuals *or groups of people* the equality of treatment that they wish for. The Sub-Commission held that differential treatment of such groups or of individuals was justified only when it was exercised in the interest of their contentment and the welfare of the community as a whole.

In 1965 the International Convention on the Elimination of All Forms of Racial Discrimination defined the relationship between the principles of equality and non-discrimination. Article 1 of the Convention established that "the term 'racial discrimination' shall mean any distinction, exclusion, restriction or preference based on race, colour, descent, or national or ethnic origin *which has the purpose*

---

17 On the role and the abuse of indirect rule in Africa, see Mahmood Mamdani, *Citizen and Subject: Contemporary Africa and the Legacy of Late Colonialism* (Princeton, NJ: Princeton University Press, 1996), 22–54.
18 Ann F. Bayefsky, "The Principle of Equality or Non-Discrimination in International Law," *Human Rights Law Journal* 11.1–2 (1990): 1–34, 5.

or effect of nullifying or impairing the recognition, enjoyment or exercise, on an equal footing, of human rights and fundamental freedoms in the political, economic, social, cultural or any other field of public life."[19]

Clearly, in Kenyatta's case we can consider the violation of the principle of equality as defined by the UN and the International Convention on the Elimination of All Forms of Racial Discrimination with reference both to the individual (Jomo Kenyatta) and to the group (the ethnic group of Kikuyu). Furthermore, we should note that this concept of equality in general, and with reference to the African oral culture in particular, includes *the respect* of human rights as defined by oral traditions. This is further supported by the terms of the Constitution of Kenya which entered into force in 2010.

Article 1 of the 2010 Constitution (*Sovereignty of the people and supremacy of the Constitution*) establishes that: "Any law, *including customary law*, that is inconsistent with the Constitution is void to the extent of the inconsistency, and any act or omission in contravention of this Constitution is invalid." We can clearly see a complete equal treatment between the law codified in the usual positive way and the customary law, as integrated in the constitutional order (either by the indirect rule method or by a direct codification). Article 27 of the Constitution (*Equality*) subsequently establishes that: "The State shall not discriminate directly or indirectly against any person or any ground, including race, sex, pregnancy, *marital status*, health status, ethnic or social origin, color, age, disability, religion, conscience, belief, culture, dress, language or birth." By way of example, in Kenya as in many African societies, *marital status* depends on the different traditions which pertain to different ethnic groups. Thus we have a constitutional disposition that guarantees respect for a culturally differentiated equality. It is an interesting example of how written law cannot, even today, preclude oral traditions of law.

As demonstrated in Kenyatta's trial, respecting this aspiration requires the establishment of rigorous checks and balances in the procedures and trials concerning the protection of human rights, most importantly to include complete equality between written and "oral" forms of legal expression. To do this, the protection of human rights in Africa has to be conscious of the territorial traditions linked to the ethnic groups, revealing again the strong connection among the principles of equality, identity and freedom of speech with the principle of democratic participation.

---

19 The International Convention on the Elimination of All Forms of Racial Discrimination influenced other international and regional human rights treaties and instruments subsequently entered into force, with particular reference to the Convention for the Protection of National Minorities, 1995 and the European Charter for Regional or Minority Languages, 1992.

Matteo Nicolini

'n Droë Wit Seisoen in die Stormkaap: André Brink and the Fundamental Rights of the Afrikaners in Apartheid South Africa

1 "White" Fundamental Rights? Overturning the Legal Examination of the Apartheid Regime

Scholars – with either a background in the humanities or in law – probably would not choose to dedicate an essay to the fundamental rights *Afrikaners* were entitled under the South African apartheid regime. On the one hand, they might consider bizarre the idea of examining the legal status of the *Afrikaners* – i.e., the descendants of the Dutch colonists who had been settling in the Cape peninsula from the seventeenth century onwards. The odd thing about it is that *Afrikaners'* fundamental rights will be scrutinized through the literary works of André Brink, one of the most renowned *Afrikaanse skrywers* (Afrikaans writers). On the other hand, it could be disputable whether the two constitutive parts of the law-and-literature movement – that is to say, the literary and the legal ones – could contribute to the analysis of such topic.

From a legal perspective, it is obvious that white people, in general, and *Afrikaners*, in particular,[1] were the sole groups who enjoyed *all* the fundamental rights set forth in the *South Africa Act 1909* and in the subsequent Constitutions (the *Republic of South Africa Constitution Act, 1961* and the *Republic of South Africa Act, 1983*). The white, racially dominated South Africa provided for a "separate-but-not-equal" constitutional legal framework. The same word *apartheid* (apartness) connotes the "entire complex of superior-subordinate relationships between Europeans and non-Europeans."[2]

Afrikaner politicians conceived apartheid to be a form of work-in-progress process of State-building. The process began in the seventeenth century during

---

1 Within the whites, Afrikaners form a separate group, juxtaposed to the English one. Indeed, "Afrikaner is a speaker of Afrikaans with a special loyalty to South Africa": Brian M. du Toit, "Afrikaners, Nationalists, and Apartheid," *The Journal of Modern African Studies* 8.4 (December 1970): 531–551, 532. On English as the language of the oppressors see André P. Brink, "English and the Afrikaans Writer," *English in Africa* 3.1 (March 1976): 34–46, 35.
2 Colin Rhys Lovell, "Afrikaner Nationalism and Apartheid," *The American Historical Review* 61.2 (January 1956): 308–330, 308.

the rule of the *Vereenigde Oost-Indische Compagnie* (VOC) – the Netherlands East Indian Company –; it was the official policy of the *Boer* Republics (1854–1902). From 1910 to 1948 the South African Dominion fostered "social apartheid"[3] by progressively depriving the subordinate ethnic groups of their fundamental rights.[4] The segregationist policies were influenced by the *Afrikaner Broederbond*, a secret society with the professed aim of "promotion of all the interests of the Afrikaner nation."[5]

The apartheid system was strengthened after the Second World War – i.e., when the Afrikaner *Nasionale Party* won the 1948 general elections.[6] The national government passed several legislative acts and administrative measures, which established a legal system based on racial separateness and limitation of black people's rights. The flexible character of South African Constitutions favored the approval of such measures: hence, the sole clauses entrenched in the Constitution dealt with suffrage and Afrikaans and English as official languages. Segregationist policies eventually culminated in the so-called "territorial apartheid",[7] which led to the creation of *Bantustans* – i.e., quasi-independent Homelands for the blacks. Additional legislative provisions abolished the fundamental rights of Indians and colored people.[8]

---

3 On "social" apartheid see Colin Rhys Lovell, "Afrikaner Nationalism and Apartheid," 308 ff. The first recorded use of the term "apartheid" occurred in 1929 by Rev. J.C. du Plessis, pastor of the *Gereformeerde Nededuitse Kerk*, but "the idea of apartheid became crystallised" in the early 1940s (Hermann Giliomee, "The Making of the Apartheid Plan, 1929–1948," *Journal of South African Studies* 29.2 (June 2003): 373–392, 373–374).

4 See among others, the *Mines and Works Act* (No 12 of 1911), the *Native Land Law* (No 27 of 1913), the *Native (Urban Areas) Act* (No 21 of 1923).

5 See the *Bond Constitution*, clause 4c, in *Die Nederduitsch Hervormde Kerk en die Afrikaner Broderbond*, submitted to the General Synod of 23 April 1964, Chapter 3, section 15, quoted by Dan O'Meara, "The Afrikaner Broederbond 1927–1948: Class Vanguard of Afrikaner Nationalism", *Journal of Southern African Studies* 3.2 (April 1977): 156–186, 156 and 164 ("membership was restricted to financially sound, white, Afrikaans-speaking, Protestant males, over age 25, of 'unimpeachable character,' who actively accepted South Africa as their sole homeland, containing a separate Afrikaner nation with its own language and culture").

6 The first *Nasionale Party* was erected by General Hertzog in 1913: see Dan O'Meara, "The Afrikaner Broederbond," 159. According to Brian M. du Toit, "Afrikaners, Nationalists," 540 note 1, the first party "should not be confused with the [...] 'purified' national party [...] set up by Dr Malan in 1934," which won the 1948 general elections. On Hertzog's role in shaping apartheid policies see Colin Rhys Lovell, "Afrikaner Nationalism," 324.

7 *Afrikaner Broederbond* first recommended territorial apartheid in 1933. See Saul Dubow, "Afrikaner Nationalism, Apartheid and the Conceptualization of 'Race'," *The Journal of African History* 33.2 (1992): 209–237, 211–212.

8 Indians and colored were deprived of the electoral suffrage by *The Separate Representation of Voters Act* (No 46 of 1951). The act was declared invalid [*Harris and Others v Minister of the Interior*

Moreover, the regime aimed at subduing every single aspect of private and public life – individual ethical and moral behaviors, marriages, facilities, education, public health and so forth – to a strict and detailed regulation. The regime pursued the segregationist policies according to "visible" and "invisible" mechanisms of enforcement. *Visible mechanisms* were, for example, the massacres in Sharpeville (1960) and Soweto (1976). The *invisible ones* were represented by a parallel system of secret police entrusted with the protection and supervision of apartheid core values and principles. It had frequent recourse to torture and inhuman and degrading treatments thus reversing the structure of criminal proceedings – i.e., the process as a trial of fact-finding, which tends to represent events in their absence. On the contrary, the regime preferred sudden disappearances and hidden slayings of white dissenters and blacks charged with terrorism.

In legal terms, disappearance not only caused the physical removal of the body; it also deleted the proof of evidence. Paraphrasing Peter Schneck, disappearance impeded the production of images of oppression to the mind and inhibited the recognition of the body as the essential piece of evidence: the representation of reality was thus incomplete.[9] The way the parallel police operated impeded the performance of the body itself as evidence and the right to a fair proceeding. As Mark Sanders stresses, apartheid policies and the Afrikaner nationalists sought to render "black bodies undesirable to whites, and white bodies undesirable to blacks."[10] The outcome was a legalistic, multi-level and hierarchically organized legal system, within which the whites and the blacks were set at the top and at the lowest tier of the caste-like system respectively. The separate-but-not-equal rule ended up with the transition to democracy between 1990 and 1996. As a backlash, the result is "the overriding importance of equality in the constitution itself and in the project of transformation envisaged by the [same] constitution."[11]

---

and Another 1952 (2) SA 428 (AD)], because it infringed the "Cape franchise" entrenched in ss 35 and 52 of the 1909 Constitution. The Parliament approved the *Senate Act* (No 53 of 1955) and modified the composition of the Upper Chamber. This allowed the *Nasionale Party* to pack the Senate and circumvent the entrenched clauses by passing the *South Africa Amendment Act* (No. 9 of 1956). The Indian and colored franchise was restored by s 101(1) of the *Republic of South Africa Constitution Act, 1983*.

9 Peter Schneck, *Rhetoric and Evidence. Legal Conflict and Literary Representation in U.S. American Culture* (Berlin et al.: De Gruyter, 2011), 187–188.

10 Mark Sanders, "Undesirable Publications. J.M. Coetzee on Censorship an Apartheid," *Law and Literature* 18.1 (Spring 2006): 101–114, 102.

11 Evadné Grant, "Human Rights, Cultural Diversity and Customary Law in South Africa," *Journal of African Law* 50.1 (2006): 2–23, 9.

2 The Political Engagement Against Apartheid: André Brink's Literary Works

As for the literary perspective, the examination of *Afrikaners'* fundamental rights in apartheid South Africa highlights a more complicated reality. Indeed, South African society was "a society in which the culture of the majority, including the legal culture, has, over a long period of time, been disparaged and subjected to a minority "Western" culture, first under colonialism and subsequently under apartheid."[12]

The contradiction between human rights and the caste-like system in the separate-but-not-equal South Africa has been closely examined. The impossibility of creating an "official" opposition to the regime encouraged several authors to resort to their literary production in order to criticize apartheid. Among them, we can mention Ingrid Jonker and Breyten Breytenbach, prominent figures in the Afrikaans literary movement known as *Die Sestigers*, which used Afrikaans to speak against the apartheid government.[13] Nonetheless, we will concentrate on André Philippus Brink: Afrikaner, eminent scholar, professor of English literature, worldwide known dramatist and novelist writing in both English and Afrikaans. His literary production stands out for the subtle criticism towards apartheid. Hence, his novel *Kennis van die aand* was the first book written in Afrikaans to be banned by the South African government.[14] Moreover, the novels *Gerugte van Reën* and *'n Droë Wit Seisoen* represent his most lucid and clear depiction of the hypocritical *Afrikaner* society in the 1970s – i.e., during the period in which apartheid policies reached their heights.[15]

As a consequence, there is nothing contradictory in making recourse to Brink's works in order to examine the fundamental rights attributed to *Afrikaners* in Apartheid South Africa. Since Brink acted as a dissenter and fought against the regime, his works can support the examination of the rights conferred upon the whiteness under the racial regime.

---

12 Grant, "Human Rights," 3.
13 Brink, "English and the Afrikaans Writer," 40.
14 André P. Brink, *Looking on Darkness* (New York: Morrow, 1975).
15 André P. Brink, *Rumors of Rain* (London: Penguin, 1984) and *A Dry White Season* (London: Fontana, 1984): further references in the text, abbreviated as *RR* and *DWS* respectively.

3 The Linguistic Contradiction: Afrikaans, White But Multicultural

The essay does not intend to analyze *Afrikaners* fundamental rights. On the contrary, it focuses on the specific presuppositions apartheid rested on. The purpose is to ascertain whether such rights were consistent either with apartheid ideology or with the "universal" notion of fundamental rights, the foundations of which can be traced back to *equality* and *liberty*.

The "white" South African legal system relied on manifold contradictions, and André Brink's literary works contribute to highlight them. Furthermore, his literary and political engagement supports the idea that such contradictions modeled the "fundamental rights" whites were entitled to by the regime. The first contradiction refers to Afrikaans – i.e., the language spoken by *Afrikaners*. Afrikaans – the world's youngest "natural" language – cannot be considered a "pure" language for a "pure" white race. It is well known that *Afrikaners* protected the purity of Afrikaans having recourse to different institutions, such as the *Genootskap van Regte Afrikaners* (Society of Real Afrikaners) founded in 1875. Moreover, Afrikaans gained recognition as an official language with the *The Official Languages of the Union Act, 1925* (No 8 of 1925). In addition, s 108(1) of the *Republic of South Africa Constitution Act, 1961* stated that "English and Afrikaans shall be the official languages of the Republic, and shall be treated on a footing of equality, and possess and enjoy equal freedom, rights and privileges". As already said, the flexible South African Constitution set forth only few entrenched clauses: those concerning the equality of English and Dutch (including Afrikaans) as official languages; those related to the possibility of limiting the qualification necessary to entitle persons to vote on the grounds of race and color; those setting the amending procedure (s 35, 37 and 152 *South Africa Act, 1909*; ss 108 and 118 *Republic of South Africa Constitution Act 1961*). Such clauses were "valid unless the Bill embodying such repeal or alteration [should] be passed by both Houses of Parliament sitting together, and at the third reading be agreed to by not less than two thirds of the total number of members of both Houses".[16] The contradiction here is represented

---

16 s 118(1) *Republic of South Africa Constitution Act 1961*. For the *South Africa Act, 1909*, see Ben Beinart, "The South African Senate," *The Modern Law Review* 20.6 (November 1957): 549–565, 558. As for the electoral suffrage, the 1908 National Convention (which drafted the 1909 Constitution) preserved the "Cape franchise principle", which allowed non-Europeans to be eligible for the Cape provincial council. The Convention did not extend it to the Union parliament. This was due to the strong opposition of *Transvaal, Oranjerivierkolonie*, and Natal. As stated by Colin Rhys Lovell, "Afrikaner Nationalism and Apartheid," 321, "the Cape franchise was doubly entrenched by sections 35 and 152." Under s 35 of the 1909 Constitution, the removal of voters from the Cape

by the fact that Afrikaans is a multicultural language, which was shaped by Dutch colonists, immigrants and refugees (like the French Huguenots), slaves (such as those from Malaysia), missionaries coming from Germany and Scotland, South African native groups – among them, the Khoisan and the Nguni.

Despite these origins, Afrikaners aimed at establishing a linguistic purism, as Brink underlined in his works. The *recherche* of such linguistic purism was particularly evident in the Thirties, when purism degenerated into "puritanism: an exaggerated and often ridiculous fear of English influences on Afrikaans, resulting in a witch-hunt to eradicate all Anglicism from the language."[17] Paradoxically, puritanism did not deprive Afrikaans of the words, which it had borrowed from the other South African "inferior" languages.

4 A Second Contradiction: a White Rule Based (Also) on African Legal Systems

Let us now consider the title of the essay: *'n Droë Wit Seisoen in die Stormkaap*. The recourse to the adjectives *Wit* (white), *Droë* (dry), on the one hand, and to the noun *Stormkaap* (Cape of Storms), on the other, reveals a second contradiction in the apartheid conception of *Afrikaners'* fundamental rights. The heading merges words from the title of the most-renowned novel by Brink (*'n Droë Wit Seisoen*) and the Afrikaans denomination of the place where the Dutch people founded their first South African colony in 1652. The outcome is an oxymoron: how is it possible that "Storm" and "Dry" coexist in the same place and in the same time? Despite the oxymoron, it is possible: the *Droë Seisoen* in the *Stormkaap* is determined by the racial regime established by the whites and, in particular, by its

---

roll solely by reason of race or color had to respect s 152, which required a two-thirds vote of parliamentary membership in joint session to amend either these foregoing sections or itself. The Parliament deprived Africans of their active franchise in the Cape by the *Representation of Natives Act* (No 12 of 1396): "four Europeans would be elected by Africans to represent them in the Senate, and for this purpose the Union was divided into four constituencies." See Ben Beinart, "The South African Senate," 558–559. Moreover, the *Asiatic Land Tenure And Indian Representation Act* (Act 28 of 19646) disenfranchised the Indians in Natal. The representation of Indians at the national level was repealed under the *Nasionale Party* government: see the *Asiatic Laws Amendment Act* (No 47 of 1948).

17 Brink, "English and the Afrikaans Writer," 36: purism survived in the 1970s "mainly as a symptom of a political (extreme Right) attitude." Originally the aims were "laudable and positive enough – namely to avoid the 'easy way out' in coping, linguistically, with new challenges; and, instead of simply borrowing solutions from English, the syntactic, semantic and morphological possibilities of Afrikaans itself were explored."

segregationist policy. In this respect, the *Wit Droë Seisoen* – i.e., the rule of the whites in the Cape – withers the blending of cultures enriching the pluralistic mosaic which is South Africa.

Moreover, *Stormkaap* refers to the geographical territory falling under the Dutch administration, the legal system of which was represented by the Roman-Dutch law. To this extent, there is no correspondence between the purity and superiority of whiteness and the related legal system. Roman-Dutch law is only a part of the legal tradition known as *jus commune*. Nor it is a pure legal system: it blends Roman law, Canon law and the Germanic customary law. Thus, the alleged superiority of Dutch law stems from an apodictic equation. If the whites are the superior and pure race, it follows that both their language and legal system necessarily share such superiority and purity.

Such an assumption was compromised by the subsequent evolution of the South African constitutional history. From the eighteenth century onward, the South African legal system developed into what scholars define as a *mixed legal system*: a blending of Roman-Dutch law, Common law coexisting with African customary law. Moreover, both the language and the legal system of the oppressors did not correspond to the idea of "apartness" preserving the white race. As a matter of fact, Afrikaans is the mother tongue of the colored; moreover, Roman-Dutch law has become the legal system applicable to *all* the groups – whites, colored, Indians, blacks – living in the country.

In order to create their own identity, Afrikaners forged a literary language idealizing the *Boer* tradition, upon which they modeled a legal language expressing unequal law. The prevailing attitude was favorable to assert the inferiority of African customary and indigenous legal systems. Hence, differentiation between the juridical systems – Roman-Dutch law and customary law – had recourse to the criterion of racial separatism and exclusion, subsequently confirmed by apartheid. Separatism, however, did not eliminate African customary law.

The attitude towards customary law changed in nineteenth and twentieth centuries. In the Boer Republics (*Transvaal* and *Oranje-Vrystaat*) customary law was eventually recognized in 1885. In the Cape and Natal colonies, "the application of customary law was subject to a requirement of compatibility with principles of 'civilization'".[18] Thus, when the Union of South Africa was established (1910), approaches to customary law diverged throughout the country: there was "complete non-recognition in the Cape, limited application in the Transvaal and full recognition and application in Natal and the Transkeian territories."[19] Only

---

18 Grant, "Human Rights," 14.
19 Grant, "Human Rights," 13.

the *Native Administration Act* (No 38 of 1927) recognized customary law and established a separate system of courts for Africans. This was due to the fact that each racial group had to possess its own legal system. However, apartheid did not prevent mutual influences between the legal systems.

5 A Third Contradiction: Limitations as Collective Rights

A third contradiction derives from the foundations upon which apartheid was established. Such foundations can be traced back to a misleading and distorted interpretation of both morality and religion. In this respect, the regime exercised a strict scrutiny over ethic and individual behavior as part of the apartheid policy.[20] As already said, the regime had recourse to both *visible* and *invisible* mechanisms in order to monitor the behavior of colored and black people, as well as of the *Afrikaners*, thus limiting their civil liberties.

Through *invisible mechanisms* of control, *Afrikaners* were secretly controlled and tailed in order to check the consistency of their moral conducts – as well as of their political attitudes – with the core values of Afrikanerdom. This is evident in Brink's *'n Wit Droë Seisoen*, where Ben du Toit, the main character, realizes the ubiquity of such mechanisms of control:

> What is set up against me is not a man, not even a group of people, but a thing, a something a vague amorphous something, an ubiquitous power [...] a power that follows me wherever I go, day and night, day and night frustrating me, intimidating me, playing with me according to rules devised and physically changed by itself. (*WDS*, 233)

Such methods of control were conceived as mechanisms of self-preservation of Afrikanerdom. Indeed, protection of whiteness necessarily entailed a guardianship over public and private behaviors. As for *visible* control, we might here note the scrutiny exercised by the government over freedom of expression. Thus, the use of Afrikaans "began to bear a stamp of exclusiveness – White Afrikaner Nationalist Calvinist exclusiveness."[21]

On the one hand, the already mentioned *Genootskap van Regte Afrikaners* and the *Federasie van Afrikaanse Kultuurverenigings* (established in 1929) strictly monitored the use of Afrikaans. On the other, the *Publications and Entertainments Act* (No 26 of 1963) and the *Publications Act* (No 42 of 74) introduced severe

---

20 For apartheid legislation passed after 1951, see Elizabeth S. Landis, "Apartheid Legislation," *Africa Today* 4.6 (November-December 1957): 45–48.
21 Brink, "English and the Afrikaans Writer," 44.

mechanisms of censorship.[22] Under the *Publications Act, 1974* several Committees performed censorship scrutiny (s 4 ff), and the rulings were appealable to the Publications Appeal Board (ss 35–39). Publications – as well as films, representations of public entertainment, etc. – were banned if, in the Committee's opinion, they were 'undesirable' [s 9(1)]. Censorship was accomplished according to the core values of apartheid: according to s 1, "in the application of the Act, the constant endeavour of the population of the Republic of South Africa to uphold a Christian view of life shall be recognized."

Hence, the moral, ethical and racial presuppositions of the constitutional legal system directly affected *Afrikaners'* fundamental rights. In this respect, apartheid overturned the traditional conception of fundamental rights. Indeed, ethical and moral control over individuals operated as limits to the rights of the individuals. The contradiction lay in the fact that limitations stemming from both religious and legal foundations of apartheid were turned into *Afrikaner* collective rights: the right to individual morality; freedom of art, expression and speech, which had to be consistent with Afrikanerdom.

Such collective rights were epitomized in the banning of Etienne Leroux's novel *Magersfontein, O Magersfontein!* in 1978. The Publications Appeal Board, chaired by Judge H.J. Snyman, was extremely aggressive toward Afrikaans-speaking intellectuals:

> The point at issue is whether the position of the literary scholars [*letterkundiges*] regarding unsavoury language (however revolting [*vieslik*]) can really be justified. *The law protects the morals of the entire public* [*gemeenskap*]. The Appeal Board wishes to state expressly that, according to its assessment of the community view [*gemeenskapsopvatting*] of public morals, this approach of the literary scholars is at odds with the Publications Act [...] The general opinion of the literary scholars is that the goal of the book is to satirize [...] our own age against the background of a heroic past. *Nevertheless, the central question remains whether the public* [...] *is prepared to tolerate the manner in which this goal is attained.*

The Board concluded:

> The writer built into [the] novel excessive filthy language, excessive idle use of the Lord's name, vulgar references to excretion, masturbation, [etc.] [...] This novel is highly regarded by literary scholars. The *broad public*, however, as personified by the *average man*, regards the use [of such language] as an *infringement of the dignity of the individual and an invasion of his respect for sexual privacy.*[23]

---

22 On the relations between André Brink and censorship see John Maxwell Coetzee, "André Brink and the Censor," *Research in African Literatures* 21.3 (Autumn 1990): 59–74.

23 Jacobus Christoffel Willem Van Rooyen, *Publikasiebeheer in Suid-Afrika* (Kaapstad: Juta, 1978), 14–18, quoted by John Maxwell Coetzee, "André Brink and the Censor," 67 [italics mine].

244 —— Matteo Nicolini

The ambiguity of such collective fundamental Afrikaner rights is perfectly depicted in *Gerugte van Reën*. The main character expresses his lack of comprehension of the betrayal of Afrikanerdom:

- He had everything a man could wish for. Friends, women, money, travels, success in his career, recognition, fame, the lot. I fail to understand how a man in his position could willingly give up everything to go and fight for the sake of others.
- There's one thing you forgot, Martin.
- What's that?
- Morality. (*RR*, 69)

Hence, the legal system compensated the loss of "individual" fundamental rights: Afrikaners were set at the top of the hierarchical, caste-like society and provided with *everything a man could wish for*. This, however, could not affect the conscience of individuals. Opening up their eyes, *Afrikaners* realized that apartheid had only hushed up an inhuman reality: the white dry season had already turned in a dreadful Storm in the Cape.

6 A Fourth Contradiction: From the *Groot Trek* to Mythology, via Calvinism

The most relevant contradiction stems from the intertwining of the historical affirmation of the Afrikanerdom and its religious foundations. *Afrikaner* mythology traces back to the so-called *Groot Trek* (Great Trek), "the national epic-formal proof of God's election of the Afrikaner people and His special destiny for them."[24] To this extent, *Afrikaners* perceived themselves as *the* Chosen People. Self-identification with the Israelites can be understood within the broader context of Calvinism and the theological conception of predestination related thereto.[25]

Indeed, *Afrikaners* had recourse to the Holy Bible in order to explicate the rationale of apartheid. Seen through the lens of the oppressors, however, the underlying values and essential aims of Calvinism were completely distorted. This is particularly evident if we consider how the *Nederduitse Gereformeerde Kerk* (Dutch Reformed Church) asserted that apartheid was biblically justified:

---

24 T. Dunbar Moodie, *The Rise of Afrikanerdom Power, Apartheid, and the Afrikaner Civil Religion* (Berkeley et al.: University of California Press, 1975), 3.
25 For the incidence of Calvinism over Afrikaner ethical (and political) beliefs see Timothy M. Renick, "From Apartheid to Liberation: Calvinism and the Shaping of Ethical Belief in South Africa," *Sociological Focus* 24.2 (May 1991), 129–143, 132 et seq.; Colin Rhys Lovell, "Afrikaner Nationalism and Apartheid," 309.

Every nation and race will be able to perform the greatest service to God and the world if it keeps its own national attributes, received from God's own hand, pure with honour and gratitude [...] Equality between natives, coloureds and Europeans includes a misappreciation of the fact that God, in His Providence, made people into different races and nations.[26]

The creation of the *Afrikaner* mythology commenced at the beginning of the nineteenth century, when the British Army first occupied the Cape (1806), and then imposed its rule over the whole colony (1814)[27]. Such mythology was indirectly determined by the British colonial administration. Under the British rule, English was established as the official language of Cape colony (1813). Furthermore, the British administration introduced legal equality notwithstanding race or color (1828) and abolished slavery (1833).

Such alterations in the Cape legal system were perceived as threat for Afrikaner culture and society. As a consequence, thousands of Afrikaners – or *Boers*, since they were descendants of Dutch farmers – started to flee northward in the interior of the country. This migration is generally known as the *Groot Trek*, a long exodus towards the Promised Land, which lead to the foundation of *Boer* republics.[28]

The self-identification of the Chosen people was confirmed in 1838, when the *Trekboers* defeated the Zulus in the so-called Blood River battle. In November 1838, Andries Pretorius – the *Boer* founder of Pretoria – assembled around 500 men, women, and children along the banks of the river: "the whole force joining in prayers and the singing of psalms. The army made a vow that if victorious they would build a church, and set apart a thanksgiving day each year to commemorate it."[29] This is known as the "Vow of Covenant at Blood River":

---

26 Commission for Current Problems of the Federated *Nederduitse Gereformeerde Kerk*, 1954 quoted in Trevor Huddleston, *Naught For Your Comfort* (New York: Doubleday & Company Inc., Garden City, 1956): 61. As Neville Richardson, "Apartheid, Heresy and the Church in South Africa," *The Journal of Religious Ethics* 14.1 (Spring 1986), 1–21, 21, states, in 1982 "The World Alliance of Reformed Churches (WARC) suspended the membership of two of its South African member churches – the *Nederdutise Gereformeerde Kerk* (NGK) and the *Nederdutisch Hervormde Kerk* (NHK) [because] the latter church, by its constitution, admits only whites [...] the former [...] has a racially-based structure".
27 For a brief sketch of the Dutch rule before the British invasion, and of the British attempts to eradicate Afrikaner language and culture, see du Toit, "Afrikaners, Nationalists," 533–535.
28 Stephen Crane, *The Great Boer Trek* (New York: Hearst Corp., 1956): 158. See also Timothy M. Renick, "From Apartheid to Liberation," 133. For a stringent critique over *Afrikaner* Calvinistic self-identification with the Israelites see Trevor Huddleston, *Naught For Your Comfort*, 62ff.
29 Renick, "From Apartheid to Liberation," 134.

> Here we stand before the holy God of heaven and earth, to make a vow to Him that, if He will protect us and give our enemy into our hand, we shall keep this day and date every year as a day of thanksgiving like a sabbath, and that we shall erect a house to His honour wherever it should please Him, and that we also will tell our children that they should share in that with us in memory for future generations. For the honour of His name will be glorified by giving Him the fame and honour for the victory[30]

On December 16, between 10,000 and 15,000 Zulus attacked the little Boer army. After only a few hours, the *Boers* defeated the Zulus. The Afrikaners had finally been unchained from the oppressive Egypt of the Pharaoh – i.e., the Cape British administration. Moreover, God had given them victory over the Zulus and they were going to enter the "Promised Land." The commencement of the white dominance is an effect of the self-identification with the Israelites; they also took Israel's hierarchical order. The Afrikaner victory at Blood River became a way of ordering human existence. In Genesis, Ham sins against his father, and consequently, all of his descendants are cursed:[31]

> And [Noah] said, Cursed be Canaan; a servant of servants shall he be unto his brethren.
> And he said, Blessed be the Lord God of Shem; and Canaan shall be his servant.
> God shall enlarge Japheth, and he shall dwell in the tents of Shem; and Canaan shall be his servant (*Genesis* 9:25–27)

In Afrikaner interpretation, Ham's descendants, the Canaanites, were the African blacks. The scriptures set the divine ordering of humanity, and through this ordering apartheid found its structure.

The biblical foundations of apartheid set the legal framework, within which Afrikaners could uphold their special relationship with God, preserve mutual solidarity and the order to be retained by successive generations. Furthermore, they had to safeguard the radical purity of God's Chosen People through means of separation from the inferior races. Calvinist interpretation of the Bible provided an additional limitation to "white" individual rights, which shaped another *Afrikaner* collective right: the right (perhaps a duty) to participate in preserving "the divine order for one genetic line to serve another, and this [was] not unjust, it [was] simply the way the Almighty [had] arranged things."[32]

This was the most striking outcome of a biblical interpretation inconsistent with the New Testament. In legal terms, biblical justification for apartheid led to

---

30 Available at http://sa.travel-directory.co/62/sub-places/kwazulu-%20%3E%20natal/battle fields-region/voortrekker-zulu-%20%3E%20conflict/attractions/blood-river (October 30, 2013).
31 See Lovell, "Afrikaner Nationalism and Apartheid," 309.
32 Donald Harman Akenson, *God's Peoples: Covenant and Land in South Africa, Israel, and Ulster* (London: Cornell University Press:, 1992), 95.

negation of equality. Calvinist explanation of the *Trek* not only validated the equation between *Afrikaners* and Chosen People; it also legitimated racial inequality and oppression. From the foundations of the *Boer* Republics onward, *Afrikaners* rejected any form of *gelykstelling* (equality) as "un-Christian" and "contrary to the law of God and natural subordination by birth and faith."[33] Hence, the distinction between elect and non-elect people precluded putting whites and blacks on equal footing.

Thus, the negation of *gelykstelling* was justified on religious grounds and legally recognized. Indeed, the Constitutions of the Boer Republics expressly acknowledged European supremacy. For example, s 1 of the *Oranje-Vrystaat Konstitusie* (1854) reserved citizenship and landownership only to Europeans.[34] Moreover, the Rustenburg *Grondwet* (1858) – which would became the Constitution of the South African Republic (1860) – expressly established that "The people desire to permit no equality between colored people and the white inhabitants either in church or state."[35]

7 From *Die Groot Trek* Back to Pre-Colonial Africa. André Brink and the Reversal of the *Afrikaner* Mythology

André Brink's literary works expressly depart from *Trekboers'* self-identification with the Chosen People and biblical justification of apartheid. On the contrary, he prefers to re-examine pre-colonial South African history rather than to refer to the *Voortrekker* mythology. This strategy revises history by overturning the perspective: according to post-colonial studies, history must be examined through the lenses of the peripheries of the colonial empires. Thus, Brink bypasses *Afrikaner* history and gives voice to those who have been traditionally disregarded by "official" colonial historiography. This is particular evident in *Die Eertse Lewe van Adamastor* (1988),[36] conceived and written in Afrikaans only a few years before the dismantlement of apartheid.

---

33 The quotations are from Louis S. Steenkamp, Anna Elizabeth Steenkamp, André G. du Toit, Martin Basson eds., *Die Dagboek van Anna Steenkamp en Fragmentjies oor die Groot-Trek* (Natalse Pers: Pietermaritzburg, 1939), 10, quoted in Lovell, "Afrikaner nationalism," 314.

34 See Gert Daniel Scholtz, *Die Konstitusie En Die Staatsinstellings Van Die Oranje-Vrystaat, 1854–1902* (Amsterdam: Swets & Zettlinger, 1937).

35 André du Toit, "No Chosen People: The Myth of the Calvinist Origins of Afrikaner Nationalism and Racial Ideology," *The American Historical Review* 88.4 (October 1983): 920–952, 926–927.

36 André Brink, *The First Life of Adamastor* (London: Secker & Warburg, 1993).

The *Boer* perspective is totally reversed. First, the narrator is a South African native pertaining to the Khoikhoi ethnic group. Second, he describes events traditionally referred to by Europeans: "the first contact between European discoverers' and the colonial 'other'."[37] Third, the narrator is Adamastor, the mythical giant described in Luiz de Camoes' *Lusiads* (1572). Fourth, this is the first "constitutional history" of South Africa narrated through the eyes of black people. To put it another way, Brink sets aside the "official version of Afrikaner history" and has recourse to the point of view of those marginalized by European history, a point of view "directed against an established master-narrative valorizing the European 'discovery' of Africa."[38] The result is remarkable: Adamastor narrates the history of the arrival of the Europeans. To this extent, Brink challenges the traditional assumptions held in the "Afrikaner" epic poem *Hoe die Hollanders die Kaap ingeneem het* (How the Dutch people took the Cape), which was written by Stephanus Jacobus du Toit in 1897.[39] This is a total reversal in approaching the history of *Stormkaap*.

The re-examination of pre-colonial South African history in the light of postcolonialism is relevant from a legal perspective as well. Indeed, *Die Eerste Lewe van Adamastor* can be considered to be a form of escapism from *Trekboer* mythology and apartheid racist ideology – a literary *escamotage* in order to recover André Brink's freedom of art and expression. Such an assumption is validated if we consider that such escapism affected manifold *Afrikaner* novelists and poets: "for the Afrikaans writer, [English is] not only [...] a source of inspiration but also [...] a form of expression, [which] can be established without any problem."[40] As the renowned poet Nicolaas Petrus Van Wyk Louw (1906–1970) wrote to the newspaper *Die Burger* (18 March 1963):

> At a recent prize-giving ceremony I happened to find myself in the proximity (spiritually at least) of a compatriot who writes in English. She publishes her books abroad and apparently earns good money with them; no South African censorship can touch her (it may even be to her advantage!); she can bring her royalties into South Africa from all over the world and the government will welcome this 'influx of capital'. It occurred to me: She can ignore our censorship. *But what about me and my Afrikaans colleagues? We shall have to try and bow under this yoke.* Or ...?

---

37 Jochen Petzold, "André Brink's Magical History Tour: Postmodern and Postcolonial Influences in 'The First Life of Adamastor'," *English in Africa* 27.2 (October 2000): 45–58, 48.

38 Petzold, "André Brink's Magical History Tour," 52.

39 Stephanus Jacobus du Toit, *Hoe die Hollanders die Kaap ingeneem het* (Kaapstad: Human & Rousseau, 1966).

40 Brink, "English and the Afrikaner Writer," 38.

I doubt whether even Lord Milner could have devised a more effective way of hamstringing Afrikaans and allowing English a free rein. It is as if the aspiring young writer (including the Afrikaans writer) were told: 'If you have something to say, my boy, then write in English! And if you don't know English well enough, then learn it like Joseph Conrad: but write in English and save your T soul!.'
Truly, as an Afrikaner who has never made a secret of his Afrikaner nationalism [...] I find it impossible to grasp the motive which could have seduced a Nationalist government into formulating a Bill [the *Publications and Entertainment Act, 1963*] of such dubious 'morality' and so utterly anti-Afrikaans.[41]

The same escapism can be found in *Sandkastele*[42] set around the time of the first democratic elections (1994). In the novel, the centenarian *Ouma* Kristina completely reverses the history of South Africa. As Isidore Diala acutely observes, it is "an affront to the orthodox conception of history in many ways": first, Brink gives voice to another category of marginalized people – the women – "usually silenced in patriarchal reconstructions of the past". Second, *Ouma* Kristina narrates "her history" by tracing "the genealogy of an Afrikaner family from an unusual but more revealing and dependable perspective, the female lineage". Moreover, *Ouma* "Kristina's history, deeply anchored in myth, makes no pretension to a recoverable single version that lays claim to the authenticity and inviolability" of the divine revelation and of the Calvinist pretension to a hierarchical order between races established by God.[43]

8 Shaping Afrikaners' Fundamental Rights. The Role of Boer Mythology and Apartheid Ideology

It is quite evident that apartheid encapsulated *Boer* mythology and ideology in legal provisions. Thus, the regime created a legal system grounded both on the

---

41 "That two sets of factors are involved [...] Censorship, as viewed by Louw, is negative: using English as a form of escape, as the only means of survival. But the other is positive: turning to English to complement the experience lived in Afrikaans; and using the Afrikaans expression to complement the English. It becomes a dual exploration of a single experience – that of living in (South) Africa. In order to appreciate this, more is required than a simple historical survey. For in order to find an answer to the question: *Why should an Afrikaans writer write in English?* It is first necessary to examine the situation implied by the question: *Why write in Afrikaans?*" (André P. Brink, "English and the Afrikaans Writer," 39).
42 André Brink, *Imaginings of Sands* (London: Secker & Warburg, 1996): further references in the text, abbreviated as *IS*.
43 Isidore Diala, "André Brink and the Implications of Tragedy for Apartheid South Africa," *Journal of Southern African Studies* 29.4 (December 2003): 903–919, 916.

demystification of Calvinist theology and on the distortion of its legal (Roman-Dutch law) and extra-juridical (language, race, religion) presuppositions. The transplant of racial values and its subsequent incorporation into legal norms generated a legal system totally pervaded by the necessity of preserving a racial (divine) order, which had to be retained in its radical purity by the successive generations.

Two mechanisms ensured the preservation and protection of the apartheid regime. The first one was the same solidarity *Afrikaners* had already experienced in *die Slag van Bloedrivier*. *Afrikaners'* individual commitment in the protection of their own race and religion necessarily operated as a limitation to human rights traditionally bestowed to individuals. We have already said that such limitations turned into *Afrikaners* collective rights: the right to individual morality; freedom of art, expression and speech consistent with Afrikanerdom; the right to participate in preserving the order for one genetic line to serve another, according to the way God arranged the world.

The second mechanism of preservation operated at the institutional level. Indeed, the regime legally entrenched solidarity and preservation of Afrikanerdom terming them *the* "constitutional" foundations of the *Afrikaner* identity and of the legal system. Thus, the government had to monitor, foster and promote the individual commitment and participation in the achievement of the legal and extra-juridical presuppositions of apartness, superiority and pureness of the white race.

This gave rise to a new fundamental right, embracing and absorbing those of the individuals. We can term it as *"Afrikaner"* institutionalized solidarity. As a consequence, collective Afrikaner rights are not granted to the individuals, but are allocated at the governmental level, in order to ensure the preservation of racial purity and a caste-like social and political order for successive generations.

It follows that *Afrikaner* institutionalized solidarity influenced individual fundamental rights in two ways. On the one side, the regime entitled whites to fundamental rights, which had to be consistent with the core values of apartheid and with the ideology encapsulated in the segregationist legislation. On the other, apartheid did not directly affect the *form* and *denomination* of Afrikaner fundamental rights. The most contentious effects of apartheid over fundamental rights were evident in their exercise. Thus, the incidence of apartheid over fundamental right was "indirect" and "invisible". The apartheid regime shaped the fundamental rights by orienting their content and exercise. Moreover, such rights were enforceable provided that their exercise respected the collective rights conferred upon the regime on behalf of the *Afrikaner* community.

Brink offers an example of such performative attitude of apartheid over *Afrikaner* rights in *Censorship and Literature* (1982):

Outlining an ideal dynamic between the writer who threatens the anarchy of "total freedom" and the state whose system of justice holds the potential for overriding all private interests, Brink postulates "an intricate system of checks and balances" to allow their co-existence. What happens all too often in reality, however, is that power seeks blindly to maintain itself, forcing the writer of conscience to react; or else that the writer threatens, or is felt to threaten, the interests of the state, which then reacts against him. "This is when taboo, which fulfills a creative and possibly indispensable function in primitive society, expresses itself in the form of censorship: what used to be constructive and wholesome now becomes destructive and a symptom of sickness."[44]

To put it differently: Afrikanerdom not only affects the exercise of fundamental rights, but also pervades their content. This is the outcome of the institutionalized solidarity the government had to preserve. As a result, the *Kernbereich* of *Afrikaner* fundamental rights were monitored by the guardianship of the regime, and Afrikanerdom defined them as *Afrikaner apartheid-oriented rights*.

Hence, the core values of apartheid overturned the structure of fundamental rights. We cannot have recourse to the "classical" and "traditional" concepts in order to qualify the rights conferred upon *Afrikaners*. First, institutionalized solidarity pervaded the rights by re-determining their content; second limitations to individual rights led to a reversal in their structure: in case of conflict between the "classical" contents of rights and Afrikanerdom the latter prevailed.

Thus, Afrikanerdom limited both the content and the exercise of fundamental rights. Indeed, *Afrikaners'* individual commitment to the protection of racial supremacy subdued both their content and exercise to individual responsibility and societal solidarity. The sole right entitled to *Afrikaners* was the right to have Afrikanerdom protected from those activities which might be deemed to be inconsistent with the core values of apartheid.

Moreover, the enhancement of such right was allocated at the governmental level. The regime was then entrusted with its enforcement: it had to ensure the preservation of the radical purity and the caste-like order for successive generations. In *'n Droë Wit Seisoen* the main character is fully aware of this: he perceives "A vast, clumsy, shapeless thing"; he has "gnawing awareness of that invisible and shapeless power pursuing him." The institutionalized society makes him feel as if he was "living in an aquarium [...] your every move scrutinised by eyes watching you through glass and water, surveying even the motion of your gills as you breathe" (*WDS*, 161, 262, 222). Furthermore, the performative attitude of institutionalized *Boer* solidarity is brightly described in *Gerugte van Reën*:

---

44 Coetzee, "André Brink and the Censor," 61.

> In order to survive in South Africa, I realise today, more than ever before, it is necessary to shut one's eyes and one's conscience. One has to learn not to feel or think, else it becomes unbearable. In other words, the paradox obtains that one should really learn not to live, in order to go on living. (*RR*, 116)

Nor the color, the race and the language will impede the prosecution of those acting against the apartheid. In this respect, "acting against apartheid" means the exercise of the classical fundamental right we are used to. Moreover, it means the possibility of dissenting. However, a non-apartheid-oriented fundamental right is a betrayal of Afrikanerdom, as well as a violation of the individual commitment and responsibility in enforcing the ideology.

In other words, *it implies the loss of fundamental rights*; in most cases, of the same life:

> The end seems ineluctable failure, defeat, loss. The only choice I have left is whether I am prepared to salvage a little honour, a little decency, a little humanity – or nothing. It seems as if a sacrifice is impossible to avoid, whatever way one looks at it. But at least one has the choice between a wholly futile sacrifice and one that might, in the long run, open up a however or possibility, negligible or dubious, something better, less sordid, and more noble for our children. (*WDS*, 304)

9 Afrikanerdom After The Dismantlement of Apartheid: Towards a Renewed Calvinist Commitment in a Democratic South Africa

The main characteristic of Calvinistic moral belief is the necessity for individuals to assume their own responsibilities within society. This can be termed the *content* of the fundamental rights attributed to *Afrikaners*: the commitment of the individual to act in order to preserve and strengthen the institutionalized *Trekboer* solidarity.

As an Afrikaner, Brink himself shares such an assumption: humans must assume their responsibilities. His concern is evident in the novels written after the dismantlement of apartheid. In this respect, South Africans are committed to the establishment of a new country and a renewed society. The new core values are set forth in the 1996 Constitution, which is based on a non-ideological conception of human rights, on liberty and equality.

To this extent, the post-apartheid Constitution encompasses manifold references to *gelykstelling* – i.e., to *the* principle the new South Africa rests on. First, the Constitution describes the Bill of Rights as *the* "cornerstone of democracy" [s. 7(1)]. Second, the Bill protects "the rights of all people [...] and affirms the democratic values of human dignity, equality and freedom". Third, it applies, without exception, to all law in South Africa [s 8(1)]. Fourth, the interpretation of the Bill of Rights "must promote the values that underlie an open and democratic society based on human dignity, equality and freedom" [s 39]. Fifth, limitation of rights must be "reasonable and justifiable in an open and democratic society based on human dignity, equality and freedom" [s 36(1)]. Finally, s 9 of the 1996 Constitution promotes equality and non-discrimination.

To put it another way, there is an "overriding importance of equality in the constitution [...] and in the project of transformation envisaged by the Constitution itself." The assumption is held if we consider s 1 of the Constitution, which lists "achievement of equality," non-racialism and non-sexism as founding values of South African democracy[45].

The total overturn of the South African constitutional legal system does not mean, however, the termination of the *Afrikaner* and Calvinistic sense of responsibility. The transition to democracy necessarily entails a strong individual commitment in order to enhance and implement the universal core values set forth in the Constitution.

Hence, Brink's individual commitment is to call for Afrikanerdom to participate in the edification of the new South African Rainbow Nation. This is the sense of the new "responsibility of the Afrikaner." As Kristien, the main character of *Sandkastele* states:

> I have chosen this place, not because I was born here and feel destined to remain; but because I went away and then came back and now am here by choice. Perhaps for the first time in my life it is a decision that has not been forced on me from outside, by circumstances, but which has been shaped inside myself, like a child in the womb. This one I shall not deny. It is mine. (*IS*, 338, 349)

This is an individual responsibility different from that stemming from institutionalized *Trekboer* solidarity. The commitment to participating in the edification of a new South Africa is not imposed, but derives from an individual choice, from liberty.

The discovery of such human commitment and responsibility is also at stake in *The Rights of Desire*.[46] At the end of the book, Reuben Olivier sets aside the *Afrikaner's* estrangement arising from the so-called "white dispensation." Hence,

---

45 The quotations are from Grant, "Human Rights," 8–9.
46 André Brink, *The Rights of Desire* (London: Secker & Warburg, 2000): further references in the text, abbreviated as *RD*.

he retires from the world and seeks refuge in his library. Brink stigmatizes Reuben's evasion from his social responsibilities:

> My main regret [...] was that after having been against so much for so long – all the violence and lies of the previous regime, from Malan and Verwoerd all the way down to de Klerk – one would have hoped that in the new dispensation there would at last be the possibility of being *for* some things. (*RD*, 262)

The end of apartheid requires a new sense of responsibility from the whites. In post-apartheid South Africa, the *Afrikaners* do have to participate in recreating the society and in the rewriting the history of the Country. Like Reuben, Afrikaners in post-Apartheid South Africa must accept the challenge "[t]o face what has to be faced, what all my life I've tried to turn away from. There is the world outside – how did Rilke phrase it? – which requires me and strangely concerns me" (*RD*, 306).

Alessandra Tomaselli and Lino Panzeri
The Definition of "Linguistic Minority"

Linguistic *versus* Legal Perspectives[*]

The concept of "linguistic minority" constitutes the topic of different fields of research, among which linguistics and law represent the most prominent ones. In fact, it is well known that human rights include, among the others, the right of linguistic minorities to maintain their own language and culture. In the past, the linguistic and legal perspectives have not (sufficiently) interacted, with evident negative consequences. The normative apparatus which should guarantee linguistic minorities is far from being adequate (i.e. inefficient in most cases) with respect to the complexity of the phenomena represented by "minorities." This considera- tion suggests, at least for the future, a much stronger and more effective interaction between the legal and the linguistic perspectives which should rely, first of all, on an agreed definition of the concept and typology of "linguistic minority."

This paper tries to compare the different typologies of "linguistic minorities," which emerge from a classification based on one side on linguistic criteria, on the other side on legal ones providing a further step towards the desired harmoniza- tion.

1 From a linguistic perspective

1.1 Towards a typology of linguistic minorities from the linguistic perspective

A first important step towards a typology of linguistic minorities is due to the seminal work by Toso in 2008.[1] Focusing our attention on the German(ic) varieties spoken in Northern Italy, it is quite evident that: i) the German community in South Tyrol is "different," in a way that can be easily defined, from the so-called historical Germanic minorities which survive in isolated contexts (linguistic islands) in the Alp region; ii) each historical minority is characterized *per se* by both a different history and specific linguistic features. In order to make these assumptions more concrete we will first briefly sketch the main characteristics of

---

[*] For the formal definition of scholar responsibility, Part 1 is attributed to Alessandra Tomaselli; Part 2 to Lino Panzeri; Part 3 to both authors.
[1] Fiorenzo Toso, *Le minoranze linguistiche in Italia* (Bologna: Il Mulino, 2008).

the German community in South Tyrol (Alto Adige/Südtirol) and later those of two different historical Germanic minorities spoken in the Triveneto geographic region, i.e. the Mocheni and the Cimbrians.

The German linguistic minority in South Tyrol is a minority in Italy but a majority in the Province of Bolzano/Bozen,[2] which is characterized by territorial contiguity with Austria (in this perspective we are allowed to call South Tyrol a linguistic peninsula). The German community relies on an educational system in German language (from Kindergarten to University) and a local literature with a long tradition, from the Middle High German period (Walter von der Vogelweide, Oswald von Wolkenstein) to contemporary writers (among all, Zoderer, Stecher and Innerhofer)[3]. From a sociolinguistic point of view, South Tyrol is characterized by both a diatopic variation, i.e. a rich (German) Dialect variation,[4] and a diglossic situation (Standard *versus* Dialect) whithin a multilingual context (German, Italian, Ladin varieties).

The so-called Mocheni (from the German verb *machen* "to make") represent an historical linguistic minority settled in the Fersina valley (Val dei Mocheni/Fersental), a well delimited territory in the Province of Trento without contiguity with respect to a German speaking community/Nation (i.e. a "linguistic island"). The German language could be considered just as a potential standard. Commercial activities with South Tyrol (by the so-called "Krumeri") are well attested until the end of the last century. Not surprisingly, Mocheno and Tyrolean dialects are mutually comprehensible, Mocheno and Standard German are not. With the exception of an extremely low number of children, no new generation of speakers learn Mocheno as a mother language. The number of inhabitants in the relevant district is around 1000, but the Mocheno speakers may be fewer.[5] In recent times, thanks to a far-sighted educational politics, Mocheno has been introduced at primary school level: just a few hours per week and only in some schools, where Standard German has also been introduced.[6] The most relevant activities for

2 Among 453.272 interviews collected during the period 2001–2011, 69,41% of the population declared to belong to the German group, 26,06% to the Italian group and just 4,53% to the Ladin one. See http://www.provincia.bz.it/astat/it/censimento-popolazione/default.asp (September 16, 2013).
3 Birgit Alber, "Die Integration des Dialektes in den literarischen Text," *Tribune* 2 (2008): 16–18.
4 Kurt Klein, Ludwig Erich Schmitt, eds. *Tirolischer Sprachatlas*, vol. 3 (Innsbruck: Tyrolia – Marburg: Elwert, 1965–1971).
5 The number of native speakers of Mocheno could be approximated around 600: see Birgit Alber, "Past Participle in Mòcheno: Allomorphy, alignment and the distribution of obstruents" in *Studies on German-Language Islands*, ed. Michael Putnam (Amsterdam: John Benjamins, 2011), 33–63.
6 Ed. Federica Ricci Garotti, *L'acquisizione del tedesco per i bambini* (Trento: Unitn Labirinti, 2012).

maintaining the language and culture of this small linguistic minority are promoted by the local cultural Institution *Bersntoler Kulturinstitut – Istituto Culturale Mocheno*: among all, the project of a descriptive grammar of the Mocheno variety (1997–2003) directed by Anthony Rowley, which resulted in the production of the first reference grammar for this minority language.[7] This community, in fact, does not rely on either a grammatical tradition or a literature of its own.

The so-called Cimbrian survives in three linguistic islands distributed in three different Provinces (Trento, Verona and Vicenza) which belong to two different administrative Regions (Trentino-AltoAdige/Südtirol and Veneto): Luserna/Lusern near Trento, Giazza/Ljetzan near Verona and Roana/Roban near Vicenza. There is no territorial contiguity either among the three Cimbrian communities or with a German speaking community/Nation. German is "too far" to be taken as a reference Standard Language. All speakers learnt Italian at school and are fluent in the relevant Romance dialect of the Venetian area. The mutual comprehension between the Cimbrian varieties and Mocheno is often assumed but not always "effective." The number of inhabitants is around 238 in Luserna,[8] around 30 in Giazza[9] and even less in Roana. There is no new generation of speakers who learn Cimbrian as a mother language (with one or two exceptions just in Luserna). Cimbrian language and culture is studied at primary school level (just one hour per week in very few schools, where English is eventually learnt as second language). The Cimbrian community relies on both a relevant literary tradition (starting with the first Cimbrian translation of the Italian Catechism in 1602) and an important grammatical tradition (from Slaviero, second half of the XVIII century, to the Cimbrian Grammar by Cappelletti-Schweizer edited in 1942).[10] The most relevant activities to maintain the Cimbrian language and culture are promoted by the local cultural Institutions: *Kulturinstitut Lusérn – Curatorium Cimbricum Veronese – Istituto di Cultura Cimbra (Roana)*: among all, the project of a descriptive grammar of the Cimbrian variety of Luserna.[11]

---

7 Anthony Rowley, *Liacht as de Sproch – Grammatica della lingua mòchena – Grammatik des Deutsch-Fersentalerischen* (Istituto Culturale Mòcheno-Cimbro, 2003). It is interesting to note that only the title is written in Mocheno. The Grammar itself is written in both Italian and German.
8 For a detailed statistics see the data published on line by the *Servizio statistica della Provincia autonoma di Trento*, available at http://www.statistica.provincia.tn.it (September 16, 2013).
9 Antonia Stringher, *Censimento dei parlanti Cimbro nell'isola linguistica di Giazza* (Comune di Selva di Progno, 2012), available at http://www.sportellocimbri.it (September 16, 2013).
10 For a brief survey of the Cimbrian literature see, among all, Ermenegildo Bidese, "Alle fonti scritte del cimbro: la 'letteratura' cimbra come esempio di genesi d'una tradizione scrittoria alloglotta" in *Il cimbro negli studi di linguistica*, ed. E. Bidese (Padova: Unipress, 2010), 61–85.
11 Luca Panieri et al., *Bar lirnen z'schraiba un zo reda az be biar* (Regione Autonoma Trentino-Alto Adige/Autonome Region Trentino-Südtirol and Istituto Cimbro/Kulturinstitut Lusérn, 2006).

If on one side the differences among the three German(ic) minorities just considered are quite obvious from both a historical and a socio-cultural perspective, on the other side a closer linguistic investigation confirms a different typological classification based on "pure" grammatical criteria.

1.2 The grammar of minority languages: focusing on syntactic variation

If we compare some relevant syntactic aspects of the Tyrolean dialects with the syntax of Mocheno on one side and with the syntax of Cimbrian varieties on the other side the variations from standard German becomes immediately clear.

A coherent classification emerges, in particular, with respect to two syntactic aspects which linguists consider peculiar of German grammar, i.e.: i) the V2 linear word order restriction (just one constituent to the left of the finite verbal form):

(1)   a. ok Heute **hackt** Hans das Holz im Wald
          Today-cuts-Hans-the-wood-in+the-forest
       b. * Heute Hans **hackt** das Holz im Wald

ii) the OV/VO typology (complements to the right or to the left of the past participle verbal form):

(2)   a. Hans **hat** das Holz im Wald **gehackt**
       b. Hans **hat gehackt** das Holz im Wald

As the following data show, Tyrolean dialects (here exemplified by the variety spoken in Merano-Meran) respect both respect both the V2 restriction and the OV typology, coherently with Standard German:

(3)   Der Hons **hot** a puach **gekaft**
      The-Hons-has-a-book-bought
(4)   Di Mama hot mi kfrok, ob si di aufgobm **gmocht hot**
      The-mother-has-me-asked-if-she-the-exercises-done-has
(5)   Geschtern **hot** der Hons es holz in wold **khockt**
      Yesterday-has-the-Hons-the-wood-in-the-forest-cut
(6)   Haint **hot** di Mama di teller **gwaschn**
      Today-has-the-mother-the-dishes-washed
(7)   I **hon** niamand (net) **ksechn**
      I-have-nobody-(not)-seen

The Grammar is written in both Italian and German and only the title is written in Cimbrian, exactly as noted before with respect to Rowley's work on Mocheno (see note 7).

Contrary to the varieties spoken in South Tyrol, both Mocheno and all three Cimbrian varieties have lost the V2 restriction,[12] acquiring an exceptional status within the so called continental West Germanic varieties. Furthermore we can establish an interesting sub classification with respect to the OV/VO typology:

a) in the Mocheno variety both order possibilities are still attested, with a strong preference for the VO typology (VO: 85% – OV: 15%)[13]:

(8) Der Mario **hòt** (a puach) **kaft** (a puach)
The Mario has (a book) bought (a book)

(9) (De Mama hòt mer pfrok,) asbia as se de compiti **gamocht** asbia as se **hòt gamocht** de compiti
(The mother has me asked) whether that she has done the homework.

b) in the Cimbrian variety of Luserna/Lusern (TN) the OV typology survives in very specific contexts (i.e. with quantified/negative objects like *niamat* "nobody" in ex. (11)):

(10) Haüte die Mome **hat gebäscht** di Piattn Today the mother has washed the dishes
Today the mother has washed the dishes

(11) I **hon** niamat **gesek**
I have nobody seen

c) in the Cimbrian variety of Giazza/Ljetzan (VR) just the VO order is attested:

(12) Gheistar in Giani **hat gahakat** iz holtz ime balje (/in balt)
Yesterday the Giani has cut the wood in the forest

In conclusion, from a linguistic point of view, we can propose the following classification, based on the syntactic distance from Standard German[14]:

(13) Linguistic distance from Standard German

---

12 As for the loss of the V2 restriction in Cimbrian, see Ermenegildo Bidese, Alessandra Tomaselli, "Diachronic Development in Isolation: The Loss of V2 Phenomena in Cimbrian," *Linguistische Berichte* 210 (2007): 209–228.

13 For a detailed analysis of the VO/OV syntax in Mocheno see Federica Cognola, "Ordini OV/VO in mòcheno" in *L'influsso dell'italiano sul sistema del verbo delle lingue minoritarie: resistenza e mutamento nella morfologia e nella sintassi*, ed. Walter Breu (Bochum: Brockmeyer, 2010), 41–66.

14 It is interesting to note that the different degrees of linguistic distance from Standard German correspond both to the geographic distance from the German speaking country and to the evident decreasing number of speakers.

	V2	OV
Standard German	+	+
Tyrolean dialects	+	+
Mocheno	-	+
Cimbrian (Luserna)	-	-/+
Cimbrian (Giazza)	-	-

This "fine-grained" linguistic classification leads us to reflect on the different status of the so-called "endangered languages" like Mocheno and the Cimbrian varieties with respect to linguistic minorities which are "protected" by a Standard Language of reference like the German varieties of South Tyrol. Furthermore, the linguistic approach will help us to define the proper subset of linguistic rights to be adopted in order to preserve the language and culture of each specific minority group.

1.3 The right to preserve one's own language and culture

The preservation of a minority language as "cultural value" implies some important premises:
–   First of all, the possibility of identifying a common linguistic code. German varieties spoken in South Tyrol do not present any problem under this respect since Standard German acts as some sort of "parachute" (i.e.: high normativity). The situation is quite different as far as the historical Germanic minorities are concerned. Dialectal micro-variation within a small isolated geographic area is always characterized by "low normativity."[15] As a matter of fact, both Cimbrian and Mocheno present a number of "sub-variants" which are characterized by slight differences concerning in particular the lexicon and the morpho-phonological levels of grammar.[16] If the process of code-degradation has gone too far, there is in fact very little to do, at least as far as the language maintenance is involved.
–   The description of the code represents the subsequent step. Descriptive grammars should precede normative/scholastic grammars. As already noted before, the local cultural institutions already played a crucial role in this

---

15 Ed. Nancy C. Dorian, *Investigating Obsolescence* (Cambridge: Cambridge University Press, 1989).
16 Ed. Stefan Rabanus, *Bruno Schweizer – Zimbrischer und Fersentalerischer Sprachatlas* (Verona: Fiorini, 2012).

respect. Both Mocheno and the Cimbrian variety spoken in Luserna (TN) can rely on a good descriptive grammar. Nevertheless the big "orthographic question" which has accompanied the process of standardization in both cases is highly representative of the potential danger of disaggregation of the "common linguistic code."

–   If the process of codification obtains a positive result, teaching the language at school is the first linguistic right to be guaranteed in order to maintain (or at least "revitalize") both language and cultural transmission to the younger generations.

If on one hand educational politics represent a priority in order to protect and preserve a minority, "endangered" language, on the other hand a big question arises in contexts where cultural minorities are identified independently from the language itself. When a common code does not exist anymore we enter a dangerous field. The cultural value of certain linguistic aspects is relevant independently from the preservation of the linguistic code itself. Just to make an easy example, let us think about the relevance of historical/native geographical names and the discussion about their preservation in street signals. Nevertheless the border between the relevance of the cultural factor *per se* and what has been recently called "ethno-business phenomena" is far from being clearly defined. We do not want to deny at all the strong relation between linguistic/cultural minorities and their territorial integrity but the relevance of this relation could produce completely different results. In order to confirm these reflections it is sufficient to cite the arbitrary administrative extension of the Occitan area on one side and the still undervalued "Cimbrian factor" as a potential tourism attractor for specific geographic areas.[17] We will not enter here the topic of the (quite obvious but never "innocent") mutual relevance of cultural and economic development. This goes beyond the scope of our contribution: nevertheless we are ready to open a window on the protection of linguistic minorities from a legal perspective.

---

17 Marta Ugolini, Ketty Costa, "I Cimbri come fattore di attrattiva turistica?" in *L'eredità cimbra di Monsignor Cappelletti*, eds. Arnaldo Petterlini, Alessandra Tomaselli (Verona: Fiorini, 2009), 113–133.

2 From a legal perspective

2.1 The complexity of defining the concept of "linguistic minority"

From a legal perspective, the concept of "minority" (considered in general terms, regardless of its possible forms) is very hard to define. According to a shared orientation, it can be defined as a

> community of citizens in lower numbers than the rest of the population of a country, in a non-dominant position, whose members have different ethnic, religious or linguistic features from the rest of the population and implicitly or explicitly express their will to maintain their cultural heritage, traditions, religion or language.[18]

As regards linguistic minorities, the distinguishing feature consists in using a native language different from that of the majority, which is normally identified with the speakers whose mother-tongue is the official language of the State of which they are citizens.[19]

The linguistic factor, as objective as it may be, is not always useful to clearly define a minority, not only because using a language instead of another is always a matter of individual choice – which can lead to the use of different/multiple linguistic codes (bilingualism, diglossism, etc.) – but also because this feature combines with other distinguishing features of a community, making it hard to distinguish the concepts of "linguistic minority," "ethnic minority," or "national minority" (the latter being linked to the existence of a reference Nation to whom minority citizens claim to belong).

The overlap between these concepts is confirmed by the same international documents aimed at protecting the minority. In identifying some groups as minorities for their protection, these documents use, along with a quantitative parameter, various distinguishing criteria, without reaching, however, univocal and shared conclusions.

The same linguistic affiliation, which in itself would be an objectively detectable *discrimen*, was considered by only a few international instruments (first of all

---

18 This definition, proposed by Francesco Capotorti and for a long time shared by the doctrine, now puts on a relative meaning, having to be specified on the basis of choices made by every legal system: about the problems in defining the term "minority", moving from that given in the text, see Francesco Palermo, Jens Woelk, *Diritto costituzionale dei gruppi e delle minoranze* (Padova: Cedam, 2011), 18–21. [Our translation].

19 Fiorenzo Toso, "Minoranze linguistiche" in *Enciclopedia dell'Italiano* (Roma: Treccani, 2011), 891.

by those adopted by the UN, which also identify linguistic minorities as recipients of their measures). Others (for example, those adopted by the OECD and the Council of Europe) focused on national membership – of which the linguistic affiliation may constitute an expression – thus recognizing means of protection of a community not as a "linguistic minority," but, possibly, as a "national minority."[20]

2.2 The concept of "linguistic minority" within the Italian constitutional system: classification limits and drawbacks on its protection

The complexity of defining the concept of "linguistic minority" is also reflected in the actual level of protection, as well exemplified by references to the linguistic factor within the Italian Constitution.

Pursuant to Section 3, language, along with other factors, cannot constitute cause of discrimination among citizens. This statement, at the very beginning of the works of the Constituent Assembly, took on a meaning of strong discontinuity with the past – taking into account that, during the Fascist era, an action of forced Italianisation was conducted – and somebody initially considered this statement as sufficient guarantee, deeming any further provisions on the topic as superfluous. However, during the preparatory works of the Constitution, a different approach was suggested according to which the only "negative" protection offered by Section 3 would not have been adequate to ensure effective protection because this requires not only the formal prohibition of linguistic discrimination, but also the "positive" affirmation of functional standards for concrete actions. This approach gradually prevailed and it oriented the formulation of Section 6 of the Constitution, which forces the Republic (including all its members and not only the State) to adopt "specific rules" to ensure the fundamental equality of people belonging to linguistic minorities. Therefore, its protection is not limited to banning discrimination but involves actions to ensure, for example, the use of minority languages in the fields of teaching, contacts with the Public Administration, administration of justice or even toponymy.

When implemented, the meaning of "linguistic minority" contained in Sections 6 lent itself to different interpretations.

Initially, also because of specific international engagements by Italy, the concept of linguistic minority overlapped with that of national minority and only linguistic communities which had a "Nation" of reference obtained protection.

---

20 Lino Panzeri, Maria Paola Viviani Schlein, *Lo statuto giuridico della lingua italiana in Europa. I casi di Croazia, Slovenia e Svizzera a confronto* (Milano: Giuffrè, 2011), IX–X.

Only the special Statutes of Trentino-Alto Adige, Valle d'Aosta and, partially, Friuli-Venezia Giulia (having the nature of constitutional laws) introduced some important safeguards for the use of German, French and Slovene, so that these groups were defined as "highly protected minorities."[21] The many other minority communities living in Italy – including the Albanian, Greek and Slavic linguistic islands in the south of the country, the Franco-Provençal and Occitan communities in Piedmont and the Alpine German ones scattered outside Trentino-Alto Adige[22] and, again, the Catalan group in Sardinia – although historically settled in their local areas, did not benefit from any protection, except for some regional measures often disputed by the central Government, which, consequently, contained only some economic aid.[23]

A broader interpretation of the term "linguistic minority", open to ensure protection to "any community which presents, in fact, ethnic and linguistic differences such as to justify its protection"[24], was accepted by Law no. 482 of 15 December 1999 ("Rules on protection of historical linguistic minorities"), which implemented Section 6 after more than fifty years since the entry into force of the Constitution. The Law – which provided for a cohesive use of minority languages in the fields of education (Sections 4–6), local government and public administration (Sections 7–9), toponymy and onomasticon (Sections 10–11) and communication (Sections 12 and 14)[25] – identified minorities to be protected, specifying that the object of protection were "the languages and cultures of Albanian, Catalan, German, Greek, Slovenian and Croatian populations and the French, Franco-Provençal, Friulian, Ladin, Occitan and Sardinian speaking populations" (Section 2).

---

21 Elisabetta Palici di Suni Prat, *Intorno alle minoranze* (Torino: Giappichelli, 2002), 33. Other authors proposed the term "strong minorities," to be considered as opposed to the much lower status accorded to "weak minorities": Massimo Stipo, "Minoranze etnico-linguistiche (I, Diritto pubblico)" in *Enciclopedia giuridica* (Roma: Treccani, 1990), XXII, 10.

22 Cimbrian speakers in Veneto (Provinces of Belluno and Vicenza), some Bavarian-Carinthian variants in Veneto (Sappada) and Friuli-Venezia Giulia (Sauris, Timau, Val Canale) and Walser speakers in Valle d'Aosta (Valle del Lys) and in Northern Piedmont (Provinces of Verbano-Cusio-Ossola and Vercelli).

23 Lino Panzeri, "Le prospettive di tutela delle minoranze linguistiche in Italia: il ruolo delle Regioni ordinarie," *Le Regioni* 5 (2009): 983–984.

24 Alessandro Pizzorusso, "La tutela delle minoranze linguistiche nell'ordinamento giuridico italiano," *Città & Regione* 3 (1980): 36.

25 On the contents of Law no. 482/1999 see Valeria Piergigli, "La legge 15 dicembre 1999, n. 482 ('Norme in materia di tutela delle minoranze linguistiche storiche') ovvero dall'agnosticismo al riconoscimento," *Rassegna parlamentare* 3 (2000): 623–657.

Therefore, the Parliament started to focus not only on national minorities (already protected by special Statutes), but also on some other linguistic minorities (though not all of them).

Today, the regulatory framework suggests this classification[26]:

- "highly protected" minorities: German speakers in Alto Adige/Südtirol, French speakers in Valle d'Aosta, (partially) Slovenian speakers in Friuli-Venezia Giulia;
- recognized minorities with "possible protection": linguistic groups included in Section 2 of Law no. 482/1999;
- "not recognized" minorities: linguistic groups essentially unprotected.

Although Law no. 482/1999 expanded the number of protected linguistic minorities, the adopted rules were criticized by scholars of linguistics, as regards: a) the introduction of a closed list of protected linguistic varieties, which contrasts with the dynamic evolution of the linguistic phenomenon[27]; b) the relativity and obsolescence of the adopted selection criteria, which led to inconsistent and even counter-productive choices, such as in particular:

- the inclusion and equalization of linguistic minorities having a different degree of codification[28]: the Law was based on the false assumption of reliable levels of standardization, forgetting that most of the protected minority languages have never evolved from a vernacular level and often cannot count on a unified cultural reference basis[29];
- the assimilation of different groups from a socio-linguistic perspective: the Law, for example, reduced to the description of "Germanic populations" very different communities, ranging from the compact German speakers of Alto Adige/Südtirol (who are already protected by the special regional Statute) to

---

26 For more on this classification today, see Palermo, Woelk, *Diritto costituzionale dei gruppi e delle minoranze*, 297–307.

27 Vincenzo Orioles, *Le minoranze linguistiche. Profili sociolinguistici e quadro dei documenti di tutela* (Roma: Il Calamo, 2003), 21.

28 Toso, *Le minoranze linguistiche in Italia*, 54.

29 Overcoming this obstacle implies defining a reference grammar accepted by all the communities who identify themselves with the same minority: from this perspective, it is worth appreciating the efforts of both the *Bersntoler Kulturinstitut – Istituto Culturale Mocheno* and the *Kulturinstitut Lusérn – Curatorium Cimbricum Veronese – Istituto di Cultura Cimbra*, which focused on the draft of a reference grammar, respectively, for the Mocheno and Cimbrian varieties (see, *supra*, Part 1, fn. 7 and 11).

the other small German speaking communities in the Alps, where several local varieties are used[30];

- the exclusion from the protection measures of both idiomatic varieties with a strong link with their territories and an *animus* of community (such as the Tabarchino speaking minority in Sardinia) and the Roma minority, which, although it lacks a stable link with the territory, has been present for centuries in Italy.[31]

However, the most criticized aspect of the complex legislative framework, which is intertwined with the limits of the approach adopted by Section 2, is the possibility given by the Law to all the historical linguistic minorities to ask for protective measures similar to those already granted by the special Statutes to the languages of border national minorities. The Law, in particular, identified as an objective to be pursued in implementing Section 6 of the Constitution the access to linguistic rights by all recognized minorities, involving the public use of the minority language alongside the Italian one.

This approach has been met with much perplexity. First of all, in general terms, these rules, which are effective for groups that have always claimed a different historical, linguistic and cultural identity (such as the German speakers of Alto Adige/Südtirol) is rather inadequate for other linguistic groups[32]: in these cases, the widespread and accepted use of the Italian language makes it possible for any dialect speaker or any speaker of one of the recognized languages to fully integrate into its social context.[33] Even where the use of a local dialect or a minority language is widespread, the imposition of a standard language does not prove of any use to protect the minority, because it imposes a linguistic code which is perceived as a distant and foreign idiom (even more than the Italian

---

30 With reference to the Cimbrian and Mocheno linguistic features compared to the Standard German ones see, *supra*, Part 1, Table 13.

31 In critical terms on the exclusion of these minorities, see Elena Malfatti, "La nuova legge di tutela delle minoranze linguistiche: le prospettive ed i problemi ancora aperti," *Rivista di diritto costituzionale* (2001): 124.

32 In critical terms on the extension of the model of protection introduced for national minorities living in border Regions to other linguistic groups more recently considered worthy of protection (but having very different features) see Matteo Cosulich, "Minoranze linguistiche e istruzione nell'ordinamento italiano" in *Tutela delle identità culturali, diritti linguistici e istruzione. Dal Trentino-Alto Adige/Südtirol alla prospettiva comparata*, eds. Eleonora Ceccherini, Matteo Cosulich (Padova: Cedam, 2012), 44 and 48–49.

33 Fiorenzo Toso, "Patrimoni linguistici e lingue minoritarie: la prospettiva europea e quella italiana," *Annali della Facoltà di Lingue e letterature straniere dell'Università di Sassari* 5 (2005 pubbl. 2009): 115–124, 116–117.

language itself, now assimilated) within the specific local context: for a Cimbrian speaker, for example, the German language is almost a foreign language[34] and forcing its public use may be completely unrealistic and may contribute to the process of assimilation rather than to the preservation of this local idiom.

Secondly, in practice, this model fostered the "bureaucratization" of minority protection. Some measures have often been taken to recognize the presence of a linguistic minority in a specific area (on the basis of the "zoning" mechanism provided by Section 3 of Law no. 482/1999)[35] even where the minority language has never been spoken or has been extinct for a long time for mere economic purposes (access to the funds provided by the Law) or to enhance the tourist appeal (the so-called "ethnobusiness").[36]

The goal of accessing some protection measures has also had the further consequence, which is often dictated by political and economic reasons instead of aiming at minority protection, of trying to further expand the range of protected linguistic minorities through both the integration of the list of Section 2[37] and the actions of the Regions, in the exercise of the powers conferred on them by the new Section 117 of the Constitution.[38] This approach increases the risk of an uncon-

---

34 See *supra*, Part 1.

35 Section 3 set out the methods to define the territorial application of Law no. 482/1999, especially providing for a special resolution of the Provincial Council, after consulting the Municipalities concerned, at the request of at least 15% of the citizens registered to vote and living in the same Municipalities or a third of the councillors of the same (Paragraph 1); where none of these conditions is met but a minority recognized pursuant to Section 2 lives in the Municipality, the procedure can be started if approved by the resident population, through an appropriate consultation promoted by the eligible people in the manner required by municipal Statutes and regulations (Paragraph 2).

36 "Zoning" led to a number of paradoxes, such as the extent of the Occitan speakers area in Municipalities in which this language has never been used or is limited to the use of several expressions; in some cases, the concerned local governments merely "invented some minorities," as they did with the German speakers in Ischia or Occitan speakers in Liguria: for a review of the distorted application of Section 3 of Law no. 482/1999 see Fiorenzo Toso, "Alcuni episodi di applicazione delle norme di tutela delle minoranze linguistiche in Italia," *Ladinia* XXXII (2008): 165–222.

37 See, among the bills brought before the previous Parliament, A.S. 697, A.S. 1113 and A.S. 1216, which included into Section 2 of Law no. 482/1999 the "Slavic languages called 'Natisonian,' 'Ponasen' and 'Resian,' historically present in the Province of Udine" as well as the "Piedmontian" and "regional Venetian" speaking populations.

38 This is the case of the "Piedmontian," which the Piedmontian regional Law no. 11 of 7 April 2009 ("Protection, enhancement and promotion of Piedmont's linguistic heritage") assimilated to other historical linguistic minorities in the Region already recognized by Section 2 of Law no. 482/ 1999. This assimilation, however, was ruled illegal by the Constitutional Court with decision no. 170/2010: as regards this problem see Lino Panzeri, "Il riconoscimento giuridico delle mino-

trolled proliferation of protected minority languages, which could have detrimental effects for those minorities who are really worthy of protection and are more exposed to the danger of assimilation.

3 The prospects of protection of linguistic minorities in Italy: short concluding remarks

The limits of the Italian legislation on linguistic minorities suggest, as of now, the need for some corrective action and, above all, a considered reflection on the approach followed so far.

From a general perspective, the identification of the protection of linguistic minorities with the recognition of the linguistic rights of its speakers must be overcome. This approach has proved to be useful for the groups of the border Regions with special autonomy but it cannot be mechanically applied to all the minority groups living in Italy, which are very different, *inter alia*, in terms of the level of preservation of language and identity awareness. The protection of linguistic minorities (in its broadest sense, which includes the simple dialects and the languages of immigrants) can also be achieved in other ways, for example by considering it in its cultural dimension: language, indeed, performs not only a communicative function, but also a symbolic and identity one, so that there may be linguistic continuity even without language because a culture could well continue to exist even when a language is no longer used.[39] These possible measures should be distinguished and combined, modulating them according to the specificity of each linguistic group. In general, title to traditional linguistic rights should only be granted to the groups that specifically ask for it while the others should be assisted with the enhancement of their local languages as cultural assets, by way of measures such as the setting up of museums and libraries or by financing research groups or cultural centres involved in the study and preservation of individual linguistic varieties.

The amendment to Title V of the Constitution created interesting opportunities in this respect,[40] which, if properly cultivated, could also help overcome

---

ranze linguistiche tra unità nazionale ed istanze territoriali," *Foro amministrativo C.d.S.*10 (2010): 2093–2101.

39 Sergio Bonato, "I Cimbri del Veneto fra persistenze e cambiamenti," in *Le minoranze del Veneto: Ladini, Cimbri e Germanofoni di Sappada, Atti del Convegno di Arabba (Belluno), 7–8 novembre 1997*, ed. Luciana Palla (Cortina: Ghedina, 1998), 98.

40 Ludovico A. Mazzarolli, "La tutela delle minoranze linguistiche nella Costituzione del nuovo Titolo V," *Le Regioni* 5 (2003): 727–736.

the limits of Law no. 482/1999, for example through the provision of some forms of protection, within the limits of responsibility of each entity involved, for linguistic groups so far overlooked and, above all, for the more recently immigrated groups from outside of the EU.

These opportunities could also mitigate the differences in treatment among different groups due to the different areas of settlement. In the case of minority communities which, in spite of being characterized by historical and linguistic continuity, are settled in the territories of different Regions, there is, in general, a high level of protection in favour of the speakers residing in Regions with special autonomy and, conversely, a much less favourable treatment for those who reside in the ordinary Regions. As regards the "Germanic populations" described in Section 2 of Law no. 482/1982, for example, the different regional distribution of the individual settlement areas leads to further complication of the classification itself, which distinguishes "highly protected" minorities, minorities with "possible protection" and "not recognized" minorities: the German speakers of Alto Adige/Südtirol, whose protection is based on their special Statute, constitute a "highly protected" minority; the Cimbrian speakers are a minority with "variable protection" due to their different Regions of settlement. The groups living in the Province of Trento, in fact, benefit from a better treatment, granted by the greater powers constitutionally conferred on the Provinces of Trentino-Alto Adige/Südtirol; differently, the Cimbrian speakers who live in the Provinces of Verona and Vicenza are minorities with "possible protection", within the limits established by Law no. 482/1999, whose treatment is, on the whole, much worse.[41] Just by exercising some of the powers established by the new Section 117 of the Constitution,[42] the ordinary Regions (as regards Cimbrian speakers, the Veneto Region) could greatly improve the protection standards of the minority communities living in their territories, overcoming a now unacceptable inequality of treatment.

Significant results, however, can only be achieved if the various constituent entities of the Republic (State, Regions and local authorities) – formally put on an equal footing by Section 114 of the Constitution – will refrain from repeating the mistakes made in the past, avoiding the diversion of protective actions to meet

---

41 From this perspective, the conclusions emerged from the linguistic classification, based on the syntactic distance from Standard German, are fully confirmed: also from a legal point of view, in fact, levels of protection vary according to the distance from the German speaking country and to the evident decreasing number of speakers.

42 Valeria Piergigli, "Articolo 6," in *Commentario alla Costituzione*, eds. Raffaele Bifulco, Alfonso Celotto, Marco Olivetti (Torino: Utet, 2006), 170, dealing with the powers regarding "education," "government of territory," "promotion of cultural heritage" and "promotion and organization of cultural activities" established by Section 117, Paragraph 3.

local or electoral interests. This new approach could lead not only to significant results in simple terms of linguistic protection, but also, as it has been long authoritatively argued,[43] to encourage the interiorization of the equal dignity of the various languages and to create a climate of tolerance and mutual respect between all the components (including linguistic ones) of the Italian society.

---

43 Alessandro Pizzorusso, *Minoranze e maggioranze* (Torino: Einaudi, 1993), 201.

Valentina Adami
Rights of Humans/Rights of Nature: The Language of Environmental Rights in UN Documents

1 Human rights and the environment

Human rights and the environment are inextricably intertwined. Their relationship can be understood according to three main perspectives. The first perspective – which is the closest to the ideas expressed by the 1972 "Declaration of the United Nations Conference on the Human Environment" (usually referred to as "the Stockholm Declaration")[1] – considers the environment as a precondition for the enjoyment of human rights rather than as a specific right in itself.[2] Within this approach, according to which destroying the environment is not a crime against nature but against human rights, two different ways of protecting the environment have been suggested: one proposes that the environment should be protected through existing human rights laws, while the other advocates the creation of a new, specific human right, the "right to environment." The second approach – mainly inspired by the 1992 "Rio Declaration on Environment and Development"[3] – considers certain human rights as a precondition for achieving environmental protection and focuses on the recognition of procedural rights such as

---

1 "Declaration of the United Nations Conference on the Human Environment," Chapter I of the "Report of the United Nations Conference on the Human Environment," A/CONF.48/14/Rev.1 (June 16, 1972), available at http://www.un-documents.net/unchedec.htm (October 18, 2013).
2 See James R. May and Erin Daly, "Vindicating Fundamental Environmental Rights Worldwide," *Oregon Review of International Law* 11 (2009): 365–439, 366–367 [footnotes omitted]: "Advancing the human condition entails recognizing a fundamental constitutional right to a quality environment. [...] Courts worldwide are with growing frequency recognizing that human rights and the environment are inextricably intertwined. Fundamental human rights to life and liberty, for example, cannot be achieved without adequate environmental conditions of clean water, air, and land. A fair amount has been written about the link between human and environmental rights: whether there is a fundamental right to a quality environment, whether and the extent to which countries have entrenched environmental rights constitutionally, and the emergence of such rights in the global order of environmental law."
3 "Rio Declaration on Environment and Development," Annex 1 of the "Report of the United Nations Conference on Environment and Development," A/CONF.151/26 (August 12, 1992), available at http://www.un-documents.net/rio-dec.htm (October 18, 2013).

access to environmental information, participation in environmental decision-making and access to justice in environmental matters. Finally, the third and most debated perspective – sustained by most environmentalists around the world and by some Governments (mainly in South America), but apparently not by the United Nations (as my linguistic analysis will reveal)[4] – sees the environment (or, better, "Nature" or "the Earth") as a living entity that should be guaranteed certain rights in itself and protected by law not just for its usefulness for humans but as a good in its own right. This is the approach, for instance, of the "Universal Declaration of the Rights of Mother Earth,"[5] adopted by the World People's Conference on Climate Change and the Rights of Mother Earth in Bolivia on April 22, 2010, in the wake of the failed 2009 UN Climate Change Conference (the "Copenhagen Summit"), and submitted to the UN by the Bolivian government for consideration but never ratified because of the opposition by most Western countries.

These three approaches have been extensively debated from a philosophical, legal and political point of view,[6] but the linguistic perspective is also particularly relevant in this context. In fact, as Alan Boyle has rightly argued, "definitional problems are inherent in any attempt to postulate environmental rights in qualitative terms."[7] In particular, I think that the linguistic choices of the United

---

4 See, for instance, Dinah L. Shelton, "Human Rights and the Environment: What Specific Environmental Rights Have Been Recognized?," *Denver Journal of International Law and Policy* 35.1 (2006): 129–171, 163: "recognizing a right to environment could encompass elements of nature protection and ecological balance, substantive areas not generally protected under human rights law because of its anthropocentric focus." In this paper, Shelton also provides an interesting examination of the different approaches to environmental rights.

5 "Universal Declaration of the Rights of Mother Earth" [2010], available at http://therightsofnature.org/universal-declaration (October 18, 2013).

6 See, among others: Donald K. Anton and Dinah L. Shelton, *Environmental Protection and Human Rights* (New York: Cambridge University Press, 2011); Alan Boyle, "Human Rights and the Environment: Where Next?," *The European Journal of International Law* 23.3 (2012): 613–642; Alan Boyle, "Human Rights and the Environment: A Reassessment," UNEP (United Nations Environment Programme) working paper for the High Level Expert Meeting on the Future of Human Rights and Environment (2010), available at http://www.unep.org/delc/Portals/24151/Towardsthedeclarationhumanrights.pdf (October 18, 2013); Alan Boyle and Michael Anderson eds., *Human Rights Approaches to Environmental Protection* (Oxford: Clarendon Press, 1996); Jan Hancock, *Environmental Human Rigths: Power, Ethics and Law* (Aldershot: Ashgate, 2003); Romina Picolotti and Jorge Daniel Taillant eds., *Linking Human Rights and the Environment* (Tucson: University of Arizona Press, 2003); Shelton, "Human Rights and the Environment"; Lyuba Zarsky, *Human Rights and the Environment: Conflicts and Norms in a Globalizing World* (Abingdon: Earthscan, 2002).

7 Boyle, "Human Rights and the Environment: A Reassessment," 33.

Nations bear relevant implications for the public understanding of environmental rights within a human rights context. For example, as we will see in more detail in the next paragraphs, the use of the ambiguous expression "sustainable development" instead of "environmental rights" shifts the emphasis from ecological to economic and social concerns.[8] More in general, the use of an anthropocentric or economic-centred (rather than nature-centred) vocabulary, of passive structures and of nominalizations objectifies nature as a "thing" and sets humans apart and above nature, instead of within it.

The United Nations has repeatedly highlighted the interdependence of human and environmental rights.[9] However, the protection of human rights and that of the environment sometimes seem to be conflicting: while the United Nations, with its focus on the rights of humans, aims to protect the environment *for* people, environmentalists aim to create laws that protect the environment *from* people. My analysis of the vocabulary used by the United Nations in its declarations (or draft declarations) about environmental rights released between 1972 ("Stockholm Declaration on the Human Environment") and 2012 (Rio+20's Outcome Document "The Future We Want") – going through the 1982 "World Charter for Nature," the 1987 "Brundtland Report," the 1992 "Rio Declaration," the 1994 "Draft Principles on Human Rights and the Environment" (never ratified by the UN), the 2002 "Johannesburg Declaration" and the "Universal Declaration of the Rights of Mother Earth" – will reveal precisely how the United Nations seems to favour the first, more anthropocentric, approach.

Through the methodological perspective of ecolinguistics, this essay will analyse the lexical uncertainties in the definition of a right to environment in the

---

8 The expression "sustainable development" has been aptly defined as a "floating signifier" because of its ambiguity in: Helen Tregidga, Markus Milne and Kate Kearins, "Sustainable Development as a Floating Signifier: Recognising Space for Resistance," presented at the 10th Australasian Conference on Social and Environmental Accounting Research, Launceston, Australia, December 5–7, 2011, available at http://www.utas.edu.au/__data/assets/pdf_file/0010/188434/ Tregidga_Milne_Kearins.pdf (October 18, 2013).

9 See, for instance, the first Report of the "Independent Expert on the issue of human rights obligations relating to the enjoyment of a safe, clean, healthy and sustainable environment" (Professor John H. Knox) to the Human Rights Council, A/HRC/22/43 (December 24, 2012), available at http://www.ohchr.org/Documents/HRBodies/HRCouncil/RegularSession/Session22/A-HRC-22-43_en.pdf (October 18, 2013). See also the press release of the UN Office for the High Commissioner of Human Rights (Geneva, March 7, 2013), available at http://www.ohchr.org/en/NewsEvents/Pages/DisplayNews.aspx?NewsID=13089&LangID=E (October 18, 2013): "'Human rights and the environment are not only interrelated, they are also interdependent,' Mr. Knox noted during the presentation of his preliminary report to the Human Rights Council. 'A healthy environment is fundamentally important to the enjoyment of human rights, and the exercise of human rights is necessary for a healthy environment'."

eight aforementioned documents (revealed for instance by the use of different expressions such as "environmental rights," "right to [a healthy, safe, quality, enabling...] environment," or "sustainable development") and examines whether such linguistic variability reflects changes in political, legal and cultural approaches to environmental issues, thereby revealing the ideologies and power structures embedded within the language of the United Nations.

2 A brief history of the relationship between human and environmental rights in UN documents

As stated in the 2009 "Report of the Office of the United Nations High Commissioner for Human Rights on the relationship between climate change and human rights,"

> While the universal human rights treaties do not refer to a specific right to a safe and healthy environment, the United Nations human rights treaty bodies all recognize the intrinsic link between the environment and the realization of a range of human rights, such as the right to life, to health, to food, to water, and to housing.[10]

The link between human rights and environmental protection was first explicitly recognized in 1972 by the already-mentioned "Stockholm Declaration," which set out 25 principles for the preservation and enhancement of the human environment. Since then, environmental protection has become a matter of international concern and there have been numerous UN declarations, reports and resolutions about the environment, albeit most of those dealing *explicitly* with environmental matters are non-binding documents.

Nonetheless, there are some binding human rights treaties that can be interpreted so as to *implicitly* acknowledge environmental rights – that is, acknowledging them in relation to other rights such as the right to life, food, health, housing, property and so on. Among them, the most important is indeed the "Universal Declaration of Human Rights" (1948), which makes no open reference to the environment but – nonetheless indirectly recognizes a right to environment in Article 25, which states that "Everyone has the right to a standard of living adequate for the health and well-being of himself and of his family." Similarly, the "Convention on the Elimination of All Forms of Discrimination against Wo-

---

10 "Report of the Office of the United Nations High Commissioner for Human Rights on the relationship between climate change and human rights," A/HRC/10/61 (January 15, 2009), available at http://daccess-dds-ny.un.org/doc/UNDOC/GEN/G09/103/44/PDF/G0910344.pdf?OpenE lement (October 18, 2013).

men" (1979) states that women must be guaranteed "adequate living condition, particularly in relation to housing, sanitation, electricity and water supply, transport and communications" (Article 14 (2)(h)), which could be considered as environmental rights (even though also this convention never actually mentions the environment). The "Convention on the Rights of the Child" (1989), on the other hand, makes a more explicit reference to environmental protection in Article 24, which mentions "the provision of adequate nutritious foods and clean drinking water" and the need to take into consideration "the dangers and risks of environmental pollution." In this Convention, the words "environment/environmental" appear nine times, thus revealing the increasing importance of environmental matters within a human rights context. Moreover, the links between human rights and the environment have been explicitly recognized with reference to the rights of indigenous peoples in the "Declaration on the Rights of Indigenous Peoples" (2007), which includes explicit references to the lands, resources, and environment of indigenous peoples.

However, as I have mentioned before, most of the UN documents dealing explicitly with environmental rights are non-binding instruments that depend, for their effectiveness, on informal pressures. Since the 1972 Stockholm Conference, "the United Nations [...] has taken the lead in generating international discourse on environmental issues, by organizing conferences, commissioning reports and setting up research and development programmes."[11] The most significant documents coming out of these initiatives are the 1982 "World Charter for Nature"[12]; the 1987 "Brundtland Report"[13]; the 1992 "Report of the United Nations Conference on Environment and Development"[14]; the so-called "Ksentini Reports"[15]; the

11 Kay Milton, *Environmentalism and Cultural Theory: Exploring the Role of Anthropology in Environmental Discourse* (New York: Routledge, 1996), 180.

12 "World Charter for Nature," A/RES/37/7 (October 28, 1982), available at http://www.un.org/documents/ga/res/37/a37r007.htm (September 1, 2013).

13 "Report of the World Commission on Environment and Development: Our Common Future," A/42/427 (August 4, 1987), available at http://www.un-documents.net/wced-ocf.htm (September 1, 2013). The so-called "Brundtland Report" was the result of the work of the World Commission on Environment and Development (WCED), an independent body established by the UN General Assembly in 1983 (Resolution 38/161, "Process of preparation of the Environmental Perspective to the Year 2000 and Beyond," A/RES/38/161).

14 "Report of the United Nations Conference on Environment and Development," A/CONF.151/26 (August 12, 1992), available at http://www.un.org/documents/ga/conf151/aconf15126-1 (September 1, 2013). The Report includes the already-mentioned "Rio Declaration."

15 The Special Rapporteur on Human Rights and the Environment for the UN Sub-Commission on Prevention of Discrimination and Protection of Minorities, Ms. Fatma Zohra Ksentini, released four reports between 1991 and 1994: a Preliminary Report in 1991 (E/CN.4/Sub.2/1991/8), two Progress Reports in 1992 (E/CN.4/Sub.2/1992/7) and 1993 (E/CN.4/Sub.2/1993/7) and the Final

2002 "Report of the World Summit on Sustainable Development,"[16]; and, finally, the outcome document of Rio+20 "The Future We Want."[17]

The 1972 "Stockholm Declaration" stated that "Man has the fundamental right to freedom, equality and adequate conditions of life, in an environment of a quality that permits a life of dignity and well-being, and he bears a solemn responsibility to protect and improve the environment for present and future generations." This "grand statement"[18] was not repeated at the Rio Summit in 1992, when there was a shift away from human-rights emphasis and a retreat into procedural rights. The language adopted by the UN Special Rapporteur in the 1994 "Draft Principles" signals instead a return to the previous conception of the environment as a human right articulated in Stockholm. In fact, in the "Draft Principles" it is stated that "All persons have the right to a secure, healthy and ecologically sound environment" and to "an environment adequate to meet equitably the needs of present generations and that does not impair the rights of future generations to meet equitably their needs." This formulation stresses "the close link between the right to a decent environment and the right to development, but it also relies on the indivisibility and interdependence of all human rights."[19] In her Report, the Special Rapporteur also recalled the 1982 "World

---

Report in 1994 (E/CN.4/Sub.2/1994/9). The latter was presented at the 46th Session of the Sub-Commission on Prevention of Discrimination and Protection of Minorities, and it still today the most comprehensive study of human rights and the environment. The Report examined the legal foundations of a right to environment contained in international human rights instruments, noting that there had been "a shift from environmental law to the right to a healthy and decent environment," and proposed a series of examples of the interconnectedness of human rights and the environment. In its conclusions, the Report emphasized the need for a global approach to environmental rights and the twofold relationship between environmental degradation and human rights violations, arguing that environmental damage has direct effects on the enjoyment of a series of human rights and that human rights violations in turn may damage the environment. The final recommendations called once again for the immediate implementation of the right to environment by relevant human rights bodies and, most importantly, for the adoption of the "Draft Principles on Human Rights and the Environment" set out in Annex 1. Special Rapporteur on Human Rights and the Environment, "Final Report," E/CN.4/Sub.2/1994/9 (July 6, 1994), available at http://www.unhchr.ch/Huridocda/Huridoca.nsf/0/eeab2b6937bccaa18025675c0057 79c3 (September 1, 2013).

16 "Report of the World Summit on Sustainable Development," A/CONF.199/20 (September 4, 2002), available at http://www.un-documents.net/aconf199-20.pdf (October 18, 2013). The Reports includes the "Johannesburg Declaration on Sustainable Development."

17 "The Future We Want," A/RES/66/288 (July 27, 2012), available at http://daccess-dds-ny.un. org/doc/UNDOC/GEN/N11/476/10/PDF/N1147610.pdf?OpenElement (October 18, 2013).

18 Boyle, "Human Rights and the Environment: A Reassessment," 3.

19 Boyle, "Human Rights and the Environment: A Reassessment," 11.

Charter for Nature," particularly principles 11, 15, 23 and 24, which are – as stated in the Report – "directly linked to the rights set out in the international human rights instruments (right to health, to well-being, to an education, to participate in decision-making)." Finally, she called for the adoption of an autonomous right to a healthy environment, which would give more relevance to environmental quality and highlight the vital role of the environment as a basic condition for human dignity and well-being. However, this shift towards the notion of a human right to environment was not met favourably by most governments, and the subsequent declarations (Johannesburg 2002 and Rio 2012) went back to the Rio 1992 procedural approach and developed new, more and more economics-centred, views of environmental rights, with a clear focus on sustainable development.

3 Corpus and methodology

The "Environment" section of the UN Research Guide about UN Documentation[20] names the following six initiatives as those that have driven UN activity in the field of environment[21]:
- United Nations Conference on the Human Environment (Stockholm, 1972)
- World Commission on Environment and Development ("Brundtland Commission," 1987)
- United Nations Conference on Environment and Development (Rio de Janeiro, 1992)
- General Assembly Special Session on the Environment (New York, 1997)
- World Summit on Sustainable Development (Johannesburg, 2002)
- United Nations Conference on Sustainable Development (Rio de Janeiro, 2012)

The Outcome Documents of the aforementioned conferences include one Resolution (1997) and five Reports – four of which are classified as Reports of UN Bodies, while one is a Report transmitted by letter by a specialized agency (the Brundtland Commission, 1987):
- 1972: "Report of the United Nations Conference on the Human Environment" (A/CONF.48/14/Rev.1)

---

20 Available at http://research.un.org/en/docs/environment (October 18, 2013).
21 See http://research.un.org/content.php?pid=405645&sid=3326935 (October 18, 2013).

- 1987: "Report of the World Commission on Environment and Development: Our Common Future" (A/42/427)
- 1992: "Report of the United Nations Conference on Environment and Development" (A/CONF.151/26)
- 1997: "Programme for the Further Implementation of Agenda 21" (A/RES/S-19/2)
- 2002: "Report of the World Summit on Sustainable Development" (A/CONF.199/20)
- 2012: "Report of the United Nations Conference on Sustainable Development" (A/CONF.216/16), which includes "The Future We Want" (A/RES/66/288)

In order to have a more uniform and manageable corpus for what concerns documents' size, typology and structure, I have decided to focus my analysis on Reports only (thus excluding the General Assembly Resolution), and particularly on the "declaration"[22] sections within the Reports.[23] Moreover, to the list provided by the UN Research Guide I have added the 1982 "World Charter for Nature," particularly relevant because it is the only non-anthropocentric statement of the United Nations about environmental rights, the 1994 "Draft Principles," which are probably the most comprehensive UN statement on environmental rights and represent a sort of mediation between human-rights and nature-rights approaches, and the 2010 "Universal Declaration of the Rights of Mother Earth," an ecocentric declaration debated by the UN General Assembly on April 20, 2011, but never ratified because of the opposition by most Western countries. These last three documents, particularly the World Charter and the Universal Declaration, will allow me to compare the anthropocentric approach of official UN Declarations with alternative, more ecocentric, approaches.

---

22 The term "declaration" is commonly used for various international instruments: the term is often deliberately chosen to indicate that the parties merely want to declare certain aspirations; however, declarations can also be binding treaties. Moreover, some documents called "declarations" were not originally intended to be binding, but they have gained binding character at a later stage, such as the 1948 Universal Declaration of Human Rights. For the purposes of this paper, any document that enunciates some principles or political commitment will be treated and analysed as a "declaration."

23 "The Future We Want" is sometimes called "Declaration" and others simply "Outcome Document." It does not have the formal structure of a declaration, and it is much longer than the other Declarations under analysis, but I have nonetheless included it in my analysis because it represents the most recent expression of the UN political commitment to environmental rights issues.

So, to sum up, the corpus on which this analysis is based is the following:

1. "Declaration of the United Nations Conference on the Human Environment" (1972)
2. "World Charter for Nature" (1982)
3. "Summary of Proposed Legal Principles for Environmental Protection and Sustainable Development" – Annexe 1 of the "Brundtland Report" (1987)
4. "Rio Declaration on Environment and Development" (1992)
5. "Draft Principles on Human Rights and the Environment" (1994)
6. "Johannesburg Declaration on Sustainable Development" (2002)
7. "Universal Declaration of the Rights of Mother Earth" (2010)
8. "The Future We Want" (2012)

These eight documents will be analysed according to the theoretical perspective and methods of ecolinguistics, particularly of Ecocritical Discourse Analysis,[24] in order to criticise the ideologies hidden behind – or revealed by – the use of certain words and expressions by the United Nations. Since, as stated by Norman Fairclough, "the most obvious distinguishing features of a discourse are likely to be features of vocabulary – discourses 'word' or 'lexicalize' the world in particular ways,"[25] the analysis will focus in particular on the continuities and discontinuities in the lexical choices of the United Nations in its declarations about the environment, with particular reference to the differences between the declarations that have been ratified by the UN and those that have not.

4 Defining a human right to environment?

The terminology used by the United Nations to define environmental rights reveals a degree of uncertainty regarding the concept. In most instances, the word "environment" is qualified with an adjective such as "satisfactory," "decent," "safe" or "clean" or with some other expression such as "of a quality that permits" or "adequate for." As May and Daly have rightly argued, the recognition of environmental rights

---

24 See, among others: Valentina Adami, "Culture, Language and Environmental Rights: The Anthropocentrism of English," *Pólemos* 7.2 (2013): 335–355; Alwin Fill and Peter Mühlhäusler eds., *The Ecolinguistics Reader* (London and New York: Continuum, 2001); Alwin Fill, "Ecolinguistics as a European Idea," *The European Legacy* 2.3 (1997): 450–455; Peter Mühlhäusler and Adrian Peace, "Environmental Discourses," *Annual Review of Anthropology* 35 (2006): 457–479.
25 Norman Fairclough, *Analysing Discourse: Textual Analysis for Social Research* (London and New York: Routledge, 2003), 129.

comes with certain unavoidable challenges. New concepts and vocabulary need to be developed. Does the noun "environment" mean human environment, natural environment, or both? And which adjective to choose: "quality," "healthful," "clean," "adequate," or something else? What does a fundamental right to a quality environment entail?[26]

These definitional issues are inherent in any attempt to conceptualise environmental rights. In fact,

> there is little international consensus on the correct terminology. Even the UN Sub-Commission could not make up its mind, referring variously to the right to a "healthy and flourishing environment" or to a "satisfactory environment" in its report and to the right to a "secure, healthy and ecologically sound environment" in the draft principles. [...] What any of these mean is largely a subjective value judgment.[27]

As mentioned in the quote by Boyle, even within one single document such as the 1994 Ksentini Report we encounter a variety of expressions such as: "a healthy and flourishing environment," "a healthy and balanced environment," "a satisfactory environment," "a healthy and decent environment," "a healthy environment," "a healthy and balanced environment." The annexed "Principles on Human Rights and the Environment" speak instead of "an ecologically sound environment" (Principle 1: "Human rights, an ecologically sound environment, sustainable development and peace are interdependent and indivisible"); "a secure, healthy and ecologically sound environment" (Principle 2: "All persons have the right to a secure, healthy and ecologically sound environment")"; and "the right to an environment adequate to meet equitably the needs of present generations and that does not impair the rights of future generations to meet equitably their needs" (Principle 4). Ms. Ksentini herself seems aware of these language issues, because in the Report she explicitly comments on the use of the term "healthy," stating that:

> When asserting the right to the environment, current provisions express it in terms of the right to a healthy environment. This qualification of the environment has been generally interpreted to mean that the environment must be healthy in itself – free from "diseases" that hinder its ecological balance and sustainability – and that it must be healthful, that is conducive to healthy living.[28]

---

26 May and Daly, "Vindicating Fundamental Environmental Rights Worldwide," 370.
27 Boyle, "Human Rights and the Environment: A Reassessment," 33.
28 Special Rapporteur on Human Rights and the Environment, "Final Report," §180

Other documents adopt equally diverse formulations. Considering, for instance, Principle 1 of each Declaration, we find that the "Stockholm Declaration" recognizes "the fundamental right to freedom, equality and adequate conditions of life, in an environment of a quality that permits a life of dignity and well-being"; the "Proposed Legal Principles for Environmental Protection and Sustainable Development" annexed to the Brundtland Report state that "All human beings have the fundamental right to an environment adequate for their health and well being"; the "Rio Declaration" sets human beings "at the centre of concerns for sustainable development" and entitles them to "a healthy and productive life in harmony with nature"; the "Draft Principles" underline the interdependence and indivisibility of "human rights, an ecologically sound environment, sustainable development and peace"; the "Johannesburg Declaration" generally reaffirms a "commitment to sustainable development", as does the "The Future We Want," which then adds a commitment to "the promotion of an economically, socially and environmentally sustainable future for our planet and for present and future generations." All of these formulations contrast sharply with the perspectives of the "World Charter for Nature," whose first principles is that "Nature shall be respected and its essential processes shall not be impaired", and of the "Universal Declaration of the Rights of Mother Earth," which opens with the statement that "Mother Earth is a living being."

Expressions such as "sustainable development," "ecologically sound environment," and "an economically, socially and environmentally sustainable future" could be defined as "empty" or "floating signifiers"[29] that point to "a vague, highly variable, unspecifiable or non-existent signified."[30] In fact, their meaning is a matter of subjective interpretation, because the qualifying adjectives used to (attempt to) clarify the concept of "a right to environment" are themselves vague and imprecise.[31]

> What constitutes a *satisfactory, decent* or *ecologically sound* environment is bound to suffer from uncertainty. At best, it may result in cultural relativism, particularly from a North-South perspective, and lack the universal value normally thought to be inherent in human rights. Indeterminacy is an important reason, it is often argued, for not rushing to embrace new rights without considering their implications.[32]

---

29 Claude Lévi-Strauss, *Introduction to the Work of Marcel Mauss* [*Introduction à l'oeuvre de Marcel Mauss*, 1950], trans. Felicity Baker (London: Routledge, 1987), 61. Lévi-Strauss coined the notion of "floating signifier" to define "mana."
30 Daniel Chandlers, *Semiotics: The Basics* [2002] (New York: Routledge, 2007), 78.
31 See Tregidga, Milne and Kearins, "Sustainable Development as a Floating Signifier."
32 Boyle, "Human Rights and the Environment: A Reassessment," 33. [My emphasis].

In the light of these observations, the questions that arise are:

> Should we continue to think about human rights and the environment within the existing framework of human rights law in which the protection of humans is the central focus – essentially a greening of the rights to life, private life, and property – or has the time come to talk directly about environmental rights – in other words a right to have the environment itself protected? Should we transcend the anthropocentric in favour of the ecocentric?[33]

While these questions remain unanswered, I would like to briefly comment on the current uncertainties in the definition of a human right to environment. From a practical legal point of view, such terminological vagueness indeed constitutes an obstacle for its recognition, and "looking at environmental protection through other human rights" would be more convenient, because it would avoid "the need to define such notions as a satisfactory or decent environment."[34] However, the protection of the environment achieved through existing human rights laws would only represent an incidental consequence of decisions taken to protect other rights, rather than the result of a broader commitment to the environment.

On the other hand, the establishment of a right to environment would give environmental issues greater relevance in competition with other rights and enable courts to protect the environment on public interest grounds, and thus benefit society as a whole. Moreover, from a purely theoretical point of view, such uncertainty in the definition allows for a certain flexibility and thus favours a less rigid approach to environmental rights, an approach that avoids categorizations and oversimplifications. The variability in the formulation of a human right to environment is in fact best suited to address the complexities of environmental issues. For example, the use of different adjectives and expressions makes clear that the right to environment cannot be categorized as a civil and political right, or as an economic, social and cultural right, or as a collective right, because it transcends such distinctions: each adjective or expression points to a different aspect of the right to environment, which can thus be seen as belonging to different categories of rights.

---

33 Boyle, "Human Rights and the Environment: A Reassessment," 2–3.
34 Boyle, "Human Rights and the Environment: A Reassessment," 33.

5 Environment, nature, earth or sustainable development? Power struggles in environmental rights discourse

An analysis of the occurrences of the words "environment," "nature" and "earth" and of the expression "sustainable development" in the eight documents under consideration can reveal the main concern of each document and thus the perspective from which it was written. Rather than counting the number of occurrences of these words and expressions, it is interesting to observe the prevalence of one over the other and the contexts in which each word appears in each document.

First of all, it has to be noted that the documents under examination were the result of complex negotiations among the parties involved. The variability and uncertainties in the linguistic choices of the United Nations, both within a single document and across different documents, are evidence of the power struggles at work in environmental rights discourse at international level. As we will see, these power struggles are particularly evident in "The Future We Want," which seems to be attempting to express all possible positions and approaches to environmental rights, from the ecocentric idea of "the rights of nature" or even "of Mother Earth" to the anthropocentric concept of "sustainable development."

The word "environment" is frequently used in all of the eight documents, albeit with different understandings and in different contexts: its use can in fact indicate either a human-rights approach to environmental protection or a "sustainable-development" approach. The use of the terms "nature" or "earth," on the other hand, clearly indicates a "nature-rights" approach, and it is in fact much less frequent in UN documents. Finally, the focus on "sustainable development" reveals an economics-based approach, which considers environmental protection merely (or mainly) as an instrument for reaching other economic, social and political goals.

In the 1972 "Stockholm Declaration," "environment" is often qualified with the adjective "human" and in connection with the idea of improvement (as in "the preservation and enhancement of the human environment"). The declaration underlines the active role of "man" [sic] in transforming the environment (as in "man has acquired the power to transform his environment"), but also, albeit with less emphasis, our dependence on the environment: "Man is both creature and moulder of his environment" and "the earthly environment on which our life and well being depend." The power struggles and the attempts at making the declaration slightly more ecocentric are also revealed by the reference to the idea of cooperation with nature, as in the phrase "to build, in collaboration with nature, a better environment." There are two more references to "nature" in the declaration ("attaining freedom in the world of nature" and "nature conservation"), and six occurrences of "earth" ("in many regions of the earth," "pollution in water, air, earth and living beings," "The natural resources of the earth," "The capacity of the earth to produce vital renewable resources," and "The non-renewable resources of the earth," and "creating conditions on earth that are necessary for the improvement of the quality of life"). However, all in all the declaration appears to be definitely anthropocentric, focusing clearly on the protection of the environment (or nature, or the earth) *for* humans, as revealed by the phrases "a better life in an environment more in keeping with human needs and hopes," "the preservation and improvement of the human environment, for the benefit of all the people and for their posterity," and the already-quoted "in an environment of a quality that permits a life of dignity and well-being."

In the 1982 "World Charter for Nature," as suggested by the title, the focus is on nature rather than on environment. Accordingly, the term "environment" only appears three times, in the expressions "the protection of the environment," "decisions of direct concern to their environment," and "when their environment has suffered damage or degradation." Thus, two out of the three occurrences do not actually refer to "the environment" in general but to "*their* environment," thereby referring to the specific environment of certain individuals or groups. The hugely predominant use of the word "nature," as well as the focus on concepts of harmony and ecological unity (as in "protecting and safeguarding the balance and quality of nature," "Mankind is a part of nature," "Civilization is rooted in nature," "living in harmony with nature" and "Nature shall be respected"), reveal the ecocentric approach of the World Charter, which is in fact the only "nature-rights" document ever ratified by the United Nations.

The 1987 "Brundtland Report" (with the annexed "Proposed Legal Principles for Environmental Protection and Sustainable Development") is the first one to mention "sustainable development," an expression that was in fact coined by the Brundtland commission in this report. As indicated by the title, the "Proposed Legal Principles" deal with environmental protection and sustainable development, while "nature" and "earth" are never mentioned: the perspective is thus definitely economics-centred and human-centred, with most of the principles beginning with the phrase "States shall." The term "environment" usually appears in relation to the concept of human rights (in the already-mentioned principle 1, "All human beings have the fundamental right to an environment adequate for their health and well being") and to the usefulness of the environment for humans (as in principle 2: "States shall conserve and use the environment and natural resources for the benefit of present and future generations" and, twice, "interferences with their use of a natural resource or the environment").

In the 1992 "Rio Declaration," the use of the word "environment" partly recalls the perspective of Stockholm 1972, with expressions such as "to protect the environment" and "impact on the environment." It also refers to procedural issues ("access to information concerning the environment") and to specific concerns in the context of environmental protection ("The environment and natural resources of people under oppression, domination and occupation" and "protection for the environment in times of armed conflict"). However, unlike the "Stockholm Declaration," the "Rio Declaration" does not explicitly speak of a "right to environment," a concept which is here substituted by the idea of a right to development, but with a distinctive human-centred rather than economics-centred inclination, as revealed by principle 1 ("Human beings are at the centre of concerns for sustainable development"). Nonetheless, "nature" and "Earth" are also mentioned in this document, in the expressions "the integral and interdependent nature of the Earth, our home," "the health and integrity of the Earth's ecosystem," and "in harmony with nature." This reveals that, while the focus has indeed shifted from environmental rights to sustainable development and socio-economic issues, the "Rio Declaration" is the outcome of significant power struggles between the countries that supported a human-centred and economics-centred approach and those that sustained a more holistic and ecocentric view of environmental issues.

The 1994 "Draft Principles" recall more closely the "Stockholm Declaration," focussing on a human right to environment. Despite the already-mentioned variability in the adjectives used to qualify the environment in the Report to which the "Draft Principles" are annexed, the attempt to postulate the recognition of environmental rights from a human-rights perspective is evident in the statement of "the right to a secure, healthy and ecologically sound environment," "the right to an environment adequate to meet equitably the needs of present generations and that does not impair the rights of future generations to meet equitably their needs" and of the "duty to protect and preserve the environment." Nonetheless, the other two, contrasting perspectives (nature-centred and economic-centred) are also present in the "Draft Principles," as revealed by the (occasional) use of both "nature" ("the conservation and sustainable use of nature" and "ecologically sound access to nature") and "sustainable development" ("sustainable development links the right to development and the right to a secure, healthy and ecologically sound environment," "Human rights, an ecologically sound environment, sustainable development and peace are interdependent and indivisible," "environmental protection, sustainable development and respect for human rights").

In the 2002 "Johannesburg Declaration," the focus is definitely on sustainable development. In fact, "nature" is never mentioned while "earth" is mentioned only once (albeit with a capital letter!) in the phrase "the generations that will surely inherit this Earth"; even the less ecocentric word "environment" only appears three times in the whole declaration (although the adjective "environmental" is more frequent). Of these three occurrences of the noun "environment," the first refers to the environment as one of the pillars of sustainable development ("the protection of the environment and social and economic development are fundamental to sustainable development"), the second appears in the general statement "The global environment continues to suffer," and, finally, the third uses the word "environment" with a different acceptation in the phrase "within a transparent and stable regulatory environment." So, the environment is not the main concern of the Johannesburg Declaration, which is instead very much focused on the interaction between economic development, social development and environmental protection, as demonstrated by the 18 occurrences of "sustainable development" (plus 1 "unsustainable development").

In the 2010 "Universal Declaration of the Rights of Mother Earth," neither environment nor nature nor sustainable development are mentioned. The eco-centric, deep-ecology approach of the Declaration is confirmed by the exclusive use of the term "Earth," always with a capital letter and often in the collocation "Mother Earth." Moreover, this document differs from the UN-approved declarations for its focus on concepts of harmony, balance and all-togetherness, in expressions such as: "we are all part of Mother Earth," "Mother Earth is the source of life, nourishment and learning," "the integrity, balance and health of Mother Earth," "respecting and living in harmony with Mother Earth."

Finally, the most recent UN declaration about the environment, "The Future We Want," displays the widest variety of lexical choices. This is in part due to the fact that it is a much longer document than the others (and, as underlined before, perhaps not even a "proper" declaration in its structure), but also to the particularly strong power struggles that took place before, during and after the Rio+20 Summit. The most interesting choice for what concerns the use of the term "environment" is its collocation with the adjective "enabling" (9 times), as in "the continued need for an enabling environment" and "We underline the need for enabling environments." However, the environment is mainly conceived of as one of the pillars of sustainable development, in phrases such as "democracy, good governance and the rule of law [...] as well as an enabling environment are essential for sustainable development" and "we reaffirm the need to achieve economic stability, sustained economic growth, the promotion of social equity and the protection of the environment." In fact, sustainable development is indeed the main focus of "The Future We Want," which in the first three paragraphs defines the commitments of the Rio Conference: "the promotion of an economically, socially and environmentally sustainable future," "the eradication of poverty" and "the need to further mainstream sustainable development at all levels, integrating economic, social and environmental aspects and recognizing their interlinkages, so as to achieve sustainable development in all its dimensions." The terms "nature" and "Earth" are also used in the document, but the contexts in which they appear reveal that they were used not because of a real commitment to an ecocentric approach, but rather in the attempt to fulfill the expectations of certain (mainly South American) countries – as in "we note that some countries recognize the rights of nature in the context of the promotion of sustainable development" and "We recognize that [...] 'Mother Earth' is a common expression in a number of countries and regions." Nonetheless, "The Future We Want" displays a moderate opening towards a more holistic approach to environmental issues, with expressions such as "to promote harmony with nature," "We call for holistic and integrated approaches to sustainable development," and "to restore the health and integrity of the Earth's ecosystem."

6 Conclusion

Despite the discrepancies in the linguistic – and thus also conceptual – formulation of a right to environment, what all the documents I have analysed have in common (albeit in different ways and at different levels) is a general aspiration to environmental protection. However, from an ecocritical perspective it must be noted that UN formulations of the right to environment follow mainly anthropocentric, or even economics-centred, approaches that protect the environment only for its usefulness for humans or as one of the pillars of sustainable development. Such approaches disregard a more holistic and ecocentric view of environmental rights (expressed instead by the 2010 "Universal Declaration," never ratified by the United Nations precisely because of its ecocentrism), based on the recognition that environmental protection can represent an end in itself, not only an instrument for the realization of other human rights. By contrasting the United Nations' human-centred and economic-centred formulations of environmental rights with the ecocentrism of other documents, ecocritical discourse analysis reveals the possibility of a different approach, based on a different vocabulary.

Mara Logaldo
On Crimes, Punishments, and Words: Legal and Language Issues in Cesare Beccaria's Works

1 Premise

> If Voltaire's and Beccaria's outcries against torture often fell on deaf ears in the eighteenth century, they were very much in the drafters of the major twentieth-century international legal documents on human rights.[1]

Many of the standards set forth in the *Universal Declaration of Human Rights* of 1948, particularly in the first ten articles, owe something to Cesare Beccaria's theory of justice. The statements that all human beings are equal and equally entitled to the right to life, freedom, security and to the fair exercise of the law were already contained in *An Essay on Crimes and Punishments* (1764).

The following passage highlights how for the Italian political writer human rights represented the groundwork on which he founded all his theories concerning specific issues of criminal justice.

> If it can only be proved, that the severity of punishments, though not immediately contrary to the public good, or to the end for which they were intended, viz. to prevent crimes, be useless, then such severity would be contrary to those beneficent virtues, which are the consequence of enlightened reason, which instructs the sovereign to wish rather to govern men in a state of freedom and happiness than of slavery. It would also be contrary to justice and the social compact.[2]

It is important to underline that for Beccaria human rights are intertwined with natural rights, a notion he inherited from Thomas Hobbes.[3] But Beccaria took the

---

1 Micheline R. Ishay, *The History of Human Rights: From Ancient Times to the Globalization Era* (Berkeley, CA: University of California Press, 2008), 87.

2 Cesare Beccaria, *An Essay on Crimes and Punishments* (Boston, MA: International Pocket Library, 1992), 22: further references in the text, abbreviated as *CP*.

3 "each man has to use his own power, as he will himself for the preservation of his own nature – that is to say of his own life." Thomas Hobbes, *Leviathan* (Oxford: Oxford University Press, 1998 [1651]), 86. Significantly, the connection will be reasserted in article 3 of the *Universal Declaration of Human Rights*, which claims that "everyone has the right to life, liberty and security of person." On this connection, see Micheline R. Ishay, *The History of Human Rights*, 87.

imperative of the right to life to its furthest extent, for he used it as a starting point in order to adamantly condemn capital punishment, a topic on which, unfortunately, even the *Universal Declaration of Human Rights* seems to fall short. This shows how far-reaching Beccaria's position was. In fact Hobbes' idea could be interpreted in two opposite ways: as a justification for sentencing to the death penalty those who endanger other individuals' right to life or, conversely, as a condemnation of all possible ways of inflicting death, including legal ones.[4] On the contrary, by linking the *jus naturale* to the social contract Beccaria bends Hobbes's view to his own reformist intent, making it fit into a more neatly defined framework of human rights. As Ishay remarks:

> Following Hobbes, Beccaria believes that, in the social contract, we negotiate away only the minimal number of rights necessary to bring about peace. Thus, people hold onto their right to life, and do not hand this over to the public good. Given the fact that capital punishment cannot be justified by Locke's reasoning, Beccaria argues that the only other justification is that it is either necessary or useful for public good. He contests both of these claims.[5]

We see, moreover, how for Beccaria the idea of liberty itself is inseparable from both natural and human rights. The social contract should prevail over any kind of external impediments to the free manifestation of one's own nature, being the only legitimate buffers to the negative effects that may derive from an excess of freedom either internal faculties, namely reason and judgment, or social regulations codified by the law. In doing so, he manages to reach a relative balance between nature and norm.

That the law should be universal, rational, and fair is the prerequisite for a society in which happiness is guaranteed not just to the powerful few but to "the greatest number" (*CP*, 14). This idea of justice is inseparable from the belief that human rights should always be given the priority. The declaredly utilitarian view and the principles of the Enlightenment supported by Beccaria would disintegrate if sovereigns, who are the spokesmen of society's will, lost sight of this goal.

---

4 The idea that the capital punishment is legitimate whenever someone violates natural rights was held by John Locke in his *Second Treatise* (1690) and was still supported by Rousseau in the section entitled "The Right of Life and Death" contained in *The Social Contract* (1762). Even Montesquieu in *De l'esprit des lois* (1748) declared himself favourable to the capital punishment in the case of crimes against security. Beccaria makes an exception only for individuals who constitute a danger for the state. This exception was recalled by Robespierre as a justification for the execution of Louis XVI; ironically, when Robespierre pleaded against the capital punishment (cf. "Gazette nationale, ou Le Moniteur universel" (162, Wednesday 1st June 1791): 630–631), the same argumentation was used against himself.

5 Ishay, *The History of Human Rights*, 87.

Beside the rejection of the death penalty, the principal reforms endorsed by Beccaria were that punishments should be proportionate to the crime committed, certain and prompt, and that torture ought to be abolished, since it is evidence of "the coldest insensibility" (*CP*, 69). Trials should be public and general rather than "private and particular" (*CP*, 25). He underlined that a search for fairness in criminal procedures was totally neglected in eighteenth-century Europe, in spite of the progress made in other areas, such as trade and industry. "What must we think of mankind" he declared "when we reflect, that such is the established custom of the greatest part of our polished and enlightened Europe?" (*CP*, 25).

As is well known the response to Beccaria's principles all over the old Continent and, later on, in America[6] was enormous. More than fifty editions of *On Crimes and Punishments* in sixteen different languages appeared in the next few decades. André Morellet, who translated the text into French for the edition that contained the famous preface by Voltaire, claimed that while working at it he actually felt "the rattling chain of superstition" being shaken and the "howls of fanaticism" being choked.[7]

Half a century later Ugo Foscolo, in his essay entitled *The Italian Periodical Literature* (1824) wrote:

> The Marchese Beccaria, impelled by an irresistible love of truth and of his country, had the courage to compose his work on Crimes and Punishments; but alarmed by the spirit of the times and of the country in which he lived, he wrote it in secret, and published it without his name. All the governments of Italy offered a reward, the same as for the head of a malefactor, to any one who should discover the author. [...] Some princes have succeeded in imposing silence upon [these] subjects;[8] but neither their censures nor their inquisitions, either religious or political, nor their arbitrary punishments, have ever been able to prevent the inhabitants, either of the palaces, the cottages, or the prisons of their dominions, from reading almost every thing that is written in other nations. In our days, the whole of Europe appears one immense assembly, in which many expose their opinions, and all listen with eagerness. To read, to think, and to reason, has become in the present day an irresistible

---

6 We might recall Thomas Jefferson's references to *On Crimes and Punishment*. As Blackstone remarked "While the [state constitutional] provision suggests the immunities of the Great Charter, its language seems due rather to the influence of Beccaria, whose treatise on Crimes and Punishments was translated into English in 1768, and was read avidly by lawyers and jurists everywhere in the latter part of the eighteenth and the earlier part of the nineteenth centuries." See John D. Bessler, "Revisiting Beccaria's Vision: The Enlightenment, America's Death Penalty, and the Abolition Movement," *Northwestern Journal of Law and Social Policy* 4.2 (2009): 207.

7 Morellet was here repeating the same expressions used by Beccaria in the letter addressed to him. Beside translating *On Crimes and Punishments*, Morellet slightly changed Beccaria's book and divided it into sections with the aim to make its structure more systematic.

8 With one exception: admittedly inspired by Beccaria's principles, the Duke of Tuscany abolished the death penalty in 1786.

necessity. [...] if the torture began to be abolished in Europe, and if the criminal process appeared in all its native and horrid deformity, Beccaria alone has the merit.[9]

Beccaria's next treatise, *Ricerche intorno alla natura dello stile* (*Disquisitions on the Nature of Style*), published in 1770,[10] was possibly composed as a reaction to all the criticism which had followed, along with its renown, the appearance of *An Essay on Crimes and Punishments*.[11] In this book the criminologist apparently turned to metaphysics. Nonetheless, reflections on society and the function of the law were still present, though associated with language and style rather than overtly with juridical matters. The ideas contained in the *Disquisitions* were as revolutionary as those presented in the more famous pamphlet. As John Gorton argues, Beccaria went so far there as to build his argument on "the paradoxical notion that nature had implanted in every individual an equal degree of genius and that education was all in all."[12]

Given the evident coincidence of intent between the two works, I would argue that for Beccaria law and language are closely interrelated issues. *On Crimes and Punishments* actually presents numerous reflections upon language, while, conversely, the *Disquisitions on the Nature of Style*, which mainly revolve around words and literature, also throw light on Beccaria's general theory of government and society.[13] In the attempt to draw some significant parallels, I will focus on the following points: the theory of the association of ideas, the notion of normativity, the historical evolution of language and the law, Beccaria's criticism to abstraction and emphasis on the body, his mistrust towards tradition and interpretation,

---

9 Ugo Foscolo, *La letteratura periodica italiana* (1824). Italian and English text available at http://www.bibliotecaitaliana.it/xtf/view?docId=bibit000879/bibit000879.xml&chunk.id=d41e217&toc.depth=1&toc.id=&brand=default (February 5, 2013).

10 Cesare Beccaria, *Ricerche intorno alla natura dello stile* (Milano: Giovanni Silvestri, 1809). The full text of the essay is available at http://books.google.it/books?id=TzgPAQAAMAAJ&pg=PR14&lpg=PR14&dq#v=onepage&q&f (05/02/13). Further references in the text abbreviated as *RS*. [all translations into English are mine.]

11 John Gorton, *A General Biographical Dictionary*, I (London: Whittaker and co., 1833). The only other major work published by Beccaria was a collection of lectures on economics (*Elements of Public Economy*, 1784).

12 Gorton, *A General Biographical Dictionary*.

13 This cross-referential attitude has obvious historical reasons: in the eighteenth century, morality, politics, jurisprudence, literature and the arts were all considered as the different facets of one single science, the science of man. Montesquieu himself, whose influence was so strong on Beccaria, had written both on laws and style. In the *Disquisitions* the frequent tributes paid by Beccaria to his master include a praise of the unfinished "Essai sur le goût dans les choses de la nature et de l'art," a fragment of Montesquieu's article entitled "Goût," which appeared posthumously in Diderot's and d'Alembert's *Encyclopédie* (1757).

his condemnation of metaphoric excess and, finally, his position in relation to the arbitrariness of the sign and of the law.

2 The association of ideas

Though Beccaria acknowledges his intellectual indebtedness to several philosophers of the time, from Monstesquieu to Hélvetius and Condillac, his main source of inspiration is John Locke. Indeed, Locke's theories represent a unifying framework both for *An Essay on Crimes and Punishments* and the *Disquisitions*. There are passages in the former in which Beccaria quotes, almost literally, from *An Essay Concerning Human Understanding* (1690), particularly when he denies the existence of innate ideas and stresses the importance of sensory experience. Neither the laws nor language can do without a close relationship with the empirical way of feeling and perceiving things, "for no advantage in moral policy can be lasting which is not founded on the indelible sentiments of the heart of man" (*CP*, 20). The difficult task of the law is to counterbalance the negative effects deriving from the overwhelming flood of sensations by turning them to advantage. Style has a similar task: as part of eloquence, it is subject to sensations, though these have been internalized and converted into a philosophy of the soul (*RS*, 13).

Locke's influence becomes even more blatant with reference to simple and complex ideas, a connection which is at the core of Beccaria's political view as well as of his theory of language. In *On Crimes and Punishments* he claims that our "knowledge is in proportion to the number of our ideas. The more complex these are, the greater is the variety of positions in which they may be considered" (*CP*, 23). Since the multitude tends to be impressed only by "motives that are the immediate objects of sense" (*CP*, 19), the law ought to act without delay, so that the two ideas of crime and punishment may be closely associated (*CP*, 72).

Similarly, in the *Disquisitions* Beccaria argues that the writer has to choose the precise word that awakens a precise sensation: this search for the perfect "match" (*accozzamento*) should reflect a process that occurs not only between words and sensible ideas but also, respectively, between the ideas and between the words that belong to a language (*RS*, 218, 221).

Hence law and language have a similar task: that of opposing the compelling and continually renovated drive for sensations which presses on mankind with a high degree of intensity by turning that very drive to moral and social advantage, so that "the smallest force continually applied will overcome the most violent motion communicated to bodies" (*CP*, 20).

3 Normativity in law and language

In Beccaria's utilitarian view, the association of ideas could prove a powerful tool both to ensure freedom and to contain it. On the one hand the process embodies a form of freedom. For instance, it is the free association of ideas that allows language to be creative. Thanks to this liberty, writers may enrich their language with new words and phrases (*RS*, 221). This creative side should however be counterbalanced by a normative one, lest wit might overtake judgment. In Beccaria's empirical perspective the association of ideas is a positive process; however, an excess of it may blur the lines of separation that are necessary to the spirit of geometry, which, rather than measure abstract categories, is meant here to gauge the phenomena of human sensibility.

The idea is clearly expressed in the *Disquisitions*, where he acknowledges having been inspired only by those philosophers, such as Locke and d'Alembert who founded their rigorous analyses on a close observation of human nature (*RS*, viii). As is often the case with eighteenth-century theories, laws are searched for to provide an answer to the subtle mechanisms by which sensations appeal to the soul. If the reasons behind aesthetic pleasure can be explored, then style can also become the object of rational investigation.[14]

The taste for symmetry and order could be explained as one such phenomenon. On the one hand too much symmetry would have a dull, negative effect. In the *Disquisitions* Beccaria blames those who have the habit of accompanying every noun with an adjective, "so that you may count as many adjectives as nouns". "Such formal symmetry", he writes, "tires out the soul" (*RS*, 81). On the other hand he warns against using language so as to recall too many sensations at once, because this would produce a confusing effect. There is only a limited number of sensations that can be taken in simultaneously: this limit, beyond which language ceases to make sense, is presented as an unquestionable fact (*RS*, 27).[15]

In the same years a similar aesthetic theory was expressed by several artists and writers. In *The Analysis of Beauty* (1757), for instance, William Hogarth claimed that an appearance of natural asymmetry is to be preferred to a dull bilateral identity of patterns. He underlined that "it is a constant rule in composition to avoid regularity;" on the other hand, a complete lack of symmetry would

---

14 The idea had clearly been expressed by David Hume in *Enquiry Concerning Human Understanding* (1748) and by Edmund Burke in *Philosophical Enquiry into the Origin of our Ideas of the Sublime and Beautiful* (1757).

15 In the twentieth century this idea will be discussed in terms of entropy. See Claude Elwood Shannon; Warren Weaver, *Mathematical Model of Communication* (Urbana: University of Illinois Press, 1949).

suggest unfitness and make a figure chaotic and unpleasant. He therefore praised the "line of beauty," which has to be neither too straight nor too twisted.[16]

The idea of the middle line is also stressed by Beccaria in *On Crimes and Punishments* with reference to the law, when he writes that, in the life of the nations, periods of prosperity are followed by periods of scantiness and that the law has the function of accelerating the intermediate states between these two opposites. More relevantly he applies the idea to punishment, stressing that it should be not only proportionate to the crime committed but also halfway between extremes.[17]

Yet, Beccaria is also aware of the fact that a mathematical search for the perfect balance between order and disorder, symmetry and asymmetry is bound to fail in the law as in any other domain of human activity.

> It is impossible to prevent entirely all the disorders which the passions of mankind cause in society. [...] In political arithmetic, it is necessary to substitute a calculation of probabilities to mathematical exactness. [...] If mathematical calculation could be applied to the obscure and infinite combinations of human actions, there might be a corresponding scale of punishments, descending from the greatest to the least; but it will be sufficient that the wise legislator mark the principal divisions, without disturbing the order, left to crimes of the *first* degree be assigned punishments of the *last*. If there were an exact and universal scale of crimes and punishments, we should there have a common measure of the degree of liberty and slavery, humanity and cruelty of different nations (*CP*, 26).

The impossibility of reducing human matters to a hard discipline ("Happy the nation where the knowledge of the law is not a science!" *CP*, 40) and the wavering between norms and exceptions fuel a distinctively eighteenth-century debate which Beccaria keeps alive both in his view of the law and in his theory of style. Although law and style are ways of coming to terms with human passions by controlling their disrupting and obscuring power (*RS*, 140), both have limits in achieving this end. As he admits in the *Disquisitions*, "in the mechanical form of the word" there are gaps that need to be filled (*RS*, 128). Therefore it is not surprising that, also in criminal matters, a momentary disorder may arise even

---

16 William Hogarth, *The Analysis of Beauty* (New Haven & London: Yale University Press, 1997), 48–49.

17 Here the immediate reference seems to be to Montesquieu, whose philosophy was founded on the ideas of mediation and moderation. The middle line could set a limit to the spirit of geometry without denying it. Even in aesthetic matters Montesquieu had reached the paradoxical conclusion according to which "art provides rules and taste provides exceptions to the rules: taste tells when art ought to prevail and when art ought to surrender." (Montesquieu, "Fragment sur le goût"). [My translation].

from "a rigorous observance of the letter of penal laws" (*CP*, 24). He concludes that "neither the power of eloquence nor the sublimest truths are sufficient to restrain, for any length of time, those passions which are excited by the lively impressions of present objects" (*CP*, 19), and that "it is a false idea of utility that would give to a multitude of sensible beings that symmetry and order which inanimate matter is alone capable of receiving" (*CP*, 91).

Neither words nor laws can do without a close relationship with empirical experience and consequently with a certain amount of disorder. As concerns language, in the *Disquisitions* Beccaria never seems to question the existence of a rule which defines the best expression to be chosen among many and discard "vicious ones" (*RS*, 141). On the other hand this norm is not founded on mere grammatical rules, the "mechanical connection of syntax" (*RS*, 219), but on logical relations between ideas and the most effective way of expressing them through words. Hence style acts as a touchstone for identifying the precise correspondence of language and sensible ideas. Also the law should be founded on the human way of associating ideas and sensations, "for all laws are useless, and in consequence destructive, which contradict the natural feelings of mankind" (*CP*, 50).

In sum, Beccaria's empirical view asserts at the same time the strength and weakness of law and language: although both have a normative ground, neither of them can ultimately be reduced to abstract, steady formulations.

4 The three stages of society

In the *Disquisition* we read that humanity has gone through three different stages. At the first stage, or state of nature, human beings had *more ideas than words*. During that primitive and savage phase, man resorted to the repetition of formulae and verbal patterns. Society mainly expressed itself through dances and pantomimes, which imitated objects and immediate sensations as they were, instead of submitting them to a rational process of elaboration and articulation through language. At the second stage a balance was reached: human beings started to possess *as many ideas as words*. This is also described as the "poetic stage," which was "eloquent and full of imagery". Implicitly starting from the Lockean assumption that sounds are signs of ideas, Beccaria underlines that signs became more perfect along with the evolution of ideas. No longer prone to mere immediate sensations, people started to use their imagination to combine ideas and express them through words. Finally humanity reached the third stage, in which human beings started to have *more words than ideas* (*RS*, 208–214).

On the one hand this process has been a positive one. General terms appeared to describe ideas which, combining together, became more and more complex, while abstractions were made necessary by the increasingly faster way of reasoning. On the other hand the evolution of language has had negative implications. First, impressions themselves have become vaguer and vaguer. Secondly, also language has became weaker, making any succession and combination of signs acceptable, as long as it complies with the rules of syntax, considered as a set of arithmetic signs rather than as a system of logical connections (*RS*, 215–216). Most of all, we note in Beccaria's theory the awareness that in the third stage of society signifiers may exist and be used without any relation to the signified. Words may outlive objects and ideas, leaving room for mere nominalism.

A similar three-phase evolution may be detected in *On Crimes and Punishments*. In fact, also in this text we see how mankind has gone through different stages, from anarchy to the present social contract. In the introduction Beccaria writes that the original function of the law was that of preventing society from dissolving or plunging into chaos. At this primitive stage a lawless society was prey to the immediate impressions left by objects. Little by little, ideas started to prevail over mere sensations, giving rise to the second stage of society and to general laws. Eventually, we have reached a further stage in which the law seems to have exceeded human needs, cutting the thread that linked the senses and the intellect in a harmonic way.

Nowadays abstract ideals, as for instance the ancient value attributed to the concept of "honour", have no longer any connection with actual experience; nonetheless, severe punishments are routinely performed to preserve them. As Beccaria also remarked in his *Disquisitions*, the words "justice, honour, law, etc." are moral terms related not only to physical sensations but to internal feelings connected to them; therefore these "moral words" owe their legitimacy only to the complex ideas they slowly arouse and should be used only as long as this process of gradual recognition occurs (*RS*, 39).[18]

> Honour, then, is one of those complex ideas which are an aggregate not only of simple ones, but of others so complicated, that, in their various modes of affecting the human mind, they sometimes admit and sometimes exclude part of the elements of which they are composed,

───────

18 Less subtly, or more pragmatically, Locke had written that these ideals and practices (such as, for instance, duels fought to defend honour) are only made acceptable by culture: "Where then are those innate principles of justice, piety, gratitude, equity, chastity? Or where is that universal consent that assures us there are such inbred rules? Murders in duels, when fashion has made them honourable, are committed without remorse of conscience: nay, in many places innocence in this case is the greatest ignominy. And if we look abroad to take a view of men as they are, we shall find that they have remorse, in one place, for doing or omitting that which others, in another place, think they merit by" (John Locke, *An Essay Concerning Human Understanding* (London, Tegg and Son, 1836, 26).

retaining only some few of the most common, as many algebraic quantities admit one common divisor. To find this common divisor of the different ideas attached to the word honour, it will be necessary to go back to the original formation of society. (*CP*, 32)

Hence he blames his time for fighting duels and punishing men in the name of ideals that no longer generated any feeling or retained any meaning. In the Age of Reason these void and dangerous practices constituted an anachronistic return to the first stage, or state of nature.

The first laws and the first magistrates owed their existence to the necessity of preventing the disorders which the natural despotism of individuals would unavoidably produce. This was the object of the establishment of society, and was, either in reality or in appearance, the principal design of all codes of laws, even the most pernicious. [...]

Honour, being produced after the formation of society, could not be a part of the common deposit, and therefore, whilst we act under its influence, we return, for that instant, to a state of nature and withdraw ourselves from the laws, which, in this case, are insufficient for our protection.

Hence it follows, that, in extreme political liberty, and in absolute despotism, all ideas of honour disappear, or are confounded with others. In the first case, reputation becomes useless from the despotism of the laws; and in the second, the despotism of one man, annulling all civil existence, reduces the rest to a precarious and temporary personality. Honour, then, is one of the fundamental principles of those monarchies which are a limited despotism; and in those, like revolutions in despotic states, it is a momentary return to state of nature and original equality. (*CP*, 33)

Since they can also exist independently from concrete objects or ideas, words may be deceptive. Therefore no man should be condemned merely on the ground of words said or reported, particularly in the case of secret accusations. Nor should oaths be considered as a reliable way for obtaining the truth from witnesses:

for [...] violent and uncommon actions, such as real crimes, leave a trace in the multitude of circumstances that attend them, and in their effects; but words remain only in the memory of the hearers, who are commonly negligent or prejudiced. It is infinitely easier, then, to found an accusation on the words than on the actions of a man; for in these the number of circumstances urged against the accused afford him a variety of means of justification (*CP*, 39).

As Steven Lynn points out:

the uncertainty of our notions of honour and virtue, [...] is an uncertainty made inevitable by the arbitrary connection between "names" and "the things they originally signified" [...]. Beccaria, tacitly following Locke, is so much aware of the prison house of Language that he would have no one placed in a more substantial prison house on the basis of words: "when the question relates to the words of a criminal, the credibility of a witness is null." Actions, res, must found an accusation, not verba – which, as Locke tells us, "stand for nothing but the Ideas in the Mind of him that uses them."[19]

Unfortunately, as Beccaria argues when dealing with the subject of confessions extorted by means of torture, "men are influenced more by the names than the nature of things" (*CP*, 89).

5 Law, language and the body

Beccaria's empirical approach is reflected in his stress on the human body. The emphasis given to the application of *habeas corpus* rights is clear: the physical presence of the defendant is necessary during trials. Also acts of accusation, beside being public, should never be anonymous. It will also be apt to report here his definition of the law as a tangible truth (*CP*, 30) whose contradictions are also "palpable" (*CP*, 50, 88); his vivid description of tortures and executions; his claim that there is no liberty when the law allows man to cease being a person and become a thing (*CP*, 53); his discourses on suicide (punishing a suicide would be like "scourging a statue", *CP*, 77) and exile, the latter considered as a way of depriving society of one's own body; finally, his statement that the power of the laws "should follow every subject, as the shadow follows the body" (*CP*, 84).

Beccaria shows a tendency to emphasize the importance of the body also in his reading of other kinds of experience, including the experience of language. He often hints at the fact that language and ideas have a body. He also argues that during the second stage of society words acquired the capacity to make objects exist within the human imagination. More generally, words suggest movement and by evoking the body they evoke the image of other bodies and spaces, an endless propagation of the "copies of sensation" (*RS*, 69).

Even words denoting abstract concepts must have their origin in sensation. Abstract terms should seldom be used or at least they ought to be surrounded by other expressions that immediately recall feelings; for they are acceptable only as long as they are useful to produce new combinations of sensible ideas. Moral objects, such as "law" and "justice", which are not the immediate outcome of sensations but of complex ideas and processes involving personal feelings, acquire a more intense and persisting effect when they are associated with

---

19 Steven Lynn, "Locke and Beccaria: Faculty Psychology and Capital Punishment," *Postscript* 5 (1988): 1–12, 4.

physical objects (*RS*, 42). In fact, images that recall bodily experience "receive from time and space an amplitude and a presence which makes the impression immutable and more constantly fixed" so that the moral idea they excite will "be given the time to be internalized more deeply and long-lastingly" (*RS*, 42).

However, when dealing with the law as a practice Beccaria underlines that justice cannot be embodied by a physical being who has the power to impose him or herself in a coercive way: "we should be cautious how we associate with the word *justice* an idea of any thing real, such as a physical power, or a being that actually exists" (*CP*, 21).

Beccaria's theory is actually founded on a tripartite structure: the sovereign, the defendant and the magistrate. The law cannot be identified with the magistrate, though the latter plays a fundamental role in the application of the laws: the magistrate is a third party who has to decide the contest unappealingly; and his determination "should consist of a simple affirmation or negation of fact" (*CP*, 22). The only person who, metaphorically, can embody justice and has "the authority of making penal laws" is the sovereign, but only insofar as he represents the whole society united by the social compact, for "laws receive their force and authority from an oath of fidelity, either tacit or expressed, which living subjects have sworn to their sovereign" (*CP*, 23).

Hence in juridical matters the idea of the body becomes acceptable only if we consider the collective body of society. It is interesting to note that language is also described in similar terms: in the *Disquisitions* Beccaria never refers to single linguistic phenomena within a particular idiom, but always to "the whole corpus of a language" (*RS*, 220), which is the expression of the entire society of speakers.

6 Against tradition

Beccaria considers language as a living organism. First of all from a synchronic point of view. Indeed, when he talks about the arrangement of words produced by the combination of simple ideas into complex ones, he seems to refer to language in terms of a sort of transformational-generative grammar. Of course, also from a diachronic perspective language is a live body that grows and modifies along with the evolution of ideas.

In a similar way, the law is conceived by Beccaria as a living organism, which must evolve with the transformations of society. Codes are the living expression of the social contract. It follows that the laws are not something given once and for all, a corpus of inert texts inherited from the past. As typical of the Enlightenment, the authority of tradition is strongly questioned, while emphasis is given to the cultural and social distance from the past. Indeed, erroneous principles may not only be "driven by the gales of passion" but also "received and transmitted by ignorance!" (*CP*, 32).

For this reason, the repositories of society's will are not the judges but the sovereigns.

> [Magistrates] have not received the laws from our ancestors as a domestic tradition, or as the will of a testator, which his heirs and executors are to obey; but they receive them from a society actually existing, or from the sovereign, its representative. (*CP*, 22)

This is another point of contact between laws and language: laws cannot be inherited "as a domestic tradition," just as style cannot be inherited from the authors of the past but has to derive from a process of constant creation and re-creation. In the *Disquisitions* he praised D'Alembert, Condillac "and others, even more famous thinkers" because they had "changed a situation in which eloquence had been made "sterile and bare on account of gloomy pedantry and servile imitation" and had started to look "into our faculties, into our way of feeling, the origin of taste, laws as invariable as the human soul" (*RS*, xv).

Here we find one of the contradictory tenets of eighteenth-century theory: the negation of innate ideas and, at the same time, the confirmation of universal principles on which those very ideas are based. How can standards (for instance the standard of taste) be alive and changeable if the human soul is invariable? The debate, involving both the idea of the language and the idea of the law, was already present in Edmund Burke, where it was ultimately expressed as an insolvable one: for, on the one hand, he claimed that concepts crystallized by tradition needed to be redefined, while, on the other hand, he asserted that if there are "no fixed principles, if the imagination is not affected according to some invariable and certain laws, our labour is like to be employed to very little purpose; as it may be judged as useless, if not an absurd undertaking, to lay down rules for caprice, and to set up for a legislator of whims and fancies."[20]

Beccaria expressed the debate in analogous terms: the law, as well as language and style, has written rules which must be literally complied with, though those very rules, be they fixed in legal codes or in grammars, should never cease being the living expression of society and the human soul.

---

20 Edmund Burke, "On Taste" in *An Inquiry into the Origin of Our Ideas of the Sublime and Beautiful*.

7 Against interpretation

With this caveat, Beccaria legitimizes written rules so incontestably that he denies the possibility that there may be room left for the judge's interpretation.

> When the code of laws is once fixed, it should be observed in the literal sense, and nothing more is left to the judge than to determine whether an action be or be not conformable to the written law. (*CP*, 24)

Judges "in criminal cases, have no right to interpret the penal laws, because they are not legislators" (*CP*, 22). Interpretation, when necessary, can only derive from the needs of society, which, by turn, can only be expressed through the figure of the sovereign: "Who then is their lawful interpreter? The sovereign, that is, the representative of society, and not the judge, whose office is only to examine if a man have or have not committed an action contrary to the laws" (*CP*, 23).

The task of the magistrate is to apply the laws literally, after finding out whether the defendant is innocent or guilty. In doing so, he should reason according to the following syllogism:

> In every criminal cause the judge should reason syllogistically. The *major* should be the general law; the *minor*, the conformity of the action, or its opposition to the laws; the *conclusion*, liberty, or punishment. If the judge be obliged by the imperfection of the laws, or chooses to make any other or more syllogisms than this, it will be an introduction to uncertainty. (*CP*, 7)

The "letter" of the law should be constant and unchanging. It seems to follow that the language of justice should be totally denotative and referential, literal to the highest degree.

> The disorders that may arise from a rigorous observance of the letter of penal laws are not to be compared with those produced by the interpretation of them. The first are temporary inconveniences which will oblige the legislature to correct the letter of the law, the want of preciseness and uncertainty of which has occasioned these disorders; and this will put a stop to the fatal liberty of explaining, the source of arbitrary and venal declamations. When the code of laws is once fixed, it should be observed in the literal sense, and nothing more is left to the judge than to determine whether an action be or be not conformable to the written law. (*CP*, 24)

In the ensuing chapter he warns against the use of obscure language: "If the power of interpreting laws be an evil, obscurity in them must be another, as the former is the consequence of the latter" (*CP*, 25).

He also shows great awareness of the problems that may derive from the language in which the laws are written. If the language is unknown to the people involved in a case, there is the necessity of resorting to mediators during trials. But Beccaria does not seem to trust this kind of interpreter either: he considers written translations far more reliable. He claims that codes should be translated into every European language, for the laws should be written in words all the people can read and understand.

> This evil will be still greater if the laws be written in a language unknown to the people; who, being ignorant of the consequences of their own actions, become necessarily depen-dent on a few, who are interpreters of the laws, which, instead of being public and general, are thus rendered private and particular. What must we think of mankind when we reflect, that such is the established custom of the greatest part of our polished and enlightened Europe? Crimes will be less frequent in proportion as the code of laws is more universally read, and understood; for there is no doubt but that the eloquence of the passions is greatly assisted by the ignorance and uncertainty of punishments. (*CP*, 25)

But the problem of interpretation is, more generally, an ontological one that involves both the nature of the law and the nature of language: "There is nothing more dangerous than the common axiom; *the spirit of the laws is to be considered.* To adopt it is to give way to the torrent of opinions" (*CP*, 23). Opinions, as Sterne's *The Life and Opinions of Tristram Shandy, Gentleman* confirmed, are the source of all forms of uncertainty. As Beccaria remarks:

> Every man hath his own particular point of view, and, at different times, sees the same objects in very different lights. The spirit of the laws will then be the result of the good or bad logic of the judge; and this will depend on his good or bad digestion, on the violence of his passions, on the rank or condition of the accused, or on his connections with the judge, and on all those little circumstances which change the appearance of objects in the fluctuat-ing mind of man. Hence we see the fate of a delinquent changed many times in passing through the different courts of judicature, and his life and liberty victims to the false ideas or ill humour of the judge, who mistakes the vague result of his own confused reasoning for the just interpretation of the laws. We see the same crimes punished in a different manner at different times in the same tribunals, the consequence of not having consulted the constant and invariable voice of the laws, but the erring instability of arbitrary interpretation. (*CP*, 7)

Just as in *On Crimes and Punishment* the right to interpret is denied to the magistrate and granted only to the sovereign, in the *Disquisitions* this privilege seems to be bestowed only on the artist. And just as in the former context the sovereign becomes the embodiment of society as a whole, in the latter the writer becomes the repository of the whole corpus of the language, the profound connoisseur of the power of words. Here by 'interpreting' Beccaria does not mean turning away from the literal meaning of words but, on the contrary, delving deeply into their essence. Only eloquence can set off a search around the nature of things. He makes this point through an amazingly modern description of the process, which resonates with the manifesto of the Russian formalists that would appear more than a century and a half later.[21]

> While obscure opinions on objects continually change, and investigations into their nature may so greatly differ from one another and lead farther from their actual appearance, only eloquence can recall and recombine the real appearance of objects so at to awaken our dulled attention and, by clothing them with permanent and immediately eye-catching colours, multiply them for universal research and make them popular and ever-lasting. (*RS*, xvi)

In language we look for the unexpected. Beccaria goes so far as to say that we do not pay attention to words that are totally predictable, to the extent that they become meaningless to us (*RS*, 81). These words are reduced to a mere succession of sounds for they awaken "no sensible or aural sensation" (*RS*, 81). This idea is strikingly modern, for it foreshadows studies in informativeness and non informativeness.[22] Uniformity is to be avoided: "white snow," for instance, is unbearably dull, while "cold snow" is slightly better. In any case, "additions" of qualities (whiteness and coldness) are to be enhanced. General names have fewer qualities in common than proper names, where qualities identify with one single person or thing (*RS*, 71–72). As permanent qualities are well-known, figures of speech that evoke different movements and extensions of the words are to be praised, for they reinforce the main idea we want to convey. Metaphors are an example of these figurative extensions: they multiply sensations, which is the main aim of style.

8 On metaphor

On the one hand Beccaria seems to believe in a one-to-one correspondence between sign and referent. Words should immediately, almost mechanically, bring to mind ideas when we utter them. No word can replace another word; only *that* word expresses and recalls *that* particular idea. For this reason, synonymy and metaphor are to be used sparingly: writers should not resort to a synonym instead of choosing the exact word, just as they should not express an analogous idea instead of the principal one.

---

21 It may sound anachronistic to define Beccaria a forerunner of the Russian formalists, but here he actually seems to express the idea of *ostranenie*, which resides in the assumption that, by a process of defamiliarization, art brings objects back to life, thus rescuing them from the oblivion of habit. See Viktor Shklovsky, *The Theory of Prose* (New York: Yale University Press, 1976), 12.
22 In *The Mathematical Model of Communication*, Shannon and Weaver claimed that informativeness is inversely proportional to predictability.

In the *Disquisitions* he seems to suggest that this is the result of both the denotative and connotative function of language: "within the immense array of words that form the body of a language, there are some that immediately and truly arouse feelings in the soul" (*RS*, 9). This belief entails a reflection upon the relation between sound and meaning as well as upon discourse patterns, "the correspondence between the sound and collocation of words and the idea they represent" (*RS*, 147). The statement has nothing to do with a mere search for euphonic effects[23] or with the conviction of the all-pervasive power of onomato-poeia, though the existence of this phenomenon is widely acknowledged. This awareness does not infringe Beccaria's belief in the conventionality of the sign either (see section below). Yet, it establishes a deep correlation between sound and meaning, emphasizing the capacity of language to make manifest the con-nection between ideas and feelings by virtue of its phonic substance. Hence, for instance, harmonic or clashing ideas can be expressed by harmonic or clashing combinations of words (*RS*, 150). Similarly, the reference to *collocation* does not simply hint at conventions, but considers semantic and syntactical choices as a sign of coherent argumentation. As we have seen, for Beccaria logic and grammar are two distinct things: he blames a "tied up style" in which words are linked by connectors that are grammatically, rather than logically, correct (*RS*, 140). Once again, this shows how modern Beccaria's theory of language was.[24]

A certain gap between word and idea is nonetheless acknowledged: there is an excess of meaning, with particular reference to complex ideas, which actually allows the existence of a metaphorical level. Still, there is a wide range of shades by which an utterance can take a distance from the idea figuratively associated to it. The image used by Beccaria is that of a painter: writers can play with tones up and down the whole scale of colors and they can do so just because ideas themselves have "shades" (*RS*, 98). Figures of speech should be used so as to create "beautiful" connections not only between words but also between words and ideas. From this perspective they act as links, as knots that bind together, almost synaesthetically, language, sensations and ideas (*RS*, 152–160).

As he argues in the *Disquisitions*, a metaphor is effective only if a common quality between the two objects being compared prevails over the differences

---

23 However, a whole section is devoted to the sound of words, which should never overwhelm ideas. The sound of words should be used to convey ideas as effectively as possible, like the rings of a chain. Too many sounds have a confusing effect. Words have a "mechanical and physical charm" and as such they can be used to capture the attention of an audience (*RS*, 151).

24 In *Syntactic Structures* (1957), linguist Noam Chomsky would use the famous sentence "colour-less green ideas sleep furiously" to show how a statement can be grammatically correct but semantically nonsensical.

between them. This common quality, which ancient rhetoric defined as *tertium comparationis* should actually be able to recall a "third idea" to which the two different objects can be related (*RS*, 47, 55).[25] Metaphors that fall short of generating a third idea, because the resemblance between the two objects is too plain, or, conversely, metaphors that compare objects that are too distant and therefore have nothing in common, are to be avoided. In the former case the deriving image would be "false or weak;"[26] in the latter, it would be "gigantic and strange" (*RS*, 84).

Metaphorical processes implying either a separation from actual facts or the association of concepts on the ground of far-fetched analogies dubitably detected in different fields and subjected to the deceiving action of opinion are obviously to be discarded. In fact rather than bring to light an associated idea this kind of metaphor makes discourse more obscure, just as too much brightness has a dazzling effect (*RS*, 90–91).

Beccaria lingers on this problem both in the *Disquisitions* and in *On Crimes and Punishment:* in the former he speaks about the "weakest flicker of a far-fetched analogy mistaken for the clear light of evidence" (*RS*, 193). In the latter he expresses the same idea with reference to penal decisions. An excess of metaphoric associations is identified with obscurity and therefore perceived as utterly negative. Significantly, the image of metaphor is associated to torture, which is defined as "a *metaphorical* and incomprehensible purgation of infamy."[27] The fact that torture is actually a *figurative* way of punishing is something Beccaria and his contemporaries were perfectly aware of.

> Contemporary political philosophers distinguish between two principle theories of justifying punishment. First, the retributive approach maintains that punishment should be equal to the harm done, either *literally* an eye for an eye, or *more figuratively* which allows for alternative forms of compensation. The retributive approach tends to be retaliatory and vengeance-oriented. The second approach is utilitarian which maintains that punishment should increase the total amount of happiness in the world. This often involves punishment as a means of reforming the criminal, incapacitating him from repeating his crime, and deterring others. Beccaria clearly takes a utilitarian stance. For Beccaria, the purpose of

---

25 It is interesting to notice that the notion of *tertium comparationis* is both a linguistic and legal term. In Italian jurisprudence the term was introduced in 1804 to indicate the possibility of referring to a third norm to assess whether a constitutional norm complies both with the principle of legitimacy and with the principle of equity.

26 Beccaria is clearly aware of the process by which tropes may die by repeated usage within a culture. See Paul Ricoeur, *The Rule of Metaphor* (London: Routledge and Kegan Paul, 1978).

27 In the English edition (*CP*, 43), the adjective "metaforica" in the original text is imprecisely translated as "metaphysical."

punishment is to create a better society, not revenge. Punishment serves to deter others from committing crimes, and to prevent the criminal from repeating his crime.[28]

Beccaria denies the utility of metaphorical forms of compensation, which dissociate crimes and punishments, just as they dissociate ideas from sensations and words.

9 The arbitrariness of the sign and of the law

The emphasis on literalness seems to suggest that Beccaria considers language an efficient tool: it is only up to the good writer or legislator to find the precise words to communicate precise ideas. This conviction seems to clash not only with Locke's awareness of the difficulty of finding the right expression to articulate an idea, but also with the possibility that that expression would arouse exactly the same idea both in the mind of the speaker and in the mind of the hearer.[29] Locke also distinguishes between civil and philosophical uses of language, claiming that in the former a certain degree of imperfection does not prevent a reasonably accurate way of communicating, while in the latter it does, because words have "to convey the precise notions of things."[30]

At a superficial level Beccaria's view of language appears less problematic. He actually seems to rely on the possibility that communication is possible, both in civil and philosophical matters, in legal cases as well as in works of art.[31] Although he acknowledges that, historically, ideas become more difficult to convey as long as they become increasingly complex, he believes that language, behind its different manifestations, has the power to retain the trace of a common way of feeling founded on the senses (see, for instance, *RS*, 109). The inevitable and unvaried repetition of principal ideas is an example of this process (*RS*, 33). Hence written rules, both in the law and in style, are acceptable only if they are means of complying with that primeval, universal way of feeling, and not just empty canons that suffocate man's "original energy" (*RS*, xix).

---

28 *Internet Encyclopedia of Philosophy*, last updated April 11, 2001, available at http://www.iep. utm.edu/beccaria/ (February 10, 2013) [italics mine].
29 As Locke put it, "it is easy to perceive what imperfection there is in language, and how the very nature of words makes it almost unavoidable for many of them to be doubtful and uncertain in their significations." (Locke, *An Essay Concerning Human Understanding*, 348.)
30 Locke, *An Essay Concerning Human Understanding*, 348.
31 In *RS* he actually mentions in passing a distinction between *figure di sentenza* (statements) and *figure di parole* (tropes) but never describes the former, he develops his elaborate discourse only on the latter (*RS*, 83).

On the other hand, Locke and Beccaria share the same consciousness of the arbitrariness of language, which, twinned with the absence of an innate moral code, makes our convictions "suspect and tentative."[32]

> Now, since sounds have no natural connexion with our ideas, but have all their signification from the arbitrary imposition of men, the doubtfulness and uncertainty of their signification, which is the imperfection we here are speaking of, has its cause more in the ideas they stand for than in any incapacity there is in one sound more than in another to signify any idea: for in that regard they are all equally perfect. That then which makes doubtfulness and uncertainty in the signification of some more than other words, is the difference of ideas they stand for.[33]

Language originates from the experience of the senses; therefore, there must be some kind of relationship between words and objects. On the other hand words stand for ideas that are inside our minds, hence the relationship is constantly transformed, attaining a more conventional status.

The ancient debate surrounding the conventionality of the sign acquired a completely new meaning in the eighteenth century,[34] affecting both language and the law. As Steven Lynn remarks:

> By acknowledging, like Locke, the gap between res and verba, Beccaria reminds us that "justice" is an arbitrary construct, which for him means "nothing more, than that bond which is necessary to keep the interest of individuals united."[35]

And with this observation, the circle is somehow closed. Codes and grammars may not exhaust, respectively, all the facets of law and language. A certain degree of arbitrariness is never questioned by Beccaria: it is the very condition for freedom and progress. However, the conventionality of the sign and of the law should be accepted only to a certain extent. Otherwise arbitrariness would sever the social contract, turning the workings of the minds into a pretext for tyranny and the negation of human rights.

---

32 Lynn, *Locke and Beccaria*, 5.

33 Locke, *An Essay Concerning Human Understanding*, 349.

34 On the one hand words are connected to ideas and ideas are the outcome of the impressions made by objects on the senses, a process which we are almost passive. On the other hand the intellect is active in elaborating simple ideas into complex ones. This process, for instance, allows the creative use of language, and is particularly evident in word-formation. If words are directly connected to sensation they are not conventional; but, if we recognize the role of the intellect in generating abstract and universal concepts, then the non conventionality of the sign is overtly questioned. See Ugo Volli, *I filosofi e il linguaggio* (Bologna: Progetto Leonardo, 1993).

35 Lynn, *Locke and Beccaria*, 4.

Jeanne Gaakeer
Dignity and Disgrace in Law and Literature

> I call on you Old Masters
> in my moments of doubt.
> Zbigniew Herbert

1 Alike in dignity?

In the text of the Preamble of the 1948 Universal Declaration of Human Rights the concept of dignity is placed prior to those of human rights and the rule of law. This has always intrigued me in view of the variety of theories of law invoked in contemporary human rights discourse, from pre-modern natural law drawing on Greek Stoicism and the iconic example of Antigone's defiance of Creon[1] and the Roman lawyer Ulpian's principle of rendering to each man his due[2] to modernity's forms of positivism with an emphasis on the social contract, reason rather than nature and rights rather than duties, and beyond. For is not such word order a sure sign of begging the question with respect to the connection between dignity and the very idea of law, both generally and specifically in the form of human rights?

What is more, the term human dignity is itself problematic in a legal context. It is more often than not used as a container concept in that it is formulated as a negative as well as a positive "right" and at the same time referred to in terms of a foundational value for (other) human rights. What, for example, are we to distil from the definition given in the Charter of Fundamental Rights of the European Union: "Human dignity is inviolable. It must be respected and protected,"[3] or

---

1 E.g., Burns H. Weston, "Human Rights" in *Human Rights in the World Community, Issues and Action*, eds. Richard Pierre Claude and Burns H. Weston (Philadelphia: University of Pennsylvania Press, 1989), 12–29, 13, who refers to the philosopher Zeno of Citium's claim that "a universal working force pervades all creation and that human conduct therefore should be judged according to, and brought into harmony with, the law of nature."

2 On the basis of Ulpian's principle Gregory Vlastos, "Justice and Equality" in *Theories of Rights*, ed. Jeremy Waldron (Oxford: Oxford University Press, 1989), 41–76, 45 uses the term natural rights and human rights interchangeably. For an extensive study of Ulpian's importance for human rights, see Tony Honoré, *Ulpian, Pioneer of Human Rights* (Oxford: Oxford University Press, 2002).

3 2000/C 364/01, Chapter 1: Dignity, Article 1: Human Dignity.

from article 1 of the German Grundgesetz (1949) "Human dignity is inviolable. To respect it and protect it is the duty of all state power"?[4]

And what are we – against the background of a truth called self-evident in the American Declaration of Independence that all people are equal – to make of the fact that the U.S. Constitution does not even contain the word dignity and hence "a jurisprudence of dignity" is a doctrine mainly developed by means of judicial decisions in the context of the Eight Amendment?[5] Or that Common article 3 of the Geneva Conventions prohibits "outrages upon *personal* dignity, in particular humiliating and degrading treatment" in the case of armed conflict? [italics mine]

Human dignity is a contested concept as far as its nature (e.g., community-based or individual; an "Is" or an "Ought" value) and contents (e.g., an aspect of civil and political rights only or also of cultural and solidarity rights)[6] are concerned now that there is no agreement on their source and substantive scope. The problem of justification comes to the fore when judicial decisions have to be made about alleged violations of human dignity and subsequently holdings about pecuniary and non-pecuniary damages to be paid by nation states held responsible for such violations.[7]

---

4 The original German text: "Die Würde des Menschen ist unantastbar. Sie zu achten und zu schützen ist Verpflichtung aller staatlichen Gewalt."

5 Leslie Meltzer Henry, "The Jurisprudence of Dignity," *University of Pennsylvania Law Review* 160 (2011):169–233, 171.

6 For an extended overview of the historical development of the concept, see Weston, "Rights," 16ff. See also Samantha Besson and Alain Zysset, "Human Rights Theory and Human Rights History: Two Odd Bedfellows," *Ancilla Iuris* special issue on international law and ethics (anci.ch) (2012): 204–219.

7 For an example of the indignity of the applicant's treatment in Russian detention see ECHR Third Section, *Kalashnikov v. Russia*, (Application no.47095/99), 15 October 2002; comparable cases are *Selmouni v. France*, (Application no.25803/94), 28 July 1999, *Idalov v. Russia*, (Application no. 5826/03), 22 May 2012 (Grand Chamber); *Enea v. Italy* (Application no. 74912/01) 17 September 2009 (Grand Chamber); *Jalloh v. Germany* (Application no.54810/00) 11 July 2006 (Grand Chamber) with a concurring opinion by judge Zupančič concluding that the issue was not just the inhuman and degrading treatment of the individual but that "[T]he whole system of law enforcement was exposed to degradation that was far more critical and perilous." See also ECHR, Case C-36/02, (First Chamber) 14 October 2004, a preliminary ruling under article 234 EC in the case of *Omega Spielhallen -und Automatenaufstellungs-GmbH v. Oberbürgermeisterin der Bundesstadt Bonn*, on whether or not a lasergame in which participants "play at killing" people by hitting sensory targets placed on players' jackets could be prohibited by local authorities, ruling that "Community law does not preclude an economic activity consisting of the commercial exploitation of games simulating acts of homicide from being made subject to a national prohibition measure adopted on grounds of protecting public policy by reason of the fact that that activity is an affront to human dignity."

Quite rightly, therefore, Jeremy Waldron has recently asked us to consider the ambiguous and/or tautologous uses of the word dignity in various treaties and warned against a mere decorative use of the language of dignity,

> On the one hand, it is stated that humans have dignity and that this dignity inhering in the human person is the source and ground of rights. And on the other hand, it is said that people have a right to dignity, or a right to have their dignity protected. In the former usage, dignity is presented as the ground of human rights; in the latter usage "dignity" is presented as the content of human rights, that is what the human rights are rights *to*.[8]

On the view that the contingency[9] of the existing connections between law and dignity may cause scepticism about the relevance of dignity in human rights discourse, Waldron elaborates[10] on the idea of dignity as a *status*-concept, though not in the sense of the rank of the human species *per se* but building on the concept of *dignitas* as associated with the language of respect, claiming that:

> Dignity is the status of a person predicated on the fact that she is recognized as having the ability to control and regulate her actions in accordance with her own apprehension of norms and reasons that apply to her; it assumes that she is capable of giving and entitled to give an account of herself (and of the way in which she is regulating her actions and organizing her life), an account that others are to pay attention to; and it means finally that she has the wherewithal to demand that her agency and her presence among us as human being be taken seriously and accommodated in the lives of others, in others' attitudes and actions towards her, and in social life generally.[11]

---

8 Jeremy Waldron, "Dignity and Rank," *Archives Européennes de Sociologie* XLVIII.2 (2007): 201–237, 203–204, emphasis in the original.

9 On the contingency of the definitions of dignity, see also Henk Botha, "Human Dignity in Comparative Perspective," *Stellenbosch Law Review* 2 (2009):171–220.

10 Waldron, "Rank," 222ff.; see also Jeremy Waldron, "Dignity, Rank, and Rights: the 2009 Tanner Lectures at UC," Berkeley Working Public Law & Legal Theory Research Paper Series, working paper no.09–50 New York University School of Law, September 2009, available at http://ssrn.com/abstract (the number of the abstract is 1461220, accessed July 1, 2012): 1–69, especially 22 and 62, for Waldron's earlier argument that we should differentiate between ordinary and stipulative uses of the term dignity, hence the importance of context, and his exploration of the meaning of dignity as the rank we hold people to have, i.e. comparable to the Roman concept of *dignitas* as the honor and privileges due to rank or office (one pervasive in Western society, cfr., the opening lines of Shakespeare's *Romeo and Juliet*, "Two households, both alike in dignity/In fair Verona, where we lay our scene"), so as to better understand the failure of the norm in actual political situations such as slavery and racism in U.S. history. For an overview of the meaning of dignity thought the ages, see also Christopher McCrudden, "Human Dignity and Judicial Interpretation of Human Rights," *The European Journal of International Law* 19.4 (2008): 655–724.

11 Jeremy Waldron, "How Law Protects Dignity," *New York University Public Law and Legal Theory Working Papers* (2012): Paper 317, available at http://lsr.nellco.org/nyu_plltwp/317 (July 1,

Recognition is indeed the crucial aspect in human rights discourse with which the concept of dignity is inextricably intertwined, for what matters most is how the other, individual or nation state, treats you. Waldron's definition of dignity has the advantage that it encompasses the legal idea of standing. As such it is a step further than dignity as a value idea in the sense attributed to it by Immanuel Kant in his 1785 *Groundwork of the Metaphysics of Morals*, and the rights-as-claims discourse of Hart, Dworkin and Feinberg; or so Waldron suggests.[12]

Another proposal to get us out of the definitional morass, more or less I would claim in the same way that the illustrious Baron von Münchhausen pulled his horse and himself up by his own periwig's tail, is proferred by Leslie Meltzer Henry. On the view that jurists are more often than not semantic essentialists, she turns to Wittgenstein's approach of meaning being found in the use of a word, so that "To conceptualize dignity, we therefore must observe how the word is employed in our discourse," on the view that "[A] context-driven view of dignity develops with societal change; it does not hold society to static meanings. More-over, it recognizes that understanding is, to use Hans-Georg Gadamer's words, 'a historically effected event'."[13]

What matters to me here is not just that human rights scholarship abounds in references to philosophical sources, i.e., to the *litterae humaniores*, but, more importantly, that from the start of the development of human rights as we now know them, literary authors such as Mary Wollstonecraft, Percy Bysshe Shelley and William Wordsworth immediately joined the debate and contributed their views on human rights and human dignity.[14] If we combine the argument so far

---

2012): 1–25, 2–3. For a related discussion of dignity from a bioethical perspective, see Patrick Lee and Robert P. George, "The Nature and Basis of Human Dignity," *Ratio Juris* 21 (2008):173–193, 174, who start from the premise that "Human beings are rational creatures by virtue of possessing natural capacities for conceptual thought, deliberation, and free choice, that is, the natural capacity to shape their own lives."

12 The importance of Kant for Waldron's thought, however, cannot be underestimated. Kant's idea that only humans so far as they are capable of morality can have dignity also pervades Michael Rosen, *Dignity, Its History and Meaning* (Cambridge (Mass.) and London: Harvard University Press, 2012).

13 Meltzer Henry, "Jurisprudence," 187–189. On a comparable view McCrudden, "Interpretation," 679, asks us to try and discover Wittgensteinian family resemblances in the different ways of looking upon the contents of dignity. He points to the ontological claim made that being human means possessing an intrinsic worth, to the relational claim of the recognition of such worth by others, and the political claim that the recognition of the intrinsic worth of the individual means that the state exists for the sake of the individual, not the other way around.

14 See Mary Wollstonecraft, *A Vindication of the Rights of Men* and *A Vindication of the Rights of Woman* in *The Works of Mary Wollstonecraft* vol. 5, eds. Janet Todd and Marilyn Butler (London: William Pickering, 1989). Percy Bysshe Shelly's *Declaration of Rights* [1812], available at http://

with Kevin Crotty's observation that the troubling paradox of legal theory is that the legitimacy of law rests in part on fictive idealizations[15] and that literature can help out legal theory by showing how the fictive works and with Jeremy Waldon's cautious remark about unearthing semantic deference in our usage of the word dignity,[16] the case for a literary-legal investigation of dignity speaks for itself.[17] Literary examples (personal and fictional) of – hopefully past – violations of dignity abound, from Federico García Lorca on Franco's Falangist Spain, Ántonio Lobo Antunes on Salazar's Portugal to Kiran Desai's inheritance of loss in India and Vladimir Bukovsky's life as a dissenter in the former USSR, to name but a few. Inspired by Waldron's claim that because "[T]he discipline of dignity is a normative discipline and [...] it presents itself on the one hand as an aspiration, and on the other hand as a reproach to our shortcomings" each legal system "has to cope with the burden of its own history,"[18] in what follows I will use Joseph Slaughter's ideas on the *Bildungsroman* as a background for a discussion of John M. Coetzee's novel *Disgrace*, hoping to show that and how an education in the humanities is indispensable to human rights discourse.

---

www.rc.umd.edu/editions/shelley/devil/declright.html (July 3, 2012), significantly ends with a sobering reference to the frailty of human dignity, urging the individual to capitalize the rights Shelley distinguishes, for "They are declared to thee by one who knows thy *dignity*, for every hour does his heart swell with honourable pride in the contemplation of what thou mayest attain, by one who is not forgetful of thy degeneracy, for every moment brings home to him the bitter conviction of what thou art. Awake! – Arise! – or be for ever fallen" [italics mine]. William Wordsworth's 1805 poem "The Prelude" emphasizes the dignity of the individual person.

15 Kevin M. Crotty, *Law's Interior, Legal and Literary Constructions of the Self* (Ithaca and London: Cornell University Press, 2001), 166.

16 Waldron, "Rank," 234, n. 58, semantic deference being the circumstance "that most people's use of a term presupposes implicit reference to the expertise of a few who know more about the condition of its proper application than they do."

17 As a topic in *Law and Literature*, attention to human rights dates back to at least the 1983 *Human Rights Quarterly* (vol. 5) special issue. For the bioethical perspective on dignity via literary works see Richard F. Storrow, "Therapeutic Reproduction and Human Dignity,"*Law & Literature* 21.2 (2009): 257–274, and Jeanne Gaakeer, "Ishiguro's Legal Chimera: *Never Let Me Go* and the Legal Fiction of Personhood," *Pólemos* 2 (2007): 119–132. See also *Being Human: Readings from the President's Council on Bioethics* (Washington D.C.: 2003), available at http://www.bioethics.gov/bookshelf/reader (July 1, 2012), chapter 10 for literary sources of human dignity discussions and *World Literature for Equal Dignity*, available at http://www.humiliationstudies.org/literaturelist.php (July 2, 2012).

18 Waldron, "Law," 23.

2 Being and becoming

On the view that "The nature of our understanding of human subjectivity is central to any thorough discussion of human rights," Slaughter suggests that one of the problems in human rights discourse is that conflicting views on subjectivity, i.e., juridical subjectivity as an artificial construct versus identity as something an individual can choose to assume, are not sufficiently brought to the surface; to him, then, in order to provide a remedy, human rights "can be productively formulated in terms of narrative genres and narrative voices."[19] Resonating behind the conflict as Slaughter defines it, is, of course, the age-old dichotomy of law being made or being found. And given that the schism in legal theory between natural law thought and positivism is a product of the Enlightenment, it comes as no surprise that Slaughter proposes the perspective of the literary genre of the *Bildungsroman* as a lens through which to view human rights abuse "as an infringement on the modern subject's ability to narrate her story," and as an instrument with which to evaluate the various degrees of abuse "on a continuum of narratability, with oppressive voicelessness on one end and bellicose vociferousness on the other."[20] In short, the idea of narrative self-determination or, more generally, an independence of voice is crucial and that, too, can be looked upon in terms of modernity's emphasis on the individual.

What matters to me here is that Slaughter's premise and its impressive elaboration in *Human Rights Inc.*[21] can be fruitfully connected to the requirements of dignity in law, both in the sense of the integrity of the legal process and the dignity of the act of judging, and more generally to issues of legal standing, and, at another level, to other scholarly work in the broader field of law and the humanities on voice and narrative since James Boyd White first emphasized the importance in law of telling one's story and being heard.[22] What is more, the very idea of *Bildung* as expressed in the genre of the *Bildungsroman* obviously ties in with ongoing debates in literary-legal studies, e.g., on the value of an humanistic

---

19 Joseph R. Slaughter, "A Question of Narration: the Voice of International Human Rights Law," *Human Rights Quarterly* 19 (1997): 406–430, 407 footnote omitted. For an early application of literary categories to the narratives of legal theories, using Northrop Frye's critical framework as developed in *Anatomy of Criticism*, see Robin West, "Jurisprudence as Narrative: An Aesthetic Analysis of Modern Legal Theory," *New York University Law Review* 60 (1985): 145–211, repr. in Robin West, *Narrative, Authority & Law* (Ann Arbor: University of Michigan Press, 1993), 345–418.
20 Slaughter, "Question," 413.
21 Joseph R. Slaughter, *Human Rights Inc. The World Novel, Narrative Form, and International Law* (New York: Fordham University Press, 2007).
22 E.g., James Boyd White, *Heracles' Bow, Essays on the Rhetoric and Poetics of the Law* (Madison: University of Wisconsin Press, 1985).

education,[23] the function and (ab)use of the Western canon, and related topics of in- and exclusionary strategies in law and literature, as well as the new dichotomy of high culture versus popular culture. Not incidentally the epigraph to Slaughter's discussion of the topic of "Human rights literacy: Scenes of Narrative Recognition and Self-Determination" is Hans-Georg Gadamer's phenomenological premise that "Education (*Erziehung*) is to educate oneself; cultivation, or formation, (*Bildung*) is self-cultivation [...] Cultivation (*Bildung*) cultivates itself [...] All that is involved here is what has already formed itself in a hidden way."[24]

Reasons of space prevent my doing full justice to Slaughter's treatment of his subject. Suffice it to say that starting from the definition of the *Bildungsroman* as "the coming-of-age genre [...] whose plot we could provisionally gloss as the didactic story of an individual who is socialized in the process of learning for oneself what everyone else (including the reader) presumably already knows," Slaughter develops the claim that what goes for the protagonist of the *Bildungsroman* also goes for the development of the individual human rights personality, namely "to recognize what one already is by right," and with respect to the latter, doing so by taking responsibility for the plot of the development of human rights in a local or national context as well as by sticking to narrative rather than violence as a means of self-determination.[25] He gives specific attention to various concepts of dignity, including dignity as an aristocratic quality (with Goethe's *Wilhelm Meister* as the exemplary "novelistic reformation that rearticulates aristocratic privileges and dignity as bourgeois rights"[26]) and dignity as both basis and goal of human rights. Slaughter, too, recognizes the risks of tautology involved in the natural-law focus on inalienability of human rights. Rather than rejecting the self-referentiality of such thought, he wants to make it productive, "because tautology delimits the margins of a culturally situated logos, signaling the site where culture-bound knowledge confronts its own limits."[27] So while for some "'person,' by definition, is the proper name of creatures with dignity," "'person' also signifies whatever culture makes it signify."[28] Obviously, when it comes to solving human rights issues at the level of politics, cultural-situatedness is important in any context. More specifically, it can be thought of in terms of a conceptual wrench in those situations where a political reversal such as the

---

23 For an important, recent contribution see Marett Leiboff, "Ghosts of Law and Humanities (Past, Present, Future)," *The Australian Feminist Law Journal* 36 (2012): 3–17.
24 Slaughter, *Human Rights*, 245.
25 Slaughter, *Human Rights*, 3 and 249–250.
26 Slaughter, *Human Rights*, 105.
27 Slaughter, *Human Rights*, 78.
28 Slaughter, *Human Rights*, 332 n. 45 and 18.

overthrow of a repressive regime and the (re)introduction of human rights necessitate the introduction of a new language with which to speak of both past and future.

With this in mind as an overture for an investigation of narrative conferral and narrative acknowledgement of dignity, I read Coetzee's novel *Disgrace*, set in post-apartheid South Africa, as a human rights *Bildungsroman* in a double sense, i.e. as the narrative of the protagonist David Lurie's self-destruction and subsequent self-recreation on the one hand, and on the other as the narrative of violence and the possibility of redemption and reconciliation that the novel holds before us in its depiction of Lurie's daughter Lucy's plight.

Central to the novel are parallel narratives of violations of human dignity, a literary microcosm so to speak of human rights issues. The tone is set at the very start when David Lurie, a former professor of modern languages in Capetown recently demoted to adjunct professor of communications, is ironically described as a professional failure who lacks personal dignity with as a result that "Because he has no respect for the material he teaches, he makes no impression on his students," while at the same time the possibility of personal *Bildung* is introduced as well, for Lurie continues to teach "because it teaches him humility."[29] His weekly visits to Soraya of Discreet Escorts, a woman classified as "Exotic," reveal both his instrumental, demeaning, egocentric view on women and his desire to engage in a personal relationship. When he calls her at home, he sees himself as a predator intruding who knows what reaction to expect, for Soraya breaks off their business relation. Yet he immediately forgets his consideration to "retire from the game" (*DG*, 9) when he chances upon Melanie Isaacs, a student of his, thirty years his junior. She is coloured, with "wide, almost Chinese cheekbones, large, dark eyes" (*DG*, 11). He invites her for supper and asks her to stay and spend the night with him which she refuses. Lurie knows "that is where he ought to end it. But he does not" (*DG*, 18). He takes her out for lunch and back at his house he makes love to her on the living-room floor, realizing she is no more than a child but unable to check his own desire. A week later he goes to her flat. Unlike Soraya "she is too surprised to resist the intruder" (*DG*, 24) so "All she does is avert herself [...] Not rape, not quite that, but undesired nevertheless, undesired to the core" (*DG*, 25). Lurie realises his mistake. Yet, when she later asks whether she can stay at his place for a while, he agrees. The whole thing explodes in his face when she lodges a complaint against him and it turns out that he also drew up a fraudulent record, because Melanie skipped classes and yet her record is "unblemished" (*DG*, 41).

---

29 John M. Coetzee, *Disgrace* (London: Vintage/Random House, 2000), 4–5: further references in the text, abbreviated as *DG*.

Symbol and symptom of domination Lurie sorely lacks *dignitas*. He does not fulfil the duties proper to his rank as a university teacher, and when having to face the committee examining the complaint, he does not exhibit the proper language of respect, i.e., the deference required in the situation.[30] While Lurie pleads guilty to both charges – it is important to note that only the attendance fraud is explicitly mentioned, the sexual harassment is not voiced – he refuses to say he is sorry about what happened,

> What goes on in my mind is my business, not yours [...] Frankly, what you want from me is not a response but a confession. Well, I make no confession. I put forward a plea, as is my right. Guilty as charged. That is my plea. That is as far as I am prepared to go. [...] Suffice it to say that Eros entered. After that I was not the same. [...] I became a servant of Eros. [...] This is not a defence. You want a confession, I give you a confession. As for the impulse, it was far from ungovernable. (*DG*, 51–52)

The committee immediately understands what he is after, "Don't play games with us, David. There is a difference between pleading guilty to a charge and admitting you were wrong, and you know that" (*DG*, 54). Lurie, however, refuses to sign the statement reading

> I acknowledge without reservation serious abuses of the *human rights* of the complainant, as well as abuse of the authority delegated to me by the University. I sincerely apologize to both parties and accept whatever appropriate penalty may be imposed (*DG*, 57 [emphasis mine]),

for the very reason that it contains an apology. His guilty plea should suffice, for "Repentance is neither here nor there. Repentance belongs to another world, to another universe of discourse"(*DG*, 58). In the same way that the concept of human rights is depicted here as existing horizontally between private individuals rather than between the state and the individual – the violation of Melanie's physical integrity is not treated in terms of crime whereas most jurisdictions have specific provisions for the teacher-student relationship – Lurie gives priority to the private rather than the public sphere. He asks what the point is when his apology is not sincere. The answer? "The criterion is not whether you are sincere. That is a matter, as I say, for your own conscience. The criterion is whether you are prepared to acknowledge your fault in a public manner and take steps to remedy it"(*DG*, 58). And so "The whole thing is disgraceful from beginning to end. Disgraceful and vulgar too" (*DG*, 45).

---

30 On the association of dignity with respect see also Waldron, "Rank," esp. 222 n.35 and 223.

This scene is of great importance not only for what follows in the narrative as far as Lucy's rape is concerned, but also for broader issues of law when it comes to dealing with truth and reconciliation that the eponymous South-African committee had to confront. I am thinking here of the place of the victim in legal procedure. There is, of course, the problem that criminal law starts from the premise of individual responsibility whereas systemic violations of human rights of the kind perpetrated by oppressive, totalitarian regimes are much harder to redress when the perpetrators are either no longer alive or pleading that they merely obeyed higher authorities, if we recall the Nuremberg trials. When viewed from the perspective of the victim, it is exactly because of the dominant asymmetrical vertical relation between state and individual in human rights that resembles the one in criminal law between the state and the defendant that finding a language with which to give voice to the victim is so hard. Or, as Benjamin Berger put it succinctly, "The point here is that the gravamen of victimhood lies in the senselessness of suffering, not in the fate or blame of the perpetrator. Criminal law can speak to the latter, but has nothing to say about the former" and as a result "though embedded in the pursuit and affirmation of justice, the gesture of recognizing the victim is always also a gesture towards recognizing its [i.e. criminal law's] own inability to speak to the gravamen of crime, the experience of senseless suffering. In seeking to restore order and reason, the criminal law inescapably exposes the chaos and injustice of experience."[31] That, in turn, affects the human capacity to forgive, for if modernity's individualism thinks in terms of reciprocity only, i.e., like the Roman *do ut des* or "I respect you only in so far as you respect me" rather than in terms of human beings' mutual dependence, "forgive so that you too will be forgiven." This affects not only our private lives, as Lurie painfully realizes at the end of the novel because he is unable to forgive himself, but, more importantly, it affects our public lives when human rights are at stake.[32]

After having been asked to resign Lurie leaves for a visit to his daughter Lucy who lives on a smallholding in the Eastern Cape in Salem, a name that does not augur well for what follows, reminiscent as it is of seventeenth-century juridical errors.[33] Lucy has boarding kennels for dogs and on Saturdays she sells her garden produce at the market together with the black man Petrus, her assistant

---

31 Benjamin L. Berger, "On the Book of Job, Justice, and the Precariousness of the Criminal Law," *Law, Culture and the Humanities* 4 (2008): 98–118, 108–109.

32 I am inspired here by the point made by Hannah Arendt that lack of forgiveness is "a clear symptom of the increasing depersonalization of public and social life," Hannah Arendt, *The Human Condition* [1958] (Chicago: University of Chicago Press, 1998), 236–243, 243.

33 Compare Henry Miller's *The Crucible* and the judicial errors and violations of the defendants' human rights in the Outreau case (with charges of incest and paedophilia) in France a couple of

and co-proprietor who takes care of the dogs, the narrative of whose fates runs parallel with the events on the farm. Lurie meets Lucy's acquaintance Bev Shaw who runs a dog shelter where she has to put down the animals that no one wants because nobody else likes to do the job. Bev is convinced of the equality of all creatures, i.e., that "This is the only life there is. Which we share with the animals," to which Lurie responds "We are of a different order of creation of the animals. Not higher, necessarily, but different" (*DG*, 74). When asked whether she minds euthanizing the dogs, she responds "I do mind. I mind deeply. I wouldn't want someone doing it for me who didn't mind. Would you?" (*DG*, 85)

It is to Bev that Lurie confesses that he is staying with Lucy because he is "[N] ot just in trouble. In what I suppose one would call disgrace" (*DG*, 85), a confession that is the first sign of his recreation of the self, his *Bildung* that develops more fully after the horrible experience he and Lucy have when two black men and a boy come to the farm, hit Lurie on the head, and lock him in the lavatory after which they rape Lucy, shoot all the dogs and leave them to die, and steal what little Lucy owns of material value. This violent reversal of fates, or of ranks if we recall Lurie's treatment of Melanie, does not lead to legal action however. Lucy's earlier remark to Lurie about Melanie, i.e., "you have paid your price. Perhaps, looking back, she won't think too harshly on you. Women can be surprisingly forgiving" (*DG*, 69) proves to have been prospective. Not only does Lucy refuse at first to tell Lurie what happened, mirroring Lurie's view on the distinction between the public and the private,[34] and not only is the story of her being raped not voiced in the newspapers comparable to Melanie's harassment being reduced to an incident, but she also decides to keep the baby rather than have an abortion.

Initially, Lurie is extremely upset, "Lucy's secret; his disgrace" (i.e., of having been unable to protect her, Dg 109). But when he recognizes Lucy's emotion of shame and disgrace when she hides instead of resuming her Saturday routine of going to the market, he enters a new level of *Bildung*. He begins to help Bev Shaw with euthanizing the superfluous dogs and feels as if "[H]is whole being is gripped by what happens in the theatre. He is convinced the dogs know their time has come. [...] They flatten their ears, they droop their tails, as if they too feel the disgrace of dying" (*DG*, 143). What is more, he also takes up the task of bringing

---

years ago, discussed by Antoine Garapon and Denis Salas under the revealing title *Les nouvelles sorcières de Salem, leçons d'Outreau* (Paris: Seuil, 2006).

34 "You want to know why I have not laid a particular charge with the police. I will tell you, as long as you agree not to raise the subject again. The reason is that, as far as I am concerned, what happened to me is a purely private matter. In another time, in another place, it might be held to be a public matter. But in this place, at this time, it is not. It is my business, mine alone."(*DG*, 112)

the bodies to the incinerator because he is offended by the way in which the incinerator crew beat the bags with the backs of their shovels,

> "For the sake of the dogs? But the dogs are dead; and what do dogs know of honour and dishonour anyway?" [...] He saves the honour of the corpses because there is no one else stupid enough to do it. (*DG*, 146)

When Lucy speaks for the first time about her ordeal, the crux of her narrative is that "[I]t was so personal [...] It was done with such personal hatred. That was what stunned me more than anything. The rest was [...] expected. But why did they hate me so? I had never set eyes on them" (*DG*, 156). This is, of course, the heart of the general issue of retribution for human rights violations and of that of reconciliation: who eventually has to pay the prize for what the state does to some of its citizens? Obviously there is no such simple thing as institutionalized solace, neither for victims nor for perpetrators. Lucy's solution is to accept publicly by marriage to the perpetrator what is done to her privately, rather than taking her case to a court of law.[35] Even though her existence is initially disintegrated by the events, her further development is not at risk, contrary to what one would expect in view of the Aristotelian idea as expressed in the *Nicomachean Ethics* (Books III-IV) that adverse personal circumstances may seriously hamper our ability to maintain a dignified, virtuous bearing. Lucy realizes that "if I leave the farm now I will leave defeated, and will taste that defeat for the rest of my life"(*DG*, 161). So she opts for agency and presence instead, more or less of the kind Jeremy Waldron puts forward in his definition of dignity as noted above in paragraph 1. She does not stand on her seemingly *prima facie* rights as a victim. On the contrary, she is going to marry the father of the baby, or rather, because he is too young, become Petrus' third wife. This is a moral rather than juridical act that at least resembles if not forgiveness, then at least acceptance of the new situation. Lucy will start again from scratch, "With nothing. No cards, no weapons, no property, no rights, no dignity [...] Like a dog" (*DG*, 205). Not like Joseph K. at the end of Kafka's *The Trial* but rather with hope for the future after she has been able overcome the initial humiliation of what happened to her.

This is the start of redemption and reconciliation for Lurie as well. He acknowledges the rape word and is able to make a double confession to his daughter and to the Isaacs family, i.e., that he did not save Lucy and that he did

---

35 See Robert Meister, "Forgiving and Forgetting: Lincoln and the Politics of National Recovery" in *Human Rights in Political Transitions: Gettysburg to Bosnia*, eds. Carla Hesse and Robert Post (New Yook: Zone Books, 1999), 135–176, 159, that the fundamental question that remains is still, "Is the sharing of guilt for the crimes that one did not commit more important to the moral foundation of national recovery than accountability for the crimes that actually occurred?"

Melanie wrong, explaining that he is "sunk in a state of disgrace from which it will not be easy to lift [himself]" (*DG*, 172). The apogee of *his Bildung*, as I see it, is in the penultimate chapter of the novel where Lurie thinks "Du muss dein Leben ändern!: you must change your life" (*DG*, 209). The German line is taken from Rainer Maria Rilke's poem "Archaïscher Torso Apollos," the poem that opens his 1908 cycle *Neue Gedichte. Anderer Teil*, dedicated to the French sculptor Rodin. In it Rilke describes how an ancient Greek statue of Apollo that he saw in the Louvre spoke to him and admonished him to change.[36] The effect of the change in Lurie, i.e., that like Lucy he is able to overcome the fear of crisis situations, acknowledge his agency and understand that his worldview needs reconsideration, is best seen in his changed attitude toward the dogs. That is to say, from indifference to their lives and fates to an attitude of care, that finally moves beyond his earlier egocentrism. For when he returns to the shelter to assist Bev Shaw he gives up on the young, crippled dog named Driepoot that he has grown attached to, rather than save him for another week, thus acknowledging the dog's right as a fellow creature with an equal right to dignified treatment and dignified death. Lurie, in short, has become what Bruno Latour, in his discussion of the "redistribution" of humanism in the context of modern science, called a true "Lévinas of animals," that is to say a human being, one who acknowledges the Other creature and their common equality, if not before the law, then at least in a moral sense.[37]

3 Lost narratives, lost voices

In much the same sense as the statue of Apollo spoke to Rilke, the literary work speaks to us, can speak to us or, even more tentatively and as an implicit assignment to those of us who aim to show the value of literary-legal studies, should be shown to speak to us. That, at least, is my premise and I would argue that the concept of *Bildung* associated with humanism broadly conceived still has an important function, and thus a chance to survive even postmodernism.

The novel *Disgrace* does not prioritize the natural-law logic of inherent human rights that prevails in human rights discourse, aimed as it is at validating rights and obligations. Neither does it take the comparable universalistic, normative approach that all human beings have the right to have their dignity respected

---

36 The German philosopher Peter Sloterdijk took this line as a title for his book on the need for change in contemporary societies, *Du muss dein Leben ändern* (Frankfurt am Main: Suhrkamp, 2009), in English translation *You Must Change Your Life* (Cambridge, Polity Books, 2012).
37 Bruno Latour, *We Have Never Been Modern* (Hempel Hempstead UK: Harvester Wheatsheaf, 1993), 136.

under all circumstances. Rather, the focus of its fictional reality is "case-oriented," one that Richard Rorty also advocates with respect to our stories about moral dilemmas and human rights.[38] In its focus on the contingency of the human condition, so to speak, it does not aim at providing rules for behaviour. Rather, it aims at offering alternative versions of looking at human experience.[39] This is not to read *Disgrace* in terms of a representation of an actual situation, a kind of correspondence theory of literature, but metaphorically, that is to say in the Aristotelian tradition that the literary work shows what it has to say to us by pointing to what may happen, to what may be the case. This suggested meaning must of course be worth our while as Owen Barfield argued and the author must actually have something to say.[40] This Coetzee certainly has, as can also be seen from his other works such as *The Lives of Animals* and *Elizabeth Costello*.

To me, Coetzee unfolds *in* the competing perspectives of the narrative of *Disgrace* what he wants to demonstrate *with* the novel. Therein lies the epistemological significance of the literary narrative. It is what Habermas called a counterfactual interpretation,

> A literary text is marked by the fact that it does not come forth with the claim that it documents an occurrence in the world; nonetheless, it does want to draw the reader into the spell of an imagined occurrence step by step, until he follows the narrated events *as if* they *were* real. Even the fabricated reality must be capable of being experienced by the reader as a reality that is real – otherwise a novel does not accomplish what it is supposed to do.[41]

---

38 Richard Rorty, "Human Rights, Rationality, and Sentimentality" in *On Human Rights, the Oxford Amnesty Lectures 1993*, eds. Stephen Shute and Susan Hurley (New York: Basic Books, 1993), 111–134, 133–134, "A better sort of answer is the sort of long, sad, sentimental story which begins 'Because this is what it is like to be in her situation – to be far from home, among strangers,' or 'Because she might become your daughter-in-law,' or 'Because her mother would grieve for her.' Such stories, repeated and varied over the centuries, have induced us, the rich, safe, powerful, people, to tolerate, and even to cherish, powerless people – people whose appearance or habits of beliefs at first seemed an insult to our own moral identity, our sense of the limits of permissible human variation."

39 See Jerome S. Bruner, "The Reality of Fiction," Keynote at the 27–28 May 2009 conference of the Italian Society for Law and Literature, 1–9, 5, "we become better able to understand the real world of experience by seeing it in the light of fictional worlds of possibility." Available at www.lawandliterature.org (June 1, 2011).

40 Owen Barfield, "Poetic Diction and Legal Fiction" in Owen Barfield, *The Rediscovery of Meaning and Other Essays* (Middleton (Ct): Wesleyan University Press, 1977), 44–64, 48.

41 Jürgen Habermas, "Philosophy and Science as Literature?" in Jürgen Habermas, *Postmetaphysical Thinking: Philosophical Essays*, trans. William Mark Hohengarten (Cambridge, Mass.: MIT Press, 1992), 205–227, 211.

Looked upon in this way, the interpretation of *Disgrace* is written in the text as much as it allows the reader the opportunity to ascribe meaning. Its importance for law is that it can also help (re-) open a debate on the uses and abuses of legal concepts and categories, one that always looms large behind human rights discourse. We can ask whether we found human rights discourse on the premise that law's "classificatory schemes provide a science of the concrete," or whether we will allow "narrative schemes [to] provide a science of the imagination."[42] Habermas argued that when we understand that any form of theory is firmly rooted in our social and cultural environments so that our understanding of theory is necessarily contextual, we will see that there is truth in narrative.[43] As a consequence, we have to accept that there is no immediate, i.e., unmediated access to truth and reality. Such access only comes into being by the mediation that is the result of the dialectics of the private and the public, of the subject and the object.

It also ties in with Waldron's definition of dignity noted above and Slaughter's point about culture-bound knowledge. In showing the characters' initial inability to come to terms with what happened to them, i.e. their inability to tell their own stories, the narrative of *Disgrace* is emblematic of what Slaughter proposes as a way to formulate human rights differently, "one that focuses on the voice of the juridical subject and the possibility of narration. That is, stressing the voice of the subject, positing the voice as an emblem of subjectivity, allows for a conception of human rights that does not rely upon some essential, inherent human quality."[44] And so "conceptions of human rights that guarantee the subject's ability to narrate herself" are open to change because "conceptions of the speaking self" are culturally determined, as Lucy's initial reluctance to speak to her father about what violations she has had to endure clearly shows. On this view, Slaughter emphasizes the need for commitment to voice, "as a tool to guarantee recourse to individual narration."[45]

---

42 Edward M. Bruner, "Ethnography as Narrative" in *The Anthropology of Experience*, eds. Victor W. Turner and Edward M. Bruner (Urbana: University of Illinois Press, 1986), 139–155, 140.
43 Habermas, "Philosophy," 225.
44 Slaughter, "Question," 412.
45 Slaughter, "Question," 429, and also "While postmodern theory posits the unknowability of the self, because subjectivity is the nexus of complex relationships, the testimony offered by victims of human rights abuses tends to suggest that, even if the subject is ultimately unknowable, the individual, through self-narration, experiences herself as a distinct spatio-historical being." See Slaughter, *Human Rights*, 142 on the Truth and Reconciliation Commission's "ability to identify by name both victims and perpetrators of violence [...] its capacity to trade amnesty for truth [...] and its emphasis on the 'healing potential of telling stories' for the survivors of human rights abuse" (endnote omitted). See also Jean-François Lyotard, "The Other's Rights" in *On*

On this view too, I would further suggest, we will therefore do well as readers to develop a literary sensibility to recognize situations in which voices and narratives are lost. And that is also to say that especially as jurists we must be aware of the need for professional and private self-reflection. For all too often we misjudge discursive situations, both literary and actual, for instance when our own preconceived interpretative framework becomes dominant and we forget about our own prejudices. What is more, individual narration of the kind Slaughter distinguishes may be seriously hampered when a person is simply unable to make any sense of, and hence no story about, what happened to her in terms of her own (social) experiences. Such hermeneutical injustice[46] results in marginalization of those who cannot find the words to express themselves on account of there being a lack of collective understanding of a specific experience in their specific (cultural) context. That, in turn, may lead to situations of "testimonial injustice"[47] when as readers or hearers we do not recognize such situations and either disbelieve entirely what such a person writes or says, or give her too much credit. In *Disgrace*, David Lurie may be looked upon as one lacking in testimonial sensibility and one who falls short of decency in his treatment of Soraya and Melanie. In the same sense that individual voices are lost because they remain unexpressed, whole (topics for) narratives may be lost when for whatever reason it is either (totally) impossible or no longer possible to discuss what is deemed important to some people, for example when a change in a professional culture makes it "not done" to put certain topics up for discussion.[48]

When these circumstances occur simultaneously they mutually reinforce the risk of adding to linguistic imperialism of the kind that James Boyd White warns against in *Living Speech*.[49] Sure signs of such development are the occurrence of tautology and/or changes of meaning while signifiers remain the same. An example of the former can be found in the South African "Immorality Act" (1957, amended 1969), where it says that "'coloured person' means any person other

---

Human Rights, the Oxford Amnesty Lectures 1993, eds. Stephen Shute and Susan Hurley (New York: Basic Books, 1993), 135–147, on the Other that I recognize in myself and the ordeal of being silenced.

46 The term "hermeneutical injustice" is coined by Miranda Fricker, *Epistemic Injustice, Power and the Ethics of Knowing* (Oxford: Oxford University Press, 2007), 7, and also 154–155 and 162 for an elaboration.

47 Fricker, *Injustice*, 117.

48 On "lost narratives" see Jean-François Lyotard, *The Postmodern Condition: A Report on Knowledge*, trans. Geoff Bennington and Brian Massini (Minneapolis: University of Minnesota Press, 1991), 31.

49 James Boyd White, *Living Speech, resisting the empire of force* (Princeton and Oxford: Princeton University Press, 2006).

than a white person; 'white person' means any person who in appearance obviously is or who by general acceptance and repute is a white person."[50] The tautology is patent. Further examples abound. The term "enemy-combatant" is but one recent form of linguistic subversion of reality that is a sign of totalitarian tendencies. In his personal account of the language of Nazi Germany Victor Klemperer shows how this ideology could maintain its position because a special service guarded every linguistic detail and decided what could and could not be "said." In this language web of the Minister of Propaganda the first Nazi words were "Strafexpedition" "as a kind of punitive expedition against all kinds of despised peoples" and "Staatsakt," the term for a state occasion, i.e., a party rally organised by Goebbels to legitimize any state action aimed at eliminating those who were deemed unwanted.[51] After Dresden was bombed in February 1945, Klemperer on his flight through Germany found that the Nazi language had spread in all regions of Germany, in all layers of society. Trying to further his knowledge of this *Lingua Tertii Imperii* Klemperer explains, "I read whatever I could catch sight of, and everywhere I saw traces of this language. It was truly totalitarian."[52] Obviously it is of immense importance to develop an appreciation of the power of language, because "Whatever it is that people are determined to hide, be it only from others, or from themselves, even things they carry around unconsciously – language reveals all."[53]

A literary rendering of the same linguistic perversion is given by Jonathan Littell in *The Kindly Ones* in which we can truly detect the truth in the metaphoric of the narrative. When the main character Max Aue is appointed to the personal staff of the Reichsführer, he is told by the Obersturmbannführer, "For your reports, the Reichsführer has issued *Sprachregelungen*, language regulations. Any report that doesn't conform to them will be returned to you."[54] Behind that is the logic of the *Führerprinzip*,

> It's up to the recipient to recognize the intentions of the one who gives the command, and to act accordingly. The ones who insist on having clear orders or who want legislative measures haven't understood that it's the will of the leader, and not his orders, that counts,

---

50 As cited by Slaughter, *Human Rights*, 256.
51 Victor Klemperer, *The Language of the Third Reich, LTI – Lingua Tertii Imperii, a philologist's notebook* [1957], trans. Martin Brady (London and New Brunswick (NJ): The Athlone Press, 2000), 43.
52 Klemperer, *Language*, 260–261.
53 Klemperer, *Language*, 11. Cfr. Jorge Semprun, *Literature or Life*, trans. Linda Coverdale (New York: Viking, 1997) on comparable language experiences during his captivity in camp Buchenwald.
54 Jonathan Littell, *The Kindly Ones*, trans. Charlotte Mandell (London: Vintage, 2010), 546.

and that it's up to the receiver of the orders to know how to decipher and even anticipate that will.[55]

And so in the course of time words lose their meaning.[56] *"Endlösung"*(final solution), *"völlige Lösung* (complete solution)" and *"allgemeine Lösung* (general solution),"

> according to the period, [...] meant exclusion from public life or exclusion from economic life or, finally, emigration. Then, little by little, the signification had slid toward the abyss, but without the signifier changing, and it seemed almost as if this final meaning had always lived in the heart of the word [...] and then we had passed the event horizon, beyond which there is no return.[57]

In other words, the denial of the other's humanity is the first step on the road to humiliation and destruction. Exit dignity, exit civil, political, and human rights.

4 A literary turn of mind

In a way comparable to Lurie's realization that he has to change his life, these examples, in showing us that linguistic corruption is intertwined with acts of degradation and violations of human rights, admonish us as jurists, if we read well, to pay careful attention to this aspect of our tool of trade, language.

On a different level the same also goes for legal procedure. Not only in the sense that being allowed to tell one's story and being heard is a way to be recognized as a human being but also in the way such procedure confers, if only for the moment in court, dignity on the speaker in that it honors her autonomy as a legal subject. That is to say that in order to demand one's rights, both a forum to do so and an individual voice are required. The latter requirement is made poignantly clear in Yael Farber's play *Molora*, based on Aeschylus' *Oresteia* and to be understood against the background of the Truth and Reconciliation Commission convened in Cape Town 1995.[58] In it one of the characters is tortured by

---

55 Littell, *Kindly Ones*, 548.
56 See James Boyd White, *When Words Lose Their Meaning* (Chicago: University of Chicago Press, 1984).
57 Littell, *Kindly Ones*, 630–631.
58 Yael Farber, *Molora, based on the Oresteia by Aeschylus* (London: Oberon Books, 2008). The central argument of the play takes place between Klytemnestra and Elektra, and is heard by the Chorus, Xhosa tribeswomen who function as witnesses, having come to hear the testimonies as Farber explains in the *mise en scène*. Of related interest is Astrid van Weyenberg, *The Politics of*

means of the infamous wet-bag method that not only deprives that person of breath but more importantly makes it impossible for that person to testify to his experience so that he "is denied not just the right to speak but the right to be heard."[59] With respect to the forum on which to realize the right to be heard there is also the risk of our ignoring or simply not recognizing in the courtroom those people who are hermeneutically marginalized persons, that is to say those who suffer a "situated hermeneutical inequality" because they simply have not been assigned a place in our collective understanding given the dominance of various sorts of social, cultural and professional identity prejudices.[60] Although obviously judges always have to strike a balance between personal and institutional contexts, their respectfulness toward the people before them is always required, as can also be seen from various codes of judicial conduct that demand a respect for the legal subject's dignity.[61]

Taken together this is all the more reason to investigate the possible contributions of the humanities in order to maintain the integrity not only of law itself and those subject to it, but also of the judge, on the view that a literary turn of mind is what is required of the judge to remain whole and integrated rather than succumb

---

Adaptation, Contemporary African Drama and Greek Tragedy (privately published Ph.D. thesis, Amsterdam: Off Page Printing, 2011). See David Luban, *Legal Ethics and Human Dignity* (Cambridge: Cambridge University Press, 2009), 68–70, 70 on the subject of litigants given the possibility to tell their stories because human dignity requires them to be heard, "honoring a litigant's human dignity means suspending disbelief and hearing the story she has to tell. So [...] having human dignity means, roughly, *having a story of one's own*"[italics in the original].

59 Sophie Nield, "Introduction: The Power of Speech" in Farber, *Molora, based on the Oresteia by Aeschylus*, 9–11, 9. See also Farber, scene viii, "wet bag method," 43 ff.

60 See Fricker, *Injustice*, 154–162, 162. I elaborate on the role of the judge in Jeanne Gaakeer, "Configuring Justice," *No Foundations, An Interdisciplinary Journal of Law and Justice* 9 (2012): 20–44.

61 See the *Recommendation CM/REC (2010)12 of the Committee of Ministers to Member States on Judges: independence, efficiency and responsibilities*, a European Code adopted on 17 November 2010 by the Committee of Ministers, that reads in Chapter VII – Duties and responsibilities under the topic of Duties, "59. Judges should protect the rights and freedoms of all persons equally, respecting their dignity in the conduct of court proceedings"; the *ENCJ* (i.e., European Network of Councils for the Judiciary) *Working Group Judicial Ethics Report 2009–2010, Judicial Ethics: principles, values and qualities*, adopted 2010 by the ENCJ General Assembly, in Part I – The values/merits, about what society and citizens may expect of a judge, reads "The judge exercises his functions by applying loyally the rules of procedure, by showing concern for the dignity of individuals and by acting within the framework of the law" and "The judge's sense of humanity is manifested by his respect for persons and their dignity in all circumstances of his professional and private life"; the Dutch *NVVR Guide to Judicial Conduct* under the heading Expertise and professionalism also reads, "2.4.3 The judge's conduct vis-à-vis parties to the proceedings and any other parties involved, such as victims in a criminal case, is one of respect."

to the pressures of instrumentalist, economic views in law or to the vice of professional *hubris* that leads to the humiliation of the other in word and deed.[62] This is even more so now that judges are the authors of law in the decisions they take, i.e., by means of language they constitute new worlds for the people subject to their authoritative decisions, the legitimacy of which depends on criteria comparable to what Calvino called the levels of reality in literature. To Calvino, what matters is the credibility of the narrative as a criterion for the success of the text, both on the internal level of the world that is shown in it and on the external level of what the reader can accept and believe.[63] The literary turn of mind as already advocated by Aristotle in his *Poetics* as the best way to learn about the lives and experiences of others and subsequently to develop an attitude of empathy is so very important because the judge mediates between the abstract world of the rule of law in democratic societies and the lives of their citizens. In this mediation lies her duty. She mediates understanding that she fulfils her duties in an imperfect world in which "Law never is, but is always about to be."[64] In this understanding lies her challenge.

---

62 Steven L. Winter, "Law, Culture and Humility" in *Law and the Humanities: An Introduction*, eds. Austin Sarat, Matthew Anderson and Cathrine O. Frank (Cambridge: Cambridge University Press, 2010), 98–121, 115 note 63, "A literary turn of mind is vital to morality because it is through narrative enactment that we imagine how various situations might be carried forward and, thus, are able to assess their ethical implications." For a sobering thought on the limits of the human ability to imagine and emphatize as well as on the contribution of literature, see Elaine Scarry, "The Difficulty of Imagining Other People" in *For Love of Country, Debating the Limits of Patriotism, Martha C. Nussbaum with respondents*, ed. Joshua Cohen (Boston: Beacon Press, 1996), 98–110 (originally published in *Human Rights in Political Transitions: Gettysburg to Bosnia*, eds. Carla Hesse and Robert Post (New Yook: Zone Books, 1999), 277–309), (references are to the 1996 publication), 104, "we must recognize the severe limits of imaginative accomplishment" because there are "limits on solving real-world otherness through literary representation alone" and these include our tendency to read for self-identification and the fact that too often an appeal to our imagination does not lead to a concrete willingness to act and change the law.
63 Italo Calvino, "Levels of Reality in Literature" in Italo Calvino, *The Uses of Literature* (New York: Harvest, 1987), 101–121; see the comparison Calvino makes with the Coleridgean concept of suspension of disbelief, "different levels of reality may be matched by different levels of credibility – or, to put it better, a different suspension of disbelief" (108).
64 Benjamin N. Cardozo, *The Nature of the Judicial Process* (New Haven: Yale University Press, 1921), 126.

Contributors

Valentina Adami is Adjunct Professor of English at the University of Verona and at the Free University of Bolzano/Bozen. Her research interests include trauma studies, law and literature, bioethics, medicine and literature, ecolinguistics and ecocriticism. Her publications include *Trauma Studies and Literature: Martin Amis's* Time's Arrow (Peter Lang, 2008), and *Bioethics through Literature: Margaret Atwood's Cautionary Tales* (WVT, 2011).

Maria Aristodemou is Professor of Law at Birkbeck College London. Her research interests move around the relation of law and psychoanalysis in legal and cultural texts. Her publications include *Law and Literature: From Her to Eternity* (Oxford UP, 2000). Her *Law, Psychoanalysis, Society: Taking the Unconscious Seriously* will be published by Routledge in 2014.

Riccardo Baldissone is an honorary fellow at the Birkbeck Institute for the Humanities in the University of London and an adjunct researcher at the Centre for Human Rights Education, Curtin University, Perth. His current research addresses the denial of multiplicity in western political thought.

Charia Battisti is Researcher in English literature in the Department of Foreign Literature at the University of Verona. Her research interests include literature and the visual arts, with a particular focus on literature and cinema, literature and science, literature and law, gender studies and the study of fashion. Her publications include *La traduzione filmico: il romanzo e la sua trasposizione cinematografica* (Ombre Corte, 2008) and *Civiltà come manipulazione: cultura come redenzione in* Brave New World *e* Metropolis (Longo, 2004).

Patrizia Nerozzi Bellman is Emeritus Professor of English Literature at IULM Milan. Her research interests include the history of the novel, eighteenth century British literature and art, new communication technologies and visual arts, and literature and law. She is presently director of the Tristram Shandy web (http://www.tristramshandyweb.it/) and is a member of the editorial board of Polemos.

Paola Carbone is Associate Professor of English Literature at IULM Milan. Her fields of research include narrative theory, contemporary British culture and the novel, and the relationship between literature and new communication technologies. She has published several works on postmodern literature and digital art. In 2008 she published *La lanterna magica di Tristram Shandy: Visualità e informa-*

zione, ordine ed entropia, paradossi e trompe-l'oeil nel romanzo di Laurence Sterne (Ombre Corte).

Daniela Carpi is Professor of English Literature at the University of Verona. Her research interests include Renaissance theatre, critical theory, postmodernism, law and literature, law and science, and literature and the visual arts. She is a founder member of AIDEL and is managing director of *Polemos*. She has edited a number of books including *The Concept of Equity: an interdisciplinary Assessment* (Winter, 2007), *Practising Equity, Addressing Law* (Winter, 2008), *Bioethics and Biolaw through Literature* (De Gruyter, 2011) and, with Jeanne Gaakeer, *Liminal Discourses: Subliminal Tensions in Law and Literature* (De Gruyter, 2013).

Carla Dente is Professor of English Literature and Theatre Studies at the University of Pisa. Her research interests are focussed on conversation and rhetorical argumentation in dramatic text, migrant theatre, theatre and reception, Shakespearian re-writings and anti-theatrical discourse in the Restoration. She has edited a number of volumes including *Proteus: the Languages of Metamorphism* (Ashgate, 2005) and *Marginal Textualities: Shakespeare in Conflict* (Palgrave, 2013). She is co-founder and former president of the Italian Association of Shakespearian and Early Modern Studies.

Roxanne Barbara Doerr is Adjunct Professor of English Literature at the University of Modena and Reggio Emilia, and of English Language at the Universities of Milan, Verona and Padua and Doctor Europaeus. She holds a Phd from the University of Verona and the title of Dr.Phil from the University of Cologne. Her research interests include literature and visual arts, law and literature, law and culture, language and the new media, the legal thriller, postmodern literature and multiculturalism.

Sidia Fiorato is Researcher in English Literature in the Department of Foreign Literature at the University of Verona. Her research interests include the postmodern novel, detective fiction, law and literature, and literature and dance. Her publications include *Il Gioco con l'Ombra: Ambiguità e metanarrazione nella narrativa di Peter Ackroyd* (Fiorini, 2003) and *The Relationship between Literature and Science in John Banville's Scientific Tetralogy* (Peter Lang, 2007).

Jeanne Gaakeer is endowed Professor of Legal Theory and Associate Professor of Jurisprudence at Erasmus University Rotterdam. Her research interests are focussed on interdisciplinary legal studies, specifically law and literature and law and the humanities. She currently serves as a justice in the criminal law section of the Appellate Court of The Hague having previously served as a judge in the Regional Court of Middelburg. She is the co-founder of the European Network for Law and Literature (http://www.eurnll.org). She is editor, with Daniela Carpi, of *Liminal Discourses: Subliminal Tensions in Law and Literature* (De Gruyter, 2013).

Lisa Lanzoni is Adjunct Professor of Public Law in the Department of Economic Science at the University of Verona. She holds a Phd and *Doctor Europaeus* in Italian and European Constitutional Law at the University of Verona. In 2007 she was visiting Professor at UNED University Madrid. Her research interests are focussed on fundamental human rights, and regional development. Her publications include *Il territorio tra diritto nazionale ed europeo. Contesto instituzionale e politiche di sviluppo regionale* (ESI, 2013).

Mara Logaldo is Assistant Professor of English at IUML Milan. Her research interests are focussed on rhetoric and multimodality in literature and media discourse. Her publications include *Figura e Rappresentazione in Henry James 1896–1901* (Edizioni Dell'Orso, 2000), *Writing for the Media* (Arcipelago, 2003), *Cronaca come romano: Truman Capote e il New Journalism* (Arcipelago, 2003), and *Augmented Linguistics* (Arcipelago, 2012).

Richard Mullender is Professor of Law and Legal Theory at Newcastle University. His research interests are concentrated in the areas of legal philosophy, tort, law human rights and public law.

Matteo Nicolini is Assistant Professor of Comparative Public Law at the University of Verona and Senior Researcher in the Institute for Studies on Federalism and Regionalism at EURAC of Bozen. His research interests are focussed on comparative Italian and European Constitutional law, participatory and deliberative democracy, judicial review and territorial demarcation. His publications include *Partecipazione regionale e 'norme di procedura': Profili di diritto costituzionale italiano ed europeo* (ESI, 2009) and (with F.Palermo) *Il Bicameralismo: Pluralismo e limiti della rappresentanza in prospettiva comparata* (ESI, 2013).

Lino Panzeri is Researcher at the Insubria University where he teaches Elements of Public Law. He is the co-author of *Lo Statuto Giuridico della Lingua Italiana in Europa: I casi di Croazia, Slovenia e Svizzera a Confronto* (Giuffre, 2011) and *Statuti Ordinari e Legge Regionale. Contributo allo Studio del Giusto Procedimento Legislativo* (Franco Angeli, 2012).

Helle Porsdam is Professor of American Studies at the University of Copenhagen. She holds a Phd from Yale University and Dr.Phil. from the University of Southern Denmark. She has held fellowships at Harvard Law School, Wolfson College Cambridge, and the Centre for Advanced Studies Munich and is currently a Global Ethics Fellow with the Carnegie Council for Ethics in International Affairs. Her publications include *Legally Speaking: Contemporary American Culture and the Law* (University of Massachusetts Press, 1999) and *From Civil to Human Rights: Dialogues in Law and Humanities in the United States and Europe* (Edward Elgar, 2009).

Alessandra Tomaselli is Professor of German Language at the University of Verona. Her research interests include Germanic comparative syntax, linguistic contact between Romance and Germanic varieties and the history of German language. Her publications include *An Introduction to German Syntax* (BA Graphis, 2003).

Ian Ward is Professor of Law at Newcastle University. His research interests are focussed on associated areas of law, literature and history. He has held visiting positions at the Universities of Alberta, Iowa, Montpellier and Turku, and recently held a visiting fellowship at the Centre for Advanced Studies Munich. Amongst his recent publications are *Law and the Brontes* (Palgrave, 2012) and *Sex, Crime and Literature in Victorian England* (Hart, 2014).

Index

Lightning Source UK Ltd.
Milton Keynes UK
UKHW022032220719
346637UK00002B/20/P